CENSORED

CENSORED2010

The Top 25 Censored Stories

Edited by
PETER PHILLIPS and MICKEY HUFF
with PROJECT CENSORED

INTRODUCTION BY DAHR JAMAIL
CARTOONS BY KHALIL BENDIB

Seven Stories Press

New York / London / Melbourne / Toronto

Seven Stories Press
140 Watts Street
New York, NY 10013

In Canada: Publishers Group Canada, 559 College Street, Suite 402, Toronto, ON
M6G 1A9

In the U.K.: Turnaround Publisher Services Ltd., Unit 3, Olympia Trading
Estate, Coburg Road, Wood Green, London N22 6TZ

In Australia: Palgrave Macmillan, 15–19 Claremont Street, South Yarra, VIC 3141

ISBN 978-1-58322-890-6

Book design by Jon Gilbert

Printed in the U.S.A.

Contents

Dedicated to

Thomas Lough, PhD
1938–2008

Sociologist, Teacher, Feminist, Peace Activist

One of the Kent State 25

and

Long Time Friend to Project Censored
National Judge and Evaluator

Preface

by Mickey Huff and Peter Phillips

As the familiar idiom dating back to King James I of England goes, "No news is good news." For the corporate media, "no news" is becoming a reality, and not in a good way. Record numbers of daily newspapers are closing, and other major stalwarts of the press—like the *Chicago Tribune* and the *New York Times*—are fighting for their fiscal lives. One might think this would motivate these institutions to aggressively investigate hard news stories for a competitive edge in dire times. Instead, big corporate news outlets manage to get scooped by independents and the blogosphere almost every day on most major topics.

Corporate news is a dying system. It has helped make itself irrelevant with its insatiable appetite for the inane, a strong reliance on commercialism, and an inability to inform the public on crucial matters of our time. What passes for news on the 24/7 cable broadcasts is more like a gossip rag or screed sheet, a veritable three-ring circus sideshow of spectacle and distraction. Even print media have succumbed to this inevitable purging, exchanging substance for style, fact for opinion, news for propaganda. On the key issues of the past several years, from election fraud and matters of torture to leaving single-payer health care and impeachment off the table of public discourse, corporate media have failed America.

The theme of this year's *Censored* is just that: corporate media are not in the news business, so someone else had better be. Project Censored's top censored story authors are part of a changing system of independent global news. This year, once again, the Top 25 stories highlight journalism at its best by holding the powerful accountable for their decisions and actions and by telling the public what they need to know about our fractured society on a struggling planet.

We are honored to have independent journalist Dahr Jamail penning the introduction this year. Dahr is one of those brave independent journalists reporting from the field on empire and war. We need hundreds more like him to build a real world news system.

We welcome back Khalil Bendib's biting editorial cartoon commentary. Khalil's sharp wit and deep understanding of the sociopolitical hypocrisies of our time are a powerful contribution to this book.

Chapter One houses the Top 25 most significant censored stories from March 2008 to March of 2009. With the guidance of Trish Boreta, the research of Sonoma State University and Project Censored affiliated college and university students and faculty, and the expertise of our national judges, we have another year's worth of undercovered, hard-hitting news on crucial issues ranging from the financial meltdown and influence of lobbyists to the resegregation of schools and continued US global economic and military dominance. Mike Niman introduces the theme of this year's book in "Die Zombie Newspapers, Die."

In Chapter Two, a follow up from last year's Top 25 stories, future Project Censored director Ben Frymer, Kate Sims, and students update us on key reports from 2009.

In Chapter Three, Mickey Huff and Project Censored intern Frances A. Capell analyze the Infotainment Society, exploring the "issues" corporate media spend time discussing rather than important political or social issues. The Junk Food News and News Abuse chapter has been a tradition at Project Censored since Dr. Carl Jensen began looking at inconsequential stories, or fluff, as news in the mid-1980s. Sadly, this "no news" segment has much to display.

Chapter Four celebrates the good-news stories of the past year. Kate Sims, working in conjunction with Sarah van Gelder and the folks at *Yes! Magazine*, has again compiled a fine list of what's good in the news (online at http://www.yesmagazine.org). These include real stories of hope and change (unlike the promised ones from last campaign season) that the corporate media have little interest in covering.

Chapter Five is about the collusion between corporate media and the military-industrial complex in their quest to further US global dominance. Peter Phillips and Mickey Huff delve deeply into the propaganda that passes for news and argue for a bottom-up, democratic model of media reform.

Chapter Six continues with the theme of Pentagon propaganda with a compilation of first-class reporting by Diane Farsetta, the people at PR Watch, and the staff at the Center for Media Democracy (http://prwatch.org). Farsetta's coverage of the video news release (VNR) scandals in recent years led to Federal Communications Commission (FCC) investigations and fines. We hope her continued efforts yield similar results in pulling back the curtain on military message control.

Chapter Seven is the annual *Fear & Favor* report from the media watchdog group Fairness and Accuracy in Reporting (publishers of the now monthly *Extra!* magazine, http://fair.org). FAIR has been challenging media bias and censorship for over twenty years and we are proud to again have their revealing analysis in newsrooms across the country.

The Index on Censorship report is back again in Chapter Eight. This year's report looks at liability issues for journalists and the impact this has on a free press.

Chapter Nine is a study by Project Censored intern Andy Hobbs on media bias. Hobbs examines US press coverage of Venezuelan leader Hugo Chávez and applies logic and critical analysis to the broadcasts of conservative commentator Rush Limbaugh. He explores how both US coverage of Chávez and Limbaugh's broadcasts exemplify failures of corporate media.

Chapter Ten, by coeditors Peter Phillips and Mickey Huff, takes a look back at Project Censored stories under the Clinton and Bush Jr. years to respond to accusations of possible left-leaning bias at Project Censored. The authors come to an interesting conclusion.

Chapter Eleven is by Brad Freidman of *The Brad Blog*, one of the most widely read blogs on election issues and politics in the US (http://brads-blog.com). In this chapter, Brad looks at ongoing voting problems in the US, emphasizing the latest election in 2008. The reporting, analysis, and conclusion on the future of American democracy are as crucial as they are bleak. We ignore these stories at our peril.

In Chapter Twelve, Peter Phillips looks at the importance of investigative research and how universities should play a larger role in news construction in the future. This further highlights this year's theme of "no news" by heralding the significance that college and university research studies have for our society, and how they may play a key future role in global news reporting. As corporate media fails, colleges and universities have an opportunity to fill the increasing news gaps in society.

Chapter Thirteen is a study on human trafficking, prostitution and media representation by Aashika N. Damodar. This chapter is a reconsideration of a very important and ongoing problem of inequality in the US.

Former Project Censored associate director Andrew L. Roth returns for Chapter Fourteen this year. Roth looks at the ever-developing issues in the world water crisis and corporate attempts to assume private control of fresh water for political as well as financial gain.

Rounding out the book this year in Chapter Fifteen, Sonoma State University sociology professor James Dean looks at films from a gay and lesbian standpoint films and Queer Cinema. Dean's critical theory approach to media and social issues ends this year's *Censored* on a strong academic tone by looking at how media view these groups.

Judging by this year's *Censored* contents, there is plenty of news to report. If the corporate media spent more time covering these crucial stories, maybe they wouldn't be in such dire straits. Perhaps that old saying should be amended and updated for the twenty-first century: No Corporate News is Good News . . . for the rest of us.

We hope you enjoy this year's effort by the team at Project Censored. Welcome to *Censored 2010*.

Introduction

by Dahr Jamail

Make no mistake. The American Empire is in decline. We are watching the bloated lumbering beast, drunk on its own propaganda of moral, spiritual, military, social, and material superiority, hurtling down the abyss. The world is visibly multipolar today, but the United States continues to trumpet its belief of undisputed might and authority. To a discerning citizenry, it would be obvious that the contribution of the US to these dark times is quite in consonance with its notions of superiority. Be it in the realm of catastrophic climate change, depleted natural resources, global economic meltdown, or military misadventures in sovereign states, our country has indeed established itself the undisputed leader.

Despite promises of "change" and "withdrawal" by the Obama administration, Iraq remains occupied, with over 130,000 US soldiers and over 200,000 private contractors. During my most recent visit there in 2009, the only notable change I witnessed was such a dramatic decline in living conditions that superlatives are rendered superfluous. If such a thing is possible, and in Iraq it is, there is less electricity than ever before, there are fewer jobs and far less potable water, the medical system has collapsed further from its skeletal status, and the number of Iraqis killed by the US-led invasion and occupation has far exceeded 1.2 million. At the time of my visit, one out of six Iraqis remained displaced from their homes. According to the latest Oxfam International report, one in three was in need of emergency assistance.

Steadfast in its distortion of facts, the corporate press declares the exact opposite: that things in Iraq are far better than before, and that Obama is poised to bring home the troops. It is left to the gullible consumer of such "news" to reconcile it with the Obama administration's declared plans to have between 50,000 to 70,000 troops in Iraq until at least the end of his first term in 2013.

Change we can believe in.

Media, too, we can believe in, merely at some peril to our reason.

Even as the ongoing occupations of Iraq and Afghanistan daily erode what little is left of any credibility and respect for the United States, the

State Department is busy devising elaborate "negotiations," which are little more than carrot and stick strategieswith different states in the region. But the carrots hold no promise and the sticks can flatten entire villages of civilians, as they have been doing in recent months on the borders of Pakistan and Afghanistan.

Perhaps the thinking segment of the US population has tired of crying foul. "Not in our name" is not a slogan heard anymore. Dissent is a taboo topic in the media, whose goal is only to "manufacture consent."

Nor does anyone want to talk about the other elephant in the room. The corporate media is complicit in its alliance with the powers through its silence, but how do we explain the conspicuous absence of protest from the Left and liberal media groups against this country's unbridled, unquestioned support for the state of Israel?

Most of the rest of the world perceives Israel as the leading terrorist state in the Middle East, and with good reason. It is the only nuclear-armed power that by definition of its own constitution has no borders. Perhaps to justify a continued expansion into Palestinian lands?

In late 2008, Israel began a military assault on the people of Gaza, instructing soldiers to shoot women, children, and virtually anything that moved. Aerial support of the offensive was provided by US-supplied F-16 war planes dropping white phosphorous incendiary weapons on the civilian population. The support package included Apache helicopters, missiles, jet fuel, and cluster bombs, all showered abundantly on the civilian population of Gaza while the soon-to-be-inaugurated president Barack Obama stood silent.

The world watched in horror. The United States media must have been looking the other way, aside from when they dutifully defended Israel's "right to defend itself."

In 2008, special interest groups paid Washington lobbyists $3.2 billion, an amount higher than any other year on record. Subsequently, US-aided Israeli settlement activity in the West Bank doubled in the same year. By offering tax deductions for donations to these settlements, our government makes public its encouragement of Israeli tactics. Only on occasion do we hear some muted denouncements of the settlements.

It is no coincidence that Israel will be the primary financial beneficiary of the reconstruction of Gaza as the sole supplier of construction materials and the overseeing authority on the contracts to rebuild what was bombed. Joseph Heller must be writhing in his grave.

Israel has at least 200 nuclear warheads, while Iran remains years away from obtaining a single one. Yet the frightening prospect of another war in the Middle East hinges on the "threat" that Iran poses to Israel, and by implication, to the US.

So the mainstream media will have us believe.

Those who expected a change in the country's foreign policy when the occupant of the White House changed will do well to take a reality check. Let us remain mindful of the fact that the Democratic administration of President Barack Obama and a "Democrat"-controlled Congress are operating on the same policies of the Bush administration that have bankrupted the United States economically, morally, militarily, and spiritually.

Change we can believe in.

Two appropriate old adages come to mind: "What do all men with power want? More power." And, "How much is enough? Just a little more."

We may now, without hesitation, dispel from our minds whatever ambiguity may have existed there. The Siamese twin of Corporations and Wall Street still runs our government. Federal lawmakers responsible for regulating big business in the US have received, since 2001, $64.2 million. Donors include investment bankers such as Merrill Lynch, Morgan Stanley, American International Group (AIG), Bear Stearns, and Goldman Sachs. Nearly every single member of the House Financial Services Committee who oversaw hearings on how the first bailout was being spent had received contributions from these financial institutions during the 2008 election cycle. How convenient for these "too big to fail" companies. Former International Monetary Fund (IMF) chief economist Simon Johnson put it succinctly: "The finance industry has effectively captured our government."

Greed, power, and gluttony dictate US home and foreign policy. We are governed by a sick hybrid of militarized corporate capitalism that is literally consuming and burning up our planet.

The latest report portends that the Arctic may well be completely ice-free in the summer as early as 2010. Since the first Earth Day in 1970, one quarter of all species on Earth have gone extinct. Another one million species are likely to become extinct within forty years as a result of climate change.

But for the US corporate press, global climate change remains the 800-pound gorilla in the room that will disappear if it is dismissed as fiction or ignored entirely. Each year the effects become more obvious and devastating.

The ominous news for those who can stomach it is that it is business as usual for big oil and the nuclear power industry.

News of far more significance is that radioactive storage pools of spent fuel rods contaminate areas of North Carolina near the Shearn Harris nuclear plant, making it one of the most contaminated areas on the North American continent.

It is now established beyond reasonable doubt that the mainstream media in the United States is not reliable or trustworthy. It sold us the bogus justifications for the wars in Iraq and Afghanistan, and it continues to distort and disregard the human catastrophe that unfolds in those countries on a daily basis. It falsifies the role the US in the Middle East and elsewhere, and it refuses to report accurately on the impending crisis of climate change.

Project Censored is doing yeoman's service for those who are willing to be served by truth. Thanks to this project, the most important stories from each year that go either underreported or ignored by the corporate press find visibility and public life. Exhaustive research conducted over months brings together stories in an annual volume that has become a trusted research and media tool. Increasingly, international journalists, activists, scholars, and researchers rely on it.

We commemorate the progress of the project. At a time when the need for independent journalism and for media outlets unaffiliated with and untainted by the government and corporate sponsors is greater than ever, Project Censored has created a context for reporting the complete truth in all matters that matter. It has engineered a valuable bridge between those who wish to inform truthfully and transparently, and those who wish to be informed likewise.

In an interview decades ago the late journalist Martha Gellhorn commented to veteran journalist John Pilger, "All governments are bad, and some are worse."

It is therefore left to us to find sources for information we can trust, or even to collect and report on stories ourselves. It is in this task that we are fortunate to have an ally like Project Censored.

DAHR JAMAIL is an independent journalist who has been reporting from the Middle East for over five years, nine months of which he has spent in Iraq. Dahr currently writes for the Inter Press Service, *Le Monde Diplomatique*, and Truthout.org. His stories have been published with *The Nation*, the *Sunday Herald* in Scotland, Al-Jazeera, the *Guardian*, Foreign Policy in Focus, and the *Independent*, to name just a few. Dahr's reporting has earned him numerous awards, including the prestigious 2008 Martha Gellhorn Award for Journalism, the Lannan Foundation Writing Residency Fellowship, the James Aronson Award for Social Justice Journalism, the Joe A. Callaway Award for Civic Courage, and four Project Censored awards. He is the author of *Beyond the Green Zone: Dispatches from an Independent Journalist in Occupied Iraq* and *Military Resisters: Soldiers Who Refuse to Fight in Iraq and Afghanistan.*

The Top Censored Stories of 2008 and 2009

by Peter Phillips, Tricia Boreta, and Project Censored

This year's cover image, entitled "No News," is symbolic of the state of media in the United States today. Newspapers are failing because their content has collapsed. In the thirty-three years of Project Censored, the absence of real news from corporate media has never been so complete. Lies, deception, propaganda, superficial coverage, and overt censorship are on the rise. We cannot be polite about this anymore. Corporate media is irrelevant to working people and destructive to democracy. Look elsewhere for real news, as you won't find it in the mainstream press.

Project Censored's overview of top undercovered news this year reveals a surge in militarized corporate takeovers of governments and resources—not only abroad, but at home in the United States. Despite the new face Barack Obama has brought to Empire, this year's stories reveal a proliferation of battles between mismatched forces of people and multinational industries. From the buying of US Congress and the appointment of corrupt corporate insiders to key federal positions, to the fast track exploitation and subjugation of Palestine, Sudan, Somalia, Haiti, New Orleans, Appalachia, the Amazon, Nigeria, Iraq, Afghanistan, and Pakistan, new waves of imperial aggression are crashing down. And a massive worldwide resistance is growing.

Project Censored's selection of top news stories has greatly expanded this year to include the research of college and university students across the nation. Twenty-eight professors from New York to California have actively incorporated Project Censored curricula and investigative research procedures into their classrooms. The following chapter represents the work of hundreds of students and professors.

INTRODUCTION

Die Zombie Newspapers, Die: The dailies really died a generation ago, and now their corpses are following suit.

by Michael I. Niman

Headlines and TV news leads are abuzz with obituaries for the newspaper business, as if the industry had suddenly up and died. Sure, the nation's top newspapers are in financial turmoil. A few major dailies recently shuttered their doors. Most papers are downsizing staff. Some, like the *Wall Street Journal* and the *Los Angeles Times*, are physically shrinking, trimming their waistlines by about three inches. The *Detroit News/Free Press* and *Seattle Post-Intelligencer* are moving away from printed paper and going virtual. Denver's 150-year-old *Rocky Mountain News*, the 128-year-old *Cincinnati Post*, and the 87-year-old *Albuquerque Tribune* have recently closed down entirely and gone to the compost pile. Like much of what we've been reading in our daily newspapers, however, the story about the collapse of journalism is old news. Newspapers have been dead for quite a while. The only twist is that their zombie bodies have finally followed suit. I know this sounds cruel, and I'm no doubt raising the ire of legions of coupon-clippers, crossword enthusiasts, and dog-smackers, but let's look at the history here.

The collapse of the newspaper industry was predicated by its loss of biodiversity. The monopoly model grew to dominate the industry by the middle of the twentieth century. In almost every American city, the dominant paper, buoyed by a growing economy of scale, drove its competition out of business. By the end of the century, approximately 98 percent of American cities were one-newspaper towns.

The monopolies threatened democracy, with the dailies often acting as regional news gatekeepers whose spin dominated local politics. Their power put them above reproach; few politicians ever took on the local daily and lived, at least career-wise, to tell about it. And they jacked up advertising prices, sometimes to the point of threatening the very existence of struggling businesses.

With their regional monopolies, newspapers regularly generated double-digit returns for their Wall Street investors, becoming one of the nation's most profitable industries. The romance of the cub reporter out chasing hot leads, ferreting out corruption, scooping the competition, and saving democracy, however, was dead. Newspapers, as profit generators, more and more were taken over by conglomerates in business not to inform, educate, and agitate, but simply to make money. The monopoly model gave newspapers a good run financially, but it was short-lived because publishers grew fat and arrogant as they sat on their thumbs, viewing their growing profits more as an entitlement than as something they would have to work to earn. Without competition, they cut staff, even in good financial times, greedily bleeding their papers for ever-increasing profit margins. Generic wire service stories replaced hard-hitting local reporting, and papers lost their significance as sources of local news.

The profit-greed model meant that newspapers avoided biting the hands that fed them. This meant avoiding stories that pissed off advertisers, friends of advertisers, and the folks that sold out to advertisers. It also meant avoiding any controversy that could in any way upset any party that might one day think of advertising. Between these two censored categories lie most of the stories that make newspapers both necessary and vibrant.

In its more extreme form, the profit-greed model meant not only trying not to offend, but actually pandering to advertisers. Hence, newspapers replaced hard news with soft, advertising-driven fluff stories and entire advertiser-driven sections of the paper.

Think about it. When was the last time you read a story in the auto section critical of a car, or a story in the real estate section critical of irresponsible development patterns?

On the macro level, the "suck up to power and don't ask questions" mandate to which newspapers adhered left us, for example, with nearly every major newspaper in the United States shamelessly parroting subsequently discredited Bush administration propaganda in the lead-up to the 2003 invasion of Iraq. In fact, many media critics now argue that the pro-war bias of American newspapers was a key factor in allowing the Bush administration to lead the nation into war. Alternative news sources, residing mostly in cyberspace, countered this false information with what has proven to be prescient analysis and more accurate information—but they couldn't counter the misinformation disseminated by newspapers.

Look over Project Censored's tally of the most important but least reported stories of the past twenty years. They choose twenty-five mind-boggling stories each year—stuff like Halliburton selling nuclear technology to Iran, Halliburton getting contracts to build detention centers in the US, and Dick Cheney's Halliburton stock rising 3,000 percent during the Iraq war. These stories cover the gamut from government allowances for carcinogens in our food and water, to the destruction of habeas corpus and basic human rights protections, to the wholesale corporate plunder of natural resources.

Yet, in any given year, you can count the number of these stories broken by daily newspapers on your thumbs—and usually have a thumb or two left over. Newspapers have let us down. That's why we've turned to other sources for our news.

Sure, the newsprint model of squishing forests into paper pulp is dated in the digital age, but that's not why these massive news organizations are dying. Today's major newspapers have, on average, a century or so of brand-building under their belts. They should be the principal recognized players in the news industry, in every medium. These should be strong brands well placed to dominate a convergent media landscape. But after a generation of suck-up-manship, their brands, and hence, their value on Wall Street, are trash. After leading us into war with Judith Miller's mindless cheerleading for the Bush administration, why should we trust the *New York Times* for information about Iraq? And, really, why the hell should we pay for their misinformation?

Many of the stories we're reading and watching about the collapse of newspapers are authored by papers whining about their own self-induced demise, or by similarly run and equally greedy TV news organizations, prematurely gloating about the death of newspapers as they follow closely down the same path to irrelevance. Missing from this analysis is coverage about the consequent growth of democratic media organizations that actually challenge the status quo and report on dangerous and troubling news stories. In this context, the story isn't one of a generation racing toward illiteracy and apathy, but a much more hopeful story about a media revolution. Let's look at this as a market adjustment, with the value of the propaganda model plummeting. This is not a bad development.

But Big Media won't die gracefully. No. They're wheeling out a host of wonks—so-called experts—to tell us that newspapers have been killed off by, get this, Craigslist.

Think about that. It seems the mysterious loss of classified revenue turned out to be the silver bullet laying the undead to rest. But (and seldom does anyone ask) why did the dailies lose their classified ads?

Coincidentally, this loss came on the heels of their readership dwindling. And many of those ads migrated not to Craigslist, but to the weekly alternative papers that have been picking up the reporting slack as the big guys shied away from dangerous stories. This is the market at work—Milton Friedman, not Karl Marx. Where do you look when you want to rent an apartment? And the weeklies didn't inherit these ads from dead relatives—they worked for them around the same time the dailies stopped working.

For journalism to thrive, journalists need to be paid. Critics of democratic media are quick to point out that the market cannot support a million online information venues, and small media organizations can only afford small salaries for all but a handful of workers. So, the argument goes, we need a new model to finance quality media.

True indeed. But this same argument often operates on the premise that the old model—big monopoly newspapers—were doing that, and that the death of the big boys now means the end of journalism as a profession. The remuneration system by which professional journalists are paid has been way out of wack for a long time, rewarding some of the worst, most spineless, boot-licking writers, while punishing hard-working, risk-taking journalists. Let's look at the *New York Post*, for example—clearly one of the nation's most sensationalist, fear-mongering, xenophobic rags. They employ some of the highest-paid "journalists" in the industry. Meanwhile, in the same city, the hard-hitting, award-winning *Indypendent* (yes, it's spelled with a "y") relies on volunteer writers for some of the best local investigative reporting in the country. If we stop rewarding lackeys for selling out their supposed profession, that's not a bad thing. Finding revenue streams to pay good journalists is a whole other issue.

The bottom line here is that while there might not be a future for soulless, zombie monopoly newspapers, there is a future for journalism. I'm reminded of a meeting I had a few years back with a delegation of Ukrainian journalists. They were all middle-aged, which means they trained as journalists in a totalitarian Soviet society where there was no journalism. Still, generation after generation, aspiring journalists learned skills they were barred from using. Then the empire collapsed, and when it collapsed, there were journalists waiting to come out of hibernation.

Maybe that's the story here. Perhaps the collapse of self-censored monopoly papers will finally break the stronghold that mediocrity has held over journalism for a generation. Maybe this means that good journalists won't have to hold day jobs in other professions to support themselves. Perhaps it means weasels will no longer edit newspapers. Or maybe not much will change other than the venue in which misinformation and trivia is delivered. In any event, I'm not shedding any tears for corporate media.

DR. MICHAEL I. NIMAN is a professor of journalism and media studies at Buffalo State College. A version of this introduction was published in *ArtVoice* on April 28, 2009. His previous *Artvoice* columns are available at artvoice.com, archived at mediastudy.com, and available globally through syndication.

1

US Congress Sells Out to Wall Street

Sources:

Truthout, October 2, 2008
Title: "Lax Oversight? Maybe $64 Million to DC Pols Explains It"
Author: Greg Gordon

Capital Eye blog, February 10, 2009
Title: "Congressmen Hear from TARP Recipients Who Funded Their Campaigns"
Author: Lindsay Renick Mayer

Rolling Stone, March 19, 2009
Title: "The Big Takeover"
Author: Matt Taibbi

Student Researchers: Jocelyn Rapp and Caitlin Ruxton (SSU)
Faculty Evaluator: Samual Mikhail PhD, Chip McAuley, PhD
Indian River State College and Sonoma State University

Federal lawmakers responsible for overseeing the US economy have received millions of dollars from Wall Street firms. Since 2001, eight of the most troubled firms have donated $64.2 million to congressional candidates, presidential candidates, and the Republican and Democratic parties. As senators, Barack Obama and John McCain received a combined total of $3.1 million. The donors include investment bankers Bear Stearns, Goldman Sachs, Lehman Brothers, Merrill Lynch, Morgan Stanley, insurer American International Group (AIG), and mortgage giants Fannie Mae and Freddie Mac.

Some of the top recipients of contributions from companies receiv-

ing Troubled Assets Relief Program (TARP) money are the same members of Congress who chair committees charged with regulating the financial sector and overseeing the effectiveness of this unprecedented government program. In total, members of the Senate Committee on Banking, Housing and Urban Affairs, Senate Finance Committee, and House Financial Services Committee received $5.2 million from TARP recipients in the 2007–2008 election cycle. President Obama collected at least $4.3 million from employees at these companies for his presidential campaign.

Nearly every member of the House Financial Services Committee, who in February 2009 oversaw hearings on how the $700 billion of TARP bailout was being spent, received contributions associated with these financial institutions during the 2008 election cycle. "You could say that the finance industry got their money's worth by supporting members of Congress who were inclined to look the other way," said Lawrence Jacobs, the director of the University of Minnesota's Center for the Study of Politics and Governance.

For instance, in 2004 when the Securities and Exchange Commission adopted a major rule change that freed investment banks to plunge tens of billions of dollars in borrowed money into subprime mortgages and other risky plays, congressional banking committees held no oversight hearings. Congressional inaction also allowed mortgage agents to earn high fees for peddling loans to unqualified homebuyers and prevented states from toughening regulations on predatory lending practices.

Author Matt Taibbi writes that some of the most egregious selling of the US government to Wall Street happened in the late nineties, when "Democrats, tired of getting slaughtered in the fundraising arena by Republicans, decided to throw off their old reliance on unions and interest groups and become more 'business-friendly.' Wall Street responded by flooding Washington with money, buying allies in both parties." In the ten-year period beginning in 1998, financial companies spent $1.7 billion on federal campaign contributions and another $3.4 billion on lobbyists. Wise political investments enabled the nation's top bankers to effectively scrap any meaningful oversight of the financial industry.

In 1999, Texas Senator Phil Gramm cosponsored the bill that repealed key aspects of the Glass-Steagall Act, which, since the Great Depression, prevented banks from getting into the insurance business. The very next year Gramm wrote sweeping new legislation called the Commodity Futures Modernization Act, which made it impossible to regulate credit swaps as either gambling or securities. Trading in risky credit was thus deregulated.

In 1997 and 1998—the years leading up to Phil Gramm's act that gutted Glass-Steagall—the banking, brokerage, and insurance industries spent $350 million on political contributions and lobbying. Gramm, then the chairman of the Senate Banking Committee, collected $2.6 million in only five years. The law passed 90–8 in the Senate with the support of thirty-eight Democrats, including Joe Biden, John Kerry, Tom Daschle, Dick Durbin, and John Edwards. The act helped create the too-big-to-fail financial behemoths like Citigroup, AIG, and Bank of America—and in turn helped those companies slowly crush their smaller competitors, leaving the major Wall Street firms with even more money and power to lobby for further deregulation.

By early 2009, a whole series of new government operations had been invented to inject cash into the economy, most all of them under the completely secretive control of the financial sector. Taibbi points out that "While the rest of America, and most of Congress, have been bugging out about the $700 billion bailout program called TARP, newly created organisms in the Federal Reserve zoo have quietly been pumping not billions, but trillions of dollars into the hands of private companies (at least

$3 trillion so far in loans, with as much as $5.7 trillion more in guarantees of private investments)." Taibbi continues, "This new, secretive activity by the Fed completely eclipses the TARP program in terms of its influence on the economy. . . . No one knows who's getting that money or exactly how much of it is disappearing through these new holes in the hull of America's credit rating. Moreover, no one can be sure that these new institutions are really temporary, or whether they are being set up as permanent, state-aided crutches to Wall Street, designed to systematically suck bad investments off the ledgers of irresponsible lenders."

Taibbi concludes, "The reality is that the worldwide economic meltdown and the bailout that followed were together a kind of revolution, a coup d'état. They cemented and formalized a political trend that has been snowballing for decades: the gradual takeover of the government by a small class of connected insiders, who used money to control elections, buy influence and systematically weaken financial regulations."

Fraud and crisis continue to deepen and expand with significant conflicts of interest in Congress and the executive branch of the US government. Simon Johnson, former International Monetary Fund (IMF) chief economist, says, "The finance industry has effectively captured our government."

UPDATE BY LINDSAY RENICK MAYER

Even as the federal government has continued to figure out ways to help the struggling finance sector and give the economy a boost, they've been collecting input from the very companies that have accepted taxpayer dollars and are, in part, being held responsible for the current crisis. But that's not all they've collected—Congress has been busy fundraising from the finance sector, including those companies that received billions of dollars from TARP.

Since my story was written in February, the finance sector has, of course, continued to give money to candidates, party committees, and political action committees. Since the start of 2009, Wall Street has donated $12.6 million—more than any other sector this year. And 58 percent of that has gone to Democrats, marking a change, perhaps, in political strategy. Not since the 1990 election cycle have finance, insurance, and real estate companies given more than 52 percent of its overall donations to Democrats, and from 1991 to 2006, finance gave the majority of its money to Republicans.

Many of the companies, who we wrote about in this story, that sent their CEOs to testify before the House Financial Services Committee have actually scaled back their overall giving in the first quarter of 2009 compared to the first quarters of 2007 and 2005. This includes J. P. Morgan Chase, Bank of America, Goldman Sachs (which ranks No. 1 for a decline in contributions this year compared to the start of 2008), Morgan Stanley, Citigroup, and Wells Fargo. However, it is still very early in the cycle, and campaign contributions generally don't start flowing in until closer to an election. For the most part, these companies, like the rest of the industry, targeted Democrats with a majority of their political giving.

Of course, a big story this year will be whether lawmakers, especially members of the banking and finance committees, took a hit to their personal finances like much of the rest of the country, or whether they personally benefited by infusing the Wall Street companies with taxpayer cash. The 2008 personal financial disclosure reports with those answers are now available on OpenSecrets.org at http://www.opensecrets.org/pfds/search_cid.php.

To read more about how lobbying and influence peddling are shaping legislation, keep up with the Capital Eye blog at http://www.opensecrets.org/news.

And to do some investigating yourself, dive into our industry profiles: http://www.opensecrets.org/industries/index.php.

We also follow the cash flow to committees. Check out the Senate Finance Committee data here: http://www.opensecrets.org/cmteprofiles/index.php.

2

US Schools are More Segregated Today than in the 1950s

Source:
The Civil Rights Project, UCLA, January 2009
Title: "Reviving the Goal of an Integrated Society: A 21st Century Challenge"
Author: Gary Orfield

Student Researchers: Melissa Robinson and Rena Hawkins
Faculty Evaluator: Sangeeta Sinha, PhD
Southwest Minnesota State University

Schools in the United States are more segregated today than they have been in more than four decades. Millions of nonwhite students are locked into "dropout factory" high schools, where huge percentages do not graduate, and few are well prepared for college or a future in the US economy.

According to a new Civil Rights Project report published at the University of California–Los Angeles, schools in the US are 44 percent nonwhite, and minorities are rapidly emerging as the majority of public school students in the US. Latinos and blacks, the two largest minority groups, attend schools more segregated today than during the civil rights movement forty years ago. In Latino and African-American populations, two of every five students attend intensely segregated schools. For Latinos, this increase in segregation reflects growing residential segregation. For blacks, a significant part of the reversal reflects the ending of desegregation plans in public schools throughout the nation. In the 1954 case *Brown v. Board of Education*, the US Supreme Court concluded that the Southern standard of "separate but equal" was "inherently unequal," and did "irreversible" harm to black students. It later extended that ruling to Latinos.

The Civil Rights Project study shows that the most severe segregation in public schools is in the Western states, including California—not in the South, as many people believe. Unequal education leads to diminished access to college and future jobs. Most nonwhite schools are segregated by poverty as well as race. Most of the nation's dropouts occur in nonwhite public schools, leading to large numbers of virtually unemployable young people of color.

Schools in low-income communities remain highly unequal in terms of funding, qualified teachers, and curriculum. The report indicates that schools with high levels of poverty have weaker staffs, fewer high-achieving peers, health and nutrition problems, residential instability, single-parent households, high exposure to crime and gangs, and many other conditions that strongly affect student performance levels. Low-income campuses are more likely to be ignored by college and job market recruiters. The impact of funding cuts in welfare and social programs since the 1990s was partially masked by the economic boom that suddenly ended in the fall of 2008. As a consequence, conditions are likely to get even worse in the immediate future.

In California and Texas, segregation is spreading into large sections of suburbia as well. This is the social effect of years of neglect to civil rights policies that stressed equal educational opportunity for all. In California, the nation's most multiracial state, half of blacks and Asians attend segregated schools, as do one quarter of Latino and Native American students. While many cities came under desegregation court orders during the civil rights era, most suburbs, because they had few minority students at that time, did not. When minority families began to move to the suburbs in large numbers, there was no plan in place to attain or maintain desegregation, appropriately train teachers and staff, or recruit nonwhite teachers to help deal with new groups of students. Eighty-five percent of the nation's teachers are white, and little progress is being made toward diversifying the nation's teaching force.

In states that now have a substantial majority of nonwhite students, failure to provide quality education to that majority through high school and college is a direct threat to the economic and social future of the general population. In the world economy, success is linked to formal education. Major sections of the US face the threat of declining education levels as the proportion of children attending inferior segregated schools continues to increase.

Rural schools also face severe segregation. In the days of civil rights struggles, small towns and rural areas were seen as the heart of the most intense racism. Of 8.3 million rural white students, 73 percent attend schools that are 80 to 100 percent white.

Our nation's segregated schools result from decades of systematic neglect of civil rights policy and related educational and community reforms.

According to the UCLA report, what is needed are leaders who recognize that we have a common destiny in an America where our children grow up together, knowing and respecting each other, and are all given the educational tools that prepare them for success in our society. The author maintains that if we are to continue along a path of deepening separation and entrenched inequality, it will only diminish our common potential.

3

Toxic Waste Behind Somali Pirates

Sources:
Al Jazeera English, October 11, 2008
Title: "Toxic waste behind Somali piracy"
Author: Najad Abdullahi

Huffington Post, January 4, 2009
Title: "You are being lied to about pirates"
Author: Johann Hari

WardheerNews, January 8, 2009
Title: "The Two Piracies in Somalia: Why the World Ignores the Other"
Author: Mohamed Abshir Waldo

Student Researcher: Christine Wilson
Faculty Evaluator: Andre Bailey, Educational Opportunity Program Advisor
Sonoma State University

The international community has come out in force to condemn and declare war on the Somali fishermen pirates, while discreetly protecting the illegal, unreported, and unregulated (IUU) fleets from around the world that have been poaching and dumping toxic waste in Somali waters since the fall of the Somali government eighteen years ago.

In 1991, when the government of Somalia collapsed, foreign inter-

ests seized the opportunity to begin looting the country's food supply and using the country's unguarded waters as a dumping ground for nuclear and other toxic waste.

According to the High Seas Task Force (HSTF), there were over 800 IUU fishing vessels in Somali waters at one time in 2005, taking advantage of Somalia's inability to police and control its own waters and fishing grounds. The IUUs poach an estimated $450 million in seafood from Somali waters annually. In so doing, they steal an invaluable protein source from some of the world's poorest people and ruin the livelihoods of legitimate fishermen.

Allegations of the dumping of toxic waste, as well as illegal fishing, have circulated since the early 1990s, but hard evidence emerged when the tsunami of 2004 hit the country. The United Nations Environment Program (UNEP) reported that the tsunami washed rusting containers of toxic waste onto the shores of Puntland, northern Somalia.

Nick Nuttall, a UNEP spokesman, told Al Jazeera that when the barrels were smashed open by the force of the waves, the containers exposed a "frightening activity" that had been going on for more than a decade. "Somalia has been used as a dumping ground for hazardous waste starting in the early 1990s, and continuing through the civil war there," he said. "The waste is many different kinds. There is uranium radioactive waste. There is lead, and heavy metals like cadmium and mercury. There is also industrial waste, and there are hospital wastes, chemical wastes— you name it."

Nuttall also said that since the containers came ashore, hundreds of residents have fallen ill, suffering from mouth and abdominal bleeding, skin infections and other ailments. "What is most alarming here is that nuclear waste is being dumped. Radioactive uranium waste that is potentially killing Somalis and completely destroying the ocean," he said.

Ahmedou Ould-Abdallah, the United Nations (UN) envoy for Somalia, says the practice helps fuel the eighteen-year-old civil war in Somalia, as companies pay Somali government ministers and/or militia leaders to dump their waste. "There is no government control . . . and there are few people with high moral ground. . . . Yes, people in high positions are being paid off, but because of the fragility of the Transitional Federal Government, some of these companies now no longer ask the authorities—they simply dump their waste and leave."

In 1992, the countries of the European Union (EU) and 168 other countries signed the Basel Convention on the Control of Transboundary Movements of Hazardous Wastes and their Disposal. The convention prohibits waste trade between countries that have signed, as well as countries that have not signed the accord, unless a bilateral agreement had been negotiated. It also prohibits the shipping of hazardous waste to a war zone.

Surprisingly, the UN has disregarded its own findings and has ignored Somali and international appeals to act on the continued ravaging of the Somali marine resources and dumping of toxic wastes. Violations have also been largely ignored by the region's maritime authorities.

This is the context from which the men we are calling "pirates" have emerged.

Everyone agrees they were ordinary Somali fishermen who, at first, took speedboats to try to dissuade the dumpers and trawlers, or at least wage a "tax" on them. They call themselves the Volunteer Coast Guard of Somalia.

One of the pirate leaders, Sugule Ali, explains that their motive is "to stop illegal fishing and dumping in our waters. . . . We don't consider ourselves sea bandits. We consider sea bandits [to be] those who illegally fish, and dump waste, and carry weapons in our seas."

Author Johann Hari notes that, while none of this makes hostage-taking justifiable, the "pirates" have the overwhelming support of the local population for a reason. The independent Somalia news site *WardheerNews* conducted the best research we have on what ordinary Somalis are thinking. It found that 70 percent "strongly support the piracy as a form of national defense of the country's territorial waters."

Instead of taking action to protect the people and waters of Somalia from international transgressions, the UN has responded to the situation by passing aggressive resolutions that entitle and encourage transgressors to wage war on the Somali pirates.

A chorus of calls for tougher international action has resulted in a multinational and unilateral Naval stampede to invade and take control of the Somali waters. The UN Security Council (a number of whose members may have ulterior motives to indirectly protect their illegal fishing fleets in the Somali Seas) passed Resolutions 1816 and 1838 in June and October 2008 respectively, which "call upon States interested in the security of maritime activities to take part actively in the fight against piracy on the high seas off the coast of Somalia, in particular by deploying naval vessels and military aircraft . . ."

Both the North Atlantic Treaty Organization (NATO) and the EU have issued orders to the same effect. Russia, Japan, India, Malaysia, Egypt, and Yemen, along with an increasing number of countries, have joined the fray.

For years, attempts made to address piracy in the world's seas through UN resolutions have failed to pass, largely because member nations felt such resolutions would infringe on their sovereignty and security. Countries are unwilling to give up control and patrol of their own waters. UN Resolutions 1816 and 1838, to which a number of West African, Caribbean, and South American nations objected, were accordingly tailored to apply to Somalia only. Somalia doesn't have strong enough representation at the United Nations to demand amendments to protect its sovereignty, and Somali civil society objections to the draft resolutions—which makes no mention of illegal fishing or hazard waste dumping—were ignored.

Hari asks, "Do we expect starving Somalians to stand passively on their beaches, paddling in our nuclear waste, and watch us snatch their fish to eat in restaurants in London and Paris and Rome? We didn't act on those crimes—but when some of the fishermen responded by disrupting the transit-corridor for 20 percent of the world's oil supply, we begin to shriek about "evil." If we really want to deal with piracy, we need to stop its root cause—our crimes —before we send in the gun-boats to root out Somalia's criminals."

UPDATE BY MOHAMED ABSHIR WALDO

The crises of the multiple piracies in Somalia have not diminished since my previous article, "The Two Piracies in Somalia: Why the World Ignores the Other," was written in December 2008. All the illegal fishing piracy, the waste dumping piracy, and the shipping piracy continue with new zeal. Somali fishermen, turned pirates in reaction to armed foreign marine poachers, have intensified their war against all kinds of ships in the Gulf of Aden and the Indian Ocean.

On international response, foreign governments, international organizations, and mainstream media have been united in demonizing Somalia and described its fishermen as evil men pillaging ships and terrorizing sailors (even though no sailors were harmed). This presentation is lopsided. The media said relatively little on the other piracies of illegal fishing and waste dumping.

The allied navies of the world—fleets of over forty warships from over ten Asian, Arab, and African countries as well as from many NATO and EU member countries—stepped up their hunt for the Somali fishermen pirates, regardless of whether they are actually engaged in piracy or in normal fishing in the Somali waters. Various meetings of the International Contact Group on Somalia (ICGS) in New York, London, Cairo, and Rome continue to underline the demonization of the Somali fishermen and urge further punitive actions without a single mention of the violation of illegal fishing and toxic dumping by vessels from the countries of those sitting in the ICGS and UN forums in judgment of the piracy issue.

At the ICGS Anti-Piracy meeting in Cairo on May 30, 2009, Egypt and Italy were two of the loudest countries calling for severe punishment of the Somali fishermen pirates. As the ICGS met in Rome on June 10, 2009, two Egyptian trawlers full of fish illegally caught in Somali waters and an Italian barge that had been towing two huge tanks suspected of containing toxic or nuclear waste were being held in the Somali coastal town of Las Khorey by the local community, who invited the international experts to come and investigate the cases. At the time of the meeting, the international community had not yet responded to the Las Khorey community's invitation.

Somalia is not alone; both the IUUs and waste dumping are happening in other African countries. Ivory Coast, as just one example, is a victim of major international toxic dumping.

It is said that acts of piracy are actually acts of desperation, and, as in the case of Somalia, what is one man's pirate is another man's coast guard.

4

Nuclear Waste Pools in North Carolina

Source:
CounterPunch, August 9, 2008
Title: "Pools of Fire"
Author: Jeffrey St. Clair

Student Researchers: Krisden Kidd and Karene Schelert
Faculty Evaluator: Heidi LaMoreaux, PhD
Sonoma State University

One of the most lethal patches of ground in North America is located in the backwoods of North Carolina, where Shearon Harris nuclear plant is housed and owned by Progress Energy. The plant contains the largest radioactive waste storage pools in the country. It is not just a nuclear-power-generating station, but also a repository for highly radioactive spent fuel rods from two other nuclear plants. The spent fuel rods are transported by rail and stored in four densely packed pools filled with circulating cold water to keep the waste from heating. The Department of Homeland Security has marked Shearon Harris as one of the most vulnerable terrorist targets in the nation.

The threat exists, however, without the speculation of terrorist attack. Should the cooling system malfunction, the resulting fire would be virtually unquenchable and could trigger a nuclear meltdown, putting more than 200 million residents of this rapidly growing section of North Carolina in extreme peril. A recent study by Brookhaven Lab estimates that a pool fire could cause 140,000 cancers, contaminate thousands of square miles of land, and cause over $500 billion in off-site property damage.

The Nuclear Regulatory Commission (NRC) has estimated that there is a 1:100 chance of pool fire happening under the best of scenarios. And the dossier on the Shearon Harris plant is far from the best.

In 1999, the plant experienced four emergency shutdowns. A few months later, in April 2000, the plant's safety monitoring system, designed to provide early warning of a serious emergency, failed. And it

wasn't the first time. Indeed, the emergency warning system at Shearon Harris has failed fifteen times since the plant opened in 1987.

In 2002, the NRC put the plant on notice for nine unresolved safety issues detected during a fire prevention inspection by NRC investigators. When the NRC returned to the plant a few months later for reinspection, it determined that the corrective actions were "not acceptable." Between January and July of 2002, Harris plant managers were forced to manually shut down the reactors four times.

The problems continue with chilling regularity. In the spring of 2003, there were four emergency shutdowns of the plant, including three over a four-day period. One of the incidents occurred when the reactor core failed to cool down during a refueling operation while the reactor dome was off of the plant—a potentially catastrophic series of circumstances.

Between 1999 and 2003, there were twelve major problems requiring the shutdown of the plant. According to the NRC, the national average for commercial reactors is one shutdown per eighteen months.

Congressman David Price of North Carolina sent the NRC a report by scientists at Massachusetts Institute of Technology (MIT) and Princeton University that pinpointed the waste pools as the biggest risk at the plant.

"Spent fuel recently discharged from a reactor could heat up relatively rapidly and catch fire," wrote Bob Alvarez, a former advisor to the Department of Energy and coauthor of the report. "The fire could well spread to older fuel. The long-term land contamination consequences of such an event could be significantly worse than Chernobyl."

The study recommended relatively inexpensive fixes, which would have cost Progress approximately $5 million a year—less than the $6.6 million annual bonus for Progress CEO Warren Cavanaugh.

Progress scoffed at the idea and recruited the help of NRC Commissioner Edward McGaffigan to smear the MIT/Princeton report. McGaffigan is a nuclear enthusiast who has worked for both Republicans and Democrats. A veteran of the National Security Council in the Reagan administration, McGaffigan took a special interest in promoting nuclear plants to US client states. He served two terms as NRC commissioner under Clinton as a tireless proponent of nuclear plant construction and deregulation, and consistently dismissed the risks associated with the transport and storage of nuclear waste.

McGaffigan's meddling has outraged many antinuclear activists. Lewis Pitts, an environmental attorney in North Carolina says, "The NRC has directed the production of a bogus study to deny decades of science on the perils of pool fires."

Author Jeffrey St. Clair concludes, "If the worst happens, the blame will reside in Washington, which has permitted the Shearon Harris facility to become a nuclear time bomb."

5
Europe Blocks US Toxic Products

Sources:
Scientific American, September 30, 2008
Title: "European Chemical Clampdown Reaches Across Atlantic"
Author: David Biello

Environmental Defense Fund, September 30, 2008
Title: "How Europe's New Chemical Rules Affect US"

Democracy Now! February 24, 2009
Title: "US Lags Behind Europe in Regulating Toxicity of Everyday Products"
Author: Mark Schapiro

Student Researchers: Caitlin Ruxton (SSU), Annie Sexton, Gwendolyn Brack, Hallie Fischer, Bernadette Gorman, Paige Henderson, Daryl Mowrey, and Taylor Prodromos
Faculty Evaluators: Robert Girling, PhD, and Jeanette Pope, professors of geology
Sonoma State University and DePauw University

US deregulation of toxic substances, such as lead in lipsticks, mercury in electronics, and phthalates (endocrine disruptors) in baby toys, may not only pose disastrous consequences to our health, but also to our economic and political status in the world. International markets are moving toward a European model of insisting on environmental and consumer safety. A European-led revolution in chemical regulation, requiring that thousands of chemicals finally be assessed for their potentially toxic effects on human beings and the environment, signals the end of American industry's ability to withhold critical data from the public.

Europe has launched stringent new regulations that require companies seeking access to their lucrative markets eliminate toxic substances and manufacture safer electronics, automobiles, toys, and cosmetics.

Dangerous chemicals have been identified via the European Union's 2007 Registration, Evaluation, Authorization, and Restriction of Chemicals (REACH) law, which requires the disclosure of all chemicals sold in the EU in quantities of more than one metric ton per year.

Hundreds of companies located in the US produce or import hundreds of chemicals designated as dangerous by the European Union. Large amounts of these chemicals are being produced in thirty-seven states, in as many as eighty-seven sites per state, according to biochemist Richard Denison of Environmental Defense Fund, author of the report "Across the Pond: Assessing REACH's First Big Impact on US Companies and Chemicals."

Of the 267 chemicals on the potential REACH list, compiled by the International Chemical Secretariat in Sweden, only one third have ever been tested by the Environmental Protection Agency (EPA), and only two are regulated in any form under US law.

Mark Schapiro, author of *Exposed: The Toxic Chemistry of Everyday Products and What's at Stake for American Power*, writes that according to the EPA itself, only 5 percent of all chemicals in the US have undergone even minimal testing for their toxicity or environmental impact. Researchers at University of California–Berkeley's School of Public Health estimate that 42 billion pounds of chemicals enter American commerce daily. Fewer than five hundred of those substances, according to a report the school produced for the state of California, have undergone any substantive risk assessments.

Over the past decade, the industry has been either the second or the third biggest lobbying force on Capitol Hill, according to the Center for Responsive Politics. Between 1996 and 2006, the industry contributed $35 million to federal election campaigns, and spends between $2 million and $5 million each year on lobbying in Washington. This interest also spent a significant amount on lobbying at the state level. Consequently, new EPA requirements include the "costs to industry" in determining whether a substance presents an "unreasonable threat to public health" and that the "least burdensome regulation" be imposed on industry.

Industry's evisceration of the EPA, the Food and Drug Administration (FDA), and a host of regulatory agencies has placed US firms in a position of unaccountability. As a result, American products are increasingly viewed with distrust on the global market.

When Europeans started imposing standards to protect people from dangerous products, the US chemical industry began flooding Brussels with lobbyists. The European Parliament and the European Commission (which are essentially the Congress and White House of the European Union) are now surrounded by Burson-Marsteller and Hill & Knowlton companies, as well as American Chamber of Commerce executives, all lobbying for less oversight of toxic products.

Schapiro observes, however, that to a great extent US-style lobbying doesn't work in Europe, and in many cases is backfiring.

We are seeing an enormous global shift in power in which multinational companies are adapting to European standards based on the notion that regulation is actually good for business—thus rendering US standards irrelevant.

As a result of the contrast between US deregulation and the spreading European model of regulation, the US has become the dumping ground for toxic toys, electronics, and cosmetics. We produce and consume the toxic materials, from which other countries around the world are protected.

6

Business Booms for Lobbyists

Source:

OpenSecrets.org
Title: "Washington Lobbying Grew to $3.2 Billion Last Year, Despite Economy"
Authors: Center for Responsive Politics

Student Researchers: Alan Grady and Leora Johnson
Faculty Evaluator: John Kramer, PhD
Sonoma State University

According to a study by the Center for Responsive Politics (CRP), special interests paid Washington lobbyists $3.2 billion in 2008—more than any other year on record. This was a 13.7 percent increase from 2007 (which broke the record by 7.7 percent over 2006).

The CRP calculates that interest groups spent $17.4 million on lobbying for every day Congress was in session in 2008, or $32,523 per legislator per day. Center director Sheila Krumholz says, "The federal government is handing out billions of dollars by the day, and that translates into job security for lobbyists who can help companies and industries get a piece of the payout."

Health interests spent more on federal lobbying than any other economic sector. Their $478.5 million guaranteed the crown for the third year, with the finance/insurance/real estate sector a runner up, spending $453.5 million. The pharmaceutical/health products industry contributed $230.9 million, raising their last eleven-year total to over $1.6 billion. The second-biggest spender among industries in 2008 was electric utilities, which spent $156.7 million on lobbying, followed by insurance, which spent $153.2 million, and oil and gas, which paid lobbyists $133.2 million. Pro-Israel groups, food processing companies, and the oil and gas industry increased their lobbying expenditures the most (as a percentage) between 2007 and 2008.

Finance, insurance and real estate companies have been competing to get a piece of the $700 billion bailout package Congress approved late last year. The companies that reduced lobbying the most are those that declared bankruptcy or were taken over by the federal government and stopped their lobbying operations all together. "Even though some financial, insurance, and real estate interests pulled back last year, they still

managed to spend more than $450 million as a sector to lobby policy-makers. That can buy a lot of influence, and it's a fraction of what the financial sector is reaping in return through the government's bailout program," Krumholz said.

Business and real estate associations and coalitions were among the organizations that ramped up their lobbying expenditures the most last year. The National Association of Realtors increased spending by 25 percent, from $13.9 million to $17.3 million. The American Bankers Association spent $9.1 million in 2008, a 47 percent increase from 2007. Other industry groups that spent more in 2008 include the Private Equity Council, the Mortgage Bankers Association of America, and the Financial Services Roundtable.

The US Chamber of Commerce remained the number one spender on lobbying in 2008, spending nearly $92 million—more than $350,000 every weekday, and a 73 percent increase over 2007—to advocate for its members' interests. Pro-business associations as a whole increased their lobbying 47 percent between 2007 and 2008.

With record spending on lobbying, some industries face serious cut backs and have put the brakes on spending, but have not discontinued the practice. Automotive companies decreased the amount they paid lobbyists by 7.6 percent, from $70.9 million to $65.5 million. This is a big change from prior years; auto manufacturers and dealers increased lobbying spending by 21 percent between 2006 and 2007. Between 2007 and 2008, the Alliance of Automobile Manufacturers, which testified before Congress with Detroit's Big Three last year, decreased its reported lobbying by 43 percent, from $12.8 million to $7.3 million. Of the Big Three, only one company, Ford, increased its efforts, though not by much: it went from $7.1 million to $7.7 million, an 8 percent increase.

Among Washington lobbying firms, Patton Boggs reported the highest revenues from registered lobbying for the fifth year in a row: $41.9 million, an increase since 2006 of more than 20 percent. The firm's most lucrative clients included private equity firm Cerberus Capital Management, confection and pet food maker Mars, communication provider Verizon, pharmaceutical manufacturers Bristol-Myers Squibb and Roche, and the American Association for Justice (formerly the Association of Trial Lawyers of America).

UPDATE BY LINDSAY RENICK MAYER

It seems like this should be a classified ad: "Laid off and looking for work? The lobbying industry wants you!" Since we posted this story on OpenSecrets.org in January, the lobbying industry has only continued to grow, even as industries across the board have continued to shrink, forcing hundreds of thousands of Americans out of work. This growth could be attributed in part to the economy itself—many executives are looking for some help from the government to keep their businesses afloat. Others are simply taking advantage of the opportunities that a spate of government handouts has presented. But as long as there's a federal government calling the shots, lobbyists will be paid more and more each year to hold their clients' fire to lawmakers' feet.

Year after year we see increases in lobbying expenditures—in fact, 100 percent over the last decade—and the flurry of activity during the first three months of 2009 indicates that the trend won't come to an end anytime soon. Based on records from the Senate Office of Public Records, the nonpartisan Center for Responsive Politics found that from January through March, lobbying increased slightly compared to the same period of time last year, by at least $2.4 million. In the first half of 2009, unions, organizations, and companies spent at least $799.7 million on sending influence peddlers to Capitol Hill, compared to $797.2 million during the same time in 2008. That might seem like a small increase compared to the billions spent each year on this activity, but in a time of economic turmoil, that's a hefty revenue stream for a single industry.

That said, industries that have made the most headlines for seeking or receiving help from the federal government actually decreased the amount they spent on lobbying in the first three months of 2009 compared to 2008. Recipients of cash from the federal government's Troubled Asset Relief Program (TARP) handed out less money to lobbyists than they had in any quarter of 2008, in part, perhaps, because they faced new rules restricting their lobbying contact with officials in connection with the bailout program. The CRP found that TARP recipients have spent $13.9 million on lobbying so far this year, compared to $20.2 million in January through March of last year and $17.8 million in the last three months of 2008. With the government doling out billions of dollars, these sums pale in comparison to the benefit the companies are reaping.

To read more about how lobbying and influence peddling are shaping legislation, keep up with CRP's blog at http://www.opensecrets.org/news.

7

Obama's Military Appointments Have Corrupt Past

Sources:
ConsortiumNews.com, November 13, 2008
Title: "The Danger of Keeping Robert Gates"
Author: Robert Parry

Global Research, February 13, 2009
Title: "Obama's Defense Department Appointees: The 3.4 Trillion Dollar Question"
Author: Andrew Hughes

Democracy Now! January 7, 2009
Title: "Obama Nominee Admiral Dennis Blair Aided perpetrators of 1999 church
    Killings in East Timor"
Interviewee: Allan Nairn

The Hill, November 24, 2008
Title: "Ties to Chevron, Boeing Raise Concern on Possible NSA Pick"
Author: Roxana Tiron

Student Researcher: Chris McManus
Faculty Evaluator: Diana Grant, PhD
Sonoma State University

President Barack Obama's retention of Robert Gates as secretary of defense makes Gates the first appointment from an outgoing administration of the opposing party to be kept in the position. Over the last two years of the previous administration, Gates was a key implementer of Bush's Iraq War "surge"—after he replaced Donald Rumsfeld, who had opposed the escalation.

Obama's appointees to the Department of Defense and National Intelligence embody many of the worst elements of US national security policy over the past three decades, including responsibility for what Obama himself has fingered as chief concerns: "politicized intelligence" and "lack of transparency." The valued "decades of experience" these leaders bring with them are filled with ethical breeches, lies to Congress, and deep conflicts of interest and revolving doors within the US military-industrial complex. Although Obama promised to keep lobbyists out of top government posts, many of those he appointmented are former lobbyists or former board members of companies directly doing business with the Pentagon.

Robert Gates, whose career has reflected and implemented neoconservative positions, also decried Obama's plan for a phased withdrawal of US troops. Gates's history as a career intelligence officer began under Richard Nixon. But, as Robert Parry chronicles, it was as a senior Central Intelligence Agency (CIA) official in the 1980s under Ronald Reagan that Gates broke the back of the CIA analytical division's commitment to objective intelligence.

In a recent book, *Failure of Intelligence: The Decline and Fall of the CIA*, former CIA analyst Melvin A. Goodman identifies Gates as "the chief action officer for the Reagan administration's drive to tailor intelligence reporting to White House political desires." As chief analyst under CIA director William Casey, Gates "guided the first institutionalized 'cooking of the books' at the CIA in the 1980s, with a particular emphasis on tailoring intelligence dealing with the Soviet Union, Central America, and Southwest Asia," says Goodman, in order to justify increased US military spending and US support for bloody brushfire wars—central elements of Reagan's foreign policy.

Gates's 1991 confirmation hearing for George H. W. Bush's CIA director marked an extraordinary outpouring of career CIA officers going public with inside stories about how Gates had corrupted the intelligence product. There also were concerns about Gates's role in misleading Congress regarding the secret Iran-Contra operations in the mid-1980s, an obstacle that had prevented Gates from getting the top CIA job when Casey died in 1987. Gates funneled support to Saddam Hussein during the Iran-Iraq War, covertly supplying chemical weapons, arms, and equipment.

Gates served on the board of directors of Science Applications International Corporation (SAIC), which reported $7.5 billion earnings in 2005. SAIC is involved in everything from intelligence gathering to Iraq reconstruction for the Pentagon.

On January 21, 2009, Obama signed an executive order that issued more stringent ethics rules, prohibiting lobbyists from serving in agencies they have lobbied in the previous two years. Just two days later, on January 23, the White House announced that its tough new ethics rules wouldn't apply to the nominee for deputy defense secretary, William Lynn. Lynn was senior vice president for government operations and strategy at the defense giant Raytheon, and a registered Raytheon lobbyist until July 2008. Raytheon, the fifth largest defense company, sells $18 billion worth of missiles radars, sensors, munitions, space systems and other technology to the military and other government agencies annually.[1] Republican senator for Iowa, Charles Grassley, forcefully objected to the appointment of Lynn on the basis of "very questionable accounting practices that were obviously not in the public interest" while in the position of Pentagon comptroller during the Clinton administration.

In fiscal year 1999, the Department of Defense reported that it was missing $2.3 trillion. In fiscal year 2000, the department reported missing another $1.1 trillion. In total, that's $3.4 trillion in "missing" taxpayer money. This happened under the watchful eye of the same William Lynn who now passes through the revolving door between the Department of Defense and the defense industry.

As the Defense Department's chief financial officer, Lynn was responsible for all budgetary administration and reporting. He was also responsible for the publication of audited financial statements, which he failed to do during his tenure and which have not been published since.

Also newly appointed, Under Secretary of Defense (Comptroller) Robert Hale served as assistant secretary of the air force in the role of financial comptroller from 1994 to 2001. He was also responsible, along with Lynn, for the management of Defense Department funds. Hale is also a certified defense financial manager with acquisition specialty. This is his particular connection to the military-industrial complex.

Author Andrew Hughes points out that, "Between these two

appointees, they have lost enough taxpayer money to pay for Obama's stimulus plan four times over and are now, again, responsible for overseeing how the Department of Defense manages its appropriations."

Admiral Dennis Blair, Obama's pick to head National Intelligence, which oversees all sixteen intelligence agencies, was the commander of military forces in the Pacific under Bill Clinton. As such, he played a critical role in the backing of the Indonesian occupation of East Timor after the US-backed dictator Suharto fell in 1998. In 1999, when the Indonesian military terrorized the population to thwart democratic reform, Blair was sent by Clinton and the US State Department to demand that Indonesian General Wiranto stop the massacres. Instead, Admiral Blair falsely informed the general of unwavering US support. Government-sponsored atrocities escalated. Blair then lied to Congress, claiming that only small unit violence was involved, when in fact the top echelons of the Indonesian military were carrying out kidnapping, massacres, and torture. Blair essentially sided with General Wiranto in the mass killing of Indonesian civilians, against US Congress's orders and knowledge.

Blair is a member of the Trilateral Commission (see story # 22). He was on the board of the Earl Dodge Osborne (EDO) Corporation, which is the subcontractor for the F-22 raptor program. He also served on the board of Tyco International, which manufactures small electronic components used by F-22 subcontractors and other parts for the military, and Tridium, a satellite company. In 2006, Blair had to step down as president of the Institute for Defense Analyses (IDA) because of conflicts of interest. The IDA was evaluating the F-22 program for the Pentagon.

Serving under Blair, former four-star general James L. Jones has been appointed head of the National Security Agency. Jones is not only the former NATO commander and commandant of the marine corps, he is also a member of the Trilateral Commission. Jones served on the boards of directors of Chevron, Boeing, and Invacare Corp. (which produces medical equipment for the Pentagon) until December 2008. He served as a consultant to Cross Match Technologies, a biometrics company that worked with the Pentagon and Federal Bureau of Investigation (FBI) until January 2009. He also served on the board of advisors to MIC Industries, which developed the Ultimate Building Machine, a mobile construction device used exclusively in Iraq and Afghanistan to rapidly deploy steel structures for military objectives. Jones was most recently employed as president of the US Chamber of Commerce's "Institute for 21st Century Energy."

Citation:

1. William Matthews, "Lynn gets waiver from Obama lobbyist rules," *Federal Times*, January 26, 2009, http://www.federaltimes.com/index.php?S=3918762.

UPDATE BY ROBERT PARRY

As for the significance of "The Danger of Keeping Robert Gates," that early decision by President-elect Obama was the first clear indication that he would not diverge dramatically from President Bush's national security policies. It also revealed that Obama had no intention of challenging Washington's false narrative of the preceding Republican-dominated decades, since Gates had been a key figure in many of those scandals, including Iran-Contra and politicization of CIA intelligence, both important precursors to Bush's disastrous decisions this decade. Instead, by retaining Gates, Obama made clear that he would avoid the kinds of conflicts that might have put the United States on a dramatically different course. He was, in effect, bowing to the status quo.

Since the story, Obama's intentions have only become clearer. While he has rhetorically shifted away from Bush's bellicose style, Obama has kept much of the substance, with Gates and other holdovers slowing the pace of US withdrawal from Iraq and building up US forces in Afghanistan. Obama also has opposed any accountability for Gates's old superiors, much as President Clinton swept under the rug the earlier scandals that implicated Gates and the Reagan and Bush administrations.

Gates personifies the "see no evil" of the Washington Establishment—at least toward its own—so naturally the Washington news media had little interest in following up any evidence of Gates's wrongdoing, past or present. Gates was a favorite of Official Washington during his Reagan–Bush days and he remains so now.

When Gates was named defense secretary by G. W. Bush in November 2006, the mainstream press completely misinterpreted the significance. The conventional wisdom was that Gates's appointment indicated that Bush would bow to the Iraq Study Group's plan to wind down the war. In reality, Gates was far more of a hawk than Donald Rumsfeld.

But the big-name journalists never corrected their mistake. They just went on viewing Gates through the same rose-colored glasses. When

CBS's *60 Minutes* did a recent profile of Gates, it was all puffery about Gates's deep personal concern for the troops, even though his earlier government work set the stage for the G. W. Bush wars (especially the corrupting of the CIA analytical division) and his unqualified support for the Iraq surge had sent more than 1,000 more US soldiers to their deaths. The critical reporting on Gates continues to come mostly from former CIA officials who worked with Gates in his early years and know him as the consummate careerist. For instance, former CIA analyst Melvin A. Goodman devotes a large part of his book, *Failure of Intelligence: The Decline and Fall of the CIA* to Gates's role in ending the CIA's tradition of providing "bark-on" intelligence to US policymakers. During Gates's dominion over the analytical division in the 1980s, the bark came off and the intelligence was polished just the way the Reagan-era ideologues wanted it.

UPDATE BY ANDREW HUGHES
Since the original article was published in February 2009, not one single line in the mainstream media has been written to address this enormous theft of public money. In reality it has been overshadowed by the equally grievous theft of public money masquerading as "Solving the credit crisis." The figure in the latter swindle is almost five times the $3.4 trillion stolen by the Department of Defense.

The two appointees, William Lynn and Robert Hale, unveiled the proposed 2010 defense budget on May 7, 2009, that will increase defense spending by 4 percent to $663.8 billion. This comes at a time when the population is being impoverished through rising unemployment, shrinking state and federal programs, and the transfer of wealth from American households to the Wall Street banking cartel.

The issue highlighted in the original article was not just the missing $3.4 trillion from the Department of Defense but the fact that this was business as usual for an out-of-control government that, even with a change in the White House residency, continues to steal from its own citizens.

When listening to Obama's campaign speeches, in which he emphasized the importance of Afghanistan as the new front in the War on Terror—that elusive, neverending and unwinnable war—it was obvious that, behind all the stage-managed speeches and media deification, the agenda laid out by Zbigniew Brzezinski and the Project for a New American Century was in simply repackaged in a persona who represented "change we can believe in."

The developments since my story was originally published have only emphasized the lack of commitment to any solid accounting of the public coffers. No investigation has been commissioned to look into the missing trillions; Donald Rumsfeld, William Lynn, and Robert Hale have not been subject to questions regarding this crime; defense spending has increased; the war in Afghanistan has escalated; Pakistan is being destabilized by US proxies in the region; Obama has been responsible for the murder of hundreds of Pakistani civilians by Predator Drones flown by CIA operatives; and the promises to end the Iraq War have been cynically ignored, obfuscated, and recycled into political doublespeak.

This all speaks to the fact that the governmental-military-industrial organism is a symbiotic union of self interest, greed, and lust for power on a level never before seen in human history. It is important to take a bird's eye view of the corruption that has been highlighted in this article to see its true nature and how it forms the fabric that holds the system together. This system has been growing steadily over the decades and has insured itself against any real investigation or consequence by co-opting the mainstream media through acquisitions by defense contractors of corporate news companies and through the placing of Department of Defense employees and CIA personnel into these same news companies. But the quintessential achievement of this system is the fact that Donald Rumsfeld could announce at a public press conference on September 10, 2001, without any fear of prosecution or public backlash, that trillions of dollars were missing, that there would be no investigation and that nobody would be held accountable. We have seen exactly the same arrogance with regard to the torture scandal, the banker bailout scandal, the Iraq War scandal, and the advancing police state grid being established by the Department of Homeland Security to label anyone who disagrees with government policy—or who believes in the US constitution—as "terrorists."

An investigation into the missing Department of Defense trillions needs to be initiated as a matter of urgency, and as a precursor to further investigations of gross corruption perpetrated by the US government. It will only be achieved through an awakening to reality, a refusal to be lied to by mainstream media, and an understanding of the depth of the corruption and how it will destroy what remains of the Constitution, public trust, and real freedom.

8

Bailed-Out Banks and America's Wealthiest Cheat IRS Out of Billions

Sources:
Bloomberg, December 16, 2008
Title: "Goldman Sachs's Tax Rate Drops to 1% or $14 Million"
Author: Christine Harper

Huffington Post, February 23, 2009
Title "Gimme Shelter: Tax Evasion and the Obama Administration"
Author: Thomas B. Edsall

Student Researchers: Valerie Janssen and Aimee Drew
Faculty Evaluators: B. C. Franson, JD, and Robert Girling, PhD
Southwest Minnesota State University and Sonoma State University

A 2008 study done by the Government Accountability Office (GAO) reported that eighty-three of the top publicly held US companies have operations in tax havens like the Cayman Islands, Bermuda, and the Virgin Islands. Fourteen of these companies, including American International Group (AIG), Bank of America, and Citigroup, received

money from the government bailout. The GAO also reported that activities of Union Bank of Switzerland (UBS) are directly connected to tax avoidance.

Swiss banking giant UBS has enabled wealthy Americans to use tax schemes—some of which are illegal—to cheat the Internal Revenue Service (IRS) out of over $20 billion in recent years, according to the Department of Justice. UBS, a sponsor of the prestigious Miami Art Basel show, takes advantage of this public event to build relationships with the rich by helping them find ways to avoid paying taxes in the US. Art Basel Miami Beach is the most important art show in the United States, a cultural and social highlight for the Americas. Its sister event, Switzerland's Art Basel, is considered the most prestigious art show worldwide. UBS uses the show to find clients looking for advice on tax shelters and how to take advantage of bank secrecy rules in Switzerland, Lichtenstein, and other places. Other locations for hiding funds include Austria, Luxembourg, the Channel Islands, Singapore, Hong Kong, Andorra, Monaco, and Gibraltar. In the Caribbean, the established havens are the Bahamas, Bermuda, and the Cayman Islands. Some of the newer countries with bank secrecy are the Cook Islands, Turks, and Calicos.

For corporations, the process of geographic tax avoidance is fairly simple. A US corporation will sell at reduced rates, even at a loss to their own offshore subsidiaries, and then resell the products at higher prices, paying little or no taxes in the foreign country.

In December 2008, the bank holding company Goldman Sachs reported its first quarterly loss. On the heels of this announcement, Goldman Sachs issued a statement confirming that its tax rate was dropping from 34.1 percent to 1 percent. Goldman Sachs Group Inc., which got $10 billion and debt guarantees from the US government in October 2008, expects to pay only $14 million in taxes worldwide for 2008, compared with $6 billion in 2007. The New York-based Goldman Sachs cited "changes in geographic earnings mix" as the reason behind the decrease.

According to US Representative Lloyd Doggett, the shifting of income to countries with lower taxes is cause for concern. "The problem is larger than Goldman Sachs," Doggett said, "With the right hand out begging for bailout money, the left is hiding it offshore."

On February 19, 2009, UBS for the first time agreed to release to the US Department of Justice (DOJ) an as yet undetermined number of the names of bank account holders. Anywhere from just 250 to 19,000 of US taxpayers with Swiss bank accounts face the prospect of IRS examination of their bank documents with an eye to prosecution and/or civil litigation of the account holders. The DOJ has demanded UBS bank account documents for a total of 52,000 additional depositors.

UBS and Swiss banking authorities are claiming that their guarantee of absolute banking privacy will somehow survive this attack—"Banking secrecy remains intact," declared Hans-Rudolf Merz, Switzerland's president and its finance minister.

There is, however, much more money escaping taxation through entirely legal means—through provisions in the US tax code—and there is an accurate accounting of the revenues that are lost. Every year, the congressional Joint Committee on Taxation puts out an illuminating but little-read document with the bestselling title "Estimates of Federal Tax Expenditures," subtitled this year, "For Fiscal Years 2008–2012."

Citation:

1. "International Taxation: Large US Corporations and Federal Contractors with Subsidiaries in Jurisdictions Listed as Tax Havens or Financial Privacy Jurisdictions," GAO US Government Accountability Office, December 18, 2008, http://www.gao.gov/products/GAO-09-157.

UPDATE FROM RACHEL KEELER, *DOLLARS & SENSE*, MAY–JUNE 2009 ISSUE:

Over the years, trillions of dollars in both corporate profits and personal wealth have migrated offshore in search of rock bottom tax rates and the comfort of no questions asked. This was a significant contributing factor to international economic downturn in 2008. The G20 meetings in April of 2009 declared a crackdown on tax havens as the first step to financial recovery. However, the offshore banking world now harbors $11.5 trillion in individual wealth alone, and many countries will continue to resist regulation and inspections from outside their borders.

9

US Arms Used for War Crimes in Gaza

Sources:

Human Rights Watch, March 25, 2009
Title: "White Phosphorus Use Evidence of War Crimes Report: Rain of Fire: Israel's
    Unlawful Use of White Phosphorus in Gaza"
Author: Fred Abrahams

Guardian, February 23, 2009
Title: "Suspend Military Aid to Israel, Amnesty Urges Obama after Detailing US
    Weapons Used in Gaza"
Author: Rory McCarthy

Inter Press Service, January 8, 2009
Title: "US Weaponry Facilitates Killings in Gaza"
Author: Thalif Deen

International Middle East Media Center News, January 8, 2009
Title: "US military re-supplying Israel with ammunition through Greece"
Author: Saed Bannoura

Foreign Policy Journal, January 9, 2009
Title: "US Senate Endorses Israel's War on Gaza"
Author: Jeremy R. Hammond

Student Researchers: Erin Galbraith and Curtis Harrison
Faculty Evaluators: Andy Merrifield, PhD, Cynthia Boaz, PhD, and David McCuan, PhD
Sonoma State University

Israel's repeated firing of US-made white phosphorus shells over densely populated areas of Gaza during its recent military campaign was indiscriminate and is evidence of war crimes, Human Rights Watch said in a report released March 25, 2009.

The seventy-one-page report, "Rain of Fire: Israel's Unlawful Use of White Phosphorus in Gaza," provides witness accounts of the devastating effects that white phosphorus munitions had on civilians and civilian property in Gaza. Human Rights Watch researchers found spent shells, canister liners, and dozens of burnt felt wedges containing white phosphorus on city streets, apartment roofs, residential courtyards, and at a United Nations school in Gaza immediately after hostilities ended in January.

Militaries officially use white phosphorus to obscure their operations on the ground by creating thick smoke. It has also been used as an incen-

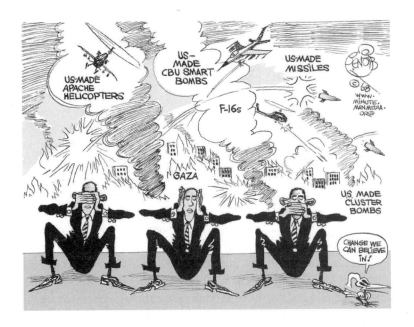

diary weapon, though such use constitutes a war crime. "In Gaza, the Israeli military didn't just use white phosphorus in open areas as a screen for its troops," said Fred Abrahams, senior emergencies researcher at Human Rights Watch and coauthor of the report. "It fired white phosphorus repeatedly over densely populated areas, even when its troops weren't in the area and safer smoke shells were available. As a result, civilians needlessly suffered and died." The report documents a pattern or policy of white phosphorus use that Human Rights Watch says must have required the approval of senior military officers.

The devastating Israeli firepower, unleashed largely on Palestinian civilians in Gaza during the three-week attack starting December 27, 2008 was fueled by US-supplied weapons paid for with US tax dollars. Washington provided F-16 fighter planes, Apache helicopters, tactical missiles, and a wide array of munitions, including white phosphorus and DIME. The weapons required for the Israeli assault were decided upon in June 2008, and the transfer of 1,000 bunker-buster GPS-guided Small Diameter Guided Bomb Unit-39s (GBU-39s) were approved by Congress in September. The GBU-39 bombs were delivered to Israel in November (prior to any claims of Hamas cease-fire violation) for use in the initial air raids on Gaza.

Researchers in Gaza found several weapon fragments after the attacks. One came from a 500-pound Mark 82 fin guided bomb, which had markings indicating parts were made by the US company Raytheon. They also found fragments of US-made white phosphorus artillery shells, marked M825A1.

In the recent Gaza operations, Israeli forces frequently airburst white phosphorus in 155-millimeter artillery shells in and near populated areas. Each airburst shell spreads 116 burning white phosphorus wedges in a radius extending up to 125 meters from the blast point. White phosphorus ignites and burns on contact with oxygen, and continues burning at up to 1,500 degrees Fahrenheit (816 degrees Celsius) until nothing is left or the oxygen supply is cut. When white phosphorus comes into contact with skin it creates intense and persistent burns that continue to ignite.

On January 15, 2009, several white phosphorus shells fired by the Israeli military hit the headquarters of the UN Relief and Works Agency in Gaza City, destroying medicine, food, and other basic aid. One fragment found at the scene had markings indicating it was made by the Pine Bluff Arsenal, based in Arkansas, in October 1991.

The UN Security Council, Amnesty International, International Red Cross, and voices of protest from around the world demanded a ceasefire. Yet, with shocking lack of regard, both houses of US Congress overwhelmingly endorsed resolutions to support a continuation of Israel's "self defense."

Four days after the carnage ensued, on December 31, 2008, the US Navy's Sealift Command hired ships to deliver another 3,000-odd tons of arms to Israel through Greece. This last shipment was halted mid-January due to Greek protest. The US has long been the largest arms supplier to Israel; under a current ten-year agreement negotiated by the Bush administration, the US will provide $30 billion in military aid to Israel.

"As the major supplier of weapons to Israel, the USA has a particular obligation to stop any supply that contributes to gross violations of the laws of war and of human rights," said Malcolm Smart, Amnesty's Middle East and North Africa program director. "To a large extent, Israel's military offensive in Gaza was carried out with weapons, munitions, and military equipment supplied by the USA and paid for with US taxpayers' money."

UPDATE BY JEREMY R. HAMMOND

On the day the US Senate passed S.R. 10, "reaffirming the United States' strong support for Israel in its battle with Hamas" (January 8, 2009), the International Committee of the Red Cross (ICRC) issued a statement demanding to be allowed to assist those in need of medical attention because the Israeli military had blocked access to wounded Palestinians, a war crime under international law. Also that same day, UN Secretary-General Ban Ki-Moon issued a statement condemning the Israeli Defense Force for firing on a UN aid convoy delivering humanitarian goods to the desperate people of Gaza, another war crime, as well as the killing of two staff members of the UN Relief and Works Agency for Palestine Refugees (UNRWA) in a separate incident.

The next day, the House passed its own version of the resolution, H.R. 34, as UNRWA announced that it had had to halt its humanitarian efforts because of numerous incidents in which its staff, convoys, and installations had come under attack by Israeli forces.

The Senate resolution was reported by foreign media agencies. The *Jerusalem Post* had a story on it, as did Reuters. In the US, it was reported by the Jewish daily *Forward* and mentioned in alternative media sources by Stephen Zunes, Robert Naiman, and several others. It was first brought to my attention by Foreign Policy in Focus (www.fpif.org), and the text was available on the American Israel Public Affairs Committee (AIPAC) website. But to my knowledge it was not reported in the mainstream media.

It's hardly a secret that the US has a "special relationship" with Israel, but the full extent of US support for Israeli crimes is a matter that is met with absolute silence by the mainstream media, and congressional support for Israel's aggression and war crimes against the people of Gaza was no exception. When reporting, the mainstream media employs euphemisms or parrots the official US government line, such as that settlements are an "obstacle to peace" rather than "illegal."

The US supports Israel financially, with upwards of $3 billion annually. This money is given with little to no oversight, but even if it is not used to directly fund Israel's illegal settlements and occupation, it allows Israel to free up other funds and divert them for that purpose.

The US supports Israel militarily. In its assault on Gaza, for instance, Israel employed US-made F-16 jets and Apache helicopter gunships. US-made bombs were dropped on Gaza during twenty-two days of violence, resulting in the deaths of over 1,300 Palestinian, nearly a third of whom were children, among other civilian victims.

The US also supports Israel diplomatically. For instance, the US delayed passage of a UN resolution calling for a cease-fire during the assault on Gaza, according to foreign diplomats.

President Obama has issued strong words in support of Palestinian statehood and against the Israeli settlements. It's up to the American people, though, to put pressure on the US government to ensure that the rhetoric is followed up with action, such as an end to financial, military, and diplomatic support for Israeli crimes.

This is among the reasons why it's so important that stories like the US congressional endorsement for Israel's "Operation Cast Lead" against Gaza be made known to the public.

10

Ecuador Declares Foreign Debt Illegitimate

Sources:
AlterNet, November 26, 2008
Title: "As Crisis Mounts, Ecuador Declares Foreign Debt Illegitimate and Illegal"
Author: Daniel Denvir

YouTube, Fall 2008
Title: "Invalid Loans to Ecuador: Who Owes Who"
Producer: Committee for the Integral Audit of Public Credit

Foreign Policy in Focus, December 15, 2008
Title: "Ecuador's Debt Default"
Authors: Neil Watkins and Sarah Anderson

Student Researcher: Rosemary Scott
Community Evaluator: Tim Ogburn
Sonoma State University

In November 2008, Ecuador became the first country to undertake an examination of the legitimacy and structure of its foreign debt. An independent debt audit commissioned by the government of Ecuador documented hundreds of allegations of irregularity, illegality, and illegitimacy in contracts of debt to predatory international lenders. The loans, according to the report, violated Ecuador's domestic laws, US Securities and Exchange Commission regulations, and general principles of international law. Ecuador's use of legitimacy as a legal argument for defaulting set a major precedent; indeed, the formation of a debt auditing commission sets a precedent.

In the 1970s, Ecuador fell victim to unscrupulous international lending, which encouraged borrowing at low interest rates. But in over thirty years the country's debt rose from $1.174 billion in 1970, to over $14.250 billion in 2006, a twelve-fold increase, due in large part to interest rates that rose at the discretion of US banks and the Federal Reserve from 6 percent in 1979 to 21 percent in 1981.

The commission revealed that Salomon Smith Barney, now part of Citigroup Inc., issued unauthorized restructuring of Ecuador's debt in 2000 that lead to exorbitant interest rates, which, combined with illegal borrowing by former dictators, has turned the country, along with many of its Southern neighbors, into a major capitol exporter to its Northern "benefactors." Over the years, the country has made debt payments that far exceed the principal it borrowed.

Of all loans made between 1989 and 2006, 14 percent was used for social development projects. The remaining 86 percent was used to pay for previously accumulated debt. Continuously from 1982 and 2006, the country paid foreign debt creditors $119.826 billion for capital and interest, while receiving over the same period $106.268 billion in new loans, which amounts to a total negative transfer of $13.558 billion.

The human costs are staggering. Every dollar spent on illegitimate international credit means fewer are available for fighting poverty. In 2007, the Ecuadorian government paid $1.75 billion in debt service

alone, more than it spent on health care, social services, the environment, and housing and urban development combined.

While the risks of default are high, Ecuador had only two options: keep paying a dubious and illegal debt at the risk of social unrest, or default and face the wrath of the international market.

Under the World Bank system, which oversees investment treaties, there are no standard judicial ethics rules, no public accountability, and no appeals process. Ecuador has thus exposed a major problem in the international financial system: the lack of an international, independent mechanism for countries to resolve disputes over potentially illegitimate and/or illegal debt. Ecuador's findings could set a precedent for the poorest of indebted countries, whose debt burden has long been criticized as predatory and inhumane.

Ecuador has called on Latin America to forge a united response to foreign debt. Venezuela, Bolivia, and Paraguay have recently created debt audit commissions. The country has also asked the United Nations to help develop international norms to regulate the foreign debt market.

A bill pending in the US Congress presents an ethical step forward. The Jubilee Act, which passed in the House of Representatives in April 2008, would require the comptroller general to undertake audits of the debt portfolios of previous regimes where there is substantial evidence of odious, onerous, or illegal loans. The legislation also instructs the secretary of the treasury to "seek the international adoption of a binding legal framework on new lending that . . . provides for decisions on irresponsible lending to be made by an entity independent from the creditors; and enables fair opportunities for the people of the affected country to be heard."

UPDATE BY DANIEL DENVIR

In June 2009, Ecuador announced that it had reached an agreement with 91 percent of creditors to buy back its debt for 35 cents on the dollar, confirming many analysts' predictions that the default was a strategic move aimed at getting a "haircut" on their debt. Ecuador's default drove down the price of their debt, making a buyback far more affordable. Many analysts believe that Ecuador had already started to quietly buy back debt on the secondary market, a claim the government has declined to comment on. Ecuador was expected to pay $1.075 billion for $3.375 billion in debt.

Following the December 2008 default on its 2012 global bonds,

Ecuador defaulted on its 2030 global bonds in March. Ecuador continued to pay its 2015 global bonds, although there is widespread speculation that the successful buyback will lead them to default on that debt, too. Some analysts disagree, noting that allied Venezuela owns some of the 2015 bonds, while others say that maintaining payment could be a way to stay in the free market's good graces.

The default and buyback received widespread coverage in the business press, but aside from my article, International Relations Center (IRC)–Americas was the only English-language outlet to dedicate in-depth analysis to the political and economic significance of the debt auditing commission, illegitimate debt, and default. The *Financial Times*, undertaking a sober analysis of the long-term impact of Ecuador's default, noted, "Analysts fear that the government's deliberate default on two bonds—almost a third of its foreign debt—could prompt other countries to follow suit as they seek to navigate the financial crisis." Investors are worried about the precedent Ecuador is setting as the first country in decades to default while technically having the ability to pay.

One prominent international investment advisor is quoted as saying that Ecuador's default was a "brilliantly run and managed process. They nailed the timing."

To get involved with the movement against illegitimate debt, contact Jubilee USA (http://www.jubileeusa.org).

UPDATE BY NEIL WATKINS AND SARAH ANDERSON
After Ecuadorian President Rafael Correa announced the default in December 2008, the financial press smoldered with condemnations and predictions of dire consequences for this small South American nation.

Most articles quoted only the harshest critics. Ecuador had "lived up to its reputation as a banana republic" (*Investor's Business Daily*). Ecuador was "one of the axis of evil in Latin America" (*Financial Times*). A separate article in the *Financial Times* did quote two sympathetic analysts, but that effort at balanced reporting was an extreme exception.

We found no examples of mainstream press reporting on the long history of Ecuadorian activists calling for action to address illegitimate debts. Indeed, Ecuadorian civil society had long advocated for the creation of a commission to examine the nature of Ecuador's debt. That commission was founded in 2007, and its results formed the basis for the Correa government's decision to default.

The mainstream media gave the overwhelming impression that this default was the result of the personal whim of a political extremist. Virtually every story labeled Correa as a leftist and emphasized his ties to Venezuelan President Hugo Chávez. The analysts quoted reinforced this message. "I think this default is nonsense. The market sees it as politically motivated" (*Euromoney*). A former International Monetary Fund official said the default reflected "a ridiculous ideology" (Bloomberg).

Meanwhile, activists associated with the global Jubilee network, which has campaigned for the cancellation of illegitimate debts in countries around the world, applauded Correa for fulfilling a campaign promise to respect the findings of the debt audit commission. And Paraguayan President Fernando Lugo announced less than a week after Ecuador's default that his government would also "exhaustively study" its debt.

In late April of this year, Correa was reelected in a landslide, and as of this writing, his government appears on the brink of successfully negotiating with the holders of defaulted bonds. Dow Jones is reporting that a very high percentage of bondholders are expected to accept Correa's offer of 35 cents on the dollar.

As part of the response to the current financial crisis, governments should establish an international mechanism to handle debt disputes in a systematic way that balances the interests of debtors and creditors and considers how debts were accumulated in the first place. A special United Nations commission on the crisis, chaired by Nobel Prize economist Joseph Stiglitz, came out in March 2009 in support of such a mechanism. But thus far, the issue is not even on the table within the G20 grouping of the most powerful nations.

With the financial crisis hitting heavily indebted poor countries hard, there will be greater pressures on developing nations to default. Instead of demonizing leaders who default, it's time for the international community to develop a fair solution that addresses the real impacts of crushing debt on the poor.

For more information, see:

Jubilee USA Network: www.jubileeusa.org

Audit Commission of Ecuador: http://www.auditoriadeuda.org.ec

Jubilee South/Americas: http://jubileosuramerica.blogspot.com/2009/03/nuevo-sitio.html

Latindadd (Latin America Network on Debt and Development): http://www.latindadd.org

Institute for Policy Studies: www.ips-dc.org

11

Private Corporations Profit from the Occupation of Palestine

Sources:

WhoProfits.org
Title: "Who Profits? Exposing the Israeli Occupation Industry"
Author: Coalition of Women for Peace

Palestine News Network, August 26, 2008
Title: "US Tax Breaks Support Israeli Settlers"

Workers World Newspaper, February 9, 2009, and Global Research, February 11, 2009
Title: "The Tunnels of Gaza: An underground economy and resistance symbol"
Author: Sara Flounders

CommonDreams.org, February 24, 2009
Title: "Can Gaza Be Rebuilt Through Tunnels? The Blockade Continues—No Supplies, No Rebuilding"
Author: Ann Wright

Student Researchers: April Rudolph, Natalie Dale, and Kerry Headley
Faculty Evaluator: Jeff Baldwin, PhD
Sonoma State University

Israeli and international corporations are directly involved in the occupation of Palestine. Along with various political, religious, and national interests, the Israeli occupation of the West Bank, Gaza, and the Golan Heights is fueled by corporate interests. These occupying companies and corporations lead real estate deals, develop the Israeli colonies and infrastructure, and contribute to the construction and operation of an ethnic separation system, including checkpoints, walls, and roads. They also design and supply equipment and tools used in the control and repression of the civilian population under occupation.

An extensive, ongoing grassroots investigation, which exposes hundreds of international companies and corporations involved in the occupation, is being conducted and posted online at www.whoprofits.org by the Israeli group Coalition of Women for Peace. The project currently focuses on three main areas of corporate involvement in the occupation:

the settlement industry, economic exploitation, and control of the population. At this stage they are not investigating the vast industry of military production and arms trade (see story # 9).

The ongoing business of construction in the occupied territories of the West Bank and Golan Heights includes housing developments as well as extensive infrastructure projects such as roads and water systems for the exclusive use of Israeli settlers, on lands confiscated from Palestinians. The construction industry includes real estate dealers, contractors, planners, suppliers of materials, as well as security, surveillance, and maintenance services.

While the US government has on numerous occasions affirmed the illegality of Israeli settlements on Palestinian land, it encourages American support by providing tax deductions for donations to these settlements, which have nearly doubled within a year and are rapidly accelerating. An audit conducted by Reuters of American tax records found that thirteen tax-exempt groups linked explicitly to settlements managed to collect more than $35 million in the past five years alone. Secretary of State Condoleezza Rice defended the tax incentives as "humanitarian" and rejected any comparison to Palestinian charities facing US sanctions for suspected links with Islamic parties, such as Hamas.

Israeli industrial zones within the occupied territories hold hundreds of companies, ranging from small businesses serving the local Israeli settlers to large factories that export their products worldwide. Settlement production benefits from low rents, special tax incentives, lax enforcement of environmental and labor protection laws, and other governmental supports. Palestinians employed in these industrial zones work under severe restrictions on movement, on organization, and with almost no government protections. These "advantages" often result in the exploitation of Palestinian labor, Palestinian natural resources, and the Palestinian consumer market.

All Palestinian imports and exports are controlled, restricting competition with Israeli producers, and making Palestinian consumers a captive market for Israeli goods. Restrictions are imposed on the development of Palestinian businesses, and all utilities and basic services are routed through Israeli firms.

Severe restrictions on movement of Palestinian labor and products inside the occupied territories and to neighboring areas have further increased the dependency of the Palestinian economy on Israeli com-

THE "ETERNAL? UNDIVIDED UNITED (BOTH HOUSES) CAPITOL OF ISRAEL

TVIEWS·COM

CAPITOL HILL WASHINGTON, D.C.

HRC 426: THE U.S. CONDEMNS PALESTINIAN VIOLENCE SUPPORTS ISRAEL? ETC..., ETC...

OCCUPIED TERRITORY

panies as employers and retailers. The growing network of checkpoints and walls has all but destroyed Palestinian local production and the Palestinian labor bargaining power.

Since mid-2007, outraged when the Palestinians of Gaza voted for the leadership of Hamas in democratic elections, Israel imposed a total lockdown on the entire population of Gaza. The Palestinians, determined to continue to resist occupation, found a way to circumvent total starvation. Author Sara Flounders notes, "The Israeli blockade led to a new economic structure, an underground economy. The besieged Palestinians have dug more than 1,000 tunnels under the totally sealed border. Many thousands of Palestinians are now employed in digging, smuggling or transporting, and reselling essential goods." Smuggling constitutes approximately 90 percent of economic activity in Gaza, according to Gazan economist Omar Shaban.

The tunnels connect the Egyptian town of Rafah with the Palestinian refugee camp of the same name inside Gaza. They have become a fantastic, life-sustaining network of corridors dug through sandy soil. Tunnels are typically three-tenths of a mile long, approximately forty-five to fifty feet deep. They cost from $50,000 to $90,000 and require several months of intense labor to dig.

Food is towed through on plastic sleighs. Livestock are herded through larger tunnels. Flour, milk, cheese, cigarettes, cooking oil, toothpaste, small generators, computers, and kerosene heaters come through the tunnels. Every day, 300 to 400 gas canisters for cooking come through the lines. On the Egyptian side, the trade sustains the ruptured economy, while corrupt or sympathetic guards and officers look the other way.

The Israeli siege of Gaza, followed by twenty-three days of systematic bombing and invasion in December 2008 and January 2009, has created massive destruction and scarcity. Food processing plants, chicken farms, grain warehouses, UN food stocks, almost all of the remaining infrastructure, and 230 small factories were destroyed. At the time of this printing, hundreds of trucks packed with essential supplies from international and humanitarian agencies sit outside the strip, refused entry to Gaza by Israeli guards.

As soon as the Israeli bombing ended, work on the tunnels resumed.

However, Ann Wright, retired US Army colonel, former State Department official, and current peace activist, asks, "How do you rebuild 5,000 homes, businesses and government buildings when the only way supplies come into the prison called Gaza is through tunnels? Will the steel I-beams for roofs bend 90 degrees to go through the tunnels from Egypt? Will the tons of cement, lumber, roofing materials, nails, drywall, and paint be hauled by hand, load after load, seventy feet underground, through a tunnel 500 to 900 feet long, and then pulled up a seventy-foot hole and put into waiting truck in Gaza?"

For the people of Gaza, rebuilding their homes, businesses, and factories is on hold. Over 5,000 homes and apartment buildings were destroyed and hundreds of government buildings, including the parliament building, were smashed. Two cement factories in northern Gaza were completely destroyed by Israeli bombs.

Building supplies, cement, wood, nails, and glass will have to be brought in from outside Gaza. Israel controls 90 percent of the land borders to Gaza, including the northern and eastern borders, and 100 percent of the ocean on the west side of Gaza. Egypt controls the southern border with Gaza.

Wright concludes, "The Israelis who bombed Gaza will be the primary financial beneficiaries of the rebuilding of Gaza. They bombed it and now will sell construction materials to rebuild what they have bombed, exactly like the United States has done in Iraq."

UPDATE BY SARA FLOUNDERS

Much has been written about the suffering of the Palestinians, and most of it is true. What gives the history of Palestine its special potency is not the suffering, however, but the indomitable will of the people to continue fighting, even when it seems impossible. This part of the story—suffering and determination—has continued in the six months since the massive Israeli bombing of Gaza ended last January.

The Israeli invasion laid waste to much of Gaza's fragile infrastructure. The siege of Gaza continues, reducing the entire strip to a prison economy with all the desperation that implies. Every effort is being made to increase the isolation. The Israelis have forbidden the entry of even the most basic building materials that are essential to reconstruct the thousands of homes that Israeli bombs destroyed during the December/January assault on Gaza's population.

Tens of millions of dollars of medical, food, clothing, and other everyday aid have been collected from people from all around the world to send to the 1.5 million Palestinians living in Gaza, the largest open-air prison in the world. The great bulk of this aid is stalled at the border crossing points, prevented by the Israeli occupation authorities from entering.

My article, "The Tunnels of Gaza," written in February 2009, was about the 1,000 tunnels that the Palestinians courageously dug and maintained to bring material in from Egypt. These tunnels built during the months of siege and reopened after the invasion continue to be an important lifeline for Gaza's population and a symbol of continued resistance. Now, they have even become a source of desperately needed building materials.

Some Gazans have turned to making dried mud bricks, a home-building material from an ancient age, to rebuild their bombed homes. And the best mud comes from the tunnels themselves, as an article in Bloomberg on June 3, 2009, pointed out. Again, a source of possible despair has become a story to inspire confidence in ultimate victory.

But it is important that the rest of the world refuse to allow the systematic isolation and total destruction of Gaza. One way to do this is to join in the work of Viva Palestina, one of several Gaza solidarity campaigns determined to bring in a small portion of supplies needed by the Gazans, and what is perhaps even more important, to keep world attention upon the continuing Israeli siege.

British Member of Parliament George Galloway organized the first Viva Palestina caravan that took off from London and in twenty-three days crossed North Africa to deliver to Gaza 107 vehicles—including ambulances and a fire engine—255 people, and $2 million of aid last March. Now Galloway and Vietnam antiwar veteran Ron Kovic are organizing a similar caravan starting from the United States that aims to bring 500 vehicles and $10 million in aid—and to impact US political policy toward Palestine and Gaza (see vivapalestina-us.org).

The International Action Center is helping the Viva Palestina effort, and hopes that more and more people and organizations from all over the world will join to help lift the siege of Gaza and show solidarity with the Palestinian people, who once again are showing that they won't give up.

12

Mysterious Death of Mike Connell—Karl Rove's Election Thief

Sources:

The Raw Story, September 29, 2008
Title: "Republican IT consultant subpoenaed in case alleging tampering with 2004 election"
Authors: Larisa Alexandrovna and Muriel Kane

The Brad Blog, December 22, 2008
Title: "OH Election Fraud Attorney Reacts to the Death of Mike Connell"
Author: Brad Friedman

Democracy Now! December 22, 2008
Title: "Republican IT Specialist Dies in Plane Crash"
Interviewee: Mark Crispin Miller

Student Researchers: Ashleigh Hvinden, Christine Wilson, and Alan Grady
Community Evaluator: Mary Ann Walker
Sonoma State University

Karl Rove's chief information technology (IT) consultant, Mike Connell—who was facing subpoena in connection with 2004 presidential election fraud in Ohio—mysteriously died in a private plane crash in 2008. Connell was allegedly the central figure in a long-standing plot to electronically flip votes to Republicans.

In July 2008, Connell was named as a key witness in the case known as *King Lincoln Bronzeville Neighborhood Association v. Blackwell*, which was filed against Ohio Secretary of State Kenneth J. Blackwell on August 31, 2006, by Columbus attorneys Clifford Arnebeck and Robert Fitrakis. It initially charged Blackwell with racially discriminatory practices— including the selective purging of voters from the election rolls and the unequal allocation of voting machines to various districts—and asked for measures to be taken to prevent similar problems during the November 2006 election.

On October 9, 2006, an amended complaint added charges of various forms of ballot rigging as also having the effect of "depriving the plaintiffs of their voting rights, including the right to have their votes successfully cast without intimidation, dilution, cancellation or reversal by voting machine or ballot tampering." A motion to dismiss the case as moot was filed following the November 2006 election, but it was instead stayed to allow for settlement discussions.

The case took on fresh momentum in July 2008 when Arnebeck announced that he was filing to "lift the stay in the case and proceed with targeted discovery in order to help protect the integrity of the 2008 election." The new filing was inspired in part when GOP IT security expert Stephen Spoonamore came forward as a whistleblower. Spoonamore said he was prepared to testify to the plausibility of electronic vote-rigging having been carried out in 2004. The stay was lifted September 19, 2008, and Connell was served a subpoena on September 22.

Spoonamore, a conservative Republican who works for big banks, international governments, and the Secret Service as an expert in the detection of computer fraud, found evidence that Karl Rove, with the help of Mike Connell and his company GovTech Solutions, electronically stole the Ohio 2004 election for Bush.

Spoonamore testified that the "vote tabulation system [which Connell designed] allowed the introduction of an additional single computer between Computer A and Computer B." This is called a "man in the middle" attack. According to Spoonamore, "this centralized collection of all incoming statewide tabulations would make it easy for a single operator, or a preprogrammed 'force balancing computer,' to change the results in any way desired by the team controlling the Computer C." Spoonamore further testified that the only purpose for such man in the middle architecture is to commit crime.

Despite Connell's efforts to quash his subpoena to testify, he was ordered to appear for a two-hour, closed-door deposition on November 3, 2008, just eighteen hours before the 2008 national election. Though Connell had expressed willingness to testify, he was reticent after receiving threats from Rove.

Arnebeck presents evidence that Karl Rove threatened Connell, cautioning that if Connell didn't "take the fall" for election fraud in Ohio, Connell would face prosecution for supposed lobby law violations. After this threat, Arnebeck sent letters to the Department of Justice, as well as messages to high-ranking members of the department, seeking protection for Connell and his family from attempts to intimidate. Despite Connell's elite status as a top-rung Republican consultant for years, whose firm New Media Communications provided IT services for the Bush-Cheney 2004 campaign, the US Chamber of Commerce, the Republican National Committee, and many Republican candidates and campaigns, witness protection requests went unheeded.

Election fraud analyst and author Mark Crispin Miller notes that the timing and circumstances of Connell's death—between deposition and trial—are too suspicious and convenient for Rove and the Bush administration not to merit a thorough investigation. Arnebeck and Fitrakis intended to both further depose and call Connell to testify as key witness in the federal conspiracy case. Connell was also to be questioned about his key role in the disappearance of thousands of White House–Republican National Committee (RNC) email transactions. These emails are believed likely to have shed light on the White House role in the political firings of US attorneys, as well as decisions to prosecute former Alabama Democratic Governor Don Siegelman. Attorneys in the case said that Connell's testimony would likely lead to the subpoenaing and under-oath questioning of Karl Rove.

Connell was an experienced pilot. His plane had been recently serviced. He had been in the nation's capital on still-unknown business before his single engine plane crashed December 22, 2008, on the way home, just three miles short of the runway in Akron, Ohio. The cause of the crash remains unknown.

Timing of Connell's deposition may have saved the 2008 presidential elections from electronic theft. However, Bev Harris at Black Box Voting notes that man in the middle systems are still in place in Illinois, Colorado, Kentucky, and likely across the nation.[1]

Citation:
1. Bev Harris, "Man in the Middle Attacks to Subvert the Vote," Black Box Voting, November 2008, http://www.blackboxvoting.org

UPDATE BY LARISA ALEXANDROVNA

The extreme vulnerability of electronic voting systems to systematic fraud has fallen out of public awareness because it did not become a major issue during the 2008 elections, but the problem has never been resolved or even seriously examined by any official body. Questions about alleged vote count irregularities in Ohio during the 2004 election remain the strongest indication of the potential for large-scale tampering with these systems. The lawsuit, which sought testimony from GOP information technology expert Michael Connell as to any personal knowledge he might have had of those irregularities, has represented the most determined effort to get at the truth beyond these allegations.

Michael Connell testified under subpoena in November 2008 but died the following month, when his single-engine plane crashed as he was attempting to land at an Ohio airport near his home. At the time of his death, the only mainstream news outlet to even mention Connell's death and the controversies surrounding his involvement in electronic voting was a single CBS/Associated Press story.

However, there appears to have been no direct response in the mainstream press to the articles on Connell published by Raw Story. In fact, a deafening silence on his alleged relationship with the Bush White House has prevailed, even after his sudden and tragic death in December of 2008.

The case of *King Lincoln Bronzeville Neighborhood Association v. Blackwell* is still ongoing.

Additional information on the King Lincoln case can be obtained here: http://moritzlaw.osu.edu/electionlaw/litigation/klbna.php.

An organization that has taken a proactive role in making public both the case of King Lincoln and the various articles on it is Velvet Revolution. See http://velvetrevolution.us.

UPDATE BY BRAD FRIEDMAN

Little of note has changed since the death of Mike Connell as this book goes to press. The National Transportation Safety Board (NTSB) is still investigating, but is likely not to release a final report until mid to late 2010. They released a preliminary report, however, indicating decreasing visibility at the Akron airport, with visibility still at 2.5 miles at the time of the crash and temperatures just above freezing. According to the NTSB report, and confirmed via transcripts and tapes received via Freedon of Information Act (FOIA) requests, Connell radioed to ask "whether there were any reports of icing, to which air traffic control [ATC] responded that there were no reports."

The tapes and transcripts indicate that *something* suddenly happened up there, as his last words to ATC, recorded on tape, were a declaration of emergency followed quickly by "Oh, fuck," before he was not heard from again.

Curiously, for a man as well connected to the very top echelons of the Republican Party as Connell was, no GOP officials, or George W. Bush, or John McCain, or Karl Rove, to my knowledge, ever issued a public statement upon his tragic death.

For the time being, the Ohio voting rights case has been stalled since Connell's death. Cliff Arnebeck continues to investigate how he plans to move forward, and is considering broader subpoenas in hopes of taking depositions from, among others, Karl Rove, as he widens the scope of his conspiracy case.

13

Katrina's Hidden Race War

Sources:
The Nation, December 17, 2008
Title: "Katrina's Hidden Race War"
Author: A. C. Thompson

The Nation, December 18, 2008
Title: "Body of Evidence"
Author: A. C. Thompson

Democracy Now! December 19, 2008
Title: "Katrina's Hidden Race War: In Aftermath of Storm, White Vigilante Groups Shot 11 African Americans in New Orleans"

Student Researcher: Aimee Drew
Evaluator: Susan Kashack
Sonoma State University

A shocking report in *The Nation* magazine exposes how white vigilante groups patrolled the streets of New Orleans after Hurricane Katrina, shooting at least eleven African-American men.

While most of New Orleans was deluged in the wake of Katrina, word spread that Algiers Point was dry. The National Guard designated the Algiers Point ferry landing an official evacuation site, where flood victims were to be loaded onto busses headed for safety in Texas. Facing an influx of refugees, a group of heavily armed white residents sought to seal the area and to rid the neighborhood of "those who didn't belong." As the government collapsed, the city fractured along racial lines. Algiers Point is largely white, while the rest of Algiers is predominantly black. Desperate people began heading toward the west bank, some walking over bridges, others traveling by boat.

While the media portrayed African Americans as looters and thugs, it is now clear that the most serious crimes were committed by gun-toting white males. Militia member Vinnie Pervel says he lost his Ford van in a carjacking the day after Katrina made landfall, when an African - American man attacked him with a hammer. Vowing to prevent further robberies, Pervel and his neighbors began amassing an arsenal. "For a day and a half we were running around getting guns," he says. "We got about forty."

Nathan Roper, another vigilante, says he was unhappy that outsiders were disturbing his corner of New Orleans and that he was annoyed by the National Guard's decision to use the Algiers Point ferry landing as an evacuation zone. "I'm telling you, it was forty, fifty people at a time getting off these boats," says Roper. The militia, according to Roper, was armed with handguns, rifles, and shotguns. "There was a few people who got shot around here," said Roper. "I know of at least three people who got shot. I know one was dead 'cause he was on the side of the road."

While white vigilantes killed an estimated total of eleven African-American victims, local police have never conducted investigations. So far, the crimes have gone unpunished.

There has also never been any investigation on the matter of the charred remains found in a burned-out car a week after Katrina hit. Inside the scorched sedan, scattered across the backseat, were ashes, charred bone, and clumps of burned flesh. Eventually, the remains were taken to a temporary morgue in the tiny St. Gabriel.

Relatives of the deceased (later identified as Henry Glover) claim the police allowed him to die and burned the car and his remains; the New Orleans parish coroner has ruled the death "unclassified."

According to witnesses, Glover was walking in the Algiers section of New Orleans when he was shot. When the two men tried to seek medical help for Glover, they were taken into police custody instead, where they were repeatedly beaten and berated.

While Glover bled to death in the backseat of the car, the officers did nothing to try to save him. When the officers finally decided to free the men who had tried to save Glover, the cops held onto the car. One witness recalls an officer saying, "The car is in police custody."

Three days after Hurricane Katrina crashed into New Orleans, Donnell Herrington, who is African American, was shot with a shotgun. "I just hit the ground. I didn't even know what happened," recalls Herrington.

When two white men drove by, Herrington begged them for help. "I said, 'Help me, help me—I'm shot,'" he recalls. According to Herrington, the response was hostile. One of the men told Herrington, "Get away from this truck, nigger. We're not gonna help you. We're liable to kill you ourselves." After collapsing on his neighbors' front porch, Herrington was finally taken to the hospital. Returning to New Orleans months later, Herrington learned there had been no police report documenting the attack.

Democracy Now! footage shows that dead bodies were left, sometimes for weeks, to rot in full view of Homeland Security, State troopers, Army personnel, private security guards, and police who "secured" the streets of New Orleans in the aftermath of Katrina.

One reporter notes, "I was startled to meet so many people with so much detailed information about potentially serious offenses, none of whom had ever been interviewed by police investigators."

14

Congress Invested in Defense Contracts

Source:
OpenSecrets.org, April 3, 2008
Title: "Strategic Assets"
Author: Lindsay Renick Mayer

Student Researchers: Leora Johnson and Michael Seramin
Faculty Evaluator: Peter Phillips, PhD
Sonoma State University

The nonpartisan Center for Responsive Politics has calculated that more than 151 members of Congress have up to $195 million invested in major defense contractors that are earning profits from the US military occupations in Iraq and Afghanistan.

When General David Petraeus, the top US military officer in Iraq, went to Capitol Hill to brief Congress in April of 2008, he was addressing lawmakers who had a lot more than just a political stake in the Iraq occupation. Along with their colleagues in the House and Senate, the politicians who got a status report from the general and the US ambassador to Iraq had millions of dollars of their own money invested in companies doing business with the Department of Defense (DoD).

In 2006, the investment portfolios of 151 current members—more than a quarter of Congress—had between $78.7 million and $195.5 million invested in companies that received major defense contracts (over $5 million). The portfolios included holdings in companies that were paid billions of dollars each month to support America's military. These companies provided almost everything the military uses, from aircraft and weapons to medical supplies and soft drinks.

Lawmakers with the most money invested in companies with DoD

contracts include Sen. John Kerry (D-MA), with up to $38,209,020; Rep. Rodney Frelinghuysen (R-NJ), with $49,140,000; Rep. Robin Hayes (R-NC), with $37,105,000; Rep. James Sensenbrenner Jr. (R-WI), with $7,612,653; Rep. Jane Harman (D-CA), with $6,260,000; Rep. Fred Upton (R-MI), with $8,360,000; Sen. Jay Rockefeller (D-WV), with $2,000,002; Rep. Tom Petri (R-WI), with $5,800,000; Rep. Kenny Ewell Marchant (R-TX), with $1,163,231; and Rep. John Carter (R-TX), with up to $5,000,000.

Forty-seven members of Congress (or 9 percent of all members of the House and Senate) in 2006 were invested in companies that are primarily in the defense sector. The average share price of these corporations today is nearly twice what it was in 2004. Lawmakers' investments in these contracting firms yielded them between $15.8 million and $62 million in income between 2004 and 2006, through dividends, capital gains, royalties, and interest.

Companies with congressional investors received more than $275.6 billion from the government in 2006. The minimum value of Congress members' personal investments in defense contracting firms increased 5 percent from 2004 to 2006, but because lawmakers are only required to report their assets in broad ranges, the value of these investments could have risen as much as 160 percent—or even dropped 51 percent. Senator John Kerry (D-MA) and House Representative James Sensenbrenner (R-WI), two of Congress's wealthiest members, were among the lawmakers who earned the most from their investments in defense contractors between 2004 and 2006, with Sensenbrenner making at least $3.2 million and Kerry reaping at least $2.6 million. The Senate Foreign Relations and Armed Services committees both have members who are major investors in defense companies. Chairs of other defense-related committees are similarly invested. Sen. Joe Lieberman (I-CT), chairman of the Senate Homeland Security and Governmental Affairs Committee, had at least $51,000 invested in defense companies in 2006. Rep. Howard Berman (D-Calif.), who heads the House Committee on Foreign Affairs, had at least $30,000 invested in defense companies.

As the military operations in Iraq and Afghanistan have expanded and transformed, so too has the need for goods and services that extend beyond helicopters, armored vehicles, and guns. Giant corporations outside of the defense sector, such as PepsiCo, IBM, Microsoft, and Johnson & Johnson, have received defense contracts and are all popular investments for both members of Congress and the general public.

A spokesman for Sensenbrenner, who has supported the administration's policy in Iraq, said the congressman's stocks were left to him by his grandparents and are managed almost entirely by his investment advisors. Kerry, who has been particularly outspoken against the Bush administration's strategy and policies in Iraq, is a beneficiary of family trusts, which he doesn't control, the senator's spokesman said.

UPDATE BY LINDSAY RENICK MAYER

When we sat down to write this story, we had in mind a few of the obvious war contractors: Boeing, Lockheed Martin, General Dynamics, and so on. But when we finished, we had a story about the fact that nearly every lawmaker was invested in war contractors because the scope of the war had grown to the point that otherwise unlikely suspects, such as Pepsi and Johnson & Johnson, were involved. This meant that not only was it difficult for lawmakers to avoid having such investments, it was equally hard for any member of the public with a diverse blue-chip portfolio to steer clear of them.

Members of the public, however, weren't making decisions about defense legislation that could affect the value of those investments. Lawmakers continue to do so, of course, and continue to hold on to these investments. In 2007, their defense-related assets were worth between $5.3 million and $11.1 million. (Because lawmakers report the value of their investments in ranges, it's impossible to calculate their exact worth.) The 2008 personal financial disclosure reports are also now available on OpenSecrets.org at http://www.opensecrets.org/pfds/search _cid.php.

Lawmakers aren't just benefiting from the defense sector personally, but also politically. In the first three months of 2009, the defense sector gave nearly $2 million to candidates, party committees, and political action committees, with 57 percent of that going to Democrats. In the 2008 election cycle, the sector gave $23.5 million. Rep. John Murtha (D-PA), House Defense Appropriations Subcommittee chairman, has collected more money from the sector than any other lawmaker since 1989 at $2.6 million. Murtha has gotten some heat—and a lot of attention—this year for his connections to now-defunct lobbying firm PMA Group, which the FBI is investigating for allegedly violating campaign finance laws. The firm's clients were primarily defense companies that sought earmarks from Murtha's subcommittee.

Should President Obama stick to his timeline to start bringing troops home from Iraq, it will be interesting to watch as lawmakers decide whether to continue investing in war contractors, especially if their need (and, therefore, lucrative DoD contracts) diminishes over the coming years.

We've been pleased that the mainstream press has been interested in covering lawmakers' personal finances, in addition to their various financial connections to the defense industry. The press—including the *Wall Street Journal, Washington Post, New York Times,* prominent bloggers, and other watchdogs—frequently pulls data from OpenSecrets.org and cites our reports, including this one. It's important that the public understands the full relationship between lawmakers and the companies affected by their legislative votes. Only then can members of the public determine whether decisions are being made based on the merits or the money.

To read more about how lobbying, personal finances, and influence peddling are shaping legislation, keep up with the Center for Responsive Politics' blog at http://www.opensecrets.org/news.

And to do some investigating yourself, dive into our personal financial disclosure database: http://www.opensecrets.org/pfds/index.php.

15

World Bank's Carbon Trade Fiasco

Source:
Upside Down World, February 11, 2009
Title: "The World Bank and Climate Change: Sustainability or Exploitation?"
Author: Mary Tharin

Student Researchers: Victoria Masucci and Christine Wilson
Faculty Evaluator: Elaine Wellin, PhD
Sonoma State University

In the name of environmental protection, the World Bank is brokering carbon emission trading arrangements that destroy indigenous farmlands around the world.

The effort to coordinate global action to reduce greenhouse gas (GHG) emissions began with the Kyoto Protocol, which was adopted in 1997 and now has been ratified by 183 nations. While many of the strategies established in the protocol are encouraging, some are proving to have fatal flaws. One such program, known as Clean Development Mechanism (CDM) investment, has become a means by which indus-

trialized countries avoid reducing their own emissions through the implementation of "emissions reduction" projects in developing nations.

In accordance with the Kyoto Protocol, many governments have established "caps," or limits, on the greenhouse gas emissions that can be produced in their countries. Industries can respond to these government-imposed limits by responsibly reducing their emissions, or they can bypass this process entirely by purchasing "carbon credits" from other industries in other parts of the world who, through CDM investment brokered by the World Bank, trade emission reduction "credits" in order to "offset" excessive emissions. Joris den Blanken, a climate change specialist with Greenpeace, says, "Offsetting means exporting responsibilities to the developing world and removes the incentive for industry to improve efficiency or to invest in renewable energy."

While the World Bank claims that this system "supports sustainable development . . . and benefits the poorer communities of the developing world," the program in reality has become little more than a corporate profit-boosting enterprise. In fact, many transnational corporations are using cap and trade programs not only to avoid emissions responsibility, but to further profit by developing environmentally and socially destructive industries in less developed countries.

In Latin America, where a long history of corporate exploitation has already taken a steep toll, environmentalists and indigenous communities are beginning to speak out about the dangers of the CDM. Because of a myopic focus on greenhouse gas reduction only, and a lack of accountability to local communities, many projects are producing other environmental and social ills that are diametrically opposed to the program's stated objectives.

Nevertheless, the United Nations Environment Programme reports that, to date, 4,364 projects have been approved for CDM funding, and the movement continues to gain momentum. According to the World Wildlife Fund, the number of new project proposals has risen drastically in just a few years, from less than ten per month in early 2005 to about one hundred per month in 2007.

Wood and pulp industries have shown great interest in harnessing the carbon market to justify and finance projects that involve expropriating indigenous farm and grazing land for planting of enormous monospecific plantations. These plantations threaten the area's biodiversity and can severely deplete water resources. According to a 2008 report by Japan Overseas Plantation for Pulpwood (JOPP), entitled "Feasibility Study of Afforestation CDM for Community Development in Extensive Grazing Lands in Uruguay," "From an ecological standpoint, planting large-scale plantations of non-native species in this area is clearly a step in the wrong direction. From a societal standpoint, this could spell cultural genocide."

The land which would be used for the JOPP's "afforestation projects," according to the report, is currently used for "extensive grazing" of cattle and sheep. The report, which elaborates on "land eligibility," makes no mention of the people who own, live on, or make a living from the use of the land in question. The only allusion to this issue is the brief assurance that all displaced cattle would be "sold on the open market." Despite the fact that "cattle and sheep production has been the traditional rural activity in the project area and all the surrounding regions since the seventeenth century," the report contends that the establishment of plantations would be a more cost-effective use for the land than pasture. The question then becomes: cost-effective for whom?

The World Bank touts the CDM as an "integral part of the Bank's mission to reduce poverty through its environment and energy strategies." However, in Latin America as in other parts of the developing world, the global carbon market is proving to be largely detrimental to the indigenous and the poor. With little or no input on how a project is conducted, local communities have virtually no control over how their land, water, and resources will be affected.

In a recent documentary by Carbon Trade Watch, villagers explained that the massive plantations—which cover about 100,000 acres—are diverting water from local streams, causing a sharp decrease in fishing and killing off medicinal plants. In an interview, one local woman lamented that corporate plantations "continue destroying our community, destroying our citizens, destroying our fauna, destroying our flora, and nobody does anything [to stop it]."

Lack of accountability to local populations is a fundamental flaw in the way CDM projects are presented, evaluated, and implemented. The official "Project Design Document Form"—which the CDM executive board uses to approve or deny funding—largely disregards the impact of projects on local communities. The document contains no binding legal language, asking only for a "report on how due account was taken of any comments received" by local stakeholders. In their assessment of four CDM projects carried out in Brazil and Bolivia, the European Environmental Press (EEP) found that "participation of local community members was found to be limited."

While the World Bank pays constant lip service to the importance of sustainability and poverty alleviation in the CDM, it continually fails to deliver positive results for either the environment or disadvantaged communities in the developing world. The global carbon market is proving to be simply another weapon used by multinational corporations to accelerate their incursion on the rights of indigenous peoples and small-scale landholders in Latin America.

The irony of this situation takes on an especially tragic hue since many of the communities at risk have been living in a sustainable manner for centuries and thus should be seen as models in the fight against environmental degradation and climate change. Instead, the World Bank has adopted a system that inadequately addresses one pressing environmental hazard at the expense of other important environmental issues and the well-being of the world's most vulnerable, and often most knowledgeable, of populations.

Janet Redman at the Institute for Policy Studies says, "Farmers [in the global south] are trading communal land rights and their ability to feed themselves for the whims and price fluctuations of the international carbon market."

UPDATE BY MARY THARIN

As governments, environmentalists, and industry leaders gear up for the UN Climate Change Conference this December in Copenhagen, the debate over carbon offsets has taken center stage. Groups including the European Commission have acknowledged the many shortcomings of the Clean Development Mechanism and are calling for reform. In late April 2009, delegates from all over the world attended the Indigenous People's Global Summit on Climate Change, producing a declaration which called on governments to abandon "false solutions to climate change that negatively impact Indigenous Peoples' rights . . . such as carbon trading, the Clean Development Mechanism, and forest offsets."

Unfortunately, the CDM executive board, instead of addressing issues of transparency and accountability, has proposed an expansion of some of the carbon offset scheme's most problematic aspects. The board has put forth plans to expand its forestry mechanism and ease the funding application process. According to Oscar Reyes of Carbon

Trade Watch, these reforms would drastically expand CDM while "lowering the already inadequate checks on environmental sustainability and social justice."

Meanwhile, the Clean Development Mechanism continues to expand. In May 2009 alone, 132 new CDM projects were submitted for approval, marking an all-time high in the application process. At the same time, more evidence is cropping up all over the globe that many "emissions reduction" projects in the developing world are doing more harm than good. In June 2009, the UK-based *Daily Mail* published an exposé on a UN-funded chemical plant that has poisoned the local water supply in Gujarat, India. According to Eva Filzmoser of CDM Watch, large hydro and gas projects are the most damaging receivers of CDM funding. These projects, she argues, rarely save additional emissions and in fact provide perverse incentives to expand environmentally degrading industries.

In the United States, debate over carbon offsets and cap and trade schemes has erupted since the American Clean Energy and Security Act, also known as the Waxman-Markey bill, was passed by the House Energy Committee in May 2009. While many environmentalist groups are heralding the bill as a huge step toward reducing greenhouse gas emissions in the United States, others point to the prominence of carbon offsetting in the bill as a way for corporations to skirt any real commitment to emissions reductions. According to the Institute for Policy Studies (IPS), up to 2 billion tons of carbon (about 30 percent of current US emissions) could be purchased as offsets under the legislation, half of which would come from developing countries through programs like the Clean Development Mechanism.

While most of the mainstream media and many environmental groups have jumped on the cap and trade bandwagon, organizations such as the Institute for Public Studies, Carbon Trade Watch, and CDM Watch continue to boost public awareness on the dangers of cap and trade. A number of voices, including *The Economist*, have come out in favor of a Carbon Tax as a more effective way to motivate emissions reductions. These groups are calling for people in the developed world to take the lead by shrinking our own carbon footprints, and demanding a real solution to climate change that starts at home.

For more information, see:

Sustainable Energy and Economy Network (Institute for Policy Studies): http://www.seen.org

Carbon Trade Watch: http://www.carbontradewatch.org
Friends of the Earth: http://www.foe.org/global-warming
CDM Watch: http://www.cdm-watch.org

16

US Repression of Haiti Continues

Sources:

Haiti Liberté, September 4, 2008
Title: "UN Military Base Expanding: What is Washington up to in Cité Soleil?"
Author: Kim Ives

Upside Down World, June 25, 2008
Title: "Bush Administration Accused of Withholding 'Lifesaving' Aid to Haiti"
Author: Cyril Mychalejko

Upside Down World, August 4, 2008
Title: "RFK Center Releases Documents Outlining US Actions to Block Life-saving
    Funds to Haiti"
Authors: RFK Memorial Center for Human Rights

Student Researchers: Elizabeth Vortman, Leora Johnson, and Rob Hunter
Faculty Evaluators: Karen Grady, PhD, and Sasha Von Meier, PhD
Sonoma State University

The US government plans to expropriate and demolish the homes of
hundreds of Haitians in the shantytown of Cité Soleil to expand the occupying UN force's military base. The US government contractor
DynCorp, a quasi-official arm of the Pentagon and the CIA, is responsible for the base expansion. The base will house the soldiers of the UN
Mission to Stabilize Haiti (MINUSTAH). Cité Soleil is the most bullet-
ridden battleground of the foreign military occupation, which began after
US Special Forces kidnapped and exiled President Jean-Bertrand Aristide on February 29, 2004. Citizens have since been victimized by
recurring massacres at the hands of MINUSTAH.

DynCorp's $5 million contracts include expansion of the principal
base, the rebuilding of the Cité Soleil police station and two other militarized outposts, as well as training support and procurement of
equipment.

According to Cité Soleil mayor Charles Joseph and a DynCorp fore-
man at the site, the State Department's US Agency for International

Development (USAID) provides funding for the base expansion—a very unorthodox use of development aid.

Lawyer Evel Fanfan, the president of the Association of University Graduates Motivated for a Haiti with Rights (AUMOHD), says that about 155 buildings would be razed as the base expansion moves forward. As of March 2009, eighty homes have been demolished. Most of the buildings targeted are homes, but one is a church.

"They started working without saying a word to the people living there," Fanfan said. "The authorities have not told them what is being done, if they will be relocated, how much they will be compensated or even if they will be compensated."

Alarmed residents of the area formed the Committee for Houses Being Demolished (KODEL), which contacted AUMOHD. Fanfan put out a press release and KODEL held a press conference.

"MINUSTAH soldiers came to our press conference and told us to get a lawyer to talk to the American Embassy because the American Embassy is responsible for the work," said pastor assistant Eddy Michel.

"Legally, the Haitian government has not authorized anybody to do anything," said Fanfan. "The Cité Soleil mayor, Charles Joseph, supposedly authorized the construction, but there is no paper, no decree, no order which authorizes it."

On March 25, 2009, the US Ambassador to Haiti, Janet Sanderson, was joined by the head of MINUSTAH, Hedi Annabi, in a ceremony to inaugurate the newly overhauled base, which will house thirty-two Haitian policemen, including a specialized antiriot counterinsurgency unit, as well as a larger number of UN troops.

On March 31, 2008, a DynCorp press release explained: "Under the Haiti Stabilization Initiative task order, DynCorp International will provide training support for up to 444 Haitian National Police. The task order includes DynCorp International procurement of the Haitian police force's basic and specialized non-lethal equipment, vehicles and communications equipment. The value of this work is $3 million. DynCorp International has also been tasked to refurbish the main police station in Cité Soleil. This station will function as the primary location for this new specialized unit. The refurbishment work will be more than $600,000."

Related evidence of US tampering with Haiti's sovereignty and democratic processes surfaced on June 23, 2008, when human rights groups Zamni Lasante (Partners in Health's flagship program in Haiti), the Center for Human Rights and Global Justice, and the Robert F. Kennedy Center for Justice & Human Rights (RFK Center) released a report revealing the Bush administration's blocking of "potentially lifesaving" aid to Haiti in order to meddle in the impoverished nation's political affairs.

In addition to being the poorest nation in the western hemisphere, Haiti also has some of the worst water in the world, ranking last in the Water Poverty Index.

The RFK Center released internal US Treasury Department documents on August 4, 2008, exposing politically motivated actions by the US government to stop the dispersal of $146 million in loans that the Inter-American Development Bank (IDB) approved for Haiti. The IDB originally approved the loans in July 1998, including $54 million for urgently needed water and sanitation projects.

However, documents show that IDB and US Department of Treasury staff sought ways to tie the loans' release to unrelated political conditions that US leaders wanted the Haitian government to comply with. This intervention was in direct violation of the IDB's charter, which bars the Bank from basing decisions upon the political affairs of member states.

"After several years of investigating the withholding of these loans, we now have clear and detailed evidence of egregious intervention by the US government and the IDB to stop life-saving funds to Haiti," said Monika Kalra Varma, director of the RFK Center. "With their transgressions now public, they must heed the call for monitoring and transparency. We urge them to implement the necessary oversight mechanisms to prevent a reoccurrence of behind-the-scenes malfeasance, and above all, to fulfill their obligations to the Haitian people."

UPDATE BY CYRIL MYCHALEJKO

When the Bush administration withheld aid to Haiti intended to fund water and sanitation projects designed to improve "the quality of life—particularly for women and children—and to reduc[e] incidence of disease and child mortality," it did so in a country that, according to Washington, DC–based International Action, is where "water is the leading cause of infant mortality and illness in children . . . Haiti now has the highest infant mortality rate in the western hemisphere . . . [and] more than half of all deaths in Haiti were due to water-borne gastrointestinal diseases."

Despite the report released in June by the RFK Center which labeled the action as "one of the most egregious examples of malfeasance by the United States in recent years," and the internal US Treasury Department documents released in August that prove the blocking of the loan was politically motivated, there was a virtual media blackout of the findings. The *New York Times* published a 487-word article ("Rights Groups Assail US for Withholding Aid to Haiti, Citing Political Motives," June 24, 2008) covering the release of the report, but it never followed up. And despite admitting that the Bush administration was displeased with former Haitian President Jean-Bertrand Aristide, and that President Bush encouraged the coup that removed Aristide from office in 2004, the *Times* was either unable to, or refused to, recognize that the blocking of aid may have been a deliberate action to create a climate that would cause political and social unrest—conditions that could encourage parts of the Haitian population to acquiesce to an overthrow of their democratically elected government. But this was something Jeffrey Sachs, former advisor to the International Monetary Fund (IMF) and World Bank, recognized. In an article in the *Los Angeles Times* ("From His First Day in Office, Bush Was Ousting Aristide," March 4, 2004) Sachs wrote, "US officials surely knew that the aid embargo would mean a balance-of-payments crisis, a rise in inflation and a collapse of living standards, all of which fed the rebellion."[1]

The fact that the Bush administration may have caused the deaths of thousands of Haitians by blocking aid for cynical and self-interested political purposes was not a story worthy of coverage by the US mainstream media. Neither was the Bush administration's role in the violent coup that removed President Aristide, or the fact that selectively rewarding or withholding aid is used as a foreign policy tool in order to influence, destabilize and overthrow governments. But there are media outlets and organizations readers can turn to in order to follow developments like these as they happen. For more information on Haiti and Latin America:

> www.UpsideDownWorld.org
> www.RFKcenter.org
> www.Haitianalysis.org
> www.Nacla.org
> www.haitiliberte.com
> www.rightsaction.org
> www.zcommunications.org

Citation:

1. Dan Beeton, "What the World Bank and IDB Owe Haiti," Global Policy Forum, July 25, 2006.

UPDATE BY ROBERT F. KENNEDY CENTER FOR JUSTICE & HUMAN RIGHTS

RFK Center and Zamni Lasante's investigation published by Upside Down World on August 26, 2008, provides new insight into the role of US officials in stalling loans destined to Haiti. The article contains an overview of documents released by the United States government, after a Freedom of Information Act (FOIA) request filed by the Robert F. Kennedy Center for Justice & Human Rights (RFK Center) and Zanmi Lasante (ZL). This FOIA request sought to expose the actions of officials at the United States Treasury Department and the Inter-American Development Bank to illegally block potentially life-saving social sector loans to Haiti. The public release of the documents marked the end of a years-long battle to expose the United States government's role.

However, it also marked the beginning of the call for accountability. This article and the related report published by RFK Center and ZL, along with the Center for Justice & Human Rights at the NYU School of Law and Partners In Health, brought a renewed level of awareness of this issue among nongovernmental organizations, the Haitian diaspora, and officials in the governments of Haiti and the United States. This summer, the report will be released in Haiti in both Creole and French.

The groundbreaking report, "Wòch nan Soley: The Denial of the Right to Water in Haiti," examines the FOIA documents and the impact of the behind-the-scene actions they detail as well as providing an account of the human costs of these actions and analyzing whether human rights were violated. This report, including the FOIA analysis, was profiled by the *New York Times*, *Miami Herald*, and other major media.

Since the release of this report, members of Congress have begun to investigate possible malfeasance around the loans and explore policy solutions to prevent it from happening again. The experience and information gained in writing the report and advocating for accountability in this instance has assisted RFK Center in developing wider advocacy efforts regarding foreign assistance reform and the human rights-based argument for donor accountability.

Despite the article and report, the people of Haiti continue to suffer due to actions taken by the United States, through the Inter-American Development Bank (IDB). The community of Port-de-Paix, first scheduled to receive funds from these loans as early as 2001, still awaits the rehabilitation of its public water system. The delays in disbursement added a new set of obstacles to the existing hurdles faced by development projects in Haiti. The lasting impact of the US interference with the loans is felt most by the young children in Haiti, as they continue to survive without access to safe, sufficient, and clean water. However, the release of the FOIA documents and report has created a constructive space for dialogue with the IDB. In the time since the report was released, the IDB in Port-au-Prince has finally begun to implement the water projects without further delay. While progress on the ground is slow, steps taken since the release of the report finally show signs that water will one day come to Port-de-Paix, and hopefully other parts of Haiti which have sought these resources since 2001.

For more information, see:

Robert F. Kennedy Center for Justice & Human Rights: http://www.rfkcenter.org/

Partners in Health/Zanmi Lasante: http://www.pih.org/where/Haiti/Haiti.html

Center for Human Rights and Global Justice at NYU Law School:
http://www.chrgj.org

Or read the entire report at http://www.rfkcenter.org/files/
080730_Haiti RighttoWater_FINAL.pdf.

17

The ICC Facilitates US Covert War in Sudan

Sources:

Inter Press Service, March 9, 2009
Title: "Aren't There War Crimes in The US? Legitimacy of Global Court Questioned
 Over Sudan"
Author: Thalif Deen

Dissindentvoice.org, *Black Star News*, and *San Francisco Bay View*, March 6, 2009
Title: "Africom's Covert War in Sudan"
Author: Keith Harmon Snow

Michelcollon.info, April 1, 2009
Title: "The Darfur crisis: blood, hunger and oil"
Author: Mohamed Hassan interview with Grégoire Lalieu and Michel Collon

Student Researcher: Curtis Harrison
Faculty Evaluator: Keith Gouveia, JD
Sonoma State University

The United States promoted the International Criminal Court's (ICC)
indictment of Sudan's President Omar al-Bashir for war crimes in Darfur, in order to justify continuing Western exploitation and military
interventions in the resource-rich region.

"America is an opportunist country," explains Sudanese Ambassador
Abdalmahmood Abdalhaleem Mohamad. "They want to use the ICC
without being a party to it." In effect, he said, US soldiers can have
immunity, but not the president of Sudan.

At a UN press conference, the ambassador also challenged reporters
to show him any photographs or film footage from Darfur that would
equal the destruction of human lives and homes in Gaza, Iraq, and
Afghanistan. "Did anybody ask who is accountable for this damage and
destruction?"

Asked why Sudan was being singled out, the Sudanese envoy said
Western nations are eyeing Sudan's newly discovered oil riches.

Western nations have been marginalized in the region, in terms of both oil exploration and arms supplies, by China, which has in recent years become one of Sudan's closest political, economic, and military allies. Mohamad explains that the US, UK, and France "harbor a desire to revive their colonial dreams in Sudan."

Keith Harmon Snow warns, "It is difficult to make sense of the war in Darfur—especially when people see it as a one-sided 'genocide' of Arabs against blacks that is being committed by the Bashir 'regime'—but such is the establishment propaganda. The real story is much more expansive, more complex, and it revolves around . . . deeper geopolitical realities."

Michel Collon explains that when the British Empire invaded and colonized Egypt in 1898, Sudan, by extension, became an Anglo-Egyptian colony. As in other African colonies, Great Britain applied the "divide-and-rule" policy. Sudan was divided into two parts. In the north, they kept Arabic as the official language and Islam as religion. In the south, the English language was imposed and missionaries converted people to Christianity. There was no trade between the two areas. The British imported Greek and Armenian minorities to create a buffer zone. Great Britain also imposed a modern economic system that we could call capitalism. They built one train line to connect Egypt and Sudan and another to connect Khartoum to Port Sudan. These looting lines were used to siphon resources from Sudan into Great Britain and to be sold on the international market. Khartoum became an economically dynamic center of colonial activity.

This imposed division of Sudan and the choice of Khartoum as its economic center led to a series of civil wars.

When Sudan gained independence in 1956, there were still no relations between the two parts of the country. The first civil war was sparked by Southern Sudan's demand for an equitable share of the control and wealth of the country, which was still concentrated in Khartoum. When in 1978 Chevron discovered important oil fields in Southern Sudan, a second civil war broke out as Northern Sudan sought control of those revenues.

Relationships soured between US and Sudan as Chevron's motives in the region conflicted with those of the new Khartoum-based president of Sudan, Omar al-Bashir.

In this setting, Colon notes, with Sudanese oil slipping away from American interests, China came in, offering to buy raw minerals and oil from Sudan at international market prices. Whereas Africa used to be the private hunting grounds of the West, China now competes for domination of the rich African continent.

The Western agenda in Darfur, Sudan, is to win back control of natural resources by weakening the Arab government and establishing a more "friendly" government that will accommodate the corporate interests of the US, Canada, Europe, Australia, and Israel.

The ICC was used in the strategy to turn world opinion against al-Bashir and the government of Sudan, and to further divide and destabilize the region. The legitimacy of the court is being questioned as it shows itself to be a tool of Western hegemony.

Following on the heels of the announcement that the ICC handed down seven war crimes charges against al-Bashir, a story broadcast into every American living room by day's end, President al-Bashir ordered the expulsion of ten international nongovernmental organizations (NGOs) that were operating in Darfur under the veneer of humanitarian aid.

Snow points out that this expulsion was used to further ramp up Western public demand for military intervention. "Mainstream broadcasters expressed moral outrage and complained that 'hundreds of thousands of innocent refugees will now be subjected to massive unassisted suffering'—as opposed to the assisted suffering they previously faced," Snow continues, "but they never ask with any serious and honest zeal, why and how the displaced persons and refugees came to be displaced to begin with. Neither do they ask about all the money, intelligence sharing, deal making, and collaboration [between many "humanitarian" NGOs and] private or governmental military agencies."

What is not reported in English-speaking press is that the US had just stepped up its ongoing war for control of Sudan. There are US Special Forces on the ground throughout the region, prompting these big questions: 1) How many of the killings are being committed by US proxy forces and blamed on al-Bashir and the government of Sudan? and 2) Who funds, arms and trains the rebel insurgents?

Colon concludes that while the Western strategy is to magnify regional conflicts in order to mobilize international opinion and destabilize the Sudanese regime, "the truth is that if Khartoum were to stop dealing with China, the US would not mention Darfur again."

UPDATE BY KEITH HARMON SNOW

How do you whitewash a whitewash? Having manufactured the massive body of propaganda needed to persuade the English- and Hebrew-speaking world that an unadulterated genocide is occurring in Darfur, Sudan, committed by the heavily armed Arab government of Sudan—and its "Janjaweed" militias—against an unarmed civilian population of black Africans; having inflated death tolls and exaggerated the levels of violence (even as violence and death tolls are diminishing or nonexistent); having masked all military involvement of Western countries behind the moral imperatives of altruistic Western charity and aid (our selfless Judeo-Christian dedication to humanitarian action); having duped millions of people into following your charade by throwing money at them, hidden behind glossy brochures, congressional lobbies, and vested-interest advertorials; having organized good-intentioned people into a "grassroots" collective falsely equated with the Apartheid movement; and having been discovered to be a massive body of deceptions, mischaracterizations, selective facts, and outright lies: where do we go from here?

The brief exposé "AFRICOM'S Covert War in Sudan" merely scratched the surface of the massive body of "Save Darfur" propaganda, one of the false narratives created by the Empire to obliterate its culpability in war crimes, crimes against humanity, and genocide. It has been completely ignored by the establishment press, and receives equally indifferent, or even hostile, treatment from the left liberal "progressive" press.

Indeed, there is no doubt that genocide has occurred in Sudan, be it Darfur or Kordofan or the mountains of Juba. But genocide is concomitant with the imperial enterprise all over Africa, and all over the world, and that is the political economy of genocide.

For some excellent news coverage and exposés of the establishment's false narratives on Sudan, or other places, see the work of Glen Ford and Bruce Dixon in *Black Agenda Report* (e.g. Dixon: "Darfur "Genocide" Lies Unraveling—Only 1,500 Darfuris Died in 2008, Says African Union," June 24, 2009); also look to editor Milton Alimadi at *Black Star News* (see, e.g. Amii Omara-Otunu, "Western Humanitarianism or Neo-Slavery," November 7, 2007; or Alimadi, "U.S. Illegally Trained Uganda on Torture," April 19, 2009; or Keith Harmon Snow, "The U.S. and Genocide of Acholi," July 5, 2007).

The true grassroots movements to help Sudan, Uganda, and Congo can be supported through the nongovernment organizations Friends of the Congo (FriendsoftheCongo.org), Campaign to End Genocide in Uganda Now (www.CEGUN.org), and UNIGHT For the Children of Uganda (ww.unight.org).

One of the final war crimes of George W. Bush was his order to the Pentagon to immediately airlift military equipment to Rwanda, destined for Darfur, to the genocidal government of Paul Kagame, one of the protagonists destabilizing Congo and Sudan. Also backing the Rwandan Defense Forces and Ugandan People's Defense Forces covert operations in Sudan, the Obama administration has escalated military involvement in all frontline states: Chad, Uganda, Kenya, and Ethiopia. Meanwhile, all the foreign-backed rebel groups in Darfur recruit and deploy child soldiers, with some 6,000 armed children in Darfur and 8,000 in Sudan.

Weapons shipped by Israelis, including radioactive shells, were not the first to be sent illegally through Kenya—most weapons shipments cross the Kenya-Uganda border at night—but the government of Kenya arrested one official who spoke freely about their true destination (*Africa Research Bulletin*, Vol. 46, No. 1). Washington was quick to point out that "it may not be illegal for Kenya to provide weapons to Sudan"—in violation of the international arms embargo—and the Pentagon continues to fortify South Sudan in advance of its scheduled "independence" (2012), while South Sudan's de facto "president," General Salva Kiir Mayardit, has an open-door in Washington (*Africa Research Bulletin*, Vol. 46, No.

1). The bulk of South Sudan's 2008 budget ($US 2.5 billion), involving huge USAID and other "aid" donors, was spent on weapons. And the International Crises Group, and its clones—ENOUGH! and Resolve Uganda and Raise Hope for Congo—are all talking about peace, but peddling war (see Milton Alimadi, "Resolve, Enough! So Called Peace Organizations Promote War in Uganda," *Black Star News*, June 17, 2009.

KEITH HARMON SNOW is the 2009 Regent's Lecturer in Law & Society at the University of California Santa Barbara, recognized for over a decade of work outside of academia contesting official narratives on war crimes, crimes against humanity, and genocide, while also working as a genocide investigator for the United Nations and other bodies. He is also a past and present (2009) Project Censored award winner. His work can be found through his website, www.allthingspass.com.

18

Ecuador's Constitutional Rights of Nature

Source:
Upside Down World, September 25, 2008
Title: "Ecuador's Constitution Gives Rights to Nature"
Author: Cyril Mychalejko

Student Researcher: Chelsea Davis
Faculty Evaluator: Elaine Wellin, PhD
Sonoma State University

In September 2008, Ecuador became the first country in the world to declare constitutional rights of nature, thus codifying a new system of environmental protection.

Reflecting the beliefs and traditions of the indigenous peoples of Ecuador, the constitution declares that nature "has the right to exist, persist, maintain and regenerate its vital cycles, structure, functions and its processes in evolution." This right, the constitution states, "is independent of the obligation on natural and juridical persons or the State to indemnify the people that depend on the natural systems."

The new constitution redefines people's relationship with nature by asserting that nature is not just an object to be appropriated and exploited by people, but is rather a rights-bearing entity that should be treated with parity under the law.

Mari Margil, associate director of the Environmental Legal Defense Fund, worked closely over the past year with members of Ecuador's constitutional assembly on drafting legally enforceable rights of nature, which mark a watershed in the trajectory of environmental law. Ecuador's leadership on this issue may have a global domino effect. Margil says that her organization is busy fielding calls from interested countries, such as Nepal, which is currently writing its first constitution.

For all of the hope and tangible progress the rights of nature articles in Ecuador's constitution represent, however, there are shortcomings and contradictions with the laws and the political reality on the ground. A fundamental flaw in the constitution also exists due to Ecuador president Rafael Correa's refusal to include a clause mandating free, prior, and informed consent by communities for development project that would affect their local ecosystems.

"I expect them [the multinational extractive industries] to fight it," says Margil. "Their bread and butter is based on being able to treat countries and ecosystems like cheap hotels. Multinational corporations are dependent on ravaging the planet in order to increase their bottom line."

The new mining law, introduced by President Correa and backed by Canadian companies, which hold the majority of mining concessions in Ecuador, is a testament to Margil's forecast. The mining law would allow for large-scale, open-pit metal mining in pristine Andean highlands and Amazon rainforest. Major nationwide demonstrations are being held in protest, with groups accusing Correa of inviting social and environmental disaster by selling out to mining interests.

Carlos Zorrilla, executive director of Defensa y Conservación Ecológica de Intag, who has been a tireless defender of the environment against transnational mining companies, says that while the new constitution looks good on paper, "in practice governments like Correa's will argue that funding his political project, which will bring 'well being and relieve poverty,' overrules the rights of nature."

Yet even as President Correa embraces the extractive economic model of development, the inclusion of the rights of nature in a national constitution sets inspiring and revolutionary precedent. If history is any indicator, Ecuadorians will successfully fight for the rights of nature, with or without their president.

UPDATE BY CYRIL MYCHALEJKO

When Ecuadorians drafted and passed a new constitution, which gave nature inalienable rights, the US media largely ignored this historic development. In the case of the *Los Angeles Times*, one of the few mainstream outlets to cover the story, the newspaper's editorial board trivialized the development ("Putting Nature in Ecuador's Constitution," September 2, 2008) by suggesting it sounded "like a stunt by the San Francisco City Council" and that it seemed "crazy."

"As ecological systems around the world collapse, we need to fundamentally change our relationship with nature. This requires changes in both law and culture, and ultimately our behavior as part of nature," said Mari Margil, associate director of the Defense Fund, who is disappointed in how the US media largely ignored the story.

In Ecuador, at the time of the constitutional vote, the optimism over how the rights of nature clauses would translate into policy was guarded.

"As exciting as these developments are, it was also inevitable that the people in power would, and will, find ways to circumvent, undermine, and ignore those rights," said Carlos Zorrilla, executive director of Defensa y Conservación Ecológica de Intag.

According to Zorrilla, a major disappointment has been President Rafael Correa's new mining law.

"The law takes rights-to-nature loopholes and widens them so that giant dirt movers could easily drive through them," said Zorrilla, who has been working with communities of Ecuador's Intag region to resist mining and promote sustainable development. "To mention a couple of examples, the law does not prohibit large-scale mining in habitats harboring endangered species, nor the dumping of heavy metals in rivers and streams."

Indigenous leaders responded by filing a lawsuit before Ecuador's constitutional court in March 2009, seeking to overturn the mining law, which they believe is unconstitutional. Article 1 of the rights of nature clauses states: "Every person, people, community or nationality, will be able to demand the recognitions of rights for nature before the public organisms. The application and interpretation of these rights will follow the related principles established in the Constitution."

Regardless of the ongoing struggles to ensure that the true meaning and scope of the constitution is upheld, Dr. Mario Melo, a lawyer specializing in environmental law and human rights and an advisor to Fundación Pachamama–Ecuador, believes that the nature clauses that reflect the traditions of indigenous peoples could offer a path to an ecologically sustainable future.

"I consider that the recognition of the 'Rights to Nature' as a progress on a global scale and one that deserves to be globally broadcast and commented on as a contribution from Ecuador towards the search of new ways of facing the environmental crisis due to climate change."

The struggles of Ecuadorian social movements and the Ecuadorian government to uphold the rights of nature and to create a new development model that places human beings as interdependent parts of nature, rather than dominant exploiters of nature, is something we should continue to monitor and learn from.

19

Bank Bailout Recipients Spent to Defeat Labor

Source:

Huffington Post, January 27, 2009
Article: "Bailout Spent to Defeat Labor"
Author: Sam Stein

Student Researchers: Ben Kaufman and Rosemary Scott
Faculty Evaluator: Kelly Bucy, PhD
Sonoma State University

On October 17, 2008, three days after Bank of America Corporation received $25 billion in federal bailout funds, they hosted a conference call to organize opposition to the Employee Free Choice Act (EFCA). Participants, including AIG, were urged to persuade their clients to send "large contributions" to groups working against the EFCA, as well as to vulnerable Senate Republicans who could be used to help block the passage of the pro-labor bill that would make it easier for employees to organize into unions.

Bernie Marcus, cofounder of Home Depot, and Rick Berman, founder of the Center for Union Facts, led the hour-long phone call that framed the legislation as a threat to American capitalism. The legislation—which would allow workers to form unions either by holding traditional elections or by having a majority of employees sign written forms—is virtually certain to face a Republican filibuster. Obama and Senate Democrats have stated their commitment to the bill.

Donations of hundreds of thousands, if not millions, of dollars were needed, it was argued, to prevent America from turning "into France." "If a retailer has not gotten involved in this, if he has not spent money on this election, if he has not sent money to [former Senator] Norm Coleman and all these other guys, they should be shot. They should be thrown out of their goddamn jobs," Marcus declared.

One of the callers suggested that participants send major contributions to Berman's organization as a way of affecting the election without violating the McCain-Feingold campaign finance law. "Some organizations have written checks for $250,000, $500,000, some for $2 million for this," said the caller, likely Steven Hantler, director of Free Enterprise and Entrepreneurship at Bernie Marcus's Marcus Foundation.

According to author Sam Stein, reform groups are sending letters to congressional committee chairs and to the head of the Congressional Oversight Panel, urging an investigation into whether bailout recipients used taxpayer money to benefit political candidates or organizations. "We're calling for Congress to investigate whether Bank of America, AIG, or other recipients of billions in bailout money, used taxpayer dollars to send 'large contributions' to any political organizations," reads the letter. "Congress has a responsibility to oversee the $700 billion bailout of the financial services sector. That means making sure that these taxpayer funds are used transparently, and in ways that benefit regular people—not special interests."

Berman said that there "was nothing on that call that spoke to funneling money to anybody." Either way, Bank of America did use time and resources to host the anti-EFCA forum, on which individuals were urged to make political donations. That alone has compelled groups advocating government reform to raise concerns with Congress.

"What they've apparently done is taken taxpayer money and siphoned it to their political servants—right-wing Republicans," said Rep. Alan Grayson. A letter read, "In our current system, special interests believe they can buy policies from Congress through campaign contributions, and the public believes this as well. Wall Street companies routinely spend millions in campaign contributions and lobbying to resist oversight of the practices that led to the current economic crisis.

"Bank of America is now not only getting bailout money. They are lending their name to participate in a campaign to stop workers from having a majority sign up [provision]," said Stephen Lerner, director of the Private Equity Project at Service Employees International Union

(SEIU). "The biggest corporations who have created the problem are, at the very time, asking us to bail them out and then using that money to stop workers from improving their lives."

20

Secret Control of the Presidential Debates

Sources:
Open Debates, September 18, 2008
Title: "Pro-democratic Groups Call on Debate Commission to Make Secret Contract Public"
Author: George Farah

Democracy Now! October 2, 2008
Title: "No Debate: How the Republican and Democratic Parties Secretly Control the Presidential Debates"
Interviewee: George Farah

Student Researchers: Erin Galbraith, Natalie Dale, and Kerry Headley
Faculty Evaluator: Mickey Huff
Sonoma State University

The Obama and McCain campaigns jointly negotiated a detailed secret contract dictating the terms of the 2008 debates. This included who got to participate, what topics were to be raised, and the structure of the debate formats.

Since 1987, a private corporation created by and for the Republican and Democratic parties called the Commission on Presidential Debates (CPD) has sponsored the US presidential debates and implemented debate contracts. In order to shield the major party candidates from criticism, CPD has refused to release debate contract information to the public.

In 1986, the Republican and Democratic National Committees ratified an agreement "to take over the presidential debates" from the nonpartisan League of Women Voters. Fifteen months later, then-Republican Party chair Frank Fahrenkopf and then-Democratic Party chair Paul Kirk incorporated the Commission on Presidential Debates. Fahrenkopf and Kirk still cochair the Commission on Presidential Debates, and every four years it implements and conceals contracts jointly drafted by the Republican and Democratic nominees.

Before the CPD's formation, the League of Women Voters served as a genuinely nonpartisan presidential debate sponsor from 1976 until 1984, ensuring the inclusion of popular independent candidates and prohibiting major party campaigns from manipulating debate formats.

In 1980, the league invited independent candidate John B. Anderson to participate in a presidential debate, even though President Jimmy Carter adamantly refused to debate him.

Four years later, when the Ronald Reagan and Walter Mondale campaigns vetoed sixty-eight proposed panelists in order to eliminate difficult questions, the league publicly lambasted the candidates for "totally abusing the process." The ensuing public outcry persuaded the candidates to accept the league's panelists for the next debate.

And in 1988, when the George Bush and Michael Dukakis campaigns drafted the first secret debate contract—a "Memorandum of Understanding" that dictated who got to participate, who would ask the questions, even the heights of the podiums—the league declined to implement it. Instead, the league issued a blistering press release claiming, "the demands of the two campaign organizations would perpetrate a fraud on the American voter."

The major parties, however, did not want a sponsor that limited their candidates' control. Consequently, the CPD was created to step in.

Since the CPD took control of the presidential debates in 1988, the debates have been primarily funded by corporate contributions. Multinational corporations with regulatory interests before Congress have donated millions of dollars in contributions to the CPD, and debate sites have become corporate carnivals, where sponsoring companies market their products, services, and political agendas. Tobacco giant Philip Morris was a major sponsor in 1992 and 1996. Major contributor Anheuser-Busch, has sponsored presidential debates in its hometown of St. Louis in 1996, 2000, 2004, and 2008.

That the CPD has been able to raise millions of dollars in corporate contributions is not surprising. Frank Fahrenkopf and Paul Kirk, who cochair and control the CPD, are registered lobbyists for multinational corporations. Kirk has collected $120,000 for lobbying on behalf of Hoechst Marion Roussel, a German pharmaceutical company. Fahrenkopf earns approximately $900,000 a year as the chief lobbyist for the nation's $54 billion gambling industry. As president of the American Gaming Association, Fahrenkopf directs enormous financial contributions to major party candidates and saturates the media with "expert" testimony extolling gambling's "many benefits." "We're not going to apologize for trying to influence political elections," said Fahrenkopf.

"These are the guys," author George Farah points out, "deciding who gets to participate in the most important political forums in the United States of America."

He adds, "Kirk and Fahrenkopf's lobbying practices demonstrate a willingness to protect corporate interests at the expense of voters' interests. It shouldn't come as a surprise, then, that the co-chairs of the CPD are willing to protect major party interests at the expense of voters' interests."

The current structure enables corporations to give money to both the Democratic and Republican parties, which essentially supports their duopoly over the political process and excludes third party voices that may be hostile to corporate power.

Historically, third party candidates have played critical roles in our democracy by introducing popular and groundbreaking issues that were eventually co-opted by major parties—such as the abolition of slavery, women's right to vote, social security, child labor laws, public schools, the direct election of senators, paid vacation, unemployment compensation, and the formation of labor unions. With third-party candidates excluded from discourse, they can't break the bipartisan silence on issues where the major parties are at odds with most Americans.

Of past debates, Farah questions, "In a country where corporations are the dominant political and economic force, why did the debates pass without the word "corporation" being spoken? . . . What about campaign finance reform? Corporate crime? Environmental devastation? Child poverty and homelessness? Free trade and globalization? Media concentration? Military spending? Immigration? Civil liberties and privacy rights?"

For the last twenty years, while the CPD has sponsored the presidential debates, challenging questions, assertive moderators, follow-up questions, candidate-to-candidate questioning, and rebuttals have been excluded from presidential debates. The CPD's formats have typically prevented in-depth examination of critical issues and allowed the candidates to recite a series of memorized sound bites.

Walter Cronkite has called CPD-sponsored presidential debates an "unconscionable fraud."

21

Recession Causes States to Cut Welfare

Sources:
Mother Jones, January 15, 2009
Title: "Brave New Welfare"
Author: Stephanie Mencimer

Associated Press, March 26, 2009
Title: "States consider drug tests for welfare recipients"
Author: Tom Breen

Student Researcher: Malana Men, Sonoma State University, and Samantha Barowsky
Faculty Evaluator: Douglas Anderson, PhD
Southwest Minnesota State University

Many states are in the midst of an aggressive action to push thousands of eligible mothers off Temporary Assistance to Needy Families (TANF), traditionally known as welfare. Families are being denied aid so that savings can be redirected in state budgets.

Nationally, the number of welfare recipients fell more than 40 percent between 2001 and June 2008. Louisiana, Texas, and Illinois have each dropped 80 percent of adult recipients since January 2001. The state of Georgia had a 90 percent drop, with fewer than 2,500 Georgian adults receiving benefits, down from 28,000 in 2004.

In Georgia last year, only 18 percent of children living below 50 percent of the poverty line—which is less than $733 a month for a family of three—were receiving TANF.

In 2006, the Georgia Coalition Against Domestic Violence conducted a survey to find out why so many women were suddenly failing to get welfare benefits. They discovered that caseworkers were actively discouraging women from applying. Welfare caseworkers were reportedly telling applicants that they would have to be surgically sterilized before they could apply for TANF. Disabled women were told they couldn't apply because they didn't meet work requirements. Others were warned that the state could take their children if they applied for benefits. Women are increasingly vulnerable to sexual assault and exploitation—sometimes by the state officials or caseworkers assigned to help them. Arrests of women for prostitution and petty crime went up as more and more families were denied welfare.

Students completing college degrees were misinformed that they would be denied aid once they turned twenty, regardless of graduation status. Students as young as sixteen were told that they must work full time or lose benefits.

Texas reduced its caseload by outsourcing applications to a call center, which not only wrongfully denied some families, but lost applications altogether.

In Florida, one innovative region started requiring TANF applicants to attend forty hours of classes before they could even apply. Clients trying to restore lost benefits had once been able to straighten out paperwork with the help of caseworkers. In 2005, officials assigned all such work to a single employee, available two hours a week. The area's TANF caseload fell by half in a year.

Because of the recession, many Americans turn to the safety net of government assistance programs such as food stamps, unemployment benefits, or welfare. In an effort to discourage applicants, lawmakers in at least eight states want recipients to submit to random drug testing.

In March 2009, the Kansas House of Representatives approved a measure that mandates drug testing for the 14,000 people getting cash assistance from the state. In February, the Oklahoma Senate unanimously passed a measure that would require drug testing as a condition of receiving TANF benefits. Similar bills have been introduced in Missouri and Hawaii. A member of Minnesota's House of Representatives has a bill requiring drug tests of people who get public assistance under a state program there.

During the Clinton era of welfare reform, states were given a fixed amount of money regardless of need. The TANF block grant was a $16.5 billion grant in which Georgia share alone was $370 million a year. States could divert the funds to any program vaguely related to serving the needy. Since states receive the same amount of federal funds regardless of how many people received assistance, states were encouraged to deny benefits. "Even if caseloads go to zero, they get the same amount of money," notes Robert Welsh of the Georgia Budget and Policy Institute.

States have used the surplus TANF money to expand child care, job training, and transportation to help recipients find jobs. The Government Accountability Office found in 2006 that many states were moving federal welfare funds away from cash assistance to the poor, or even "work supports" like child care, to plug holes in state budgets.

TANF is a gateway to education, drug rehabilitation, mental health care, child care, even transportation and disability benefits—tools for upward mobility.

"Welfare is the only cash safety-net program for single moms and their kids," notes Rebecca Blank, an economist at the Brookings Institution, "One has to worry, with a recession, about the number of women who, if they get unemployed, are not going to have anywhere to turn."

22

Obama's Trilateral Commission Team

Source:
AugustReview.com, January 30, 2009
Title: "Obama: Trilateral Commission Endgame"
Author: Patrick Wood

Student Researcher: Sarah Maddox
Faculty Evaluator: Peter Phillips
Sonoma State University

Barack Obama appointed eleven members of the Trilateral Commission to top-level and key positions in his administration within his first ten days in office. This represents a very narrow source of international leadership inside the Obama administration, with a core agenda that is not necessarily in support of working people in the United States.

Obama was groomed for the presidency by key members of the Trilateral Commission. Most notably, Zbigniew Brzezinski, cofounder of the Trilateral Commission with David Rockefeller in 1973, has been Obama's principal foreign policy advisor.

According to official Trilateral Commission membership lists, there are only eighty-seven members from the United States (the other 337 members are from other countries). Thus, within two weeks of his inauguration, Obama's appointments encompassed more than 12 percent of the Commission's entire US membership.

Trilateral appointees include:
➤ Secretary of Treasury, Timothy Geithner
➤ Ambassador to the United Nations, Susan Rice
➤ National Security Advisor, Gen. James L. Jones
➤ Deputy National Security Advisor, Thomas Donilon
➤ Chairman, Economic Recovery Committee, Paul Volcker
➤ Director of National Intelligence, Admiral Dennis C. Blair
➤ Assistant Secretary of State, Asia & Pacific, Kurt M. Campbell
➤ Deputy Secretary of State, James Steinberg

- State Department, Special Envoy, Richard Haass
- State Department, Special Envoy, Dennis Ross
- State Department, Special Envoy, Richard Holbrooke

There are many other links in the Obama administration to the Trilateral Commission. For instance, Secretary of State Hillary Clinton is married to Commission member William Jefferson Clinton.

Secretary of Treasury Tim Geithner's informal group of advisors include E. Gerald Corrigan, Paul Volcker, Alan Greenspan, and Peter G. Peterson, all members. Geithner's first job after college was with Trilateralist Henry Kissinger at Kissinger Associates.

Trilateralist Brent Scowcroft has been an unofficial advisor to Obama and was mentor to Defense Secretary Robert Gates. And Robert Zoellick, current president of the World Bank appointed during the G. W. Bush administration, is a member.

According to the Trilateral Commission's website, the Commission was formed in 1973 by private citizens of Japan, Europe (European Union countries), and North America (United States and Canada) to foster closer cooperation among these core democratic industrialized areas of the world with shared leadership responsibilities in the wider international

system. The website says, "The membership of the Trilateral Commission is composed of about 400 distinguished leaders in business, media, academia, public service (excluding current national Cabinet Ministers), labor unions, and other non-governmental organizations from the three regions. The regional chairmen, deputy chairmen, and directors constitute the leadership of the Trilateral Commission, along with an Executive Committee including about 40 other members."

Since 1973, the Trilateral Commission has met regularly in plenary sessions to discuss policy position papers developed by its members. Policies are debated in order to achieve consensuses. Respective members return to their own countries to implement policies consistent with those consensuses. The original stated purpose of the Trilateral Commission was to create a "New International Economic Order." Its current statement has morphed into fostering a "closer cooperation among these core democratic industrialized areas of the world with shared leadership responsibilities in the wider international system."

Since the Carter administration, Trilateralists have held these very influential positions: Six of the last eight World Bank presidents; presidents and vice presidents of the United States (except for Obama and Biden); over half of all US secretaries of state; and three quarters of the secretaries of defense.

Two strong convictions guide the Commission's agenda for the 2009-2012 triennium. First, the Trilateral Commission is to remain as important as ever in maintaining wealthy countries' shared leadership in the wider international system. Second, the Commission will "widen its framework to reflect broader changes in the world." Thus, the Japan Group has become a Pacific Asian Group, which includes Chinese and Indian members, and Mexican members have been added to the North American Group. The European Group continues to widen in line with the enlargement of the EU.

UPDATE BY PATRICK WOOD

The concept of "undue influence" comes to mind when considering the number of Trilateral Commission members in the Obama administration. They control the areas of our most urgent national needs: financial and economic crisis, national security, and foreign policy.

The conflict of interest is glaring. With 75 percent of the Trilateral membership consisting of non-US individuals, what influence does this super-majority have on the remaining 25 percent?

For example, when Chrysler entered bankruptcy under the oversight and control of the Obama administration, it was quickly decided that the Italian carmaker Fiat would take over Chrysler. The deal's point man, Treasury Secretary Timothy Geithner, is a member of the Trilateral Commission. Would you be surprised to know that the chairman of Fiat, Luca di Montezemolo, is *also* a fellow member?

Congress should have halted this deal the moment it was suggested.

Many European members of the Trilateral Commission are also top leaders of the European Union. What political and economic sway do they have through their American counterparts?

If asked, the vast majority of Americans would say that America's business is its own, and should be closed to foreign meddlers with non-American agendas.

But, the vast majority of Americans have no idea who or what the Trilateral Commission is, much less the power they have usurped since 1976, when Jimmy Carter became the first Trilateral member to be elected president (Project Censored Story #1, 1976).

In light of today's unprecedented financial crisis, they would be abhorred if they actually read Zbigniew Brzezinski's (cofounder of the commission with David Rockefeller) statement from his 1971 book, *Between Two Ages: America's Role in the Technetronic Era,* which states that, "The nation-state as a fundamental unit of man's organized life has ceased to be the principal creative force: International banks and multinational corporations are acting and planning in terms that are far in advance of the political concepts of the nation-state."

Yet, this is exactly what is happening. The global banks and corporations are running circles around the nation-state, including the United States. They have no regard for due process, Congress, or the will of the people.

Why have the American people been kept in the dark about a subject so great that it shakes our country to its very core?

The answer is simple: the top leadership of the media is also saturated with members of the Trilateral Commission who are able to selectively suppress the stories that are covered. They include:

➤ David Bradley, chairman, Atlantic Media Company

➤ Karen Elliot House, former senior vice president, Dow Jones & Company, and publisher, the *Wall Street Journal*

➤ Richard Plepler, copresident, HBO

➤ Charlie Rose, PBS

➤ Fareed Zakaria, editor, *Newsweek*
➤ Mortimer Zuckerman, chairman, *US News & World Report*

There are many other top-level media connections due to corporate directorships and stock ownership.

For more information, this writer's original 1978 book, *Trilaterals Over Washington*, is available in electronic form at no charge at www.August Review.com. This site also has many papers analyzing various aspects of the Trilateral Commission's hegemony in the United States and elsewhere, since it's founding in 1973.

23

Activists Slam World Water Forum as a Corporate-Driven Fraud

Sources:

AlterNet, March 17, 2009
Title: "Fifth World Water Forum Marked by Violence and Repression"
Author: Jeff Conant

AlterNet, March 18, 2009
Title: "An Inside Peek: Why the World Water Forum is a Sham"
Author: Jeff Conant

Democracy Now! March 23, 2009
Title: "Water Rights Activists Blast Istanbul World Water Forum as 'Corporate Trade Show to Promote Privatization'"
Interviewee: Maude Barlow

KPFA, *Sunday Sedition*, March 29, 2009
Title: "Andria Lewis interviews Maude Barlow"

Student Researcher: Frances Capell
Faculty Evaluator: Andrew Roth, PhD
Sonoma State University

Water rights activists blasted the World Water Forum, held in Turkey in late March of 2009, as a corporate trade show promoting privatization of water. Three hundred Turkish activists gathered near the forum's entrance and were faced with the overwhelming force of between 2,000 and 3,000 police. The forum opened with Turkish police firing tear gas and detaining protesters, who were shouting "Water for life, not for profit."

According to its website, the World Water Forum is "an open, all-inclusive, multi-stakeholder process" where governments, NGOs, businesses and others "create links, debate and attempt to find solutions to achieve water security."

However, the forum's main organizer, the World Water Council, is dominated by two of the world's largest private water corporations, Suez Environment and Veolia Environmental Services. Critics contend that the council's links to Suez and Veolia, as well as the large representation of the business industry in the council, compromise its legitimacy. Corporate interests that make up the World Water Council are in constant contact with the World Bank and other financial institutions. Each forum is set up as a quasi-United Nations event, to the extent of issuing a ministerial statement at the forum's close promoting global policy approaches to water and sanitation.

The council promotes extraordinarily expensive and destructive dam and water diversion projects as well as policies such as Public-Private Partnerships (PPPs) that put water services under private ownership. PPPs in Argentina, Bolivia, El Salvador, the US, and other countries have resulted in huge price hikes, water pollution, depletion and cutoffs which, in the language of the water justice movement, "deny people the right to water." Despite these and other harmful impacts, the Istanbul Water Consensus aims to secure the commitment of local authorities to similar water policies. This year's forum issued a communiqué that describes access to water as a "basic human need" rather than a human right, despite efforts by dissenting Latin American countries, France and Spain, to introduce the right to water. They were reportedly blocked by Egypt, Brazil, and the United States. In the minutiae of political verbiage, this apparently slight difference in terminology can have a profound significance. If water is defined as a "need" rather than a "right," it becomes a commodity subject to trade and implies no obligation on the parts of governments to ensure access to it. If it is a human right, on the other hand, mandatory government policy is activated to assure unconditional access to everyone.

Activists from the People's Water Forum—an alternative formation representing rural poor, the environment, and organized labor—slammed the official event as a noninclusive, corporate-driven fraud pushing for water privatization. They called for a more open, democratic, and transparent forum. A block of southern governments led by Uruguay is building support for an alternative, legitimate forum to be led by the United Nations.

High-profile civil society voices such as Maude Barlow, senior adviser on water issues to the United Nations General Assembly, are calling for this to be the last corporately held World Water Forum. "The security is tight, because what they're about is promoting privatization, promoting a corporate vision of the world," she said, "and they want to pretend to the world that that's the consensus of the world. And it isn't."

Barlow maintains that multinational water companies and the World Bank are not proper hosts for a World Water Forum. She proposes that it be held under the auspices of the General Assembly of the United Nations, keeping the right to clean commons in the public trust to avert a deeply inequitable situation in which water is diverted from the poor to those who can pay for it.

"The World Water Forum is bankrupt of new ways to address the growing water crisis in the world, because they have maintained an adherence to an ideology that is not working, that has dramatically failed," Barlow remarked on *Democracy Now!* "What's clear here is that the energy and the commitment and the brilliance and the ideas and the cultural change have come together. And this [the People's Water Forum] is where the future of water is coming from, this movement here."

UPDATE BY JEFF CONANT

The World Water Council, a private consortium led by two of the world's largest water corporations, has come to be seen in the global water sector as a legitimate host of the world's largest water policy gathering. But policies promoted by the corporate body have led to profound inequity in water service provision worldwide, while also serving to move huge amounts of public money into private hands. The World Water Council and its triennial gathering, the World Water Forum, strongly promote so-called Public-Private Partnerships that put water services under private ownership. PPPs in Argentina, Bolivia, Ghana, Tanzania, the US, and other countries have resulted in price hikes, decreased pollution control, and water cutoffs, patently denying people—and especially the poor—access to safe drinking water and sanitation services.

One way in which the World Water Council seeks legitimacy is through promoting the appearance that its flagship event, the World Water Forum (WWF), is sponsored or endorsed by the United Nations.

So, when Father Miguel D'Escoto Brockmann, president of the UN General Assembly, and a vocal opponent of water privatization, received no response from the directors of the World Water Council to his appeal to speak at the Fifth World Water Forum in Istanbul, Turkey, the curtain was drawn back and the council's legitimacy came into question.

Covering the WWF in Istanbul, I persistently raised the question at press events there, "Why did Father D'Escoto's letter receive no response?" The answer from Loïc Fauchon, president of the council, was that no such letter had been received.

Since then, however, we have learned that the directors of the WWC have contacted Father D'Escoto's office to meet with him, and have suggested that many of the WWF's future activities might come under the auspices of the UN. They seem to have been shaken by the attention.

The one aspect of the forum over which the council seems to want to retain control, however, is the ministerial process. As I noted in my article, "An Inside Peek: Why the World Water Forum is a Sham," "At each Forum, a series of roundtable discussions between government ministers, corporate lobbyists and NGOs leads to a final Ministerial Statement which, while it has no teeth in international law, plays a significant symbolic role in projecting policies on the ground."

I wrote at the time, "While this process happens entirely behind the scenes and is obscure to nearly all the Forum's participants, it is perhaps the most influential aspect of the event. Over the next two days we expect to see the intrigue come to a head."

In fact, the conclusion of the process resulted, on March 22, in a serious vote of dissent, with twenty-five country delegations signing a statement defending the human right to water, and an additional sixteen demanding that future Water Fora be hosted by the UN. This is the largest collective act of dissent that the WWF has seen since its inception.

There has been very little mainstream press attention to the issue; in fact, there is persistent dearth of attention to the dire issues of water and sanitation in general. One exception has been the French press, which took up the issue in a cover story in Le Monde the day after the forum's closing. In the United States, these issues receive almost no coverage at all outside of the extreme independent press—a shocking truth given that lack of access to safe water is the number one cause of disease and death worldwide.

The best sources of information on this story, and on global water policy in general, are to be found through Food & Water Watch (www.foodandwaterwatch.org), for whom I work as a researcher and advocate, World Development Movement (www.wdm.org.uk), Public Services International Research Unit (www.psiru.org) and Transnational Institute (www.tni.org).

UPDATE BY MAUDE BARLOW

One of the most contentious issues surrounding the growing global water crisis is the question of who is going to determine access and allocation: will it be the market, or will it be people through their elected governments? Is water a commodity to be put on the open market to the highest bidder or part of our commons, a public trust and a human right? This struggle is intense in communities around the world who are fighting big private water utilities delivering water on a for-profit basis or giant bottled water companies coming in and depleting local water supplies. But every three years, the fight goes global at the World Water Forum, a massive gathering of people that resembles a United Nations summit but is actually sponsored by the World Water Council, made up largely of the big water corporations, the World Bank, and pro-corporate segments of the UN.

The Fifth World Water Forum was held in Istanbul and, as you know from the story, was the target of intense criticism from activists and environmentalists from Turkey and around the world; Miguel D'Escoto Brockmann, the president of the UN General Assembly; and many nation-state representatives who disagreed with the fact that the "right to water" was not in the final declaration. In the end, twenty-five countries signed a second declaration declaring their support for the right to water and many openly stated that the next World Water Forum should be sponsored by the General Assembly of the United Nations and not by big private water operators who stand to profit from the assembly.

Since the forum, the pressure for the General Assembly to take over this role has intensified, and in my role as senior advisor to the president of the UN General Assembly, I am urging the General Assembly to adopt an emergency resolution taking upon itself the responsibility of coming up with a global framework of action to deal with both the ecological and human crisis now upon the world, one that recognizes that water is a human right and therefore cannot be denied on the basis of the inability to pay.

This story matters because the growing water crisis is one of the most pressing threats of our time. But the only international body that presumes to speak for global policies and practices is one whose members are making billions as depleting water sources become market commodities, and that denies water to those who cannot pay for it. It is a fundamental issue of democracy and of justice in deciding the future of policies that will affect the whole world.

There was very little media from North America covering this crucial story (thank heavens for Amy Goodman!) but it did get covered in Turkey and in the global south. For more information, go to Food & Water Watch, www.foodandwaterwatch.org, and the Blue Planet Project at www.canadians.org

24
Dollar Glut Finances US Military Expansion

Source:
Global Research, March 29, 2009
Title: "Economic Meltdown: The "Dollar Glut" is What Finances America's Global Military Build-up"
Author: Michael Hudson

Student Researcher: Frances Capell
Faculty Evaluator: Mickey Huff
Sonoma State University

The worldwide surplus of dollars is forcing foreign central banks to bear the costs of America's expanding military empire. Keeping international reserves in "dollars" means that when US financial speculation and deficits payment pumps "paper" into foreign economies, these banks have little option but to recycle it into US Treasury bills and bonds—which the Treasury then spends on financing an enormous, hostile military buildup to encircle the major dollar-recyclers: China, Japan, and Arab oil producers under the Organization of Petroleum Exporting Countries (OPEC). These governments are forced to recycle dollar inflows in a way that funds US military policies in which they have no say in formulating, and which threaten them more and more belligerently.

To date, countries have been powerless to defend themselves against the fact that this compulsory financing of US military spending is built into the global financial system. Neoliberal economists applaud this as

"equilibrium," as if it is part of economic nature and "free markets" rather than bare-knuckle diplomacy wielded with increasing aggressiveness by US officials. The mass media chime in, promoting the assumption that recycling the dollar to finance US military spending is the international community's way of "showing faith in US economic strength" by sending "their" dollars here to "invest." The implication is that a choice is involved. However, the foreigners in question are neither consumers buying US exports, nor private-sector "investors" buying US stocks and bonds. The largest, most important foreign entities putting "their money" here are central banks, and it is not their money at all. They are sending back the dollars that foreign exporters and other recipients turn over to their central banks for domestic currency.

The US economy can create dollars freely, now that they no longer are convertible into gold, or even into purchases of US companies. Consequently, the US remains the world's most protected economy. It alone is permitted to protect its agriculture by import quotas, having grandfathered these into world trade rules half a century ago. Congress refuses to let "sovereign wealth" funds invest in important US sectors.

US Treasury prefers foreign central banks to keep on funding its domestic budget deficit, which means financing the cost of America's war in the Near East and encirclement of foreign countries with rings of military bases. The more capital outflows US investors spend to buy up foreign economies—the most profitable sectors, where the new US owners can extract the highest monopoly rents—the more funds end up in foreign central banks to support America's global military buildup.

No textbook on political theory or international relations has suggested axioms to explain how nations act in a way so adverse to their own political, military, and economic interests. Yet this is just what has been happening for the past generation.

The ultimate question is what countries can do to counter this financial attack. How can nations act as real nations, in their own interest, rather than in America's interest? Any country trying to do what the United States has done for the past 150 years is accused of being socialist or protectionist—this from the most antisocialist economy in the world.

The problem of speculative capital movements goes beyond drawing up a set of specific regulations. It concerns the scope of national government power. The International Monetary Fund's Articles of Agreement prevent countries from restoring the "dual exchange rate" systems that many retained down through the 1950s and even into the '60s. It was widespread practice for countries to have one exchange rate for goods and services (sometimes various exchange rates for different import and export categories) and another for capital movements. Under US pressure, the IMF enforced the pretence that there is an "equilibrium" rate that just happens to be the same for goods and services as it is for capital movements. Governments that did not buy into this ideology were excluded from membership in the IMF and World Bank, or were overthrown.

The implication today is that the only way a nation can block capital movements is to withdraw from the IMF, the World Bank, and the World Trade Organization (WTO). For the first time since the 1950s this looks like a real possibility, thanks to worldwide awareness of how the US economy is glutting the global economy with surplus "paper," and US resistance to stopping its free ride. From the US perspective, this is nothing less than an attempt to curtail its international military program of global domination.

UPDATE BY MICHAEL HUDSON

The largest "free lunch" in the world is the ability of the US Treasury to issue what is now $4 trillion in paper in exchange for foreign exports, the sale of foreign companies and real estate to US buyers, and US military purchases abroad. These three dynamics make up the US balance-of-payments deficit—which is "free" to the extent that foreign central banks recycle the surplus dollars into treasury bonds and other US securities (including Fannie Mae junk mortgages between 2004 and 2007).

China has sought to limit its acquisition of dollars, and other countries are discussing how to limit further dollar inflows.

Corporate media continue to talk of a "global savings glut," as if foreign governments invest in treasury bills because they are "a good buy" and foreigners "have faith in the US economy." But treasury bills are only yielding 1 percent now, and the dollar is weakening, so it is not a good buy at all. Foreigners are trapped in the mechanics of the international financial system controlled by the US via the IMF and World Bank. At the recent G20 meeting in April, countries reached an impasse. But the press did not explain the conflict of interest behind this impasse.

I have written about the dynamics of the dollar's free ride in *Super Imperialism: The Economic Strategy of American Empire* (1972, new ed. Pluto Press, 2002). The remarkable thing is that the information is "in plain sight," in the sense of what Edgar Allan Poe meant when he discussed how to hide the purloined letter. Reporters just don't read the Federal Reserve Bulletin and the Treasury Bulletin for the month-to-month statistics that tell where the bodies are buried. Instead, they repeat handouts from the Treasury or Federal Reserve, ignoring the statistics on US government liabilities to foreign central banks and other foreign holders.

25

Fast Track Oil Exploitation in Western Amazon

Sources:
PloS One, August 2008
Title: "Oil and Gas Projects in the Western Amazon: Threats to Wilderness, Biodiversity, and Indigenous Peoples"
Authors: Matt Finer, Clinton N. Jenkins, Stuart L. Pimm, Brian Keane, and Carl Ross

Guardian, August 13, 2008
Title: "Amazon rainforest threatened by new wave of oil and gas exploration"
Author: Ian Sample

Student Researcher: Rob Hunter
Faculty Evaluator: Sasha Von Meier, PhD
Sonoma State University

The western Amazon, home to the most biodiverse and intact rainforest on Earth, may soon be covered with oilrigs and pipelines. Vast swaths of the region are to be opened for oil and gas exploration, putting some of the planet's most pristine and biodiverse forests at risk, conservationists have warned.

A new study has found that at least thirty-five multinational oil and gas companies operate over 180 oil and gas "blocks"—areas zoned for exploration and development—which now cover the Amazon in Bolivia, Colombia, Ecuador, Peru, and western Brazil.

The western Amazon is also home to many indigenous ethnic groups, including some of the world's last uncontacted peoples living in voluntary isolation. Underlying this landscape of extraordinary biological and cultural diversity, which environmental scientists refer to as the lungs of the planet, are large reserves of oil and gas. Growing global demand is stimulating unprecedented levels of new oil and gas exploration and extraction—and the threat of environmental and cultural devastation.

Researchers tracked hydrocarbon activities across the region over a four-year period and generated a comprehensive map of oil and gas activities. The maps showed that in Peru and Ecuador, regions designated for oil and gas projects already cover more than two thirds of the Amazon. Of sixty-four oil and gas blocks that cover 72 percent of the Peruvian Amazon, all but eight have been approved since 2003, and at least sixteen were signed in 2008. Major increases in activity are also expected in Bolivia and western Brazil.

"We've been following oil and gas development in the Amazon since 2004 and the picture has changed before our eyes," said Matt Finer of Save America's Forests, a US-based environment group. "When you look at where the oil and gas blocks are, they overlap perfectly on top of the peak biodiversity spots, almost as if by design, and this is in one of the most, if not the most, biodiverse places on Earth."

Some regions have established oil and gas reserves, but in others companies will need to cut into the forest to conduct speculative tests, including explosive seismic investigations and test drilling. Typically, companies have seven years to explore a region before deciding whether to go into full production.

"The real concern is when exploration is successful and a zone moves into the development phase, because that's when the roads, drilling and pipelines come in," said Finer.

Writing in the journal *PLoS One*, Finer and others from Duke University and Land is Life, a Massachusetts-based environment group, call for governments to rethink how energy reserves in the Amazon are exploited.

One issue, the authors argue, is that while companies must submit an environmental impact assessment for their project, these are often considered individually instead of collectively. "They're not looking at the bigger picture of what happens if there are lots of projects going on at the same time. You could have each individual company thinking they're being relatively responsible and keeping their own road networks under control and so on, but what happens when you have fifteen other projects around you? All of a sudden, when you look at the bigger picture, you have a sprawling road network," said Finer. The creation of widespread road networks will put previously inaccessible forest at risk of deforestation, illegal hunting, and logging, the authors argue.

Further research by the team found that many of the planned exploration and extraction projects were on land that is home to indigenous people, who whilst being consulted, have no say in whether a project goes ahead or not. At least fifty-eight of the sixty-four blocks in Peru are on land where isolated communities live, with a further seventeen infringing on areas that have existing or proposed reserves for indigenous groups.

"The way that oil development is being pursued in the western Amazon is a gross violation of the rights of the indigenous peoples of the region," said Brain Keane of Land is Life. "International agreements and inter-American human rights law recognize indigenous peoples' rights to their lands, and explicitly prohibit the granting of concessions to exploit natural resources in their territories without their free, prior and informed consent," he added.

Indigenous resistance is increasingly organized, politicized, and effective at both national and international levels.

"This expansion occurs to the detriment of our peoples and of Mother Earth," warns Jose Antunez, a leader of the Ashaninka people of Peru.

UPDATE BY MATT FINER

This story, which highlights the threats facing the western Amazon from oil and gas development, not only involves one of the most biodiverse regions on Earth, but, as we have recently seen, is literally a matter of

life and death for people in the region. While much of the previous scientific analysis and global attention has focused on the massive deforestation in the eastern Amazon in Brazil, our study was one of the first to highlight the magnitude and scope of threats facing the still largely intact western Amazon (Bolivia, Colombia, Ecuador, Peru, and western Brazil).

After its publication in the open-access scientific journal *PLoS ONE* in August 2008, the story did receive a considerable amount of international press, including pieces in the *Guardian, New Scientist*, Associated Press, and several major newspapers in South America. Our paper appeared at a particularly opportune time, when the media and public were focused on high oil prices and dependence on foreign oil. While our paper sounded the alarm about the impending crisis in the western Amazon and was noted by the scientific community, most of the complex issues raised in our paper largely continued to stay under the radar of the public and mainstream media in the United States.

In June 2009, there were deadly clashes in northern Peru between the police and indigenous peoples who had been protesting new government policies. These policies—enacted to comply with a free trade agreement with the US—promoted oil, gas, mining, logging, and biofuel projects on indigenous lands without their consent. This issue was a major topic of discussion in our paper, under the heading of Free, Prior, and Informed Consent. These events, which reportedly left over fifty people dead, resulted in a second round of press reports citing our article. The *New York Times* and Reuters, for example, highlighted our finding that the vast majority of the oil concessions in the Peruvian Amazon overlap titled indigenous lands.

The issues raised in our paper continue to be of critical importance. Oil and gas concessions (blocks) now cover more than 700,000 square kilometers in the western Amazon, even more than we estimated in 2008. The problem of new oil and gas exploration and development projects in sensitive areas is particularly severe in Peru and Bolivia, and increasingly so in Colombia. In contrast, a hopeful sign is that Ecuador continues to promote its innovative Yasuni-ITT Initiative, which we highlighted in our study. Ecuador is proposing to leave nearly 1 billion barrels of oil, 20 percent of its known reserves, locked in the ground forever in exchange for alternative sources of revenue from the international community.

As a means to make information from our research about the western Amazon more accessible, we established the WesternAmazon.org website to distribute information and the data from our studies. We also provide links to any news stories linked to our study and the issue of oil in the Amazon.

CENSORED 2010 HONORABLE MENTIONS

Demining Stops in Lebanon

Agence France Presse, August 31, 2008
Title: "Lebanon Deminers Hang Up Their Detectors as Funds Dry Up"

Efforts to clear the more than 1 million cluster bombs Israel dropped throughout south Lebanon during the last days of its devastating thirty-four-day war on Hezbollah in the summer of 2006 will stop due to lack of funding. Demining teams comprised of the Lebanese Army, UN Forces, and approximately 1,000 mostly Lebanese civilians will withdraw though only 43 percent of the areas affected by the cluster bombs dropped during the July 2006 war have been cleared and the direct threat has been eliminated from only 49 percent of contaminated areas. "Aside from the cluster bombs, we still have 300,000 landmines along the Blue Line (the frontier with Israel)," said Tyre mayor Abdel Hosn al-Husseini, referring to mines laid by Israel before its withdrawal from southern Lebanon in 2000. Forty-five thousand cluster bombs were cleared from one village alone. A spokesperson for the UN Mine Action Coordination Centre maintains that the main impediment is the fact that Israel has not revealed any information on the cluster bombs that its air forces dropped. "The United Nations has repeatedly requested cluster bomb data from Israel (including maps and the type of ordnance dropped), but in two years plus, we still haven't received the requested data."

Cuba Years Ahead in Eat Local Movement

Common Dreams, Reuters, December 16, 2008
Title: "In Eat Local Movement, Cuba is Years Ahead"
Author: Esteban Israel

After the collapse of the Soviet Union in 1991, Cuba planted thousands of urban cooperative gardens to offset reduced rations of imported food. In the wake of three hurricanes that wiped out 30 percent of Cuba's farm crops, the country has turned again to urban farming to keep its people fed. Fifteen percent of the world's food is grown in urban areas, a figure that is expected to grow as food prices rise, urban populations grow, and environmental concerns increase. In Cuba, urban gardens have bloomed in vacant lots, alongside parking lots, and even on city rooftops. They sprang from a military plan for Cuba to be self-sufficient in case of war, and have evolved into a world model for localized food sovereignty and sustainability. They have proven extremely popular, occupying 35,000 hectares (86,000 acres) of land across the Caribbean island. The gardeners sell their produce directly to the community, so are immune to the volatility of fuel and transportation costs, and, out of necessity, grow their crops organically. In September 2008, the government began renting out unused state-owned lands to farmers and cooperatives.

Military Corporate Legacy of the New Secretary of Education

TomDispatch, January 18, 2009
Title: "The Duncan Doctrine: The Military-Corporate Legacy of the New Secretary of Education"
Author: Andy Kroll

Obama's new secretary of education Arne Duncan has close ties to the US Military. While administrator of the Chicago Public Schools (CPS), Duncan offered a key role in public education to the military. Chicago's school system is currently the most militarized in the country, boasting five military academies, nearly three dozen smaller Junior Reserve Officer Training Corps (ROTC) programs within existing high schools, and numerous middle school Junior ROTC programs. Ten thousand students are enrolled in a military education program of some sort in the CPS system. The military academies Duncan started are nearly all located in low-income, minority neighborhoods. Of the 10,000 students enrolled in a military education program, only 4 percent are white.

In the Chicago school district's five military academies, affiliated with the army, navy, or marines, all students are required to enroll as well in the academy's Junior ROTC program. That means student/cadets must wear full military uniforms to school everyday. As part of each academy's curriculum, they must also take a daily ROTC course focusing on military history, map reading and navigation, drug prevention, and the branches of the Department of Defense. When the proposed Air Force Academy High School opens this fall, CPS will be the only public school system in the country with air force, army, navy, and marine corps high school academies.

Latin American Leaders Refute US Drug War

Inter Press Service, February 12, 2009
Title: "Latin American Leaders Say 'No' to US Drug War"
Author: Marina Litvinsky

The Latin American Commission on Drugs and Democracy recently issued a report, "Drugs and Democracy: Toward a Paradigm Shift," which calls for the creation of a Latin American drug policy. The commission, led by former Brazilian, Mexican, and Columbian presidents, Fernando Henrique Cardoso, Ernesto Zedillo and Cesar Gaviria, respectively, stated that the available evidence indicates that the current US war on drugs has failed. The commission proposes three specific actions under the new paradigm: treat addicts as patients in the health system, evaluate decriminalizing cannabis possession and personal use, and reduce consumption through education targeted at youth. Despite the large investment of resources that has been put into the war on drugs, especially in Colombia and Mexico, drug trafficking and narco-violence has increased. The commission states that the long-term solution is to reduce the demand for the drugs in main consumer countries, the US and in the EU. The commission calls on these countries to share in the responsibility and implement policies aimed at reducing the demand for illicit drugs.

Guantánamo Worsens Since Obama

Inter Press Service, February 24, 2009
Title: "Report Contradicts Gov't Claims of 'Humane' Detention"
Author: William Fisher

The Observer, February 8, 2009
Title: "Top US lawyer warns of deaths at Guantánamo"
Authors: Mark Townsend and Paul Harris

Abuse of prisoners at Guantánamo Bay has worsened since President Barack Obama took office. The Center for Constitutional Rights (CCR) released a report on the conditions at Guantánamo. CCR's report, "Conditions of Confinement at Guantánamo: Still in Violation of the Law," covers conditions at Guantánamo in January and February 2009. Contrary to recent US government reports, CCR and human rights lawyers have concluded that conditions violate US obligations under the Geneva

Conventions, the US Constitution, and international human rights law. Detainees are subject to isolation, insults, preemptive use of pepper spray, and those on hunger strike are being strapped to chairs and force-fed, with those who resist being beaten. At least twenty are described as being so unhealthy they are on a "critical list."

Fault Lines Intersect Nuke Plant Near NYC

Environment News Service, August 21, 2008
Title: "Earthquake Zone Intersection Threatens Indian Point Nuclear Plant"

The nuclear power plant closest to America's largest city is more likely to be hit by an earthquake than previously thought because it sits atop a newly identified intersection of two active seismic zones, earthquake scientists warn. The Indian Point nuclear power plant, with its two nuclear generating units, is situated twenty-four miles north of New York City, on the Hudson River at Buchanan, New York. Researchers from Columbia University's Lamont-Doherty Earth Observatory have located a previously unknown active seismic zone running from Stamford, Connecticut, to the Hudson Valley town of Peekskill, New York, where it passes less than a mile north of the Indian Point nuclear power plant. The Stamford-Peekskill line intersects with the known Ramapo seismic zone, which runs from eastern Pennsylvania to the mid-Hudson Valley, passing within two miles northwest of Indian Point. Nearly 10 million people live within twenty-five miles of the Indian Point nuclear plant, including the 8.2 million in the New York metropolitan area. These findings come at a time when Entergy, the owner and operator of Indian Point, is trying to relicense the two operating plants for an additional twenty years.

Battle for the Future of SEIU

Democracy Now!, January 20, 2009
Title: "SEIU Removes Leadership at Dissident California Local"

Service Employees International Union (SEIU) President Andy Stern is facing growing internal criticism that he is seeking to consolidate unions to increase size and leadership power at the expense of rank-and-file members. Most recently, the SEIU's executive board has taken over one of its largest locals, California's 150,000-member United Healthcare Workers West (UHW-W), despite overwhelming opposition from local members. The local's leader Sal Rosselli, who has vocally criticized Stern's practices as top-down, was removed from power in the takeover. Stern is accused by members of establishing top-down sweetheart deals with industry that sacrifice workers' rights, including the right to strike and, in the case of California health care workers, the right to advocate for their patients.

The questioning of the SEIU's principles is significant because the SEIU, while eliminating the voice and power of union members, is leading the "reform" movement within organized labor that may reshape unions into a very "corporate friendly" workforce.

Constitution-Free Zone for Two-thirds of US Population

The Raw Story, October 2008
Title: "ACLU highlights 'Constitution-Free Zone' 100 miles from border"
Author: Nick Juliano

ACLU, October 2008
Title: "Constitution Free Zone: The Numbers"

The Department of Homeland Security (DHS) is expanding the authority it claims at US border crossings to infringe upon Americans rights. The ACLU reports that a "Constitution-free zone" exists within 100 miles of all US borders (including ocean, Great Lake, and gulf coasts), where DHS Customs and Border Patrol claim the authority to stop, search, and detain anyone for any reason. Nearly two thirds of the US population lives within one hundred miles of this "border zone" that surrounds the US. It encompasses the vast majority of metropolitan areas and many entire coastal states. Of particular concern is the border patrol's use of massive databases and watch lists to screen travelers. Much remains unknown about how these lists are compiled, and it is exceedingly difficult for a person to be removed from such a list once he or she is added to it.

Coal vs. Wind in West Virginia

The State Journal, August 15, 2008
Title: "Raleigh County Mountain at Center of Coal vs. Wind Debate"
Author: Pam Kasey

Coal River Mountain in West Virginia may soon become the center of an energy battle that pits fossil fuels against non-fossil renewable sources. At issue is the question, "Should we develop coal resources now if that will destroy wind resources that can be harnessed forever?" Coal River Mountain offers a high-quality wind resource. "The wind rushes out of the valleys and as it hits the ridge, the higher the ridge, the more speed it gains as it goes up," explained Rory McIlmoil, who was hired from Appalachian Voices by Coal River Mountain Watch to coordinate a wind energy campaign. "By reducing the ridge altitude by hundreds of feet you change the wind patterns and therefore impact the wind speed." With the standard assumption that the wind would blow about a third of the time, a Coal River Mountain wind project could generate 1.16 million megawatt-hours per year—more than several of the state's operating coal-fired plants.

However, Massey Energy has obtained permits for two coal mines on Coal River Mountain, and has applications for two others in the works, for what McIlmoil said totals more than 6,000 acres of mountaintop removal operations—also on the highest ridges. A wind farm would create 200 jobs during construction, and forty to fifty permanent jobs indefinitely, while Massey's mines would last only fourteen years.

Father Roy Excommunicated?

National Catholic Reporter, November 11, 2008
Title: "Roy Bourgeois threatened with excommunication"

Democracy Now! November 20, 2008
Title: "Vatican Threatens to Excommunicate Catholic Priest for Supporting Ordination of Women into Priesthood"

The Vatican has threatened to excommunicate well-known Catholic priest and longtime peace advocate Father Roy Bourgeois unless he recants his support for the ordination of women into the priesthood. In August 2008, he took part in a ceremony to ordain a member of the group called Roman Catholic Womenpriests. He was informed in a letter dated October 31, 2008, that he would face the harshest form of ecclesiastical punishment—excommunication—unless he recanted within thirty days of notice. Bourgeois responded, "Over the years I have met a number of women in our Church who, like me, feel called by God to the priesthood. . . . Who are we, as men, to say to women, 'Our call is valid, but yours is not.' Who are we to tamper with God's call? Sexism, like racism, is a sin." Bourgeois continued, "Working and struggling for peace and justice are an integral part of our faith. For this reason, I speak out against the war in Iraq. And for the last eighteen years, I have been speaking out against the atrocities and suffering caused by the School of the Americas . . . I could not address the injustice of the SOA and remain silent about injustice in my Church." Bourgeois has not recanted.

Air Force Embraces Coal

Rachel's Democracy & Health News, August 7, 2008
Title: "The Military-Industrial Complex Embraces Coal-to-Liquids"
Author: Peter Montague

"Careful deliberation and thoughtful debate have been cast aside as the Air Force has set itself on a fast track mission to bail out the coal industry," notes author Peter Montague. In 2008, the US Air Force began a major effort to define the future of energy supplies for the US and for its military allies. If military brass reaches their goal, the transportation fuel of the future will be based on coal. According to Air Force Assistant Secretary William Anderson, the USAF plan is to:

1. Build a "network" of coal-to-liquid-fuels plants to supply the air force with 400 million gallons of jet fuel each year by the year 2016—enough to power half its North American fleet of aircraft. Plans for creating this network are on a "fast track," according to officials developing coal-to-liquids plants in Montana and Alaska.

2. Engage in "a major international initiative" to persuade the governments of France, England, and other nations to adopt coal-based liquid fuels.

3. Prod Wall Street investors—nervous over coal's role in climate change—to sink money into similar plants nationwide.

According to Assistant Secretary Anderson, with the air force paving the way, the private sector will follow—from commercial air fleets to long-haul trucking companies. "Because of our size, we can move the market along."

Terrorizing Dissenters at the RNC

National Lawyers Guild Minnesota, September 2008
Title: "Ramsey County Charges RNC 8 Under State Patriot Act, Alleges Acts of Terrorism"

Democracy Now! February 18, 2009
Title: "RNC Protesters Tried on Terrorism Charges Despite Acknowledgment They Didn't Commit Alleged Acts"

In September 2008, the site of the 2008 Republican National Convention was transformed into a forbidding police state. St. Paul, Minnesota, officers in full riot gear arrested hundreds of marchers, beating some and using tear gas and pepper spray on people who were not resisting arrest. Parts of the city were closed off, and the county jail resembled a fortress with its armed guards. Three days before the convention, officials directed action toward the organizing group, the RNC Welcoming Committee. Police raided the activist convergence space in West St. Paul, detaining everyone on site and seizing pamphlets and other property. Police also descended on three homes and arrested members of the group, while snatching others off the street. In addition to activists, many legal observers, journalists, and street medics were also harshly assaulted, detained and/or arrested. The arrested activists face felony charges under Minnesota's version of the federal USA PATRIOT Act that include "conspiracy to riot in furtherance of terrorism." Defendant Luce Guilen-Givins states, "It's significant that people would be prosecuted as terrorists for involving themselves in political dissent. We do have a right to protest. Any prosecution under a [USA] PATRIOT Act infringes on those rights."

UN Negligence is Killing Child Refugees in Kosovo

New Internationalist, November 2008
Title: "Death Camps: UN negligence is killing child refugees in Kosovo"

Nine years have passed since extremist Albanians destroyed homes in Mitrovica, Kosovo. Three refugee camps were created by the UN to house about 500 people whose homes were destroyed during the uprising. The camps were, however, constructed on top of a toxic waste dump. The UN promised to find new housing within forty-five days or move the families to safe clean areas. However, even after nine years, nothing has been done to move these families. Two of the camps have been closed, but the families were moved just fifty meters away. Lead poisoning has become a big issue for the families. Seventy-seven people have died in these camps, and fifty miscarriages due to suspected lead poisoning have also occurred. Many suffer from liver and brain damage, among other maladies, and many children are expected to die prematurely.

The UN says new houses for these refugees will not be built for years.

Secret US Forces Carried Out Assassinations

Democracy Now! March 31, 2009
Title: "Secret US Forces Carried Out Assassinations in a Dozen Counties"
Interviewee: Seymour Hersh

The Bush administration ran an "executive assassination ring" that reported directly to Vice President Dick Cheney. The *New Yorker's* Seymour Hersh says, "Under President Bush's authority, special operations military assassins have been going into countries—not only Iraq and Afghanistan, but Latin America and around the world—not talking to ambassadors or to the CIA station chief, finding people on a list, executing them, and leaving." The special assassination unit operated under the Special Operations Command out of Florida. One of the units that works under the umbrella of the Special Operations Command is known as Joint Special Op (JSOC). It's a special group of elite that includes Navy Seals and Delta Force—what is called a black unit. Targets were cleared through Vice President Cheney's office. Seymour Hersh does not know whether the assassination wing is still operating under President Obama.

CHAPTER 2

Censored Déjà vu: What Happened to Previous *Censored* Stories

Edited by Ben Frymer, Kate Sims
Researched by Sean Richards, Matthew Gonzalez, Ian Marlowe, Kevin Winter, Chris McManus, and Frances Capell

Censored 2009 #1

More than 1 Million Killed in Iraq

The top story for 2009 covered a study which concluded that as of 2007, approximately 1 million Iraqis had been killed as a result of the 2003 invasion. Conducted by British polling group ORB, the research was an update to the *Lancet* study from two years earlier. Employing the widely accepted survey methods used to determine the casualty count following the conflict in Congo and elsewhere, the study estimated that approximately 1,033,000 civilians were killed as a result of the conflict from March 2003 to August 2007 with a range of 946,000 and 1,112,000.

Original Sources: Michael Schwartz, "Is the United States Killing 10,000 Iraqis Every Month? Or Is It More?" After Downing Street, July 6, 2007; Joshua Holland, "Iraq death toll rivals Rwanda genocide, Cambodian killing fields," AlterNet, September 17, 2007; Luke Baker, "Iraq conflict has killed a million, says survey," Reuters (via AlterNet), January 7, 2008; Maki al-Nazzal and Dahr Jamail, "Iraq: Not our country to Return to," Inter Press Service, March 3, 2008.

Update: Coverage of the Iraqi death toll among major media sources remained largely nonexistent throughout 2008 and 2009. While debate continues regarding the specific number of Iraqi people killed, all the individuals and organizations that study Iraqi death rates on an ongoing basis—including *Lancet* researchers, the members of Iraq Body Count and icasualties.org, and the authors of the original Censored 2009 articles—agree that the subject has received, and continues to receive, very poor coverage in mainstream media outlets.

The *Lancet* and ORB studies continue to incite controversy. While the authors concede that all studies can be improved upon, there are two primary points of logic that they want critics and those with a general interest to remember:

➤ Randomized large-scale household sampling is the standard methodology used by modern epidemiology to track everything from flu epidemics to the results of natural disasters and armed conflict.

➤ The results of these studies are consistent with comparable conflicts (Vietnam, Congo, East Timor, Yugoslavia, etc.) in terms of both the development pattern and the total death toll, roughly 2.5 percent of the population.

While no new study has been conducted since 2007, ORB researchers have completed updates to the original surveys. Responding to criticisms that the first study was focused largely on urban areas, an additional 600 interviews were conducted in rural areas of Iraq. Current updates have found that 20.2 percent of households reported having lost someone during the war, with rates in rural areas lower than in urban households.

Sources:
"Lancet Study Author Assesses New Report on Iraqi Death Toll," Institute For Public Accuracy, January 11, 2008; Diane Farsetta, "Jousting with the Lancet: More Data, More Debate over Iraqi Deaths," Center for Media and Democracy, February 26, 2008; Jonathan Steele and Suzanne Goldenberg, "What is the real death toll in Iraq?" *Guardian*, March 19, 2008; http://en.wikipedia.org/wiki/ORB_survey_of_Iraq_War_casualties.

Censored 2009 #2

Security and Prosperity Partnership: Militarized NAFTA

Story #2 for *Censored 2009* covered the Security and Prosperity Partnership (SPP), an expansion of the North American Free Trade Agreement (NAFTA) with "deep integration" of a more militarized tri-national Homeland Security force. Without public knowledge or input, the stated aim of the Security and Prosperity Partnership (according to its website) is to establish "ambitious security and prosperity programs to keep our borders closed to terrorism yet open to trade." Critics note that the SPP is not a law, or a treaty, or even a signed agreement—all of which would require public debate and participation of Congress.

Original Sources: Laura Carlsen, "'Deep Integration'—the Anti-Democratic Expansion of NAFTA," Center for International Policy, May 30, 2007; Stephen Lendman, "The Militarization and Annexation of North America," Global Research, July 19, 2007; Constance Fogal, "North American Union: The SPP is a 'hostile takeover' of democratic government and an end to the Rule of Law," Global Research, August 2, 2007.

Update: On January 19, 2009, Canada's Centre for Trade Policy and Law, at Ottawa's Carleton University, outlined an agenda for the SPP in America and Canada. It said the "most pressing issue is the need to rethink the architecture for managing North 'America's common economic space." It used language like "re-imagining (and) modernizing the border" and "integrating national regulatory regimes into one that applies on both sides of the border." It called the arrival of a new Washington administration "a golden opportunity" to forge a "mutually beneficial agenda (that) will define global and North American governance for years to come."

Shortly thereafter, a report titled "North America Next," from Arizona State University's North American Center for Transborder Studies, called for "sustainable and security competitiveness" and deeper US-Canada-Mexico integration through "sustainable security and effective trade and transportation" between the three North American nations.

In March 2008, Canada's Fraser Institute published an article calling the "SPP brand" tarnished and recommending discarding the title in favor of the North American Standards and Regulatory Area (NASRA). The article goes on to say "the SPP has raised criticism from the economic and cultural nationalists in the Council of Canadians, including Maude Barlow [who claims that] the SPP offers the United States a channel to encroach on Canadian sovereignty and gain access to such resources as water."

As another part of this integration, Canadian employees of internet service providers (ISPs) Bell Canada and TELUS (formerly owned by Verizon) have claimed that by 2012, ISPs all over the globe will reduce Internet access to a TV-like subscription model, only offering access to a small standard amount of commercial sites and requiring extra fees for every other site. These "other" sites would then lose all their exposure and eventually shut down, resulting in what would be the end of the Internet as we currently know it.

Sources:
Stephen Lendman, "SPP: Updating the Militarization and Annexation of North America," Global Research, March 13, 2009; Carleton University Canada-US Project, "Blueprint for Canada-US Engagement under a New Administration," Centre for Trade Policy and Law, January 19, 2009; Alexander Moens with Michael Cust, "Saving the North American Security and Prosperity Partnership: The Case for a North American Standards and Regulatory Area," Fraser Institute, March 2008; "North America Next: a Report to President Obama," North American Center for Transborder Studies, February 6, 2009; "Obama Administration Urged to 'Seize North American Opportunities' on Security and Competitiveness," Reuters, February 10, 2009.

Censored 2009 #4

ILEA: Is the US Restarting Dirty Wars in Latin America?

Story #4 for *Censored 2009* covered the mobile, US-sponsored International Law Enforcement Academy (ILEA), which is training Salvadoran military and police personnel in tactics once confined to the infamous School of the Americas in Fort Benning, Georgia. With provision of immunity from charges of crimes against humanity, each academy trains an average of 1,500 police officers, judges, prosecutors, and other law enforcement officials per year throughout Latin America in "counterterrorism techniques." While the main US interest in ILEA is to ensure an environment that protects free trade and an interest in local natural resources, the academy's trainees have played an active role in a crackdown against civil liberties, aimed at curbing both crime and social protest.

Original Sources: Community in Solidarity with the People of El Salvador, "Exporting US 'Criminal Justice' to Latin America," Upside Down World, June 14, 2007, and "ILEA Funding Approved by Salvadoran Right Wing Legislators," Committee in Solidarity with the People of El Salvador (CISPES), March 15, 2007; Wes Enzinna, "Another SOA?: A Police Academy in El Salvador Worries Critics," *NACLA Report on the Americas*, March/April 2008; Benjamin Dangl, "Is George Bush Restarting Latin America's 'Dirty Wars'?" AlterNet, August 31, 2007.

Update: In January 2009, the US and El Salvador signed letters of agreement committing both countries to work jointly under the Merida Initiative to fight crime and drug trafficking. The Federal Bureau of Investigation (FBI) and El Salvador's National Civilian Police jointly operate the Transnational Anti-Gang unit, which addresses the growing problem of street gangs in both countries.

On March 15, 2009, FMLN party candidate Mauricio Funes won El Salvador's presidential elections, defeating ARENA candidate Rodrigo Ávila. Final vote totals were 51.3 percent for the FMLN and 48.7 percent for ARENA. These elections mark the first time since the 1992 peace agreement that ended the civil war that an FMLN candidate has been elected president and will be the first left-of-center government in El Salvador's history. For now, the new president has pledged that ILEA will stay.

Source:
"CISPES 2009 Elections Analysis: The Road to Victory and Beyond," CISPES, March 27, 2009.

Censored 2009 #6

The Homegrown Terrorism Act

H.R. 1955, the Homegrown Terrorism Prevention Act, passed through the House of Representatives with almost full consensus. S. 1959, the Violent Radicalization and Homegrown Terrorism Prevention Act, was shelved in the Senate as a result of negative press. In May 2008, Senator Joe Lieberman put pressure on Google and YouTube to take Islamist terrorism information off the Internet but was unsuccessful.

Original Sources: Jessica Lee, "Bringing the War on Terrorism Home," *Indypendent*, November 16, 2007; Lindsay Beyerstein, "Examining the Homegrown Terrorism Prevention Act," *In These Times*, November 2007; Matt Renner, "The Violent Radicalization Homegrown Terrorism Prevention Act of 2007," *Truthout*, November 29, 2007.

Update: In March 2009, the Research and Development (RAND) corporation came out with a report entitled "Considering the Creation of a Domestic Intelligence Agency in the United States." The report details their policy recommendations for intelligence-gathering practices by the

United States. One important section of the report includes the policy paper "Arguments for Change in Current Domestic Intelligence Policies." The paper recommends improving efforts in cooperative intelligence sharing among law enforcement agencies, easing public discontent about unconstitutional intelligence gathering, giving agencies more freedom to track terrorists' "rapidly changing" communication, and includes the vague recommendation of "preemptive action against preemptive terrorism."

The RAND paper refers to ever changing "behavior" and "tactics" of terrorist organizations. "To keep pace with an agile threat, intelligence organizations must be able to adapt as well. Large, bureaucratic organizations frequently face challenges in doing so, and the ability to change rapidly may conflict with other objectives—including societal goals of intelligence oversight." These "adaptable" intelligence measures include roving, warrantless wiretaps that allow government officials to follow alleged terrorists through their various communications. However, extensive methods of intelligence gathering like these often incite controversy and opposition from citizens who are being unconstitutionally monitored. RAND's position is that these controversies are an obstacle in obtaining intelligence.

Catching terrorists before they are able to carry out their objectives is a core theme of counterterrorism (CT) measures. However, the line between preemptive and unreasonable is a topic of fierce debate. According to the RAND report, "the existence of bureaus that can devote their full resources to preemptive information gathering, analysis, and dissemination is a positive feature." "[S]eparating law enforcement from domestic intelligence" has "allowed preemptive investigations to proceed without a criminal offense having been committed and without the pressure to quickly move resources elsewhere when hard evidence is not forthcoming." Under this model, people could be convicted of terrorist activities without hard evidence; the only proof that a person was guilty of preemptive terrorist activity would be intelligence gathered without warrant and hearsay by an intelligence official.

Intelligence-gathering policies such as those called for by the RAND report tend to create distrust among the public. The report, foreseeing such eventualities, also calls for programs designed to change people's minds and to cast the erosion of civil liberties in a more positive light. According to RAND, "systematically moving to break down these negative perceptions and suspicions has been vital to winning the trust of these communities and gaining their support for CT efforts." Although RAND's policy prescriptions are unconstitutional, they want to calm the symptomatic anxieties of the public in order to continue them. In other words, the policies aren't the problem—the public just doesn't understand.

Source:

Brian A. Jackson, "Considering the Creation of a Domestic Intelligence Agency in the United States," RAND Corporation, March 2009, http://www.rand.org/pubs/monographs/2009/RAND_MG805.pdf.

Censored 2009 # 7

Guest Workers Inc.: Fraud and Human Trafficking

Story #7 for 2009 was based on a groundbreaking report by Mary Bauer and Sarah Reynolds for the Southern Poverty Law Center. It brought to light the recent, growing exploitation of thousands of laborers through the "guest worker" programs originally established in 1986. Felicia Mello's piece focused on the exploitative nature of both H-2A (agricultural work) and H-2B (nonagricultural work) programs, which provide little to no rights or protections to immigrant workers and frequently entail highly deceptive and unjust recruitment practices.

Original Sources: Mary Bauer and Sarah Reynolds, "Close to Slavery: Guestworker Programs in the United States," Southern Poverty Law Center, March 2007; Felicia Mello, "Coming to America," *The Nation*, June 25, 2007; Chidanand Rajghatta, "Trafficking racket: Indian workers file case against US employer," *Times of India*, March 10, 2008.

Update: Instead of taking up the sweeping changes of existing programs backed by farmer and worker groups, in December of 2008 the Bush administration announced new rules governing the hiring of H-2A guest workers. These rules went into effect on January 18, just two days before the inauguration of Barack Obama. According to the *New York Times* ("Bush Unveils New Rules for Guest Worker Hiring," December 11, 2008), "Bruce Goldstein, executive director of Farmworker Justice, an advocacy group based in Washington, said of the changes, 'The intent is a massive expansion of the guest worker program by enticing employers into a program with low wages and poor working conditions.'"

Three states, Utah, Colorado, and Arizona, have considered resolutions asking the federal government if they could establish state-level guest worker programs, but it is not clear if states have the authority to adopt such measures.

In April of 2009, Senators Richard Durbin (D-IL) and Chuck Grassley (R-IA) introduced bipartisan legislation, the H-1B and L-1 Visa Reform Act, to provide more worker protection and higher labor standards in existing guest worker programs (April 24, 2009, http://blog .aflcio.org/2009/04/24/bipartisan-bill-would-strengthen-guest-worker-rules/).

Senate Majority Leader Harry Reid (D-NV) has recently stated that the Senate would take up immigration reform this year and that he supports a broadening of current guest worker programs as part of that reform. See http://thehill.com/leading-the-news/immigration-is-added-atop-heavy-agenda-2009-06-04.html for more information.

Sources:
James Parks, "Bipartisan Bill Would Strengthen Guest Worker Rules," AFL-CIO Now Blog, April 24, 2009; Alexander Bolton, "Immigration is added atop heavy agenda," *The Hill*, June 4, 2009.

Censored 2009 #8

Executive Orders Can Be Changed Secretly

Story #8 for 2009 looked at newly declassified documents in which the Office of Legal Counsel had made some startling declarations disclosed on the floor of the Senate in December 2007. These included that 1) there is no constitutional requirement for a president to issue a new executive order whenever he wishes to depart from the terms of a previous executive order, 2) that a president may determine his own constitutional authority under Article II, and finally, 3) that the Department of Justice is bound by the president's legal determinations.

Original Sources: "In FISA Speech, Whitehouse Sharply Criticizes Bush Administration's Assertion of Executive Power," Senator Sheldon Whitehouse Website, December 7, 2007; Marcy Wheeler, "Down The Rabbit Hole," *Guardian*, December 26, 2007.

Update: According to Mark Hosenball's *Newsweek* article "A Loophole in the Rules," the Obama administration is claiming the same powers in regard to secretly changing executive orders as the Bush administration did. Obama White House counsel Gregory Craig does not believe President Obama is required by law to follow executive orders. The top lawyer indicated to Congress that the new president reserves the right to ignore his own (and any other president's) executive order. Along with this claim comes the right to determine what his own powers are and to determine what is law.

The *Newsweek* article quoted an unnamed "veteran undercover spy" who said that Obama could "issue a secret presidential finding instructing the CIA or another agency to overstep boundaries of public policy." Intel sources were quick to explain that Obama had no plans to issue secret orders that would contradict his public anti-torture stance. They also said that the CIA doesn't "want to be asked to do something in secret which has been publicly declared taboo." But since these are secret orders to a covert agency, who would know?

Source:

Mark Hosenball, "A Loophole in the Rules," *Newsweek*, February 2, 2009, www.newsweek.com/id/125521.

Censored 2009 #10

APA Complicit in CIA Torture

In 2005, news reports surfaced that psychologists were working with the US military and the CIA to develop brutal interrogation methods as well as training interrogators in those techniques. The American Psychological Association (APA) assembled a task force to examine the issue. After just two days of deliberations, the ten-member task force concluded that psychologists were playing a "valuable and ethical role" in assisting the military. A year later, a *Salon* report revealed that six of nine voting members were from the military and intelligence agencies with direct connections to interrogations at Guantánamo and CIA black sites that operate outside of Geneva Conventions. Two psychologists in particular played a central role: James Elmer Mitchell, who was contracted to the CIA, and his colleague Bruce Jessen. Both worked in the classified military training program for Survival, Evasion, Resistance, and Escape (SERE)—which conditions soldiers to endure captivity in enemy hands. Many angry psychologists insist that the APA policy has made the organization an enabler of torture.

Original Sources: Mark Benjamin, "The CIA's torture teachers," *Salon*, June 21, 2007; Katherine Eban, "Rorschach and Awe," *Vanity Fair*, July 17, 2007; "American Psychological Association Rejects Blanket Ban on Participation in Interrogation of US Detainees," "APA Interrogation Task Force Member Dr. Jean Maria Arrigo Exposes Group's Ties to Military," "Dissident Voices: Ex-Task Force Member Dr. Michael Wessells Speaks Out on Psychologists and Torture," and "APA Members Hold Fiery Town Hall Meeting on Interrogation, Torture," *Democracy Now!*, August 20, 2007.

Update: On October 2, 2008, American Psychological Association President Alan E. Kazdin sent a letter to President Bush concerning the role of APA members at so-called CIA black sites, such as Guantánamo Bay. The letter was to inform him of a significant change in their policy, the effect of which would "prohibit psychologists from any involvement in interrogations or any other operational procedures at detention sites that are in violation of the U.S. Constitution or international law." Previous policy had offered support to psychologists refusing to work in settings where individuals were deprived of human rights and expressed grave concern about such settings. The roles of APA members at these sites are now strictly limited to working directly for detainees, working for an independent third party working to protect human rights, or treating military personnel.

The letter also called on the Bush administration to safeguard the physical and mental welfare of incarcerated individuals, to investigate their treatment, and "to establish policies and procedures to ensure the independent judicial review of these detentions and to afford the persons being detained all rights guaranteed to them under the Geneva Conventions and the UN Convention Against Torture."

Sources:

"APA Letter to Bush: New Policy Limits Psychologist Involvement in Interrogations," States News Service, October 2, 2008, http://o-www.apa.org.iii.sonoma.edu/releases/kazdin-to-bush1008.pdf.

Censored 2009 # 15

Worldwide Slavery

Twenty-seven million slaves exist in the world today, more than at any time in human history. Globalization, poverty, violence, and greed facilitate the growth of slavery, not only in the Third World, but in the most developed countries as well. Behind the façade in any major town or city in the world today, one is likely to find a thriving commerce in human beings.

Original Sources: David Batstone, "From Sex Workers to Restaurant Workers, the Global Slave Trade Is Growing," *Sojourners*, March 15, 2007; E. Benjamin Skinner, "A World Enslaved," *Foreign Policy*, March/April 2008.

Update: In February 2009, the UN Office on Drugs and Crime (UNODC) released its annual Global Report on Trafficking in Persons, in which the International Labour Organization (ILO) estimates 2 million as the yearly net addition to the total number of slaves worldwide. Subtracting the number of people rescued or who die annually, the total number is thought to be over 10 million, although hard data about the underworld of human slavery remains elusive—partly because of the reluctance of some countries to cooperate with investigations. However, the actual number of known trafficking victims is only 22,500.

The report is based on data gathered from 155 countries. Of these, 125 have signed the UN Protocol against Trafficking in Persons. However, not all of those who ratified it are enforcing the provisions of the treaty; 40 percent of the countries in the sample did not convict anyone for trafficking in the past year.

Overall, the number of convictions for human trafficking is growing, says the report, but it is still much lower than the estimated number of victims.

Many large countries like China, Saudi Arabia, Libya and Iran remain uncooperative and provided no data. The most common form of human trafficking is sexual exploitation (79 percent), followed by forced labor (18 percent). Forced labor is detected and reported less because it frequently goes unnoticed, especially in big cities. Nearly four in five victims are women and girls. Including boys, 20 percent of all trafficking victims in the world are children, but in some parts of Africa and in Asia's Mekong region, children are the majority.

The report also reveals that intra-regional and domestic trafficking are the major forms of trafficking in persons. Criminals prey on their own kin. When it comes to trafficking, women perpetrators play an important role. In 30 percent of the countries that provided evidence on the gender of traffickers, women make up the largest proportion. In regions like Eastern Europe and Central Asia, women trafficking women is the norm. Psychological, financial, and coercive reasons often induce former victims to become traffickers.

Some analysts, however, assert that slavery as an institution may be facing extinction. Never before has slavery represented such a small fraction of the global economy. Many believe that with sufficient commitment and resources, slavery is a phenomenon that can be eradicated. To liberate and rehabilitate a slave in a poor country costs around $400 to $600. Multiplied by the estimated number of slaves, the total needed, worldwide, would amount to less than $10.5 billion.

Source:

Mirela Xanthaki, "Human Slavery Thriving in the Shadows," Inter Press Service, February 14, 2009.

Censored 2009 #17

UN's Empty Declaration of Indigenous Rights

In September 2007, the United Nations General Assembly adopted the Universal Declaration on the Rights of Indigenous Peoples. The resolution called for recognition of the world's 370 million indigenous peoples' right to self-determination and control over their lands and resources. The declaration emphasizes the rights of indigenous peoples to maintain and strengthen their institutions, cultures, and traditions, and to pursue their development in keeping with their own needs and aspirations. The declaration was passed by an overwhelming majority vote of 143–4. Only the United States, Canada, Australia, and New Zealand voted against the resolution, expressing the view that strong emphasis on rights to indigenous self-determination and control over lands and resources would hinder economic development and undermine "established democratic norms."

Original Sources: Haider Rizvi, "UN Adopts Historic Statement on Native Rights," One World, September 14, 2007, and "Indigenous Peoples Shut Out of Climate Talks, Plans," Common Dreams, December 12, 2007; Brenda Norrell, "Indigenous Peoples Protest World Bank Carbon Scam in Bali," BSNorrell.blogspot.com, December 11, 2007; Tom Griffiths, "NGO Statement on the World Bank's Proposed Forest Carbon Partnership Facility," Forest Peoples Programme, November 30, 2007.

Update: In 2009, Australia, one of few countries to vote against the UN's Universal Declaration on the Rights of Indigenous Peoples, changed its mind. However, as Australia signed on to the declaration on April 3, 2009, there were protests calling for the government to put the UN resolution into action. The policies of the Australian political party in power were said to be racist and patriarchal. "The NT Intervention contravenes 25 of the 46 articles of the UN Declaration on Rights for Indigenous Peoples. The Racial Discrimination Act 1975 remains suspended and Aboriginal communities remain under the control of an explicitly racist government," said aboriginal rights activist Barbara Shaw.

Many grievances are voiced about policies dealing with aboriginal people in the Northern Territory. According to the UN, state policies are still not in accordance with the International Covenant on Civil and Political

Rights (ICCPR). The United Nations Human Rights Committee released a report that stated, "Legislation regarding mandatory imprisonment in Western Australia and the Northern Territory, which leads in many cases to imposition of punishments that are disproportionate to the seriousness of the crimes committed and would seem to be inconsistent with the strategies adopted by the State party to reduce the over representation of indigenous persons in the criminal justice system, raises serious issues of compliance with various articles in the Covenant."

Aboriginal people's right to self-determination is limited by Australia maintaining sovereignty and stability so the rights of other Australians are not infringed upon. The closest protection under Australian law for ethnic minorities is the 1975 Racial Discrimination Act, which has been suspended in the case of the Northern Territory intervention. Section 25 allows states to disqualify people from voting because of their race, while the federal Parliament's races power in section 51(26) authorizes legislation with respect to "people of any race for whom it is deemed necessary to make special laws."

Sources:

Takver, "Australian Aboriginal groups want action as well as words from Indigenous Rights Treaty," *Sydney Indymedia*, April 4, 2009; "UN report says NT intervention 'discriminatory,'" Australian Broadcast Channel News, April 6, 2009; Human Rights Committee: Concluding Observations on Australia, http://www.austlii.edu.au/au/journals/AILR/2000/38.html; George Williams, "Racist premise of our constitution remains," *Sydney Morning Herald*, April 6, 2009.

Censored 2009 #25

The Real Problem with Eliot Spitzer

Eliot Spitzer was elected as governor of New York in 2006. During most of his tenure as governor, he pursued cases against companies, accusing them of predatory lending. His article, "Predatory Lenders' Partner in Crime," first published in the *Washington Post* in 2008, was the subject of controversy because it accused the Bush administration of being the cause of the current financial crisis. Spitzer wrote, "The administration accomplished this feat through an obscure federal agency called the Office of the Comptroller of the Currency [OCC]." First established during the Civil War, the job of the OCC is to make sure the nation's banks are balanced. Spitzer accused the Bush administration of using this against consumers. In 2003, the OCC was used to stop all state predatory lending laws. The state was made unable to help consumers with protection from banks because of the National Bank Act, an act almost 150 years old. The law was greatly protested by all fifty state attorneys general. This did not slow the Bush administration, and the financial crisis ensued. Many believe Spitzer was set up in his involvement in a prostitution ring because of his comments about the Bush administration and the crisis. The *New York Times* broke the story on March 10, 2008. Two days later, Spitzer resigned from his position as governor. The sex scandal is considered to be the biggest since Monica Lewinsky and Bill Clinton.

Original Sources: "Predatory Lenders' Partner in Crime," *Washington Post*, February 14, 2008; F. William Engdahl, "Why the Bush Administration 'Watergated' Eliot Spitzer," Global Research, March 17, 2008.

Update: In November 2008, prosecutors in charge of the case announced that Spitzer would not face criminal charges for his involvement in the sex ring, citing a lack of evidence regarding any misuse of public funds. Spitzer offered an apology for his conduct, saying, "I appreciate the impartiality and thoroughness of the investigation by the US Attorney's Office, and I acknowledge and accept responsibility for the conduct it disclosed."

Later in the month, the *Washington Post* posted a Spitzer opinion piece conveying his analysis of the financial crisis of 2008 and suggesting remedies. Spitzer concluded the piece by saying that he hoped the Obama administration would make the right policy choices and not repeat the mistakes made by the Bush administration.

On December 3, 2008, *Slate* published the first of a new column by Spitzer dedicated to the economy. In March 2009, Spitzer was interviewed by Fareed Zakaria about the current financial crisis. Spitzer argued that as attorney general he was active in pursuing white-collar crime and that, just prior to the prostitution scandal, he had investigated many of the investment banks that have been blamed for contributing to the crisis.

Sources:
Danny Hakim and William K. Rashbaum, "No Federal Prostitution Charges for Spitzer," *New York Times*, November 6, 2008; Eliot Spitzer, "How to Ground the Street," *Washington Post*, November 16, 2008; Eliot Spitzer, "Too Big Not To Fail," *Slate*, December 3, 2008.

Censored 2008 # 3

AFRICOM: US Military Control of Africa's Resources

In February 2007, the White House announced the formation of the US African Command (AFRICOM), a new unified Pentagon command center in Africa, to be established by September 2008. This military penetration of Africa was presented as a humanitarian guard in the Global War on Terror. The real objective, however, was the procurement and control of Africa's oil and its global delivery systems.

Original Source: Bryan Hunt, "Understanding AFRICOM," MoonofAlabama.org, February 2, 2007.

Update: In 2008, plans to base the much-talked-about United States Africa Command (AFRICOM) in Africa were put on hold and the US government acknowledged defeat in its all-out campaign to convince any African ally to welcome the installation on its territory. The corporate media were relatively quiet about this setback to the so-called War on Terror. Only a few months prior, news reports highlighted America's desire to establish AFRICOM somewhere on the continent as one of the main reasons for President Bush's Africa tour. In February 2008, Bush visited five African nations, all considered allies, hoping to persuade one to accept AFRICOM. With the sole exception of Liberia, Bush was met with a resounding "no" throughout his trip. Even a proposal to locate five smaller regional offices, to coordinate with AFRICOM in Germany, were rejected by African countries.

Source:
Dennis Lauman, "Africa Says No to AFRICOM," *People's Weekly World*, June 28–July 4, 2008.

Censored 2008 #7

Behind Blackwater Inc.

In 2007, Jeremy Scahill wrote *Blackwater: The Rise of the World's Most Powerful Mercenary Army*, in which he outlined the corruption and cronyism surrounding their meteoric rise to power. Critics often characterized the book as "hard-left" and said that Scahill had overplayed the dangers of private military contracting.

Original Source: Jeremy Scahill, "Our Mercenaries in Iraq: Blackwater Inc and Bush's Undeclared Surge," *Democracy Now!*, January 26, 2007.

Update: On February 13, 2009, the Blackwater private security firm announced that it would be changing its name to Xe, which is pronounced like the letter "z." The company could no longer operate under the name that came to be known worldwide as a caustic moniker for private security, dropping the tarnished brand for something new and improved. Following a deadly shooting in Baghdad's Nisoor Square, the multinational corporation had changed its name to Blackwater Worldwide. The new decision to give up the name entirely underscores how badly the North Carolina–based company's brand was damaged by that incident and other security work in Iraq.

"They have established themselves as the bad guys," said Katy Helvenston, who sued the company following her son's death during a mission in Fallujah while working for Blackwater in 2004. "They've established such a horrible reputation. Why else would they change their name?"

The issue came to a head last month, when the State Department said it would not rehire Blackwater to protect its diplomats in Iraq after its current contract with the company expires in May. The company has one other major security contract, details of which are classified.

The company is also replacing its bear paw logo with a sleeker black-and-white graphic based on letters that make up the company's new name. In a note to employees, President Gary Jackson said the name change reflects the company's new focus, and he indicated Xe would not actively pursue new security business. However, it has expanded other businesses such as aviation support, recently building a fleet of seventy-six aircraft that it has deployed to such hotspots as West Africa and Afghanistan.

Late last year, prosecutors charged five of the company's contractors—but not Blackwater itself—with manslaughter and weapons violations. In January, Iraqi officials said they would not give the company a license to operate. The State Department responded by informing Blackwater it would not renew a contract that comprises a third of the company's nearly $1 billion in annual revenue.

Illinois Rep. Jan Schakowsky, chair of the Intelligence Subcommittee on Oversight and Investigations and a longtime Blackwater critic, said the new name won't change the fact that its actions have resulted in the deaths of innocent civilians.

Source:
Mike Baker, "In shift, Blackwater dumps tarnished brand name," Associated Press, February 13, 2009.

Censored 2007 #1

Future of Internet Debate Ignored by Media

Throughout 2005 and 2006, a large underground debate raged regarding the future of the Internet, an issue that became known as "network neutrality." The battle is a tug of war with cable companies on the one hand and consumers and Internet service providers (ISPs) on the other. Most coverage of the issue framed it as an argument over regulation—but the term "regulation" in this case is somewhat misleading. Groups advocating for "net neutrality" are not promoting regulation of Internet content. What they want is a legal mandate forcing cable companies to allow ISPs free access to their cable lines (called a "common carriage" agreement). This was the model used for dial-up Internet, and it is the way content providers want to keep it. They also want to make sure that cable companies cannot screen or interrupt Internet content without a court order.

Original Source: Elliot D. Cohen, PhD, "Web of Deceit: How Internet Freedom Got the Federal Ax, and Why Corporate News Censored the Story," BuzzFlash, July 18, 2005.

Update: There is ongoing legal and political wrangling in the US regarding net neutrality. In the meantime the FCC has used their jurisdiction over the issue and has laid down guidelines that it expects the telecommunications industry to follow. On February 11, 2008, Rep. Ed Markey and Rep. Chip Pickering introduced H.R. 5353, the Internet Freedom Preservation Act, "to establish broadband policy and direct the Federal Communications Commission to conduct a proceeding and public broadband summit to assess competition, consumer protection, and consumer choice issues relating to broadband Internet access services, and for other purposes."

On August 1, 2008, the FCC formally voted 3–2 to uphold a complaint against Comcast, the largest cable company in the US, ruling that it had illegally inhibited users of its high-speed Internet service from using file-sharing software. Then–FCC chairman Kevin Martin said the order was meant to set a precedent that Internet providers, and indeed all communications companies, could not prevent customers from using their networks the way they see fit unless there is a good reason. In an interview, Martin stated, "We are preserving the open character of the Internet." The legal complaint against Comcast related to BitTorrent, software that is commonly used to download movies, television shows, music, and software on the Internet.

When in the spring of 2008 Comcast was caught paying people to fill seats at an FCC public hearing, it set off an Internet firestorm. Comcast was forced to admit to busing in the seat-fillers and has not used the tactic since.

Sources:
See http://en.wikipedia.org/wiki/Network_neutrality; Saul Hansell, "F.C.C. Vote Sets Precedent on Unfettered Web Usage," *New York Times*, August 2, 2008; Josh Stearns, "Comcast Blocking: First the Internet—anow the Public?" Media Reform News, Spring 2008.

Censored 2007 #4

Hunger and Homelessness Increasing in the US

This *Censored 2007* top 25 story focused on the 2005 US Conference of Mayors report detailing a growth in the numbers of hungry and homeless people in America's cities. The report measured the demand for food and housing assistance in twenty-four US cities and found increased levels of demand in over three quarters of the surveyed cities. This story also discussed a Bush administration plan to eliminate a highly regarded national survey, the Census Bureau's Survey of Income and Program Participation (SIPP), in use since 1984. In response, over 400 social scientists signed a letter to Congress urging full funding of the survey.

Original Sources: Brendan Coyne, "New Report Shows Increase in Urban Hunger, Homelessness," *New Standard*, December 2005; Abid Aslam, "US Plan to Eliminate Survey of Needy Families Draws Fire," OneWorld.net, March, 2006.

Update: In the midst of a major economic recession and lack of federal welfare support, rates of hunger and homelessness in the US continue to hit record highs in a number of cities and rural areas. Statistics from school districts and city census reports indicate the major crisis in homelessness has hit American children particularly hard. A 2009 report by the National Center on Family Homelessness, based on data from 2005 to 2006, indicates that one in fifty American children were homeless at one point during that year, a total of 1.5 million children. According to the *Boston Globe,* the number of homeless families in Boston increased 22 percent from December 2007 to December 2008. The number of children without a home increased from 1,850 to 2,288 in 2008. Cities across the country have witnessed similar increases in general and child homelessness.

The Bush administration's efforts to eliminate SIPP failed as Congress secured funding for 2007. After again eliminating funding for the survey program in the proposed 2008 budget, the Bush administration reversed its decision.

Sources:

Patrick Markee and Lizzy Ratner, "Homelessness Is at Record Highs: Let's Show Some Real Compassion," *The Nation,* February 3, 2009; Linda Stewart Ball, Daniel Shea, and Dionne Walker, "1 in 50 American Children Experiences Homelessness," Associated Press, March 10, 2009; Milton J. Valencia, "Homeless families rise 22% in a year," *Boston Globe,* January 6, 2009; "Baltimore's Homeless Population Grows 12 Percent," *Baltimore Sun,* January 9, 2009; Jennifer Li, "City's homeless children are "urgent" problem," *Philadelphia Inquirer,* June 9, 2009.

Censored 2007 #18

Physicist Challenges Official 9/11 Story

In the winter of 2006, Brigham Young University Professor Stephen E. Jones called for an independent, international scientific investigation into the events of 9/11 "guided not by politicized notions and constraints, but rather by observations and calculations." After research into the buildings' collapse he concluded that the official story was incomplete at best. Jones questioned the collapsing of the towers at close to free-fall speed. "Where," he asked, "is the delay that must be expected due to conservation of momentum, one of the foundational laws of physics?" Jones asserted that "as upper-falling floors strike lower floors—and intact steel support columns—the fall must be significantly impeded by the impacted mass." The paradox, he says, "is easily resolved by the explosive demolition hypothesis, whereby explosives quickly removed lower-floor material, including steel support columns, and allow near free-fall-speed collapses."

Original Sources: Elaine Jarvik, "Y. Professor Thinks Bombs, Not Planes, Toppled WTC," *Deseret Morning News*, November 10, 2005, and "BYU professor's group accuses U.S. officials of lying about 9/11," January 26, 2006; Steven E. Jones, "Why Indeed Did the WTC Buildings Collapse?" Brigham Young University website, Winter 2005.

Update: In February of 2009, Dr. Jones and a team of chemistry and physics researchers published a study, in a peer-reviewed scientific journal, that offers additional support for the controversial explosive demolition hypothesis. The team of researchers working at the University of Copenhagen, Denmark, discovered flammable thermitic materials in a number of samples of the dust produced by the destruction of the World Trade Center. The red/gray chips showed marked similarities in all four samples obtained. One sample was collected by a Manhattan resident about ten minutes after the collapse of the second World Trade Center (WTC) tower, two the next day, and a fourth about a week later. The properties of these chips were analyzed using optical microscopy, scanning electron microscopy, X-ray energy dispersive spectroscopy, and differential scanning calorimetry. Iron oxide and aluminum were intimately mixed in the red material. Numerous iron-rich spheres were clearly observed in the residue following ignition of these peculiar red/gray chips. The red portion of these chips was found to be an unreacted thermitic material and highly energetic. The research team concluded that, based on the observations, the red layer of the red/gray chips discovered in the WTC dust is active, unreacted thermitic material, incorporating nanotechnology, and is a highly energetic pyrotechnic or explosive material.

Source:
Niels H. Harrit, Jeffrey Farrer, Steven E. Jones, Kevin R. Ryan, Frank M. Legge, Daniel Farnsworth, Gregg Roberts, James R. Gourley, and Bradley R. Larsen, "Active Thermitic Material Discovered in Dust from the 9/11 World Trade Center Catastrophe," *Open Chemical Physics Journal*, February 2009, Volume 2, p. 7–31.

Mountaintop Removal Threatens Ecosystem and Economy

In 2004, *Earth First!* published an article by John Conner about a form of coal mining called mountaintop removal (MTR). Considered by many to be a dangerous undertaking, mountaintop removal is the practice of dynamiting the tops of mountains, then blowing them off. Literally millions of pounds of dynamite are used to blow up entire mountain ranges. Afterwards, the waste is then dumped into streams, valleys, and riverbeds. The process essentially destroys the entire ecosystem of an area. According to Conner, over 1,000 streams have already been destroyed in West Virginia alone. The main reason this is being done is money. Dynamite is much cheaper than hiring coal miners who are part of a union. It is estimated that over 40,000 jobs have been displaced by MTR. Big Coal has used many other names, such as cross range mining and surface mining, to mask the true meaning of MTR. As oil runs out, the demand for coal has grown exponentially. More than ninety-three new plants have been built since 2004, and demand is expected to rise along with these new facilities.

Original Source: John Conner, "See You in the Mountains: Katuah Earth First! Confronts Mountaintop Removal," *Earth First!* Nov–Dec 2004.

Update: On March 24, 2009, the Environmental Protection Agency (EPA) announced that they had called for a halt on specific MTR permits, addressing the fact that these practices could have a devastating effect on the water quality in these places. The EPA sent two letters to the US Army Corps of Engineers. This group is responsible for issuing Clean Water Act permits to various coal mining projects, to ensure they meet the set requirements. According to AlterNet, the letters express ". . . The EPA's considerable concern regarding the environmental impact these projects would have on fragile habitats and streams." These two letters specifically mentioned the projects taking place in Kentucky and West Virginia.

The EPA says it plans on writing letters addressing other projects that could cause negative effects to our environment. It is unclear whether the halt of these permits is just for these specific cases, or if this is part of a bigger movement to stop surface mining in general. In an article on Alter-

Net, Jeff Biggers said, "It is a big step for our country." Not only did the EPA send letters, they have also requested to meet with corps officials to coordinate further plans on this issue. Because of the Fourth Circuit litigations of this issue, the corps has many permits backlisted, as they have not been able to review them all in a timely manner. Since 2007, the Corps has issued far fewer permits in West Virginia and various other states because of these litigations. The EPA expects to be actively involved in the reviewing process of these permits to ensure they will not affect the environment.

Source:
Jeff Biggers, "EPA halts Mountain Top Removal Permits," AlterNet, March 24, 2009.

Censored 1999 #10

Environmental Student Activists Gunned Down on Chevron Oil Facility in Nigeria

On May 28, 1998, Nigerian soldiers were helicoptered by Chevron employees to a Chevron-owned oil facility off the coast of Nigeria in order to attack student demonstrators and villagers who had occupied a barge anchored to the facility, protesting the company's hiring and environmental practices. After multiple attacks, two protesters lay dead, and several others were wounded. The students had been peacefully protesting at the site since May 25.

Original Sources: Environmental Rights Action/Friends of the Earth Nigeria, "Chevron in Nigeria—ERA Environmental Testimonies," A-Info News Service, July 10, 1998; Amy Goodman and Jeremy Scahill, "Drilling and Killing: Chevron and Nigeria's Oil Dictatorship," *Democracy Now!*, Summer 1998.

Update: On March 5, 2009, after many court battles, the environmental protesters lost in their legal battle against Chevron Oil. A federal judge upheld an earlier San Francisco jury's verdict that cleared the Chevron Corporation of wrongdoing in the shootings of Nigerian demonstrators who occupied the offshore oil barge in 1998.

The demonstrators maintained they were unarmed and peaceful, but Chevron produced witnesses who claimed the protesters threatened violence, held crew members hostage, and demanded ransom. Chevron claimed that, after three days of negotiations, it summoned Nigerian security forces, who killed two men and wounded two others.

The suit was filed under the Alien Tort Statute, a 1789 statute giving non–US citizens the right to seek damages in US courts for international human rights violations.

On December 1, 2008, a nine-member jury had unanimously rejected the plaintiffs' claims that Chevron was responsible for assault, inhumane treatment, torture, and wrongful death. This followed a series of rulings, issued August 14, 2007, in which United States District Court Judge Susan Illston had rejected Chevron Corporation's attempts to avoid trial for its involvement in the 1998 attacks.

Sources:
Bob Egelko, "Verdict clearing Chevron upheld in Nigeria case," *San Francisco Chronicle*, March 5, 2009; "Chevron to Stand Trial For Human Rights Abuses in Nigeria," Center for Constitutional Rights, August 14, 2007.

Censored 1997 #2

Shell's Oil, Africa's Blood

In 1995, Ken Saro-Wiwa—a popular Nigerian writer who founded the Movement of the Survival of the Ogoni People (MOSOP) to protest against Shell's oil exploration in the Niger Delta—and eight fellow activists were executed after being found guilty by a three-man military tribunal on what their families and supporters claim were trumped-up charges of causing the death of four Ogoni elders.

Witnesses claim that then-managing director of Shell, Brian Anderson, offered to make a deal with Saro-Wiwa: Shell would try to prevent the executions if the activists would call off MOSOP protests. Wiwa refused, and Shell did not intervene. Publicly, Shell claimed that it was not and would not become involved in Nigeria's political affairs. Internal documents uncovered by journalists and human rights groups contradict this claim.

Beginning in 1996, the Center for Constitutional Rights, EarthRights International, and other human rights attorneys brought a series of cases against Shell under the Alien Tort Statute, a 1789 statute giving non-US citizens the right to file suits in US courts for international human rights violations, and the Torture Victim Protection Act, which allows individuals to seek damages in the US for torture or extrajudicial killing, regardless of where the violations take place.

Original Sources: Vince Bielsk, "Shell Game," *San Francisco Bay Guardian*, February 7, 1996; Ron Nixon and Michael King, "Shell's Oil, Africa's Blood," *Texas Observer*, January 12, 1996; M.L. Stein, "Rejected Ad Flap," *Editor & Publisher*, March 23, 1996; Aaron Sachs, "Dying for Oil," World Watch, May/June 1996; Chris Bright, "Eco-Justice in Nigeria," World Watch, July/August 1996; Andrea Durbin, "IFC Pulls Out of Shell Deal in Nigeria," Bank Check, February 1996.

Update: After many delays and continuances, on June 8, 2009, Royal Dutch Shell agreed to pay $15.5 million to settle a lawsuit that accused the company of colluding with Nigeria's former military regime over the execution of Ken Saro-Wiwa and other peaceful anti-oil protesters.

Shell admitted no wrongdoing in reaching the settlement, which will be used to compensate the families of the activist Mr. Saro-Wiwa and other civilians maimed or hanged by the regime. The money will also be used to set up a development trust for the Ogoni people from the Niger Delta in southern Nigeria.

The company said that it agreed to a settlement "in recognition of the tragic turn of events in Ogoni land, even though Shell had no part in the violence that took place." Malcolm Brinded, Shell's executive director for exploration and production, said: "While we were prepared to go to court to clear our name, we believe the right way forward is to focus on the future for Ogoni people, which is important for peace and stability in the region."

Sources:
"Shell settles Nigeria deaths case," BBC, June 9, 2009; Jennifer S. Altman, "Shell to Pay $15.5 Million to Settle Nigerian Case," *New York Times*, June 9, 2009; Ron Liddle, "Shell agrees to $15.5m settlement over death of Saro-Wiwa and eight others," *Times of London*, June 9, 2009; Remember Ken Saro-Wiwa Campaign, http://remembersarowiwa.com; Matthew Green and Michael Peel, "Shell faces Saro-Wiwa death claim," *Financial Times*, April 3 2009.

Infotainment Society: Junk Food News and News Abuse for 2008/2009

by Mickey Huff, Frances A. Capell, and Project Censored

> *We can do the innuendo*
> *We can dance and sing*
> *When it's said and done*
> *We haven't told you a thing*
> *We all know that crap is king*
> *Give us dirty laundry!*

—Don Henley, "Dirty Laundry," 1982

The late New York University media scholar Neil Postman once said about America: "We are the best entertained, least informed society in the world." Since the mid 1980s, Project Censored has examined this phenomenon in the culture of the 24/7 television news cycle. Looking beyond what the corporate news media undercover or ignore, Project Censored surveys what they *do* spend precious airtime and column inches on instead of covering the top censored stories. Which news stories have been found consistently by such surveys in this so-called information age? "Junk Food News," said Project Censored founder Dr. Carl Jensen. "It's like a Twinkie, not very nourishing for the consumer." This is how Jensen described it back in 1984 when he first began looking at how tabloid sensationalism had inundated the nightly news with the "Where's the Beef" campaign. Jensen still considers Junk Food News a major problem in journalism and corporate media, particularly on today's cable and television news. In that tradition, Project Censored "celebrates" the twenty-fifth anniversary of Junk Food News this year.[1]

From Jessica Simpson's weight and Brangelina's escapades to Britney Spears's sister and the Obama's First Puppy promise, the public is force-fed tripe. Americans are treated to a steady "news" diet of useless information laden with personal anecdotes or scandals, gossip, and flat-out kitsch. Topics and in-depth reports that matter little to anyone in any meaningful way are given incredible amounts of media coverage. Even when relevant stories are covered, they often easily morph into News Abuse, stories that twist and turn into stranger tales divorced from their original newsworthy criteria. From Octomom and Joe the Plumber to Barack Obama's "blackness" and inability to bowl, real yet otherwise brief stories take long detours into living rooms and stay like unwanted guests for far too long and in far too great detail.

In recent years, this has only become more obvious. For instance, CNN's coverage of celebrity Anna Nicole Smith's untimely death in early 2007 is arguably one of the most egregious examples of Junk Food and News Abuse stories of the past few years. The magnitude of corporate media attention paid to Smith's death was clearly out of sync with the coverage the story deserved, which was a simple passing mention, if that, on the entertainment portion of scheduled programming. Instead, CNN broadcast "breaking" stories of Smith's death, uninterrupted, for almost two hours, with commentary by lead anchors and journalists. This was one of the longest uninterrupted "news" broadcasts at CNN since the tragic events of September 11, 2001. Anna Nicole Smith and 9/11 are now strange bedfellows, milestone bookends of corporate news culture. While news outlets were obsessing over Smith's death, most big media giants were missing a far more important story. The US ambassador to Iraq apparently misplaced $12 billion in shrink wrapped $100 bills that were flown to Baghdad. This garnered little attention due to the media's morbid infatuation with Smith's passing. This is clearly news judgment gone terribly awry, if not an outright retreat from journalistic standards.[2]

It is important to note that CNN was not alone. Corporate rivals MSNBC and FOX struggled to keep up with the Smith saga. This is what the self-proclaimed fair and balanced most trusted names in news had to offer. Meanwhile, billions of taxpayer dollars went missing and wars raged on in Iraq and Afghanistan, American troops and Iraqi civilians died, torture went unquestioned, habeas corpus was suspended with little fanfare, and the subprime crisis loomed (while then-President Bush claimed the "fundamentals of our economy are strong"). These stories were nowhere on the intellectually barren corporate media landscape. The once trivial and absurd are now mainstreamed as "news." More young people turn to late night comics' fake news to learn the truth or tune out to so-called reality shows often scripted as Roman Holiday spectacles of the surreal. Welcome to the Infotainment Society: American Media in the twenty-first century.

Here are the Top Ten Junk Food News Stories for 2008 and 2009 as chosen by Project Censored students and the online community via http://projectcensored.org:

1. Olympic Medalist Michael Phelps Hits a Bong
2. Jessica Simpson Gains Weight
3. First Lady Michelle Obama's Fashion Sense
4. The Brangelina Twins
5. Lindsay Lohan Dates a Woman
6. The Presidential First Puppy
7. Heidi Montag "Marries" Spencer Pratt
8. Barry Bonds's Steroid Trial
9. Jamie-Lynn Spears Gives Birth
10. The Woes of Amy Winehouse

1. The British tabloid *News of the World* published an exclusive photo of Olympic gold medalist Michael Phelps smoking marijuana from a bong on Sunday, February 1, 2009, with the headline, "What a Dope." The picture was allegedly taken during a November house party while Phelps was visiting the University of South Carolina. The incident occurred nearly three months after the swimmer won eight gold medals for America at the 2008 Olympics in Beijing, China. "He grabbed the bong and a lighter and knew exactly what to do," a witness recounted of Phelps in the *News of the World* report. Phelps quickly apologized to the public for his "regrettable behavior" and was suspended for three months by USA Swimming, despite having never tested positive for banned substances during competition. In the weeks following, Phelps lost his sponsorship from Kellogg's cereal. That wasn't the only loss. Police confiscated the bong after the owner was discovered trying to sell it on eBay for $100,000. In 1998, Olympic snowboarder Ross Rebagliati and Olympic swimmer Gary Hall Jr. found themselves amid controversy after testing positive for marijuana. "It's one of those substances that every year there's debate over it," said David Howman, executive director of the World Anti-Doping Agency.

Instead of having a serious dialogue about drug use and policy in the US, the corporate media focused on celebrity scandal. Rather than reporting on the record numbers of nonviolent marijuana possession arrests in 2008 (close to one million), the press wrote about college-age, jock party bong stories. There would have likely been no story at all if these were pictures of Phelps drinking a beer or even dragging on a cigarette (nor would it be a story if it wasn't a celebrity hitting the bong). Ironically, Phelps has won the most gold medals to date of any Olympic swimmer for the US. Perhaps this sends the wrong message to the public: even champions may partake of the weed. At least the incident implies that recreational pot use may not deter significant accomplishments.

It was certainly a missed opportunity for media to moderate a national debate on marijuana policy, but this was not the only vital story the media missed that week. The same week the public was doused with discussion of the murky bong water of Phelps's party mistake and the chlorinated pool water of his many victories, a report on the dangerous effects of global climate change on California's coastal waters went virtually unnoticed. The windier than usual conditions believed by some scientists to be a result of climate change drove additional upwelling of nutrient-rich deep ocean waters. At normal levels, this upwelling sustains the abundance of marine life, but too much of these rich waters leads to a boom-and-bust cycle that ultimately creates ocean "dead zones" with little or no oxygen. Marine life that can't swim or scuttle away from these lethal zones will suffocate. Spurred by the discovery of such zones off the Oregon coast, UC Santa Cruz earth scientist Mark Snyder ran a climate simulation of the region's estimated climate from 2038 to 2070. The results showed a 40 percent increase from current wind speeds, increases of as much as two meters per second. "It was just chance they found the dead zones in Oregon," stated Snyder. Alarmed by a massive number of dead and dying crabs found in their traps, Oregon fishermen had contacted marine scientists. "It's quite possible these areas could be off the California coast," he said. Corporate media made ample time to discuss the woes of Phelps, but not an environmental shift that threatens marine life and those that rely upon it.[3]

Here are a few other news stories that were not widely covered on television network and cable news during the same period which were arguably of more significance than Michael Phelps and the bong:

> Published on Sunday, February 1, 2009, by Agence France Presse: "Israel Vows 'Disproportionate' Strike on Hamas"
> Published on Sunday, February 1, 2009, by the *Guardian*:

"Gaza Desperately Short of Food After Israel Destroys Farm-land: Officials warn of 'destruction of all means of life' after the three-week conflict leaves agriculture in the region in ruins"
> Published on Monday, February 2, 2009, by Inter Press Service: "Generals Seek to Reverse Obama Withdrawal Decision"

2. Photos of Jessica Simpson performing at a Florida Chili Cook-off looking a bit heavier than usual surfaced during the week of January 26, 2009. The purportedly unflattering shots of a curvier looking Simpson in an outfit that included "a muffin-top-inducing leopard belt" immediately made news headlines. Was she pregnant? Was she picking up eating habits from her NFL star boyfriend? Or was she simply hungry for publicity? Her sister, Ashlee Simpson-Wentz, and ex-husband, Nick Lachey, as well as seemingly unrelated celebrities, such as Kim Kardashian, were eager to weigh in on the subject. During a pre-Super Bowl interview, even President Obama quipped that Simpson was "in a weight battle apparently." One would think the leader of the free world would have more important things upon which to comment.

While Americans were concerned with what was going into Jessica Simpson's mouth, a "High Level Meeting on Food Security for All" convened by the United Nations and Spanish government was taking place in Madrid, Spain, to address the problem of one billion people suffering from hunger worldwide. During the two-day meeting, participants, including representatives from national governments, civil society, trade unions, the private sector, academia, multilateral organizations and donor agencies from approximately 100 countries expressed "the urgent need to strive even harder to achieve international commitments of increasing substantially financial resources and official development aid (ODA), particularly in relation to nutrition, food, agriculture and hunger-related program and policies." No concrete resolutions were adopted, but the final declaration of the conference urged governments and international institutions to make good on previous pledges of aid and, on a positive note, called to eliminate "competition-distorting subsidies, in order to stimulate and conduct agricultural trade in a fair way." Given that roughly 30,000 people around the globe die each day due to starvation, the media could spend more time on substantive issues surrounding food in lieu of the societal implications of Simpson's body mass index fluctuations.[4]

Here are a few other news stories that were not widely covered on television network and cable news during the same period which were arguably of more significance than Jessica Simpson's weight:

> ➤ Published on Monday, January 26, 2009, by Agence France Presse: "Study: Global Warming Effects to Last 1,000 Years"
> ➤ Published on Tuesday, January 27, 2009, by the *Independent*: "Why Would a Banker Sell his $14m House to his Wife for $100? Former Lehman boss accused of trying to hide assets from creditors"
> ➤ Published on Wednesday, January 28, 2009, by Inter Press Service: "Is Gates Undermining Another Opening to Iran?"

3. The corporate media were all abuzz over President Barack Obama's inauguration parties. In particular, the outfit the new First Lady Michelle Obama wore drew significant attention. Coverage of this historical event in American politics somehow looked more like a copy and paste job from a style column on celebrity fashion at the Academy Awards than the election of America's first African American President. "Barack Obama may have talked about hope in his inaugural address," stated a report from the *Baltimore Sun*, "but first lady Michelle Obama, wore it, quite literally, on her sleeve." Choice descriptive phrases such as "optimistic hue" and "change you can wear" epitomized the blurring of a line between meaningful commentary and useless fodder when the spotlight was on Michelle Obama. Regardless of her many prior achievements, she was now an accoutrement to the President, a First Lady with a flair for nontraditional fashion.

Despite the media's hyperfocus on the fashion sense of America's new First Lady, they failed to report a serious story concerning women's health in a Wisconsin prison. Two days after the inauguration ball, the ACLU filed a motion in federal court seeking to halt the Taycheedah Correctional Institution system from ordering and administering medication to prisoners. Taycheedah Correctional Institution is the largest women's prison in Wisconsin. According to the motion, the prison often forces women to wait weeks for medicine, and when the medicine does arrive it is often the wrong medicine in the wrong doses. Prison guards with no medical training also administered medications. This led to prisoners receiving medications intended for other prisoners with different ailments. The motion charges that prison officials have known about these problems with medical care, yet they have failed to do anything to correct them.[5]

Here are a few other news stories that were not widely covered on television network and cable news during the same period which were arguably of more significance than First Lady fashion:

> Published on Tuesday, January 20, 2009, by the *Times Online (UK)*: "Ban Ki-Moon Lambasts Shelling of UN in Gaza"
> Published on Wednesday, January 21, 2009, by the *Toronto Star*: "Tar Sands Smog Seen Worsening"
> Published on Thursday, January 22, 2009, by the *Guardian*: "US Accused of Killing 25 Afghan Civilians in Raid on Militants"

4. Hollywood power couple Angelina Jolie and Brad Pitt welcomed two new members to their ever-growing family on Saturday, July 12, 2008. That evening, Angelina gave birth to Knox Leon, a boy, and Vivienne Marcheline, a girl, at the Fondation Lenval hospital in Nice, France. The twins marked the fifth and sixth children for the couple. The following day, Mayor Christian Estrosi of Nice presented one of the birth certificates of the newborns on the steps of hospital, and stated, "It's a pride to Nice and all its citizens."

While these are fine sentiments, this celebrity affair is not news. If the US media had been inclined to keep the public informed of all the newsworthy happenings in southern France that weekend, perhaps they could have reported another story. The day before the birth of the Brangelina twins, in Lyon—a popular tourist destination less than 300 miles away from Nice—authorities ordered the temporary closure of Tricastin, a nuclear treatment plant, after a uranium leak polluted the local water supply. Residents in the region were told not to drink water or eat fish from nearby rivers because 165 pounds of untreated liquid uranium had been spilled into the ground. Swimming and water sports were prohibited, as was irrigation of crops with the contaminated water. France's ASN nuclear safety authority cited a "series of faults and human negligence that is not acceptable" when it ordered the closure following an inspection at the plant later that week.[6]

Here are a few other news stories that were not widely covered on television network and cable news during the same period which were arguably of more significance than Brangelina:

> Published on Sunday, July 13, 2008, by *The Toledo Blade*: "Community Gardens: Growing Food Brings People Together"

➤ Published on Sunday, July 13, 2008, by the *Times Herald-Record*: "Is Your Picnic Filled With 'Franken-Foods?'"

➤ Published on Tuesday, July 15, 2008, by Inter Press Service: "Israel Targets Hamas Orphanages"

5. On Monday, September 22, 2008, the syndicated radio talk show "Loveline" featured Lindsay Lohan, who confirmed what had already been widely speculated: she was in a romantic relationship with female DJ Samantha Ronson. "You guys, you and Samantha, have been going out for how long now?" DJ Ted Stryker inquired. "Like two years, one year, five months, two months?" "For a very long time," Lohan remarked after laughing. Though the pair had made public appearances and had been photographed together, the interview marked the first time that Lohan would publicly comment on the extent of their relationship. In the months after verification, the trials and tribulations of their tumultuous affair were to be covered extensively by the international news media. As of this writing, the comings and goings of Lohan and Ronson remain a staple among headlines.

While the spotlight shone on the couple's happenings and whereabouts, little attention was given to the alarming fact that a group of American citizens were being denied their right to go anywhere outside US borders. During the same week that Lilo and SamRo claimed their official couple status, Roberto Levato of *New American Media* broke a key story. Persons of Mexican descent were being subjected to unreasonable and arbitrary demands to prove that they were citizens of the United States before getting a passport. US citizens living on and around the US-Mexico border are plaintiffs in a class action lawsuit alleging that by denying them passports, the US State Department is engaging in racial discrimination. Plaintiffs say that the US government is denying them passports because they are persons of Mexican and Latino descent whose births were assisted by *parteras*, or midwives. One plaintiff, Texas native David Hernandez, a decorated US Army veteran, says, "We were all born here. We're all citizens. The only difference is that we're Hispanic, we grew up poor and we happened not to be born in a hospital. My mother had to pay a partera $40 instead." ACLU attorneys for the plaintiffs say they have documented a systematic pattern of racial discrimination among hundreds, perhaps thousands of US citizens of Mexican descent. Lovato states, according to the ACLU's Robin Goldfaden, "that although midwifery is a long-held tradition among whites, blacks and others living in Appalachia, Texas and other parts of the United States where hospital-assisted birth is unaffordable or unavailable, the denial of passports is only taking place among people of Mexican descent living along the southern border."[7]

Here are a few other news stories that were not widely covered on television network and cable news during the same period which were arguably of more significance than Lilo and SamRo:

> Published on Sunday, September 28, 2008, by the *Guardian*: "Why Are Mothers Still Dying in Childbirth? More than 500,000 women die in pregnancy or childbirth every year in the developing world due to lack of proper care"
> Published on Monday, September 29, 2008, by American News Project: "The End of Free-Market Fundamentalism—But is it really? And where is American capitalism headed?"
> Published on Tuesday, September 30, 2008, by Inter Press Service: "Bush Had No Plan to Catch Bin Laden after 9/11"

6. November 5, 2008 was the day after an historic election in which the American people voted the first African American, Barack Obama, into the nation's highest office. It had been a particularly long campaign season, starting a full two years before Election Day. Yet after two years of almost constant campaigning, there was one story corporate media felt should be the focus of post-election coverage: the imminent arrival of the new First Puppy. The new puppy had been a topic of discussion since early summer, but the coverage fervor spiked right after the election. Coverage primarily focused on what breed the Obama family would choose and whether or not the dog would come from a shelter. Rampant speculation among media elites ensued.

While Americans were checking boxes in online polls about which dog breed they felt the Obamas should adopt, reports of an American air strike on an Afghan wedding party were at first overlooked, then distorted and disputed by US government officials and the press. This US air strike killed numerous Afghans, mostly women and children. Afghan leaders estimated that up to ninety civilians died in the attack, and American military leaders, which at first denied these facts, later downplayed the losses, saying only thirty-three civilians were killed. Further, this has not been the only Afghan wedding hit by a US air strike. Rather than delve into the significance of the Afghan deaths and the plight of everyday people in the war torn country, the corporate media lamented how the strikes affected Afghan public opinion of America's presence there, thus creating a strategic hurdle for war planners. For the Pentagon and their corporate media stenographers, the air strikes were a PR problem, not a war crime or humanitarian nightmare. This is classic News Abuse.

It is true that US air strikes, especially those that kill innocent civilians, do little to encourage a favorable view of US policy in the region. However, to Afghans, this is a serious, ongoing problem, not a PR blunder. The significance of the great loss of Afghan civilian lives was a subject that, in comparison, received a mere sliver of the coverage corporate media devoted to distorting the outcome of the attacks or the introduction of one canine life into the American Presidential family. In this case, both Junk Food News and News Abuse produce a one-two punch that knocks out any chance of a legitimate debate about US war policy or international law in Afghanistan. Acquisition of the First Pup, however, is one campaign promise Obama has kept, along with his pledge to increase US military presence in Afghanistan, thus ensuring more violence in this already devastated country.[8]

Here are a few other news stories that were not widely covered on television network and cable news during the same period which were arguably of more significance than the First Puppy:

> ➤ Published on Wednesday, November 5, 2008, by Inter Press Service: "Massive Iraqi Death Toll Ignored by Tabloid Culture"
> ➤ Published on Thursday, November 6, 2008, by Inter Press Service: "For Peace, The US Will Have to Change"
> ➤ Published on Friday, November 7, 2008, by Inter Press Service: "Coca Cultivation Up Despite Six Years of Plan Colombia"

7. On November 20, 2008, Spencer Pratt and Heidi Montag—the reality TV couple whose on-off relationship has been chronicled by MTV's show *The Hills*—tied the knot near Cabo San Lucas, Mexico, after sipping margaritas on the beach. In an unprecedented feat, the ubiquitous couple known as "Speidi" managed to don the cover of *Us Weekly* magazine featuring a photo spread of the ceremony while simultaneously being described in other articles as having "quietly eloped." The couple also publicly acknowledged that their wedding was not legally binding. Upon hearing news of the elopement, Heidi's father, Bill, remarked, "then we just have to have another wedding here!" It would, indeed, be out of character for the couple—whose lives

consist of a string of endless publicity stunts—to opt for only one media spectacle of a wedding.

Not everyone was making light of the institution of marriage during that same week in late November. Quite to the contrary, on Tuesday, November 24, the chief of a California state commission that enforces election law launched an investigation of the Church of Jesus Christ of Latter-day Saints regarding alleged violations in the Proposition 8 campaign. The Fair Political Practices Commission notified the Mormon church that it would investigate a claim that the church did not disclose the value of non-monetary campaign activities, including alleged phone bank operations from Utah and Idaho that targeted California voters. The complaint was filed November 13 by Fred Karger, an activist who opposed the constitutional ban on same-sex marriage approved by 52 percent of voters on Election Day. Karger, a former political consultant who helped organize boycotts against "Yes on 8" donors, said he learned about the operations from reports in local newspapers. "Once you go out of the church membership and contact voters, that becomes a non-monetary contribution," one that must be reported to the state, Karger said. Media concentration on a staged celebrity elopement unfortunately overshadowed possible election fraud that might have had a profound impact on thousands of real California couples hoping for equal rights.[9]

Here are a few other news stories that were not widely covered on television network and cable news during the same period which were arguably of more significance than Speidi:

> Published on Thursday, November 20, 2008, by the *Baltimore Sun*: "Police Spied on Activists Through '07: Protest groups say they haven't gotten the full story from state"
> Published on Friday, November 21, 2008, by One World.net: "Economy Hitting Women Hardest, Say Experts"
> Published on Friday, November 21, 2008, by *Times Online/UK*: "National Intelligence Council Report: Sun Setting on The American Century"

8. On Monday, March 2, 2009, jury selection was expected to begin in the trial of the San Francisco Giants' Barry Bonds. The number one home-run hitter in baseball history was charged with ten counts of perjury, stemming from the 2003 testimony that he had never knowingly used performance-enhancing drugs. Prosecutors elected to appeal US

District Court Judge Susan Illston's ruling that the positive steroid tests and other key evidence were inadmissible in the proceedings after Bonds's former trainer, Greg Anderson, refused to testify. The prosecutors contended that the evidence, including alleged failed steroid tests, doping calendars, and drug ledgers seized from the home of Anderson, proves that Bonds knowingly used steroids and then lied about it before a federal grand jury during the 2003 Bay Area Laboratory Cooperative (BALCO) trial. Legal proceedings won't resume until July at the earliest.

The very same Monday that Americans—bombarded by media coverage of the Bonds case—were awaiting the determination of his fate, the Supreme Court ruled in three separate cases of a far more somber nature. The Justices offered no remarks on their move to reject appeals of American and Vietnamese victims of Agent Orange in favor of Dow Chemical, Monsanto, and other companies that made the toxic chemical defoliant and other herbicides used by the military in Vietnam. Although Agent Orange has been linked to cancer, diabetes and birth defects among Vietnamese soldiers and civilians and American veterans, the court said companies are shielded from lawsuits brought by US military veterans or their relatives because the law protects government contractors in certain circumstances who provide defective products. The news

media's ongoing interest in Bonds's case shows their commitment to infotainment. Apparently, America's favorite pastime trumps high court rulings that leave victims, particularly veterans, in the dugout while corporations keep hitting legal home runs.[10]

Here are a few other news stories that were not widely covered on television network and cable news during the same period which were arguably of more significance than Barry Bonds:

> Published on Monday, March 2, 2009, by the *Guardian*: "CIA Admits to Destroying More Interrogation Videos; Bush scandal resuscitated as pressure builds for Obama to support an investigation into the CIA's detention practices"

> Published on Monday, March 2, 2009, by *Gourmet*: "The Price of Tomatoes: Keeping Slavery Alive in Florida. If you have eaten a tomato this winter, chances are very good that it was picked by a person who lives in virtual slavery"

> Published on Thursday, March 5, 2009, by Inter Press Service: "Military Dominance in Mideast Proven a Costly Myth"

9. Following in the footsteps of older sister Britney, Jamie-Lynn Spears is making a repeat appearance on this year's list. The pregnancy of Jamie-Lynn Spears was the second place Junk Food News story last year, and the arrival of her daughter, Maddie Briann, lands at number nine this year. She gave birth to the baby girl on the morning of June 19, 2008 in a south Mississippi hospital, according to a friend of the Spears family, who disclosed the details to the Associated Press and asked not to be identified because the family had not yet announced the baby's birth. In addition to being the younger sister of Britney, Jamie-Lynn is also famous for her starring role on *Zoey 101*, a Nickelodeon sitcom about prep school friends. The network issued a statement about the birth, saying, "We wish her and her family well." Nickelodeon spokeswoman Marianne Romano said that filming of the fourth and final season of *Zoey 101* was completed the summer before Spears became pregnant.

During the same week, UN Refugee Agency (UNHCR) released a report about the increasing number of refugees worldwide. "Much of the increase in refugees in 2007 was a result of the volatile situation in Iraq," said the UNHCR in its annual survey of "Global Trends." Over 37 million people were living as refugees from conflict or persecution at the end of 2007, marking the second straight year of increases after a five-year decline. In Iraq alone, by 2008, there were close to 5 million refugees as a result of US occupation.

"We are now faced with a complex mix of global challenges that could threaten even more forced displacement in the future," said the UN's High Commissioner for Refugees Antonio Guterres. "They range from multiple new conflict-related emergencies in world hotspots to bad governance, climate-induced environmental degradation that increases competition for scarce resources, and extreme price hikes that have hit the poor the hardest and are generating instability in many places."[11]

Here are a few other news stories that were not widely covered on television network and cable news during the same period which were arguably of more significance than the Spears family:

> Published on Thursday, June 19, 2008, by the *Washington Times*: "Cheney Linked To Torture Tactics"
> Published on Friday, June 20, 2008, by the *Toronto Star*: "'Sexual Violence 'a Tactic of War,' UN Council Says"
> Published on Thursday, June 19, 2008, by the *Guardian*: "Welcome To 'The Disco': Music As Torture"

10. "The doctors have told her if she goes back to smoking drugs it won't just ruin her voice, it will kill her," said Mitch Winehouse of his daughter Amy after she collapsed and was hospitalized June 16, 2008. It was also reported that as a result of smoking crack cocaine and cigarettes, the singer had early stage emphysema, an irregular heartbeat, and would need an oxygen mask to breathe if she couldn't stop. Her publicist later said Mitch had misspoken "out of his concern for her." "She is not diagnosed with full-blown emphysema, but instead has early signs of what could lead to emphysema," Tracey Miller, her US-based representative, told the Associated Press. Winehouse, whose repertoire of hits includes an anthem vowing never to check into rehab, and who has also received treatment at a drug rehabilitation center, was reportedly covered in nicotine patches and has been "flourishing" in response to treatments. Mitch Winehouse appeared to be rather apologetic for misinforming the public in regards to the condition of his daughter.

However, an egregious lack of apology or any compensation for ex-detainees on behalf of the US government may have gone entirely unnoticed if it hadn't been reported by Tom Lasseter in the McClatchy newspapers two days after Ms. Winehouse's collapse. To date, the US government has not given any of the thirty-eight former Guantánamo detainees—who have been found not to be enemy combatants by tribunal hearings—financial compensation, or apologized for wrongfully imprisoning them, shipping them around the world and holding them without legal recourse. In January, 2009, the US Court of Appeals for the District of Columbia Circuit dismissed a case filed by four former Guantánamo detainees who alleged that their mistreatment amounted to physical torture and religious harassment. The appeals court decided that because the former detainees were foreigners who were detained outside sovereign US territory at the time, "they did not fall with(in) the definition of 'person.'" For the record, the US Constitution provides due process protections for any persons, regardless of citizenship. This has been a right in Anglo culture since the Magna Carta dating back to 1215.[12]

Here are a few other news stories that were not widely covered on television network and cable news during the same period which were arguably of more significance the woes of Winehouse:

> Published on Sunday, June 22, 2008, by the *Sunday Herald (Scotland)*: "US Military Deny That New Prison Is Planned as 'Guantánamo Two;' Afghan-US relations hit by 'climate of distrust'"
> Published on Sunday, June 22, 2008, by Inter Press Service: "Women Leaders Ask, Where Is Our Money?"
> Published on Monday, June 23, 2008, by BBC News: "Protests Over Afghanistan Deaths"

NEWS ABUSE

While the News Abuse category may be confusing in relation to Junk Food News, one distinction is that News Abuse stories are about serious issues or are genuinely newsworthy items. However, the way they are presented in the corporate press has been misrepresented in terms of how the stories have been manipulated, trivialized, distorted, personalized, or more aptly, tabloidized. Stories about aging women's fertility, domestic abuse, and views of the working class are relevant. Murders and scientific tales of wonder are significant, but they are often turned into fodder for court jesters and circus acts by corporate media instead. In this past historic election year, in lieu of sober dialogue examining

America's long held racial tensions, there were overblown stories judging the "blackness" of Barack Obama and how he symbolized the "end of racism" in America. Similar deductions were made with respect to Obama's poor bowling prowess, inferring that his inability to bowl a perfect game meant he was doomed to be an incapable leader, out of touch with the common voter. This was especially touted by the media's new electoral hero and spokesperson for the masses, Joe the Plumber. Too often important news topics are hijacked, trivialized, and made into hypothetical meta-critiques by the punditocracy. News Abuse stories are transformed from potentially newsworthy items into far more titillating yet irrelevant distractions as a result. Sadly, here are this year's News Abuse stories in detail.[13]

Top Five News Abuse Stories for 2008 and 2009:

1. Octomom
2. Chris Hits Rihanna
3. Joe the Plumber
4. Obama Can't Bowl: He's Out of Touch with Joe the Plumber
5. The Blackness of Obama

1. The number one abused story this year is the tale of Nadya Suleman, a 33-year-old single unemployed woman who, through in vitro fertilization, became pregnant with octuplets and gave birth to the second living set ever on February 26, 2009. Frequently referred to as "Octomom," Suleman was already mother to six children, all of whom were also conceived through IVF, before becoming pregnant with the octuplets. In the past, doctors have diagnosed Suleman—who has admittedly spent around $100,000 on fertility treatments—with paranoia, depression, and post-traumatic stress syndrome. The mother of fourteen children hasn't been employed since her first pregnancy, but has collected more than $165,000 in disability payments, according to workers compensation and medical records. She also receives disability payments for three of her six previous children. Apart from milking her newfound notoriety, Octomom's only current means of supporting her growing brood are student loans and a reported $460 a month in food stamps.

America's fascination and disgust with the spectacle of Octomom is clearly exacerbated by a societal increase in budget-consciousness brought on by the recession. Funding for her down payment on a $565,000, 2,583-

square-foot house in La Habra, California, largely came from selling pictures of the children and doing various interviews and appearances. In April 2009, Suleman filed for a federal trademark of the "Octomom" name. However, a Texas company not affiliated with her beat her to the punch and filed to trademark an "Octomom" game for the iPhone. Describing the forthcoming game, the company's CEO remarked, "You press on her belly and she has babies." Octomom has also signed a deal with Eyeworks, the third-largest independent television producer in the world, for a new reality show that is not yet scheduled for American broadcast. The serial mother cunningly exploits the phenomenon of News Abuse, creating a surreal and nauseating publicity cycle. By watching them on television or supporting them through limited government aid, it appears that one way or another the public will be doing its part to provide for the future of the Suleman children. Is this Octomom exploiting herself? Or is she just trying to jump on the bandwagon to take advantage of what the corporate media are doing to her anyway?

Instead of discussing the significance of fertility issues for couples, the fact that the US leads the industrialized world in infant mortality rates, growing economic hardships for single parents and children without health care, medical ethics, or that record numbers of women are having planned and unnecessary cesarean sections, the corporate media feeds off one Octomom and her children. There are clearly more important things in need of media attention that affect the lives of many.[14]

2. On the evening of February 8, 2009, a fairytale-esque story of young love blossoming in the warm glow of the Hollywood spotlight turned, suddenly, into a chilling nightmare when a conflict between young pop stars Chris Brown, nineteen, and Rihanna, twenty-one, turned physical. "I'm going to beat the . . . out of you when we get home! You wait and see," an infuriated Brown shouted at Rihanna, according to a police affidavit. The assault had occurred after a recording industry party in Beverly Hills. Though the incident was immediately all over the news, the shock value (and thus coverage worthiness) of the story escalated when a photo of a post-encounter, bruised and battered Rihanna was leaked to the public. The assault caused Rihanna's "mouth to fill with blood and blood to splatter all over her clothing," wrote a detective at the scene. Brown, who was charged with two felonies, assault, and criminal threats, faces a maximum of five years in prison if convicted.

Though subsequent public boycotts of Chris Brown's music and removal of his hits from radio airwaves in many places may have seemed appropriate, these things do not change the fact that the media egregiously abused this tragic tale of two young adults caught in unfortunate and painful circumstances (that have no doubt worsened exponentially in this climate of eagerness where the goal is to cover the most juicy and horrifying details of the incident.) Interestingly enough, hip hop star P. Diddy confirmed reports that he opened up one of his homes to Brown and Rihanna so the pair could "talk about a situation they're in," which only solidified the notion in the public eye that the lives of Hollywood celebrities are but a massive, interwoven soap opera destined to play out on televisions and newsstands. Further, rather than allowing the incident to generate a discussion on the problem of domestic violence, especially in the younger generation, the news coverage focused instead on the specific celebrity implications of the matter. Taking the issue more seriously than most, Oprah Winfrey explored issues of domestic abuse with guest co-host Tyra Banks on a show dedicated to the topic on March 12, 2009. However, what kind of message does this send to the public? When a topic as rampant and problematic in America as domestic violence is only given considerable attention when a couple of celebrities are afflicted by it, that's not just domestic abuse; it's News Abuse.[15]

3. Something magnificent happened during the campaign season of 2008; the American dream was realized and its name was Joe the Plumber. Samuel "Joe" Wurzelbacher's notoriety came to him in October after he briefly debated taxes with then-candidate Barack Obama in his own front yard. The Democratic presidential candidate was doing some neighborhood campaigning in Toledo, Ohio, when confronted by Wurzelbacher, who asked him if he believed in the American dream. "I'm getting ready to buy a company that makes $250,000 to $280,000 a year," he inquired awkwardly, "your new tax plan is going to tax me more, isn't it?" Obama responded by telling Mr. Wurzelbacher that "spreading the wealth around" was always good. The phrase was quickly seized upon by the Republican opponent John McCain, conservative bloggers, and commentators as having revealed a desire to redistribute wealth (implying some type of socialism).

At the final presidential debate, Joe began as a walk-on part in McCain's story of how Obama's taxes would hurt small business owners. "Joe wants to buy the business that he has been in for all of these years, worked ten, twelve hours a day. And he wanted to buy the business but he looked at your tax plan and he saw that he was going to pay much higher taxes," McCain started off. "Joe was trying to realize the American dream." Joe's name came up around two dozen times during the ninety-minute debate, including when the Republican nominee referred to him as "my old buddy, Joe the Plumber." After that night, Mr. Wurzelbacher was besieged with local and national news media, willingly granting interviews.

As it turned out, there wasn't much attention paid to who Joe actually was, nor to the average worker for that matter. Joe's real name was Samuel, he was not a licensed plumber, and with a reported income of $40,000 a year, he was unlikely to be buying a company any time soon, so he would probably benefit from Mr. Obama's tax plan. Ironically, the United Association of Plumbers, Steamfitters, and Service Mechanics endorsed Barack Obama, as opposed to the Republican candidate, backed by Joe the Plumber. Working class issues and union workers were sidetracked by this scripted reality sideshow made ready for primetime.

Since the election, Joe has kept himself pretty busy. Wurzelbacher's book, *Joe the Plumber: Fighting for the American Dream,* that addresses his ideas about American values, is now available for purchase. He also covered Israel's side of its offensive in Gaza (in case the US press wasn't already doing that enough) as a correspondent for the conservative website http://pjtv.com. Although foreign reporters usually need to provide proof of experience to receive government authorization to report from Israel, Wurzelbacher was escorted on his first reporting gig ever by the head of the Government Press Office and a press office photographer. He also hired a publicity team and continues making appearances, including one at an Alcohol Tobacco and Firearms party in Colorado themed "Enjoy Your Freedoms While You Still Have Them." Meanwhile, workers at places like GM are hoping to enjoy their jobs and pensions while they still have them.

It was the campaign season for Joes in 2008, from Joe the Plumber, who has said that when Obama showed up in his neighborhood he'd just been tossing the football with his son, to Joe "Lunch Pail" Biden, to Sarah Palin's Joe Six-pack. These attempts to conjure up an image that seems in touch with the "Average Joe" are hardly a new occurrence; they date back to the presidency of Andrew Jackson and the so-called era of the Common Man. Successfully resonating with those who identify as chasing after that simple American dream can be extremely helpful, especially for members of the elite who have so little in common with the majority of Americans. And what, in Joe the Plumber's words, does this dream include? "A house, a dog, a couple rifles, a bass boat." Perhaps a book deal, a press pass, and national celebrity as well. While seeming to know a lot about what's up with Joe the Plumber, Americans are still waiting to learn more about the plight of workers and what can be done to improve the lives of millions of hard working people.[16]

4. As part of a new emphasis on a more laid-back, face-to-face style of campaigning during his six-day bus tour of Pennsylvania, Barack Obama made a stop at Pleasant Valley Lanes in the town of Altoona on March 29, 2008. It was there that Obama kicked off a notorious round of bowling with a gutter ball, and ended it with a total score of 37 out of 300. "My economic plan is better than my bowling," he told fellow bowlers. "It has to be," one onlooker called out. However, in the following weeks, the amount of news coverage allotted to said economic plan paled in comparison to the fateful game of bowling in Altoona.

A fixation on Obama's ill-conceived attempt to connect with blue-collar residents of central Pennsylvania quickly became apparent throughout newspapers, magazines, the Internet, and TV, particularly on MSNBC. "You know, this cuts to 'is this person real? Do they connect with me as a voter?' You know, for someone who's in a bowling league in northeast central Pennsylvania, in Scranton and Wilkes-Barre, they can't identify with someone getting a 37 over seven frames," Reuters Washington correspondent Jon Decker declared on an April 14 edition of *MSNBC Live*. During the April 1 edition of MSNBC's *Hardball*, host Chris Matthews asked Sen. Claire McCaskill (D-MO), "Let me ask you about how he—how's he connect with regular people? Does he? Or does he only appeal to people who come from the African-American community and from the people who have college or advanced degrees?" Matthews's comment on the previous day's edition of *Hardball* was even more unconscionable: "This gets very ethnic, but the fact that he's good at basketball doesn't surprise anybody, but the fact that he's that terrible at bowling does make you wonder." Wonder about what in terms of governing a country? Perhaps the wealthy, privileged Matthews should have spent more time talking with the working people for whom he claimed to speak.

On the March 31 edition of MSNBC's *Morning Joe*, host Joe Scarborough called Obama's bowling performance "dainty," saying to co-host Willie Geist, "You know Willie, the thing is, Americans want their president, if it's a man, to be a real man. You get 150, you're a man, or a good woman." Geist replied, "Out of my president, I want a 150, at least." Everyone who could belittle Obama with a jab at his poor bowling performance did so; from opponent Hilary Clinton, who joked at a press conference on April Fool's Day, "I am challenging Senator Obama to a bowl-off," to a ten-year-old girl with a more impressive scorecard than the presidential candidate. In an April 2 article spotlighting her on NYDailyNews.com, fourth grader Gabriella Llamas of New Jersey offered some words of wisdom, "You have to look at the pins when you throw it."

Almost a full year later, Obama appeared on the *Tonight Show* to tout his economic plan and told Leno that he had been practicing in the White House bowling alley and scored an unimpressive 129. "It's like— it was like Special Olympics or something," the president said, inciting laughter from the audience. With little relevance to the majority of society, the topic of Obama's Bowl-O-Rama once again became "news." Not only was the president's joke a perpetuation of a cruel stereotype, Special Olympians said, it was factually incorrect as well. One of the nation's top Special Olympics bowlers, Kolan McConiughey stated, "He bowled a 129. I bowl a 300. I could beat that score easily."

In this case of News Abuse, Obama's opportunity to resonate with working-class voters through his economic policies was eclipsed by his recreational shortcomings. Precious airtime spent on his inability to bowl could easily have been spent analyzing labor policies, rising unemployment, or average consumer debt. Instead, the public got News Abuse. Is anyone caught in the midst of this story-run-amuck going to put it into perspective? "Being a good bowler," said young Gabriella Llamas, "doesn't make you a good president." Maybe. Or maybe she just hasn't been watching enough *Hardball*.[17]

5. In February of 2007, *Time* magazine trumpeted the following head-line question, "Is Obama Black Enough?" Had anyone asked whether Bush or Clinton where white enough? Or black enough, for that matter? No. But with a biracial man that identifies as African-American, the corporate press couldn't contain its intrigue: is he Huey Newton or Uncle Tom? Was he *really* black, as an Associated Press piece wondered with inclusion of commentator Christopher Hitchens, stating, "We do not have our first black president. He is not black. He is as black as he is white." Never mind what Obama himself said on the topic: "I identify

as African-American . . . that's how I'm treated and that's how I'm viewed. I'm proud of it." Thereafter ensued a raging debate in the nation's newspapers and cable shows: was Obama black, and if so, was he black enough? Other opportunities to discuss America's sordid history of slavery and racial tensions took a backseat.

Among the most absurd displays of concern with Obama's ethnic identification was on MSNBC's *Tucker*, with conservative host Tucker Carlson leading a discussion of Obama's blackness with an all-white panel of journalists. All mused about how certain demographics would identify with an ethnically nebulous Obama, without any evidence or expertise on the matter, let alone any personal experience with racial identity politics for African-Americans. At one point in the segment, Carlson said Obama "could just as easily identify as white [but] if he made that decision, the left would jump on him." Given that Obama identifies as African-American, it seems odd for anyone to suggest he could easily identify as something other than how he sees himself. Again, while all of this chatter persisted, looking at the racial divides in America's past and present became less important somehow. Many in the corporate press seemed far more interested in seeing how Obama stacked up to their own cultural stereotypes of African Americans and proceeded to use that as a yardstick of his blackness. FAIR media analyst Janine Jackson noted in several instances that elated pundits claimed that a more moderate (and more white?) Obama was not Al Sharpton or Jesse Jackson (and that his wife, Michelle, was no Angela Davis). The *Atlanta Journal Constitution's* Jim Wooten went so far as to say after Obama's election that it indicated that "the political system that discriminated and the people who designed it are dead and gone," and Jonah Goldberg at the *Chicago Tribune* declared that the Obama election clearly indicated America was a cured society, one of new tolerance.

Not to be outdone, NBC's Chris Matthews remarked, "No history of Jim Crow, no history of anger, no history of slavery . . . all the bad stuff in our history ain't there with this guy." Obama's election somehow vanished history. Of course, some wanted to play race both ways. Offering no evidence, GOP head Michael Steele complained the media didn't challenge Obama because he was black. Would that be the same media that was so interested in Obama's blackness, or rather, his possible whiteness, or the same media that proclaimed race was a dead issue in America of the twenty-first century?

Perhaps these folks are not paying attention to life for many people of color in America. For many in the elite press corps, a "post-racial" America seemed around the corner, yet most attention went to speculating whether or not Obama would give fair treatment to whites. Meanwhile, many parts of the US didn't get the "post-racial" memos printed in the corporate press and on cable television. Sociologist and Project Censored director Dr. Peter Phillips points out, citing a recent UCLA Civil Rights Report, "What is difficult for many whites to accept is that geographical/structural racism still serves as a significant barrier for many students of color. Whites often say racism is in the past, and we need not think about it today. Yet, inequality stares at us daily from the barrios, ghettos, and from behind prison walls." Phillips goes on to state, "Racial inequality remains in the US. People of color continue to experience high rates of poverty, significant unemployment, police profiling and repressive incarceration. School segregation is a continuing concern among race scholars as well." In fact, school segregation on racial lines is heading back to the days before *Brown v. Board of Education*, especially in the western US.

Only weeks before the unprecedented inauguration of an African-American president, the alleged ushering in of "post-racial" America, an all too commonly occurring tragedy should serve as a potent reminder of the racial divisions that still plague the US. This was the shooting to death by BART police of an unarmed, subdued young African-American man named Oscar Grant in Oakland, CA. This incident clearly illustrates how it will take more than electing a black person to the White House to end institutionalized racial violence. It will take more than hope to change course as a society and more than mere decrees from the punditocracy.

In conclusion, Phillips offers sage advice: "We are at a time in society when a majority of the population has elected a black president of the United States. This presidency is a hugely symbolic achievement for race relations in the US. We must not, however, ignore the continuing disadvantages for people of color and the resulting advantages gained by whites in our society. Institutional policies and segregation contribute to continuing inequalities that require ongoing review and discussion. Efforts against racism must continue if we are to truly attain the civil rights goal of equal opportunity for all."[18]

IN CONCLUSION: WHERE DO WE GO FROM HERE?

Unless we change direction, we are likely to end up where we are headed.
—Chinese proverb

After reviewing the Junk Food News and News Abuse stories, one thing becomes clear. The notion that corporate media are somehow serving the public good with their selection of news is both a tragedy and a farce. What they are providing are distractions and distortions that lead to a more uninformed, unaware, and unprepared electorate in a democratic society. Big media executives regularly tell Congress and the FCC they are only giving the public what the public wants. Yet survey after survey shows that the public, while liking entertainment, prefer their news to only present the facts and then to show opposing views. The past two years at regional FCC hearings on deregulation, the public overwhelmingly said they wanted more diversity, more views, and more choices. Still, every year, Americans must remain idle as they watch another season of *American Idol* or America's Toughest Sheriff on *Smile . . . You're Under Arrest*. News and entertainment lines have been blurred to the point of a new genre where news is entertainment and entertainment becomes news: that's infotainment.

The US is not only increasingly a nation of obese people, but is on the verge of another equivalent phenomenon of cultural and mental obesity. We are a nation awash in a sea of information, yet we have a paucity of understanding. We are a country where over a quarter of the population knows the names of all five members of the fictitious family from *The Simpsons,* yet only one in a thousand can name all the rights protected under the first amendment to the US Constitution. The people rely on the news to tell them what's going on. Instead, too often, We The People get news abused or are left with junk. Journalistic values have been sold out to commercial interests and not even our core national and constitutionally protected values are sacred. Garbage in, garbage out. Enough is enough. This Fourth Estate Sale is over. It's time for media revolution.

In 1976, the same year as the founding of Project Censored, there was a film released called *Network*. The main character was a disillusioned television news anchor named Howard Beale. In the film, Beale gave his viewers real advice about media bias, propaganda, and output of useless and trivial information. He shouted, "I'm as mad as hell and I'm not going to take this anymore!" Thirty-three years later, let's all scream it from the rooftops and post it to the blogosphere. It's time to escape "mediacracy" and declare our mental independence from corporate "news," which oft turns out not to be news at all.[19]

MICKEY HUFF is associate professor of history at Diablo Valley College and the associate director of Project Censored and the Media Freedom Foundation.

FRANCES A. CAPELL is a Project Censored intern, a teaching/research assistant for Professor Mickey Huff, and a junior majoring in creative writing at San Francisco State University.

Special thanks to teaching assistant Rebecca Barrett, who assisted with research, and Meg Huff, who helped edit this chapter.

Notes

1. For a more detailed introduction of Junk Food News, see Carl Jensen's *Censored: The News That Didn't Make the News—and Why* (Chapel Hill, NC: Shelburne Press, 1993, pp. 89–96, 1993). The Neil Postman quote is the general subject of his 1985 work titled *Amusing Ourselves to Death*. The "Twinkie" quote from Carl Jensen in this paragraph was from an e-mail conversation between Jensen and chapter author Mickey Huff and others on April 14, 2009. For Project Censored's more detailed history of Junk Food News and the emerging category of News Abuse see Peter Phillips, *Censored 2001* (New York: Seven Stories Press, pp. 251–264, 2001). This is project founder Carl Jensen's chapter "Junk Food News 1877–2000." Each book volume of *Censored* has had a chapter on Junk Food News since 1993 with the addition of the News Abuse category beginning in 2001. Jensen originally began looking into Junk Food News in 1984 after criticism that Project Censored was crying censorship when some journalists were saying it was merely a matter of news or editorial judgment. If that's the case, news and editorial judgment have been skewed to the trivial for some time as the trend of Junk Food News continues to grow. That said, it is also the case that the major media do sometimes break important stories, i.e., they do not always fail the public. However, they do so often enough undercover, or they ignore important issues in the name of covering Junk Food News, that it is essential to monitor this and report on it to spread awareness. The press have constitutionally protected rights to inform and hold those in power to account, regardless of ideology. If the corporate media can't do that, We the People will.

2. Peter Phillips and Andrew Roth. *Censored 2008* (New York: Seven Stories Press, 2007, pp. 184–185). For reports about skewed corporate media coverage of Anna Nicole Smith's death see http://thinkprogress.org/2007/02/09/anna-nicole-media-embarassment/ and http://www.ryersonline.ca/blogs/83/Anna-Nicole-Smith-coverage-becoming-too-much .html. For more on undercovered stories of the time, see stories #1, and #2 from *Censored 2008* and *Censored 2009* online at http://www.projectcensored.org/top-stories/ category/y-2008/ and http://www.projectcensored .org/top-stories/category/y-2009/ respectively. President Bush's comment on the economy can be found here: http://www.swamppolitics.com/news/politics/blog/2007/08/bush_fundamentals_of _our_econo.html.

3. Georgina Dickenson, "14-time Olympic gold medal winner Michael Phelps caught with cannabis pipe," *News of the World*, February 1, 2009, online at http://www.newsofthe-

world.co.uk/news/150832/14-times-Olympic-gold-medal-winner-Michael-Phelps-caught-with-bong-cannabis-pipe.html; "Phelps acknowledges photo of him smoking a bong," *FOXSports.com*, February 2nd, 2009, http://msn.foxsports.com/other/story/9160136/Report:-Picture-shows-Phelps-using-bong; "Michael Phelps escapes pot charges," *Vancouver Sun*, February 16, 2009, http://www.vancouversun.com/sports/Michael+Phelps+escapes+charges/1295645/story.html; Suzanne Bohann, "Climate Change May Be Stoking Stronger Winds, Altered Oceans," *Contra Costa Times*, February 3, 2009, http://www.commondreams.org/headline/2009/02/03-5/. On the record marijuana arrests see Peter Phillips and Andrew Roth, *Censored 2009* (New York: Seven Stories Press, pp. 99–103, 2008). This Top 25 Censored Story from 2009 is also archived at http://www.projectcensored.org/top-stories/articles/20-marijuana-arrests-set-new-record/.

4. "Please Stop Calling Jessica Simpson Fat," http://www.nbcbayarea.com/around_town/the_scene/Stop-Calling-Jessica-Simpson-Fat.html, February 6, 2009; "Jessica Simpson Shocks Fans with Noticeably Fuller Figure," *FOXNews*, January 27, 2009, http://www.foxnews.com/story/0,2933,483204,00.html; Marcus Baram, "Obama Talks Football, Troop Withdrawal, Malia and Sasha's School, and Jessica Simpson," *Huffington Post*, February 1, 2009, http://www.huffingtonpost.com/2009/02/01/obama-talks-football-troo_n_162971.html; "Call for New Focus on Food Security Ahead of Madrid Meeting," January 26, 2009, http://www.commondreams.org/headline/2009/01/26-3/. For more on global starvation, see Peter Phillips's "Global Starvation Ignored by American Policy Elites," September 10, 2008, at http://www.projectcensored.org/articles/story/global-starvation-ignored-by-american-policy-elites/.

5. Jill Rosen, "Michelle Obama's golden ensemble symbolizes hope," *Baltimore Sun*, January 20, 2009, http://www.baltimoresun.com/entertainment/news/bal-lifestyle-dress0120,0,6505702.story; Booth Moore, "Michelle Obama's style: Change you can wear," *Los Angeles Times*, January 21, 2009, http://articles.latimes.com/2009/jan/21/nation/na-inaug-fashion21; "ACLU Says Failure to Properly Administer Medicines at Wisconsin Prison puts Women's Lives as Risk," *ACLU*, January 23, 2009, http://www.commondreams.org/newswire/2009/01/23-9/.

6. Dana Kennedy and Kristin Boehm, "The Jolie-Pitts Welcome a Son and Daughter," *People*, July 13, 2008, http://www.people.com/people/article/0,,20203411,00.html; Peter Mikelbank and Pete Norman, "Mayor Makes Jolie-Pitt Birthday Official," *People*, July 13, 2008, http://www.people.com/people/article/0,,20212215,00.html; "French Nuclear Facility to Shut Down After Uranium Leak," Agence France Presse, July 12, 2008, http://www.commondreams.org/archive/2008/07/12/10317/.

7. "Lindsay Lohan Confirms She is Dating a Woman," FOXNews.com, September 29, 2008, http://www.foxnews.com/story/0,2933,426845,00.html; Roberto Lovato, "Passports Denied: Mexican Americans Can't Travel," New American Media, September 22, 2008, http://news.newamericamedia.org/news/view_article.html?article_id=a35e8db592e30dd7c7f2fc84b654a104/.

8. "Obama Family Ponders First Pup," NPR, November 6, 2008, http://www.npr.org/templates/story/story.php?storyId=96713926; Bill Graveland, "Airstrike Kills 90 in Afghan Wedding Party," *Toronto Star*, November 5, 2008, http://www.thestar.com/News/World/article/530904/. For more on the News Abuse of the US air strikes story, see Peter Hart in Fairness and Accuracy in Reporting's journal, *Extra!*, June 2009, "Treating Civilian Deaths as a 'Sore Point:' The PR war in Afghanistan and Pakistan," p. 6. Online at http://fair.org.

9. Lorena Blas, "Montag and Pratt head for the hills and elope," *USA Today*, November 24, 2008, http://www.usatoday.com/life/people/2008-11-24-montag-pratt-hills-

elope_N.htm; Kristin Boehm, "Heidi Montag and Spencer Pratt Elope," *People*, November 24, 2008, http://www.people.com/people/article/0,,20242388,00.html; Mike Swift, "State officials to Investigate Mormon Church's Prop. 8 Activities," *San Jose Mercury News*, November 26, 2008, http://www.commondreams.org/headline/2008/11/26-2/.

10. Mark Starr, "The Steroids Trial of the Century," *Newsweek*, February 26, 2009, http://www.newsweek.com/id/186723; "Bonds Trial Delayed Until at least July," *National Post*, March 2nd, 2009, http://www.nationalpost.com/related/ topics/story.html?id=1345765; "No Justice for Victims of Agent Orange," *Associated Press*, March 2, 2009, http://www.commondreams.org/headline/2009/03/02-11/.

11. "Jamie Lynn Spears gives birth to baby girl," Associated Press, June 19, 2008, http://www.msnbc.msn.com/id/25264328/; Jazmine Rodriguez, "37 Million Refugees in Spotlight This Week," *One World.net*, June 20, 2008, http://www.commondreams.org/archive/2008/06/20/9761/. For more on Iraqi refugees resulting from US occupation, see the #1 story from *Censored 2009* online at http://www.projectcensored.org/top-stories/articles/1-over-one-million-iraqi-deaths-caused-by-us-occupation/, particularly the reporting of independent journalist Dahr Jamail.

12. Gil Kaufman, "Amy Winehouse Diagnosed with Emphysema, Singer's Father Says," *MTV.com*, June 23, 2008, http://www.mtv.com/news/articles/1589756/20080623/ winehouse_amy.jhtml; "Spokeswoman: Amy Winehouse Doesn't Have Emphysema," *Associated Press*, June 23, 2008, http://abcnews.go.com/Entertainment/WireStory?id =5225321&page=1; Tom Lasseter, "Day 4: US hasn't apologized to or compensated ex-detainees," McClatchy Newspapers, June 18, 2008, http://www.mcclatchydc .com/homepage/story/38885.html/. For more on suspension of Habeas Corpus and the media, see *Censored 2008*, story #1 at http://www.projectcensored.org/top-stories/articles/1-no-habeas-corpus-for-any-person/.

13. News Abuse became a category after 2001, seen in the 2003 annual *Censored* volume and beyond.

14. Jeremy Olshan, "Looney Octomom is baby 'buggy'," *New York Post*, February 7, 2009, http://www.nypost.com/seven/02072009/news/nationalnews/loony_octomom_153939 .htm?&page=0; "Octo-mom: "Student Loans" Will Raise Kids," NBC Los Angeles, February 10, 2009, http://www.nbclosangeles.com/news/local/NATLOcto-Mom-Interviews—.html; Gayle Fee and Laura Reposa, "Octomom Nadya Suleman's new baby: $565G diggs for brood," BostonHerald.com, March 10, 2009, http://www.bostonherald.com/track/inside_track/view/2009_03_10_Octomom_s_new_baby:_565G_digs_for_brood/srvc=home&position=also; Allen Duke, "'Octomom' seeks to trademark nickname for TV, diaper line," CNN, April 15, 2009, http://www.cnn.com/ 2009/US/04/15/octuplet.mom/; Belinda Luscombe, "The Octomom's Reality Show: Not for American Eyes," *Time*, June 2, 2009, http://www.time.com/time/arts/article/0,8599,1902269,00.html/.

15. Harriet Ryan and Richard Winton, "Police records paint a violent scene between Chris Brown and Rihanna," *Los Angeles Times*, March 6, 2009, http://articles .latimes.com/2009/mar/06/local/me-chris-brown-rihanna6; "Akon says he'd work with Chris Brown; Diddy confirms rumors," Associated Press, March 11, 2009, http://www.baltimoresun.com/topic/ny-etakono310,0,1683989.story?track=rss-topicgallery; "Rihanna's Father Angry With LAPD Over Leaked Photo," *MTV News*, February 20, 2009, http://www.mtv.com/news/articles/1605481/20090220/rihanna .html; "Oprah 'Sends Love' to Chris Brown and Rihanna," FOXNews.com, March 12, 2009, http://www.foxnews.com/story/0,2933,509040,00.html/.

16. Larry Vellequette and Tom Troy, "'Joe the Plumber' isn't licensed," *Toledo Blade*, October 16, 2008, http://www.toledoblade.com/apps/pbcs.dll/article?AID=/20081016/NEWS09/810160418; Robin Abcarian, "'Joe the Plumber' becomes a national fixture," *Los Angeles Times*, October 16, 2008, http://articles.latimes.com/2008/oct/16/nation/ na-joe16; "A six-pack of Joes," BBC News, October 21, 2008, http://news.bbc.co.uk/ 2/hi/americas/us_elections_2008/7679987.stm#gi; "'Joe the Plumber' lands a book deal," BBC News, November 20, 2008, http://news.bbc.co.uk/2/hi/americas/ 7739373.stm; Amy Tiebel, "Joe Trades Wrench for Reporter's Notepad in Israel," Associated Press, January 11, 2009, http://abcnews.go.com/International/WireStory?id =6622508&page=1; John Gerome, "Joe the Plumber hires Nashville publicity team," Associated Press, October 31, 2008, http://www.usatoday.com/news/nation/2008-10-31-2677540935_x.htm; "Guns, Liquor, Cigars and Joe the Plumber," *Face the State*, May 28, 2009, http://facethestate.com/buzz/16413-guns-liquor-cigars-and-joe-plumber; Ewen MacAskill and Suzanne Goldenberg, "US Election: Who is 'Joe the Plumber' aka Joe Wurzelbacher?" *Guardian.co.uk*, October 16, 2008, http://www .guardian.co.uk/world/2008/oct/16/uselections2008-johnmccain-barackobama-debate-joe-the-plumber/.

17. Devlin Barrett, "Obama Bowls for Pennsylvania Voters," *Huffington Post*, March 30, 2008, http://www.huffingtonpost.com/2008/03/30/obama-bowling-for-voters-_n_94097 .html; "On MSNBC, Reuters's Decker on Obama's bowling: "[T]his cuts to 'is this person real? Do they connect with me as a voter?'," Media Matters for America, April 14, 2008, http://mediamatters.org/research/200804140008; "As April Fools Gag, Clinton Proposes 'Bowl-Off' With Obama to Resolve Race," Associated Press, April 1, 2008, http://www.foxnews.com/politics/elections/2008/04/01/as-april-fools-gag-clinton-proposes-bowl-off-with-obama-to-resolve-race/?wpcf7=json&wpcf7=json&wpcf7=json&wpcf7=json&wpcf7=json; Stephanie Gaskill and Michael McAuliff, "Girl who knocks down more pins than Barack Obama offers bowling advice," NYDailyNews.com, April 2, 2008, http://www.nydailynews.com/news/politics/2008/ 04/02/2008-04-02_girl_who_knocks_down_more_pins_than_bara.html; Stacy St. Clair and John McCormick, "Not bowled over by Obama's Special Olympics joke," *Los Angeles Times*, March 21, 2009, http://articles.latimes.com/2009/mar/21/nation/na-obama-special-olympics21; Corey Williams, "Kolan McConiughey, Special Olympics Bowler: I Can Beat the President!" *Huffington Post*, March 20, 2009, http://www.huffingtonpost.com/2009/03/20/kolan-mcconiughey-special_n_177591.html/.

18. Ta-Nehisi Paul Coates, *Time*, "Is Obama Black Enough?" February 1, 2007, http://www.time.com/time/nation/article/0,8599,1584736,00.html; Jesse Washington, "AP: Many Insisting That Obama Is Not Black," December 14, 2008; http://www.huffingtonpost.com/2008/12/14/ap-many-insisting-that-ob_n_150846.html; "Tucker Carlson hosted all-white panel of journalists to discuss 'Obama's blackness,'" August 9, 2007; http://mediamatters.org/mmtv/200708090005; Janine Jackson, "Let's Talk About Race—or Maybe Not: Coverage of Obama and ethnicity says more about media," *Extra!*, March 2009; http://www.fair.org/index.php?page=3725; Eric Kleefeld, "Steele: The Media Didn't Vet Obama—Because He's Black," TalkingPointsMemo.com, May 22, 2009, http://tpmdc.talkingpointsmemo.com/2009/05/steele-the-media-didnt-vet-obama——because-hes-black.php; Peter Phillips, "A Black President Doesn't Mean Racism is gone in America," May 28, 2009; http://www.projectcensored.org/articles/story/a-black-president-doesnt-mean-racism-is-gone-in-america/.

19. For further reading on some of the themes here, see Rick Shenkman. *Just How Stupid Are We? Facing the Truth About the American Voter* (New York: Basic Books, 2008); for the Beale quote from the 1976 film, *Network*, see http://www.americanrhetoric.com/MovieSpeeches/moviespeechnetwork2.html.

Signs of Health
Stories of Hope and Change from 2008 and 2009

edited by Kate Sims and the people of *Yes! Magazine*

One of the first things people do when they are told that they face a serious illness or chronic condition is to seek out information. Today they will most likely log on to the Internet and "Google" it; in the "old days," they might have read up on the condition or called an organization. Whatever the method, the goal is not just to gather data, but to obtain good information about remedies that are apt to improve one's condition. People with a serious ailment want to know what they are up against—but, more importantly, they want to know what treatments will actually work to augment their health. And the more advanced the condition the more critical it is to get good information in a timely manner!

Many people across the political spectrum have come to the conclusion that we face this kind of serious condition on a global scale. While the condition is admittedly advanced, and there is little consensus on the source of the ailment or its cure, the vast majority agree that there is still hope for recovery. People all over the world who study ecosystems, resource depletion, climate change, economic structures, and social stability, tell us that, while time is short, the prognosis is not yet terminal.

So right now, what we need is good information about the treatments and remedies within society that are actually working. In this chapter, Project Censored devotes some time to examining the strategies that appear to be improving the health of the community, whether local or global. We look for stories about *what is happening* around the world—circumstances, events or programs that are *actually working* for people and that increase the *healthy functioning* of governments, economies, the environment and the human condition.

VOTING

Iraqi Organization Successfully Promotes Peaceful Elections

In October 2008, more than 100 citizen groups in all eighteen Iraqi provinces participated in a week of activities aimed at reducing violence in the January 2009 provincial elections. A coalition called La'Onf ("No to Violence" in Arabic) led the Week of Nonviolence. During that month, Iraqis in Sadr City and Al-Anbar province held conferences to encourage peaceful elections. Youth in Salahuddin played soccer in uniforms that bore the slogan, "Nonviolence is Our Choice." La'Onf participants also appeared on Arabic radio, television, and satellite broadcasts. "Within the polarized and dangerous political environment of Iraq . . . if you speak about resistance you are accused of supporting terrorists . . . but if you speak about nonviolence you are accused of supporting the occupation," says Ismaeel Dawood, a La'Onf founder. He says La'Onf is working to create a third way in which "nonviolence is a tool to resist occupation, terrorism, and corruption." The strategy worked, and on January 31, 2009, Iraq experienced its most peaceful elections since the occupation began.

Sources: Kristin Carlsen, "Iraqis Organize for Peaceful Elections," *Yes! Magazine*, Winter 2009; Roger McShane, "A New Era in Iraq?" Slate.com, February 1, 2009.

Fusion Voting Brings Disparate Groups Together

In New York, grassroots organizers and campaign volunteers of the Working Families Party have used the state's fusion voting laws to bring together voters across the political spectrum under the banner of higher wages, fair taxes, affordable housing, civil rights, and campaign finance reform—issues too often ignored in modern politics.

Putting that principle into action requires genuine courage and selflessness, because participants in the uprising must make their own personal power a lower priority than popular control. But, says writer David Sirota, "if more people become part of this uprising, we will not only transcend the partisan divide that gridlocks our politics, but reshape the very concept of what is possible."

Source: David Sirota, "Seeing Red and Feeling Blue in Purple America," *Yes! Magazine*, Fall 2008.

Campaign Donors Strike

During the 2008 election, more than 1,500 voters pledged "not to donate to any federal candidate unless they support legislation making congressional elections citizen-funded, not special-interest funded." The "donor strike" is sponsored by Change Congress, a campaign finance reform group that advocates banning lobbyist contributions and financing campaigns solely through a combination of public funds and small-dollar donations—a proposal polls show is supported by 69 percent of Americans. The website tracks how much funding their representatives stand to lose from the strike, which stood at 1.5 million in June 2009.

Source: Brooke Jarvis, "Campaign Finance Pledge," *Yes! Magazine*, Spring 2009.

ACCOUNTABILITY

Israelis Challenge Conflict Policies

Following the Israel/Palestine conflict in December 08/January 09 that resulted in the death of 1,300 Palestinians and thirteen Israelis, pro-Israel groups like Americans for Peace Now (APN), Brit Tzedek v'Shalom, and J Street began pushing for an immediate ceasefire. Meanwhile, Israelis in growing numbers began to question their government's actions in light of emerging stories of loss and hardship suffered by Palestinians. Within Israel, there was a series of antiwar demonstrations, some numbering in the thousands. Near the Gaza border, hundreds of residents of Sderot, an Israeli town that had been hit by Hamas rocket attacks, signed a petition calling for an end to the Israeli military operations.

Source: "Activists Seek Peace in Gaza," *Yes! Magazine*, Spring 2009.

Senator Introduces Bill to Strengthen Federal Whistleblower Protections

On February 2, 2009, Daniel Akaka (D-HI) introduced the Whistleblower Protection Enhancement Act of 2009. This legislation is designed to strengthen whistleblower protections to federal employees. In his press statement, Senator Akaka said, "The Whistleblower Protection Enhancement Act addresses many court decisions that have eroded protections for federal employees and have ignored congressional intent. Our legislation ensures that federal whistleblowers are protected from retaliation if they notify the public and government leaders of waste, fraud, and abuse. This protection is crucial to our efforts to improve government management, protect the public, and secure the nation. In this time of economic crisis, we must act to make sure the government uses tax dollars efficiently and effectively. Restoring credibility to the WPA is no less than a necessity."

Source: "Senators Reintroduce Bipartisan Whistleblower Protection Bill," Press Release by Senator Akaka, February 3, 2009.

Canadian Government Apologizes for Treatment of Native Peoples

On June 11, 2008, Canadian Prime Minister Stephen Harper apologized for policies that forcibly separated aboriginal children from their families from the 1870s to the late twentieth century and placed them in boarding schools where they were subjected to abuse. He said: "The Government of Canada now recognizes it was wrong to forcibly remove children from their homes . . . to separate children from rich and vibrant traditions . . . We apologize for having done this."

Source: DeNeen L. Brown, "Canadian Government Apologizes For Abuse of Indigenous People," Washington Post, June 12, 2008.

DEMOCRACY MOVEMENTS

A Model of Sustained Success in Brazil

Brazil's fourth-largest city, Belo Horizonte, has conquered hunger with a successful "food as a right" policy by acknowledging a simple principle of government that has yet to take hold in the United States: *the principle that the status of a citizen surpasses that of a mere consumer.* In 1993, the city assembled a twenty-member council of citizen, labor, business, and church representatives to advise in the design and implementation of a new food system. The city involves regular citizens directly in allocating municipal resources—a participatory budgeting system that started in the 1970s and has since spread across Brazil. During the first six years of Belo's food-as-a-right policy, perhaps in response to the new emphasis on food security, the number of citizens engaging in the city's participatory budgeting process doubled to more than 31,000. In 1993, Belo Horizonte declared that food was a right of citizenship and started working with local farmers to make good food available to all. Between 1993 and 2002 Belo Horizonte was the only Brazilian locality in which consumption of fruits and vegetables went up. One of its programs puts local farm produce into school meals. This and other projects cost the city less than 2 percent of its budget. In less than ten years, Belo Horizonte has cut its infant mortality and malnutrition by more than half.

Source: Frances Moore Lappe, "The City that Ended Hunger," Yes! Magazine, Spring 2009.

REGULATION

Europe Leads on Chemicals

A European-led revolution in chemical regulation requires that thousands of chemicals finally be assessed for their potentially toxic effects on human beings. It may also signal the end of American industry's ability to withhold critical data from the public. American companies, especially in the electronics field, are abiding by those regulations for overseas markets. Although this creates a dangerous situation in which the US has become a dumping ground for products not welcome in Europe, it is likely to force the EPA to improve regulation standards and oversight to keep from becoming obsolete.

Source: "US Lags Behind Europe in Regulating Toxicity of Everyday Products," Democracy Now!, February 24, 2009.

EPA Is Told To Reconsider Its Standards On Pollutants

In February 2009, a federal appeals court ruled that under the Bush administration, EPA standards for pollutants such as coarse and fine particulates were "contrary to law and unsupported by adequately reasoned decision making." The court ordered the Environmental Protection Agency to reconsider its standards for the fine particulates, which are linked to premature death from lung cancer and heart disease and to other health problems including asthma.

When the agency embraced the standards in 2006, its own scientific staff rejected them as too lax. On February 24, the United States Court of Appeals for the District of Columbia Circuit said the agency "did not adequately explain" why the standards were adequate. The court also upheld a ruling against Bush-era standards on emissions of mercury and other pollutants from coal-fired power plants.

Source: Cornelia Dean, "E.P.A. Is Told To Reconsider Its Standards On Pollutants," New York Times, February 25, 2009, A0–14.

HEALTH CARE

Majority Calls for Universal System

National health plans typically involve a single, publicly administered social insurance fund that guarantees health care coverage for everyone, much like Medicare presently does for seniors. Patients go the doctors and hospitals of their choice; health care providers largely remain private. Private health insurers are eliminated or their role is substantially reduced.

Despite the timidity prevalent in Congress, the public demand for universal health care continues to grow. In February 2009, a *New York Times*/CBS News poll showed, yet again, that the majority of Americans support national health insurance. The poll, which compares answers to the same questions from thirty years ago, found that "59 percent [of Americans] say the government should provide national health insurance, including 49 percent who say such insurance should cover all medical problems." Only 32 percent thought that insurance should be left to private enterprise. A related poll shows that 73 percent of Americans believe our health care system is in crisis or has "major problems," 64 percent believe the government should provide national health insurance coverage for all Americans, even if it would raise taxes, 55 percent favor one health insurance program covering all Americans, administered by the government, and paid for by taxpayers. 69 percent believe the government should make it easier to buy prescription drugs from other countries.

Sources: Michelle Levi, "Poll: Majority Would Pay Higher Taxes For Universal Health Care," CBS News, April 6, 2009; Sarah Van Gelder, "10 Policies for a Better America," *Yes! Magazine*, Fall 2008.

Physicians Join the Effort

A majority of physicians have joined the chorus as well. A survey in the *Annals of Internal Medicine* released early in 2008 showed that 59 percent of US physicians support the idea of national health insurance, a jump of 10 percentage points from five years ago.

Following the survey, over 5,000 US physicians signed an open letter calling on the president and Congress "to stand up for the health of the American people and implement a nonprofit, single-payer national health insurance system."

A bill in Congress, the US National Health Insurance Act, HR 676, embodies the single-payer model. Sponsored by Rep. John Conyers Jr. (D-MI), it currently has over ninety co-sponsors, more than any other health reform proposal. It is said to have a slim chance in 2009, but serious consideration may not be as far in the future as the corporate media would have us believe.

Source: Text of letter can be found at https://salsa.democracyinaction.org/o/307/t/5720/shop/custom.jsp?donate_page_KEY=3304.

MENTAL HEALTH

Brain research on Buddhist monks reveals the neurology of meditation

In 2004, when Dr. Richard Davidson of the University of Wisconsin used magnetic resonance imaging to look at the brains of Buddhist monks, he saw a prefrontal cortex—the part of the brain associated with happiness and other positive emotions—lit up in a way never before seen by researchers. Buddhist monks had off-the-charts gamma wave activity, which corresponds with focused thought. Testing of 150 control subjects showed no such patterns. Importantly, however, it did show low-level changes among subjects who were newly trained in meditation techniques, indicating that this exercise can benefit everyone— not just those who have dedicated their entire lives.

Source: Matthieu Ricard, "This is Your Brain on Bliss," *Yes! Magazine,* Fall 2008.

Humans are Hardwired to Cooperate

Scientists who use advanced imaging technology to study brain function report that the human brain is wired to reward caring, cooperation, and service. According to this research, merely thinking about another person experiencing harm triggers the same reaction in our brain as when a mother sees distress in her baby's face. Conversely, the act of helping another triggers the brain's pleasure center and benefits our health by boosting our immune system, reducing our heart rate, and preparing us to approach and soothe. Positive emotions like compassion produce similar benefits. By contrast, negative emotions suppress our immune system, increase heart rate, and prepare us to fight or flee.

Sources: David Korten, "We Are Hard-Wired to Care and Connect," *Yes! Magazine*, Fall 2008; "Hardwired to Connect: The New Scientific Case for Authoritative Communities," The Commission on Children at Risk, September 2003.

FOOD

Urban Gardens

Urban gardens are becoming a significant part of the effort to expand food security. Fifteen percent of the world's food is grown in urban areas, a figure that is expected to grow as food prices rise, urban populations grow and environmental concerns increase.

In the United States, urban farms and greenhouses are cropping up in urban "food deserts" (a part of the city devoid of full-service grocery stores but lined with fast-food joints, liquor stores and convenience stores selling mostly soda and sweets). Based on the Growing Power model founded by MacArthur Foundation fellow Will Allen, these urban farms produce tons of food each year and act as food distribution hubs and training centers. Deep in the heart of depressed urban areas, these farms are producing 159 different kinds of food, including vegetables, grains, poultry and fish—and building community in the process.

Source: "Oasis in an Urban Food Desert," *Yes! Magazine*, Spring 2009.

The Gardens of Cuba

In Cuba, urban gardens have bloomed in vacant lots, alongside parking lots and even on city rooftops. Originally, they sprang from a military plan for Cuba to be self-sufficient in case of war, and have evolved into a world model for localized food sovereignty and sustainability. They have proven extremely popular, occupying 35,000 hectares (86,000 acres) of land across the Caribbean island. The gardens sell their produce directly to the community, so they are immune to the volatility of fuel and transportation costs, and, out of necessity, grow their crops organically. In September 2008, the government began renting out unused state-owned lands to farmers and cooperatives.

Source: Esteban Israel, "In Eat Local Movement, Cuba is Years Ahead," Reuters, December 16, 2008.

Community Involvement

Food policy councils are part of an effort to make food a matter of community interest and to offer local food to schools. Their work is leading to state nutrition reforms throughout the country. In New Mexico, recent bans on junk food in schools (despite heavy industry pressure) and increased funding for farmers' markets were the direct result of work done by the New Mexico Food and Agriculture Policy Council, an organized group of farmers, nutritionists, educators, activists, and others on a mission for healthier food. Similar efforts are taking place in Oregon, Connecticut, Washington, Ohio, Tennessee, Colorado, and elsewhere.

Source: "Fresh from . . . the City," *Yes! Magazine*, Spring 2009.

Progress at the Federal Level

While the farm bill passed in 2008 does nothing to replace the destructive industrial model currently in place, advocates for a good food policy have gained strength and the bill did offer some positive steps that are worth mentioning:

> ➤ A record $78 million for organic agriculture research, five times the previous funding level
> ➤ $22 million to help farmers and handlers get certified as organic
> ➤ $10.3 billion increase in funding for nutrition programs, including food stamps
> ➤ $35 billion in subsidies for agricultural commodity programs
> ➤ $33 million for the Farmers Market Promotion Program
> ➤ $1.2 billion to expand the Fresh Fruit and Vegetable Program that will enable 3 million low income children across the country to have access to healthier food options

Perhaps most importantly, new mandates strengthen USDA oversight of genetically modified organism (GMO) crops. The new regulatory framework will reduce the number of GMOs in development and reduce the potential for future GMO contamination events at field trial test sites.

Source: Debra Eschmeyer (Center for Food & Justice), "The good, bad, and ugly in our national five-year agricultural plan," *Grist*, June 4, 2008.

WATER

Community Stewardship of Water

New Mexico communities are reclaiming sustainable irrigation through the use of *acequias*, a tradition of community-controlled irrigation that is making a comeback. The term refers not only to the network of canals that brings water to farmers across the Southwest, but also to a system of traditional community management of the water—a system of sharing that is equitable to everyone in the area. Students from the cities are now being brought back to farms and taught how to maintain *acequias*. Students record the work to post on YouTube and podcast on Acequia Radio.

Source: James Trimarco, "Steward Water," *Yes! Magazine,* Spring 2009.

Bangladesh offers a model of fair water governance

Poor landless fishers in Bangladesh have benefited significantly from major reforms in the governance of inland water bodies. Inland fisheries are critically important for food security and livelihoods, but access to lakes by poor, landless fishers has historically been problematic. Wealthy people tend to dominate annual leasing arrangements, leaving poorer members of the community to work as share catchers with minimal reward.

With the introduction of the Oxbow Lakes Small-Scale Fishermen Project in the early 1990s, low-income fisher groups were able to take a more active role in management of local water resources. Since that time, the situation has improved significantly. Long-term lease arrangements for public lakes and shores have been introduced and, as a further measure to protect poor people, membership of the groups is limited to those living below a set poverty line. The case study demonstrates how reforms in leasing practices, and the empowerment of people to manage their resources sustainably, can lead to broad benefits for both poor communities and the government.

Source: "Linking Land and Better Governance," International Fund for Agricultural Development, June 2006.

Mayors Say No to Bottled Water

In 2008, the US Conference of Mayors voted to eliminate the use of bottled water by governments and to encourage the use of municipal water. The non-binding resolution was adopted at the mayors' annual gathering, held in Miami in June 2008. The mayors cited the environmental impact of bottled water and the higher cost: 40 percent comes from municipal water systems, yet bottled water typically costs 1,000 to 10,000 times more.

Source: Layla Aslani, "Mayors Lead on Bottled Water," *Yes! Magazine,* Fall 2008.

HEALTHY ENVIRONMENT

NATURAL RESOURCES

Central Appalachian Network Grows Sustainability and Local Economy

A network of local people in Appalachia have set in motion a regional economy that can last in a low-carbon world. More than a decade ago, when farmers, loggers, and entrepreneurs from Ohio, Kentucky, Virginia, Tennessee, and West Virginia set out to re-energize flagging local economies, they weren't thinking about climate change or resource management. They set up the Central Appalachian Network in an effort to create jobs and build communities. But as they rediscovered local living, they found that it had ecological benefits as well. Over the last decade, the Central Appalachian Network has developed a system of sustainable forestry, farming and craftsmanship while helping its citizens reinvest in their own communities.

Source: Madeline Ostrander, "Appalachia—Down a Greener Road," *Yes! Magazine,* Spring 2008.

Holistic Range Management Shows Results

In the 1990s, the idea of Holistic Range Management was anathema to the idea of environmental conservation. It was thought that the only way to save the grasslands was to get rid of the cattle. Over the last ten years, however, ranchers who have taken the time to practice ranching methods that allow the herds to move and the lands to rest are noticing a return on their "investment." And for those ranchers the dividends have included more productive ranches with healthy ecosystems, biodiversity, healthy water and mineral cycles, and land covered with plants instead of bare dirt.

Source: Madeline Ostrander, "Restoring the Range," *Yes! Magazine,* Spring 2008.

Native Communities in Canada Gain Power Over Resources

Indigenous communities in Canada scored a major victory in June 2008 when AbitibiBowater, one of North America's largest newsprint and forest products companies, halted logging on the traditional territory of the Grassy Narrows First Nation in Ontario. The company yielded to a campaign begun in December 2002, when two young mothers from Grassy Narrows felled two trees across the area's major logging road. Their action sparked the longest running blockade in Canadian history.

The Grassy Narrows victory is part of a thriving movement for indigenous self-determination in Canada. Dozens of First Nations from the Haida in British Columbia to the Kitchenuhmaykoosib Inninuwug (KI) in northern Ontario are asserting control over their land.

Source: Jessica Bell, "First Nations Halt Clear Cutting," *Yes! Magazine*, Fall 2008.

Congress Votes "Yes" to Sweeping Public Lands Protection

On March 25, 2009, Congress approved a massive public lands bill that protects two million acres of wilderness in nine states and a thousand miles of rivers, a 50 percent increase in the wild and scenic river system. The package of 164 separate bills bundled together, known as the Omnibus Public Lands Management Act of 2009 (H.R. 146), passed by a vote of 285 to 140. The bill was signed by President Obama on March 30.

The Act will provide the largest expansion of the National Wilderness Preservation System in fifteen years. It established new national trails, national parks, and a new national monument, and provides legal status for the National Landscape Conservation System, which will protect some of the country's most spectacular landscapes. Ocean protections are also contained in the legislation, authorizing the national ocean exploration, research, mapping and preservation programs.

The Federal Ocean Acidification Research and Monitoring Act will authorize a coordinated federal research program on ocean acidification.

Some Republicans objected to the measure because it blocks millions of acres for energy development, expands federal land holdings, and overrides private property rights.

Sources: "Congress Votes 'Yes' to Sweeping Public Lands Protection Act," Environment News Service, March 25, 2009, and "Obama Signs Public Lands Protection Bill Into Law," Environment News Service, March 30, 2009.

Nations Ban Uranium Mining

The governments of Ireland and British Columbia, Canada, have banned uranium mining, which contaminates water, soil, and air, and causes elevated cancer rates among miners and nearby residents. Ireland prohibits nuclear power generation, so it "would be hypocritical to permit the extraction of uranium for use in nuclear reactors in other countries," said natural resources minister Eamon Ryan. British Columbia does not currently have uranium mines, although mining companies have their eye on the province. Earlier this year, the northern territory of Nunatsiavut placed a three-year uranium mining moratorium on Labrador Inuit land.

Source: "Ireland and BC Ban Uranium Mining," *Yes! Magazine,* Fall 2008.

CLIMATE CHANGE POLICIES

Brazil's Pledge to Protect Rainforest Bears Watching

In December 2008, the Brazilian government made its first ever serious commitment to Amazon rainforest protection, pledging to reduce the rate of deforestation by 70 percent over the next decade. If the target is met, it will keep 4.8 billion tons of CO_2 out of the atmosphere. The announcement came just before the international climate meeting in Poznan, Poland, where negotiators debated how to reward countries that reduce deforestation. Brazil's plan seeks international funding. Norway has pledged $1 billion over seven years to the effort. Despite the pledge, however, industrial uses of the area have remained unchanged and bear watching.

Source: Brooke Jarvis and Bill McKibben, "Brazil Agrees to Protect Rainforests," *Yes! Magazine,* Spring 2009.

Nation's First Mandatory Cap and Trade Program

Policymakers and environmental groups across the country are keenly watching the progress of the nation's first mandatory carbon cap and trade program, the Regional Greenhouse Gas Initiative (RGGI), which requires power plants in the northeastern US to buy permits for carbon emission. The Initiative held its first carbon auction in September 2008. Ten northeastern and mid-Atlantic states are participating in RGGI, considered a possible test case for federal legislation to reduce greenhouse gas emissions. The auction is step one in an effort to ratchet down carbon emissions by 10 percent over ten years.

Meanwhile, seven western states, along with British Columbia, Manitoba, Ontario, and Quebec, have drafted the nation's farthest-reaching cap and trade plan to date. If approved by the state and provincial governments, the plan would reduce carbon from all major sources—including electricity, industry, transportation, and fuel use—by 15 percent by 2020. California has already granted its Air Resources Board the authority to begin instituting the program, and has also recently passed a landmark bill that will fight climate change by providing financial incentives to local governments to reduce urban sprawl, cut back car travel and encourage public transit use.

Source: Madeline Ostrander, "States Hold First Carbon Auction," *Yes! Magazine*, Winter 2009.

Using Soil to Reduce CO2

Throughout the Amazon Basin, pockets of fertile, dark soil ("terra preta" in Portuguese) can be found. Terra preta is the product of slash-and-char agriculture practiced centuries ago by indigenous farmers who baked wood to charcoal and worked it into the soil.

Terra preta is big news today because these dark soils represent the possibility of natural, long-term carbon sequestration, a way to return some of the carbon once stored in fossil fuels back to the ground. Carbon in charcoal does not reoxidize to become CO_2, as does the carbon stored in plants when they decompose. Nearly half of the carbon content of biomass that is charred and returned to the soil can remain stable for hundreds and even thousands of years—keeping carbon out of the atmosphere far longer than other, more cyclical biological sinks like no-till farming or planting trees.

Source: Brooke Jarvis, "Terra Preta, a Solution Buried in the Dirt," *Yes! Magazine*, Spring 2008.

ENERGY

US is World's Largest Wind-energy Producer

The US has surpassed Germany as the world's largest wind-energy producer. In Texas, oil tycoon T. Boone Pickens has turned to wind as the answer to the nation's energy problems. Pickens has leased hundreds of thousands of acres for a wind farm in west Texas, where he plans to build the world's largest wind farm to power the state's cities. The wind energy can displace natural gas generation, Pickens believes, freeing it up to fuel cars and trucks.

Source: "US is World's Largest Wind-energy Producer," *Yes! Magazine,* Fall 2008.

World's Biggest Solar Farm

The world's largest solar photovoltaic farm, generating electricity straight from sunlight, is taking shape near Moura, Portugal. It is expected to supply 45MW of electricity each year, enough to power 30,000 homes. Portugal is pitching to lead Europe's clean-tech revolution with some of the most ambitious targets and timetables for renewables. Its intention is to wean itself off oil within a decade and set up a low carbon economy in response to high oil prices and climate change. Portugal expects to generate 31 percent of all its energy from clean sources by 2020.

Source: John Vidal, "World's Biggest Solar Farm at Centre of Portugal's Ambitious Energy Plan," *Guardian,* June 7, 2008.

UN report details the rise in renewable energy investment

Climate change worries, growing support from world governments, rising oil prices and ongoing energy security concerns combined to fuel another record-setting year of investment in the renewable energy and energy efficiency industries in 2007, according to an analysis issued July 1, 2007 by the UN Environment Program (UNEP).

"The clean energy industry is maturing and its backers remain bullish. These findings should empower governments—both North and South—to reach a deep and meaningful new agreement by the crucial climate convention meeting in Copenhagen in late 2009," Achim Steiner, the head of UNEP, says.

"Just as thousands were drawn to . . . the Klondike in the late 1800s, the green energy gold rush is attracting legions of modern-day prospectors in all parts of the globe," says Steiner, referring to a 60 percent rise in global renewable energy investment, to $148 billion at the end of 2007. The report speaks of continued worldwide sustainable energy investment.

Source: "No Gloom In Green Energy," *Green Energy News,* July 6, 2008, Vol. 13 No. 16.

FINANCIAL INSTITUTIONS

Community banks offer financial shelter amid the fallout

Of the roughly 8,500 bank charters in the United States, 8,000 are held by community banks, which tend to be locally managed, cover relatively small geographical areas, and have under $1 billion in capital. In an informal survey released September 22, 36 percent of Independent Community Bankers of America (ICBA) members reported an increase in deposits. In addition to providing FDIC deposit insurance, offered by all US banks, community banks foster economic security for their entire communities because deposits are kept local.

"The overwhelming message is that community banks didn't have anything to do with the mess on Wall Street," said Steve Verdier, senior vice president and director of congressional affairs at ICBA. "We made common sense loans that people could pay back. The last thing that community bankers want to do is make a loan that is bad for the bank, the people, and the community."

Source: "Community Banks Provide Safe Haven in Economic Storm," *Yes! Magazine*, Winter 2009.

Proposal for Common Good Bank melds traditional bank with credit union

The establishment of the Common Good Bank is sowing the seeds of evolution in community investing. The new model in banking promotes the common good by distributing excess profits to the community and by making all lending and spending decisions through participatory democracy. While the Common Good Bank model shares elements of community investment—including a focus on community development, small business lending, and financial empowerment of populations underserved by traditional financial institutions—it breaks new ground in three areas: First, it is dedicated to advancing the good not just of certain populations, but of *all*, from the local to the global community as well as the health of our planet. Second, it will distribute returns to members while granting (not loaning) net profits to the community with priority placed on those in the most need. And third, members will control the bank's lending and spending through participatory democracy.

The bank's participatory democracy melds elements of direct voting, direct representation by revocable proxy, paired instant runoff, range voting, approval voting, internet voting, and town meeting style discussions.

Source: Bill Baue, "Common Good Bank Advances One Branch of Community Investing Evolution," *Sustainability Investment News*, April 05, 2006.

LABOR EQUITY

From Wage Slaves to Worker-Owners

Low-wage workers are gaining economic stability and dignity by becoming co-owners of a cooperative. One example is Women's Action to Gain Economic Security, or WAGES, a San Francisco Bay-area organization that helps low-income women start cooperative businesses. Under a cooperative business model, each participant is both a worker and an owner of the venture, sharing the costs and profits equally.

For corporate employers, obligations to shareholders means a never-ending search for lower costs, and that often means employees are shunted aside. But that can't happen at a cooperative, because the workers, managers, and shareholders are the same people. They don't need to make huge profits for shareholders to stay in business, and there's no pressure to keep wages low. Co-ops also have the advantage of needing only modest amounts of capital to get started. People can pool their skills and resources.

While this worker-owned model has its challenges under our current economic system, it is gaining ground and providing secure income for people all over the US and the world.

Source: "Create Your Own Workplace," *Yes! Magazine*, Fall 2008.

Call for Corporate Minimum Tax

A 2008 report by the Government Accountability Office finds that nearly two-thirds of US companies paid no corporate income taxes for at least one year between 1998 and 2005. In October, both the Institute for Policy Studies and an editorial in the *Boston Globe* cited the GAO study, calling on Congress to enact a corporate minimum tax. They projected $60 billion in revenue from the tax, which they said could be used to stimulate the real economy.

Source: "Call for Corporate Minimum Tax," *Yes! Magazine*, Summer 2009.

GLOBALIZATION

Ecuador Questions Legitimacy of Foreign Debt

In November 2008, Ecuador became the first country to undertake an examination of the legitimacy and structure of its foreign debt. An independent debt audit commissioned by the government of Ecuador documented hundreds of irregularities and illegitimate mandates in contracts of debt with predatory international lenders. The commission recommended that Ecuador default on $3.9 billion in foreign commercial debts—the result of debts restructured in 2000 after the country's 1999 default.

Although Ecuador currently has the capacity to pay, dropping oil prices and squeezed credit markets are putting President Rafael Correa's plans to boost spending on education and health care in jeopardy. Correa has pledged to prioritize the "social debt" over debt to foreign creditors. In 2007 the Ecuadorian government paid $1.75 billion in debt service alone, more than it spent on health care, social services, the environment, and housing and urban development combined. Under the World Bank system, which oversees investment treaties, there is no public accountability, no standard set of judicial ethics rules, and no appeals process.

Sources: Daniel Denvir, "As Crisis Mounts, Ecuador Declares Foreign Debt Illegitimate and Illegal," AlterNet, November 26, 2008; Committee for the Integral Audit of Public Credit, Jubilee USA, "Invalid Loans to Ecuador: Who Owes Who" Part 1: http://www.youtube.com/watch?v=UxG7YBbM5Eg&feature=related; Neil Watkins and Sarah Anderson, "Ecuador's Debt Default: Exposing a Gap in the Global Financial Architecture," *Foreign Policy in Focus*, December 15, 2008.

US Loosens its Hold on the World Bank

The US is to lose its power to appoint the president of the World Bank after the UK's development secretary, Douglas Alexander, brokered a deal to throw open the post to candidates from any country. Backed by European governments and developing countries, Alexander overcame resistance from the US and Japan to secure a reform he described as "a significant step forward." Washington has had the right to hand-pick the president of the World Bank since the institution was founded after the Second World War, with Europe choosing the managing director of the International Monetary Fund.

Source: Heather Stewart and Larry Elliot, "US surrenders power to appoint World Bank president," *Guardian*, December 13, 2008.

COMMUNICATIONS

Cautiously Optimistic about Net Neutrality

The Obama election could spell good news for the media reform movement. On May 29, 2009, President Obama defended and made clear his position on keeping the Internet free, saying "Our pursuit of cybersecurity will not—I repeat, will not—include monitoring private sector networks or Internet traffic. We will preserve and protect the personal privacy and civil liberties that we cherish as Americans. Indeed, I remain firmly committed to net neutrality so we can keep the Internet as it should be—open and free."

The White House's review of cybersecurity recognized not only a commitment to net neutrality, but also to civil liberties and privacy. Obama said that the government would start treating the nation's digital infrastructure, broadband networks and computers as strategic national assets that should be "open and free."

This speech was the second time since the 2008 election that a top administration official came out for an open Internet. In his report to Congress, "Bringing Broadband to Rural America: Report on a Rural Broadband Strategy," Acting FCC Chairman Michael Copps made the same point: "The value of open networks is not a novel concept, but the Commission must act to ensure that the genius of the open Internet is not lost."

During his campaign Obama pledged, "I am a strong supporter of net neutrality . . . What you've been seeing is some lobbying that says [Internet providers] should be able to be gatekeepers and able to charge different rates to different websites . . . so you could get much better quality from the Fox News site and you'd be getting rotten service from the mom and pop sites. And that I think destroys one of the best things about the Internet—which is that there is this incredible equality there . . . as president I'm going to make sure that is the principle that my FCC commissioners are applying as we move forward."

However, large Internet providers like Comcast and Time Warner have taken bold actions over the last two years with their efforts to block content and close off certain content providers, and it remains to be seen whether Congress will support the Obama plan. So now is a good time to be optimistic—but cautiously optimistic.

Sources: Art Brodsky, "Obama Defends Net Neutrality; Is Anyone Listening?" *Public Knowledge,* May 29, 2009; John Eggerton, "Obama Committed to Network Neutrality," *Broadcasting & Cable,* May 29, 2009; Jon Healey, "Obama Exhumes Net Neutrality from the Tomb of Forgotten Issues," *Los Angeles Times,* May 29, 2009.

HOUSING

Land trusts offer haven from the foreclosure crisis

In a community land trust, families purchase homes but a nonprofit organization owns the land. This approach "protects affordability in perpetuity," says May Louie, DSNI director of capacity building. Housing experts across the country have their eye on community land trusts as proven means of preventing foreclosures. A survey released March 2008 found only two foreclosures among a national sample of 3,115 land trust homeowners.

In the Dudley Neighbors land trust of Boston, homebuyers receive a ninety-nine-year renewable and inheritable lease for use of the land. They agree that all future sales will be made to a low- or moderate-income buyer and follow a resale formula at a price that allows them to recoup the cost of home improvements and benefit from modest price appreciation. Also, Dudley Neighbors prohibits the shoddy construction that so often undermines affordable housing. Homebuyers often qualify for down payment and closing cost assistance through the Boston Home Certificate Initiative.

Homeowners also get protection from predatory lenders. Dudley Neighbors restricts loans to reasonable terms from approved lenders and steps in to help if homeowners miss payments due to job loss or medical crises. "Turnover in the land trust is very low," says Jason Webb. "People really plant roots in the community."

Source: "No Foreclosures Here," *Yes! Magazine,* Winter 2009; "Community Land Trust Keeps Prices Affordable—for Now and Forever," *Yes! Magazine,* Fall 2008.

"Housing First" Model Reduces Homelessness

The program Pathways to Housing provides immediate housing without prerequisites. This "housing first" approach to ending chronic homelessness for people with mental disabilities or problems is proving to work.

The statistics:

> ➤ The number of chronically homeless people in the United States

dropped by almost 30 percent between 2005 and 2007. Administration officials attribute much of that one-third drop to the Housing First Strategy.

➤ Public cost of an average chronically homeless person per year, living on the streets and in shelters: $40,000. Public cost of an average chronically homeless person per year, living in a supportive housing program like Pathways to Housing: $16,000.

➤ Pathways to Housing clients have an 85 percent five-year retention rate and drastic drops in emergency room visits, contacts with law enforcement, and psychiatric hospitalizations.

➤ More than 200 cities in the US and Canada adopted ten-year plans to end chronic homelessness; 67 percent of these plans include a Housing First program.

Sources: PathwaystoHousing.org; David Brancaccio, "Home at Last," *PBS' Now*, February 2, 2007.

SOCIAL POLICIES

Latin American Commission Stands Up to US on Drug War

In February 2009, the Latin American Commission on Drugs and Democracy issued a report, "Drugs and Democracy: Toward a Paradigm Shift," calling for the creation of a Latin American drug policy. The commission, led by former Brazilian, Mexican, and Colombian presidents, Fernando Henrique Cardoso, Ernesto Zedillo and Cesar Gaviria, stated that the available evidence indicates that the current US war on drugs has failed.

The commission proposes three specific actions: treat addicts as patients in the health system, evaluate decriminalizing cannabis possession and personal use, and reduce consumption through education targeted at youth. According to the report, despite the large investment of resources into the war on drugs, especially in Columbia and Mexico, drug trafficking and narco-violence has increased. The commission states that the long-term solution is to reduce the demand for the drugs in main consumer countries, the US and EU. The commission calls on these countries to share in the responsibility and implement policies aimed at reducing the demand for illicit drugs.

Source: Marina Litvinsky, "Latin American Leaders Say 'No' to US Drug War," *IPS News*, February 12, 2009.

Ecuador Declares Constitutional Rights for Nature

In September 2008, Ecuador became the first country in the world to declare constitutional rights to nature, thus codifying a new system of environmental protection. Reflecting the beliefs and traditions of the indigenous peoples of Ecuador, the constitution declares that nature "has the right to exist, persist, maintain and regenerate its vital cycles, structure, functions and its processes in evolution." The new constitution redefines people's relationship with nature by asserting that nature is not just an object to be appropriated and exploited by people, but is rather a rights-bearing entity that should be treated with parity under the law.

Ecuador's leadership on this issue may have a global domino effect. Mari Margil, associate director of the Environmental Legal Defense Fund, says that her organization is busy fielding calls from interested countries, such as Nepal, which is currently writing its first constitution. "I expect [multinational industries] to fight it," says Margil. "Their bread and butter is based on being able to treat countries and ecosystems like cheap hotels." Yet even as Ecuadorian President Correa continues the extractive economic model of development, if history is any indicator, Ecuadorians will successfully fight for the rights of nature with or without their president.

Sources: "Ecuadorian Assembly Approves Constitutional Rights for Nature," *Climate and Capitalism*, July 10, 2008; Cyril Mychalejko, "Ecuador's Constitution Gives Rights to Nature," Upside Down World, September 25, 2008.

ACKNOWLEDGMENT TO *YES! MAGAZINE*

Each year, the people of *Yes!* contribute the majority of the stories and help to build and edit this chapter. *Yes! Magazine* is an award-winning, ad-free, nonprofit publication that supports people's active engagement in building a just and sustainable world. Author and activist Van Jones calls it "the most important publication in the United States."

Project Censored agrees, and would like to offer a special thank you to Sarah Van Gelder and Kim Eckart for their help with our chapter this year.

CHAPTER 5

Truth Emergency: Inside the Military Industrial Media Empire

by Peter Phillips and Mickey Huff

> *When it comes to the news, the corporate view is "objective," all
> else is "propaganda."*
>
> —Studs Terkel

Among the most important Project Censored news stories of the past decade, one is the fact that over one million people have died because of the United States military invasion and occupation of Iraq. This, of course, does not include the number of deaths from the first Gulf War, nor the ensuing sanctions placed upon the country of Iraq that, combined, caused close to an additional two million Iraqi deaths. In the current Iraq War, beginning in March of 2003, over a million people have died violently primarily from US bombings and neighborhood patrols. These were deaths in excess of the normal civilian death rate under the previous government. Among US military leaders and policy elites, the issue of counting the dead was dismissed before the Iraqi invasion even began. In an interview with reporters in late March of 2002 when the War on Terror was in its infancy, US General Tommy Franks stated, "You know we don't do body counts."[1] Fortunately, for those concerned about humanitarian costs of war and empire, others do.

In a January 2008 report, the British polling group Opinion Research Business (ORB) reported that "survey work confirms our earlier estimate that over 1,000,000 Iraqi citizens have died as a result of the conflict which started in 2003. We now estimate that the death toll between March 2003 and August 2007 is likely to have been of the order of 1,033,000. If one takes into account the margin of error associated with survey data of this nature then the estimated range is between 946,000 and 1,120,000."[2]

The ORB report comes on the heels of two earlier studies conducted by Johns Hopkins University and published in the *Lancet* medical journal that confirmed the continuing numbers of mass deaths in Iraq. A study done by Dr. Les Roberts from January 1, 2002 to March 18, 2003 put the civilian deaths at that time at over 100,000. A second study published in the *Lancet* in October 2006 documented over 650,000 civilian deaths in Iraq since the start of the US invasion. The 2006 study confirms that US aerial bombing in civilian neighborhoods caused over a third of these deaths and that over half the deaths are directly attributable to US forces.

The magnitude of these million-plus deaths and creation of such a vast refugee crisis is undeniable. The continuing occupation by US forces has guaranteed a monthly mass death rate of thousands of people—a carnage so severe and so concentrated as to equate it with the most heinous mass killings in world history. Further, more tons of bombs have been dropped in Iraq than all of World War II.[3]

The American people are faced with a serious moral dilemma. Murder and war crimes have been conducted in America's name. Yet most Americans have no idea of the magnitude of the deaths and tend to believe that the deaths are only in the thousands and are primarily Iraqis killing Iraqis. Corporate mainstream media is in large part to blame.

The question then becomes: how can this mass ignorance and corporate media deception exist in the United States of America, and what impact does this have on peace and social justice movements in the country?[4]

TRUTH EMERGENCY AND MEDIA REFORM

In the United States today, the rift between reality and reporting has reached its end. There is no longer a mere credibility gap, but rather a literal Truth Emergency. Americans cannot access the truth about the issues that most impact their lives by relying on the mainstream corporate media. A Truth Emergency is a culmination of the failures of the fourth estate to act as a truly free press. This Truth Emergency exists not only as a result of fraudulent elections, pseudo 9/11 investigations, illegal preemptive wars, torture camps, and doctored intelligence, but also around issues that intimately impact everyday Americans. Yet these issues are rarely reported in corporate media outlets, where a vast majority of the American people continue to turn to for news and information.

Consider that most US workers have been faced with a thirty-five year decline in real wages while the top few percent enjoy unparalleled wealth with strikingly low tax burdens, creating a vastly disparate and widening wealth distribution gap. Furthermore, the US has the highest infant mortality rate among industrialized nations, is falling behind Europe and Asia in scientific research and education, faces closing factories and schools, is laying off teachers, has an actual 15 percent unemployment rate, multi-trillion dollar national debt, and a crumbling infrastructure, and is seriously lacking in health care quality and delivery. In fact, over 50 million Americans now lack health care coverage, resulting in the deaths of 18,000 people a year. America has entered another Gilded Age. Someone should alert the media.[5]

This Truth Emergency Movement held its first national strategy summit in Santa Cruz, California from January 25 to 27, 2008. Organizers gathered key media constituencies to devise coherent decentralized models for distribution of suppressed news, synergistic truth-telling, and collaborative strategies to disclose, legitimize, and popularize deeper historical narratives on power and inequality in the US. In sum, this truth movement is seeking to discover—in this moment of Constitutional crisis, ecological peril, and widening war—ways in which top investigative journalists, whistleblowers, and independent media activists can transform the way Americans perceive and defend their world.

There is another growing national movement to address mainstream media failures and policies in government: the Free Press or Media Reform Movement. However, this movement fails to address many issues of the actual Truth Emergency. During the 2008 National Conference for Media Reform (NCMR) in Minneapolis, MN, Project Censored interns and faculty conducted a sociological survey designed to gauge conference participant thoughts on the status quo of the news media as well as the truthfulness of corporate media news and the effectiveness of the media reform movement. The survey also sought to determine the level of belief and support in a Truth Emergency in the US and the varying degrees of support for key truth issues, regardless of their coverage at the NCMR conference.

The completed survey yielded 376 randomly selected NCMR attendees out of the 3,500 people registered for the conference. The survey has a statistical accuracy of plus or minus 5 percent at a 95 percent confidence interval, in that all the people at the NCMR hold the same beliefs.

Strong support was shown for the premise of a Truth Emergency in the US. The survey asked, Has corporate media failed to keep the American people informed on important issues facing the nation? Does a Truth Emergency exist in the United States?

The response was staggering. Ninety-nine percent strongly agreed, or agreed with the first question, and only seven percent of responders disagreed with the characterization of current events as a Truth Emergency in the US. Yet few of the events, panels, or talks at the conference reflected these concerns.

Discovering the most effective ways to chisel at the bulwark of corrupt corporate media will require continuing thought and effort. It is clear from our survey that media democracy activists strongly support the continuing development of independent media combined with aggressive reform efforts and policy changes as part of an overall media democracy movement. Activists also believe that both reform and grassroots independent media efforts will fit within an ongoing truth emergency theme that conducts deep investigative research into critical social justice issues. One activist said, "we cannot be afraid, democracy is in the balance."

While recognizing that this survey was done at an independent media activist "reform" conference, fully expecting a great deal of agreement on the questions, it was still amazing that there was almost total agreement for grassroots media efforts in addition to reform work (especially given that most of the emphasis of the conference was on reform of existing mainstream media rather than direct action and a grassroots movement approach with an independent and public-focused journalistic endeavor). In other words, it was reassuring to see support for a media movement of the people, by the people, and for the people.[6]

One statement on the survey, that a military-industrial-media complex exists in the US for the promotion of the US military domination of the world, received an 87 percent approval rating among the sample. This result showed that research done by Project Censored about the continuing powerful global dominance group inside the US government, the US media, and the national policy structure is widely believed by participants at the NCMR.[7]

NCMR participants also overwhelmingly believe the leadership class in the US is now dominated by a neo-conservative group of some several hundred people who share the goal of asserting US military power worldwide. This Global Dominance Group, in cooperation with major military contractors, the corporate media, and conservative foundations, has become a powerful long-term force in military unilateralism and US political processes.

THE GLOBAL DOMINANCE GROUP AND INFORMATION CONTROL

A long thread of sociological research documents the existence of a dominant ruling class in the US, which sets policy and determines national political priorities. C. Wright Mills, in his 1956 book on the power elite, documented how World War II solidified a trinity of power in the US that comprised corporate, military, and government elites in a centralized power structure working in unison through "higher circles" of contact and agreement.[8] This power has grown through the Cold War, and, after 9/11, the Global War on Terror.

The military expansionists from within the Reagan, George H. W. Bush, Clinton, and G. W. Bush administrations put into place solid support for increased military spending. Clinton's model of supporting the US military industrial complex held steady defense spending and increased foreign weapons sales from 16 percent of global orders to over 63 pecent by the end of his administration. After 9/11, during the presidency of George W. Bush, defense spending and the national deficit climbed dramatically and federal authority became more concentrated.

The US now spends over half of its discretionary budget on military related issues.

The Barack Obama administration is continuing the neo-conservative agenda of US military domination of the world—albeit with perhaps a kinder, gentler face. While overt torture is now forbidden for the CIA and the Pentagon, and symbolic gestures like the closing of the Guantánamo prison are in evidence, a unilateral military dominance policy, expanding military budget, and wars of occupation and aggression will likely continue unabated. That has been the historical pattern.

Obama's election brought a moment of hope for many. However, the new administration is not calling for decreased military spending or a reversal of US military global dominance. Instead, Obama retained Robert Gates, thus making Obama the first president from an opposing party in US history to keep in place the outgoing administration's Secretary of Defense/War. Additionally, Obama is calling for an expanded war in Afghanistan and only minimal long-range reductions in Iraq.

Major defense contractors were seriously involved in the 2008 elections. Lockheed Martin gave $2,612,219 in total political campaign donations, with 49 percent to Democrats ($1,285,493) and 51 percent to Republicans ($1,325,159). Boeing gave $2,225,947 in 2008, with 58 percent going to Democrats, and General Dynamics provided $1,682,595 to both parties. Northrop Grumman spent over $20 million in 2008 hiring lobbyists to influence Congress, and Raytheon spent $6 million on lobbyists in the same period. In a revolving door appointment, Obama nominated William Lynn, Raytheon's senior vice president for government operations and strategy, for the number two position in the Pentagon. Lynn was formally the defense department's comptroller during the Clinton administration and was reputed to have been unable to account for over three trillion dollars in defense department spending during his administration.[9]

The US now spends as much for defense as the rest of the world combined. At the beginning of 2009 the Global Dominance Group's agenda is well established within higher circle policy councils and cunningly operationalized inside the US Government. They work hand in hand with defense contractors promoting deployment of US forces in over 1,000 bases worldwide.

The corporate media in the US like to think of themselves as the most accurate news reporting source of the day. The *New York Times* motto of "all the news that's fit to print" is a clear example of this perspective, as is CNN's "most trusted name in news" and Fox News Channel's "We Report, You Decide" or "Fair and Balanced." However, with corporate media coverage that increasingly focuses on a narrow range of celebrity updates, news from "official" government sources, and sensationalized crimes and disasters, the self-justification of being the most fit is no longer valid in the US. In fact, several studies done by Diane Farsetta at the Center for Media Democracy showed Pentagon propaganda penetration on mainstream corporate news in the guise of retired generals as "experts" or pundits who turned out to be nothing more than paid shills for government war policy. While the Pentagon claimed this was legal, the Pentagon Inspector General's office rescinded a report of the most recent propaganda investigation and even removed the report from its website because the office concluded the study "did not meet accepted quality standards for an Inspector General work product."[10]

A global dominance agenda also includes penetration into the boardrooms of the corporate media in the US. In 2006 only 118 people comprised the membership on the boards of directors of the ten big media giants. These 118 individuals in turn sat on the corporate boards of 288 national and international corporations. Four of the top ten media corporations had major defense contractors on their boards of directors, including:

> William Kennard: New York Times, Carlyle Group
> Douglas Warner III: GE (NBC), Bechtel
> John Bryson: Disney (ABC), Boeing
> Alwyn Lewis: Disney (ABC), Halliburton
> Douglas McCorkindale: Gannett, Lockheed-Martin.

Given an interlocked media network, it is safe to say that big media in the United States effectively represent the interests of corporate America. The media elite, a key component of the Higher Circle Policy Elite in the US, are the watchdogs of acceptable ideological messages, the controllers of news and information content, and the decision makers regarding media resources.

An important case of Pentagon influence over the corporate media is CNN's retraction of the story about US military use of sarin (a nerve gas) in 1970 in Laos during the Vietnam War. CNN producers April Oliver and Jack Smith, after an eight-month investigation, reported on CNN on June 7, 1998, and later in Time magazine, that sarin gas was used in

Operation Tailwind in Laos, and that American defectors were targeted. The story was based on eyewitness accounts and high military command collaboration. Under tremendous pressure from the Pentagon, Henry Kissinger, Colin Powell, and Richard Helms, CNN and *Time* retracted the story by saying, "The allegations about the use of nerve gas and the killing of defectors are not supported by the evidence." Oliver and Smith were both fired by CNN later that summer. They have steadfastly stood by their original story as accurate and substantiated. CNN and *Time*, under intense Pentagon pressure, quickly reversed their position after having fully approved the release of the story only weeks earlier. April Oliver feels that CNN and *Time* capitulated to the Pentagon's threat to lock them out of future military stories.

Even ten years later, CNN has a difficult time reporting on their own complicity with the Pentagon in creating propaganda, this time with the retired Pentagon generals pundit scandal. The Pulitzer Prize for investigative reporting, which was announced in April of 2009, went to the *New York Times*'s David Barstow for his reporting on this very subject, yet CNN, while covering the list of Pulitzer winners, made no mention of his award or his reporting on the CNN/Pentagon connection (which was also reported by Diane Farsetta at PR Watch).[11]

Not only is the corporate media deeply interlocked with the military industrial complex and global dominance policy elites in the US, but the media is increasingly dependent on various governmental and corporate sources of news. Maintenance of continuous news shows requires a constant feed and an ever-entertaining supply of stimulating events and breaking news bites. The twenty-four-hour news shows on MSNBC, Fox and CNN maintain constant contact with the White House, Pentagon, and public relations companies representing both government and private corporations.

Symbiotic global news distribution is a conscious and deliberate attempt by the powerful to control news and information in society. The Homeland Security Act Title II Section 201(d)(5) specifically asks the directorate to "develop a comprehensive plan for securing the key resources and critical infrastructure of the United States including information technology and telecommunications systems (including satellites) emergency preparedness communications systems."

Media critic and historian Norman Solomon wrote in 2005, "One way or another, a military-industrial complex now extends to much of corporate media. In the process, firms with military ties routinely advertise in news outlets. Often, media magnates and people on the boards of large media-related corporations enjoy close links—financial and social—with the military industry and Washington's foreign-policy establishment."[12]

By the time of the 1991 Gulf War, retired colonels, generals and admirals had become mainstays in network TV studios during wartime. Language such as "collateral damage" flowed effortlessly between journalists and military men, who shared perspectives on the occasionally mentioned yet more rarely seen civilians killed by US firepower.[13]

In the early 1990s, Chris Hedges covered the Gulf War for the *New York Times*. Ten years later, he wrote, "The notion that the press was used in the war is incorrect. The press wanted to be used. It saw itself as part of the war effort. Truth-seeking independence was far from the media agenda. The press was as eager to be of service to the state during the war as most everyone else. Such docility on the part of the press made it easier to do what governments do in wartime, indeed what governments do much of the time, and that is lie."[14] Of course, this critique is not new. I. F. Stone, the iconoclastic investigative journalist once wrote, "All governments lie, but disaster lies in wait for countries whose officials smoke the same hashish they give out."[15]

The problem then becomes more complex. What happens to a society that begins to believe such lies as truth? What happens to leaders that begin to believe, too? And what becomes of those in the society that do not believe the lies because they find facts to be more of a guiding light? The run-up to the current war in Iraq concerning so-called weapons of mass destruction (WMDs) is a grand example. It illustrates the power of propaganda in creating not only public support for an ill begotten war, but it promotes a languishing, if not outright impotent, peace movement even when fueled by truth to stop a war based on false pretenses. The current war in Iraq was the most globally-protested war in recorded history even before it began, and this did nothing to prevent it and has done little to end it, even under a now-Democratic president that promised such on the campaign trail. The candidate of hope and change, with many progressive and peace groups in tow, has proven to be the same caliber of a leader in foreign policy that got the US into war in the first place.[16]

UNDERSTANDING MODERN MEDIA CENSORSHIP

In order to understand modern media censorship in the US, there is a growing need to broaden its definition. The dictionary definition of direct government control of news as censorship is no longer adequate. The private corporate media in the US significantly under covers and/or deliberately censors numerous important news stories every year. A broader definition of censorship in America today needs to include any interference, deliberate or not, with the free flow of vital news information to the American people. Modern censorship can be seen as the subtle yet persistent and sophisticated manipulation of reality in our mass media outlets. On a daily basis, censorship refers to the intentional non-inclusion of a news story—or piece of a news story—based on anything other than a desire to tell the truth. Such manipulation can take the form of political pressure (from government officials and powerful individuals), economic pressure (from advertisers, funders, and underwriters), and legal pressure (the threat of lawsuits from deep-pocket individuals, corporations, and institutions).

The common theme of the most censored stories over the past few years has been the systemic erosion of human rights and civil liberties in both the US and the world at large. The corporate media ignored the fact that *habeas corpus* can now be suspended for anyone by order of the president. With the approval of Congress, the Military Commissions Act (MCA) of 2006, signed by Bush on October 17, 2006, allows for the suspension of *habeas corpus* for US citizens and non-citizens alike. While the mainstream corporate media, including the *New York Times* with it's lead editorial piece published on October 19, 2006, have given false comfort that American citizens will not be the victims of the measures legalized by this Act, the law is quite clear that 'any person' can be targeted.[17]

Additionally, under the code-name Operation FALCON (Federal and Local Cops Organized Nationally), federally coordinated mass arrests occurring since April 2005 netted over 54,000 arrests, a majority of which were actually not violent criminals, the opposite of what was initially suggested. This unprecedented move of arresting tens of thousands of "fugitives" is the largest dragnet-style operation in the nation's history. The raids, coordinated by the Justice Department and Homeland Security, directly involved over 960 agencies (state, local and federal) and mark the first time in US history that all domestic police agencies were placed under the direct control of the federal government.[18]

All these events are significant in a democratic society that alleges to cherish individual rights and due process of law. To have them occur is a tragedy and farce. To have a free press not report them or pretend they do not matter is the foundation of censorship today.

ARE AMERICANS UNFEELING TOWARDS WAR?

The failure of the corporate media to cover moral issue-raising questions—like one million deaths of Iraqis—is a contributing factor to a very limited public response to the war on terror being conducted around the world by the US. Even when activists do mobilize, the corporate media coverage of antiwar demonstrations has been negligible and denigrating from the start.

Linda Milazzo writes about the major antiwar march in Washington, DC on September 15, 2007: "I, along with 100,000 kindred activists, marched through the nation's capital where we were pretty much ignored. The minimal media we did get was distorted and untrue. When a small, sadistic band of war-hawks showed up to oppose us, the press slanted their numbers as if they equaled our own. The truth is, their numbers were one-hundreth the size of ours, although one would never know that from this deceptive headline in the *Washington Post*, "Dueling Demonstrations."[19] It's a travesty to democracy that mainstream journalists of the so-called free press ignore the antiwar movement and serve the interests of their corporate masters in the military media-industrial complex to the detriment of the nation and perhaps the world.[20]

Not only does the corporate media disregard the antiwar movement in the US, but the human costs of the war are ignored as well. An investigative research study done by Project Censored at Sonoma State University focused on news photographs appearing on the front pages of the *New York Times* and the *San Francisco Chronicle* during two periods, from March to December 2003 and from January 2006 to March 2007. Examining these data, the researchers asked, how frequently do front-page news photographs depict war in Afghanistan or Iraq? And, to what extent do these photos portray the *human cost* of those wars?

Based on content analysis of over 6,000 front-page news photos, spanning 1,389 days of coverage, researchers found that only 12.8 percent of the photos analyzed relate in some way to the wars in Afghanistan and Iraq. A mere 3.3 percent of those front page news photos represent war's most fundamental human cost, by depicting dead, injured, or missing humans. This research documents the enormous gap between the number of actual deaths in Afghanistan and Iraq during this time span, which numbers hundreds of thousands, and the number of deaths depicted visually, through front page photographs— just forty-eight images of human death. Researchers concluded that the human cost of war is permitted only a small marginal position on the front pages of US newspapers.[21]

Visuals, including news photographs, play a crucial role in how readers experience newspapers and engage the stories that they contain. For example, the Poynter Institute's ongoing "Eyes on the News" study demonstrates that 90 percent of readers enter pages through large photographs or other visual images; running a visual element increases by three times the likelihood that the reader will read at least some of the accompanying text; and readers' comprehension and recall increase when photographs or other visuals accompany stories.

The one-two combination of the negation of human suffering and a neglected antiwar movement contributes to an underlying belief that the 9/11 wars and occupations are justified. A Gallup poll conducted in March of 2009 indicated, "Forty-two percent of Americans now say the United States made a mistake in sending troops to Afghanistan, up from 30 percent earlier this year and establishing a new high. Meanwhile, the 53 percent who say the Iraq war is a mistake is down slightly from 56 percent in January, and 60 percent last summer." While over 50 percent of the public still believes it was a mistake to invade Iraq, 58 percent still thinks invading Afghanistan was the right thing to do.[22]

Further, the corporate mainstream press continue to ignore the human cost of the US war in Iraq with America's own veterans. Veteran care, wounded rates, mental disabilities, denied or delayed VA claims, firsthand accounts of soldier experiences, and more are avoided like the plague in corporate mainstream media. Short of the Walter Reed VA hospital care scandal, little has been covered. One of the most important stories missed by the corporate press was about the Winter Soldier Congressional hearings in Washington, DC. The hearings, with eyewitness testimony of US soldiers relating their experiences on the battlefield and beyond, were only covered by a scant number of major media outlets including the *Boston Globe* and NPR, but only in passing mention. In contrast to the virtual corporate media blackout on American soldiers' views of the war, the independent, listener-sponsored, community Pacifica radio network covered the hearings at length.[23]

Americans do care about human suffering and external wars when they are informed about what the powerful are doing. Millions of Americans voted for Barack Obama as a peace candidate. Barack Obama's election to the US presidency in November of 2008 added to the view that something is being done to end the 9/11 wars, as there were many promises on the campaign trial hoping for change of Bush administration policies. This *belief* that change will come belies what Obama administration actions have actually shown about war policies, especially in Afghanistan, where US troop presence is actually growing, and this *belief* further contributes to a lackluster antiwar movement in the US despite what the facts show.[24]

THE LEFT PROGRESSIVE PRESS

Where the left progressive press may have covered some of the Winter Soldier issues, most did not cover the major story of Iraqi deaths. Even the left progressive media have shown limited coverage of the human costs of the 9/11 wars. In *Manufacturing Consent*, Wharton School of Business Professor of Political Economy Edward Herman and MIT Institute Professor of Linguistics Noam Chomsky claim that because media is firmly embedded in the market system, it reflects the class values and concerns of its owners and advertisers. According to Herman and Chomsky, the media maintains a corporate class bias through five systemic filters: concentrated private ownership; a strict bottom-line profit orientation; over-reliance on governmental and corporate sources for news; a primary tendency to avoid offending the powerful; and an almost religious worship of the market economy, strongly opposing alternative beliefs. These filters limit what will become news in society and set parameters on the acceptable coverage of daily events.[25]

The danger of these filters is that they make subtle and indirect censorship all the more difficult to combat. Owners and managers share class identity with the powerful and are motivated economically to please advertisers and viewers. Social backgrounds influence their conceptions of what is "newsworthy," and their views and values seem only "common sense." Journalists and editors are not immune to the influence of owners and managers. Journalists want to see their stories approved for print or broadcast, and editors come to know the limits of their freedom to diverge from the "common sense" worldview of owners and managers. The self-discipline that this structure induces in journalists and editors comes to seem only "common sense" to them as well. Self-discipline becomes self-censorship—independence is restricted, the filtering process hidden, denied, or rationalized away.

Project Censored conducted an analysis on the top ten left progressive publications' and websites' coverage of key post-9/11 issues and found considerable limitations on coverage of specific stories. Based on the evidence presented, it can be concluded that Chomsky and Herman's understanding may well contribute to the news story selection process inside the left liberal media as well.[26]

In the case of the one million dead Iraqis, the left progressive press has shown late and limited coverage at best. The million dead number emerged in the summer of 2007 on several websites, including After Downing Street, *Huffington Post*, Counter Punch, and AlterNet. Progressive journalist stalwart Amy Goodman at *Democracy Now!* didn't cover the story until February of 2008, while *Reuters* had it a few days before. *The Nation* magazine didn't acknowledge the story until February 16, 2009 in an article by John Tirman at MIT. This underplaying and lack of reporting by the left press in America for such a critical story on the humanitarian crisis of the US occupation does not bode well for a strong public peace movement. The US is in dire need of a media democracy movement to address Truth Emergency concerns. There are examples that could be instrumental in adopting such strategies available from the international community.

INTERNATIONAL MODELS OF MEDIA DEMOCRACY IN ACTION: VENEZUELA

Democracy from the bottom is evolving as a ten-year social revolution in Venezuela. Led by President Hugo Chávez, the United Socialist Party of Venezuela (PSUV) gained over 1 million voters in the most recent elections on November 23, 2008. "It was a wonderful victory," said Professor Carmen Carrero with the communications studies department of Bolivarian University in Caracas. "We won 81 percent of the city mayor positions and seventeen of twenty-three of the state governors," Carrero reported.

The Bolivarian University is housed in the former oil ministry building and now serves 8,000 students throughout Venezuela. The university (Universidad Bolivariana de Venezuela) is symbolic of the democratic socialist changes occurring throughout the country. Before the election of Hugo Chávez as president in 1998, college attendance was primarily for the rich in Venezuela. Today over one million, eight hundred thousand students attend college, three times the rate ten years ago. "Our university was established to resist domination and imperialism," reported Principal (president) Marlene Yadira Cordova in an interview November 10, 2008. "We are a university where we have a vision of life that the oppressed people have a place on this planet." The enthusiasm for learning and the serious, thoughtful questions asked by students was certainly representative of a belief in the potential of positive social change for human betterment. The university offers a fully-staffed free health care clinic, zero tuition, and basic no-cost food for students in the cafeteria, all paid for by the oil revenues now being democratically shared by the people.

Bottom-up democracy in Venezuela starts with the 25,000 community councils elected in every neighborhood in the country. "We establish the priority needs of our area," reported community council spokesperson Carmon Aponte from the neighborhood council in the barrio Bombilla area of western Caracas. Community radio, TV and newspapers are the voice of the people, and they describe the viewers/listeners as the "users" of media instead of the passive audiences.[27]

Democratic socialism means health care, jobs, food, and security in neighborhoods where in many cases nothing but absolute poverty existed ten years ago. With unemployment down to a US level, sharing the wealth has taken real meaning in Venezuela. Despite a 50 percent increase in the price of food last year, local Mercals offer government subsidized cooking oil, corn meal, meat, and powdered milk at 30 to 50 percent off market price. Additionally, there are now 3,500 local communal banks with a $1.6 billion dollar budget offering neighborhood-based microfinancing loans for home improvements, small businesses, and personal emergencies.

"We have moved from a time of disdain [pre-revolution—when the upper classes saw working people as less than human] to a time of adjustment," proclaimed Ecuador's minister of culture Gallo Mora Witt at the opening ceremonies of the Fourth International Book Fair in Caracas November 7. Venezuela's minister of culture Hector Soto added, "We try not to leave anyone out . . . before the revolution the elites published only 60 to 80 books a year, we will publish 1,200 Venezuelan authors this year . . . the book will never stop being the important tool for cultural feelings." In fact, some twenty-five million books—classics by Victor Hugo and Miguel de Cervantes, along with Cindy Sheehan's *Letter to George Bush*—were published in 2008 and are being distributed to the community councils nationwide. The theme of the International Book Fair was books as cultural support to the construction of the Bolivarian revolution and building socialism for the twenty-first century.

In Venezuela the corporate media are still owned by the elites. The five major TV networks and nine of ten of the major newspapers maintain a continuing media effort to undermine Chávez and the socialist revolution. But despite the corporate media and continuing US taxpayer financial support to the anti-Chávez opposition institutions from USAID and National Endowment for Democracy ($20 million annually), two-thirds of the people in Venezuela continue to support President Hugo Chávez and the United Socialist Party of Venezuela. The democracies of South America are realizing that the neo-liberal formulas for capitalism are not working for the people and that new forms of resource allocation are necessary for human betterment. It is a learning process for all involved and certainly a democratic effort from the bottom up.

INTERNATIONAL MODELS OF MEDIA DEMOCRACY IN ACTION: CUBA

"You cannot kill truth by murdering journalists," said Tubal Páez, president of the Journalist Union of Cuba. In May of 2008, one hundred and fifty Cuban and South American journalists, ambassadors, politicians, and foreign guests gathered at the Jose Martí International Journalist Institute to honor the fiftieth anniversary of the death of Carlos Bastidas Arguello—the last journalist killed in Cuba. Carlos Bastidas was only twenty-three years of age when he was assassinated by Fulgencia Batista's secret police after having visited Fidel Castro's forces in the Sierra Maestra Mountains. Edmundo Bastidas, Carlos's brother, told about how a river of change flowed from the Maestra (teacher) mountains, symbolized by his brother's efforts to help secure a new future for Cuba.

The celebration in Havana was held in honor of World Press Freedom Day, which is observed every year in May. The UN first declared this day in 1993 to honor journalists who lost their lives reporting the news and to defend media freedom worldwide.

Cuban journalists share a common sense of a continuing counter-revolutionary threat by US-financed Cuban-Americans living in Miami. This is not an entirely unwarranted feeling, in that many hundreds of terrorist actions against Cuba have occurred with US backing over the past fifty years. In addition to the 1961 Bay of Pigs invasion, these attacks include the blowing up of a Cuban airlines plane in 1976 resulting in the deaths of seventy-three people, the starting in 1981 of an epidemic of dengue fever that killed 158 people, and several hotel bombings in the 1990s, one of which resulted in the death of an Italian tourist.

In the context of this external threat, Cuban journalists quietly acknowledge that some self-censorship will undoubtedly occur regarding news stories that could be used by the "enemy" against the Cuban people. Nonetheless, Cuban journalists strongly value freedom of the press and there was no evidence of overt restriction or government control.

Cuban journalists complain that the US corporate media is biased and refuses to cover the positive aspects of socialism in Cuba. Unknown to most Americans are the facts that Cuba is the number one organic country in the world, has an impressive health care system with a lower infant mortality rate than the US, trains doctors from all over the world, and has enjoyed a 43 percent increase in GDP over the past three years.

Ricardo Alarcon, President of the National Assembly, discussed bias in the US media: "How often do you see Gore Vidal interviewed on the US media?" he asked. "Vidal has recently said that the US is in its 'worst phase in history.' Perhaps Cuba uses corporate news to excess," he said. "Cuban journalists need to link more to independent news sources in the US." Alarcon went on to say that Cuba allows CNN, AP and the *Chicago Tribune* to maintain offices in Cuba, but that the US refuses to allow Cuban journalists to work in the United States.

As the Cuban socialist system improves, the US does everything it can to artificially force Cold War conditions by funding terrorist attacks, maintaining an economic boycott, launching a new anti-terrorism Caribbean naval fleet, and increasingly limiting US citizen travel to Cuba. It is time to reverse this cold war isolationist position, honor the Cuban people's choice of a socialist system, and build a positive working relationship between journalists in support of media democracy in both countries.[28]

GRASSROOTS ANTIDOTES TO CORPORATE MEDIA PROPAGANDA

George Seldes once said, "Journalism's job is not impartial, 'balanced' reporting. Journalism's job is to tell the people what is really going on." Oscar-winning filmmaker Michael Moore's top-grossing movie *Sicko* is one example of telling the people what is really going on. Health care activists know that US health insurance is an extremely large and obscenely lucrative industry with the top nine companies "earning" $38 billion in profits in 2006 alone. The health care industry represents the country's third-largest economic sector, trailing only energy and retail among the 1,000 largest US firms. Despite Moore's film, and despite the fact that an overwhelming number of doctors and a majority of Americans want a single-payer health care system for all Americans, the Obama administration, Congress, and the corporate media have been deaf to the wishes of health care practitioners and the public will in their debate to "reform" the system. Single payer, the public is told, like impeachment before it, is not on the table no matter what the facts, no matter what the percentages of public support. This is a characteristic of a failing republic, a dysfunctional democracy.

Tens of thousands of Americans engaged in various social justice issues constantly witness how corporate media marginalize, denigrate, or simply ignore their concerns. Activist groups working on issues like 9/11 truth, election fraud, impeachment, war propaganda, civil liberties/torture, the Wall Street bailouts, health care reform, and many corporate-caused environmental crises have been systematically excluded from mainstream news and the national conversation leading to a genuine Truth Emergency in the country as a whole.

Now, however, a growing number of activists are finally saying "Enough!" and joining forces to address this Truth Emergency by developing new journalistic systems and practices of their own. They are working to reveal the common corporate denominators behind the diverse crises we face and to develop networks of trustworthy news sources that tell the people what is really going on. These activists know there is a need for journalism that moves beyond forensic inquiries into particular crimes and atrocities, and exposes wider patterns of corruption, propaganda, and illicit political control to rouse the nation to reject a malignant corporate status quo.

Recent efforts at national media reform through micro-power community radio—similar to the 400 people's radio stations in Venezuela—and campaign finance changes, which would mandate access for all candidates on national media, have been strongly resisted by the National Association of Broadcasters (NAB). NAB, considered one of the most powerful corporate lobby groups in Washington, works hard to protect over $200 billion dollars of annual advertising and the several hundred million dollars political candidates spend in each election cycle.

The Truth Emergency movement now recognizes that corporate media's political power and its failure to meet its First Amendment obligation to keep the public informed leaves a huge task to be done. Citizens must mobilize resources to redevelop news and information systems from the bottom up. Citizen journalists can expand distribution of news via small independent newspapers, local magazines, independent radio, and cable access TV. Using the Internet, the public can interconnect with like-minded grassroots news organizations to share important stories. These changes are already in progress with more to come.

BECOMING THE MEDIA: MEDIA FREEDOM FOUNDATION/MEDIA FREEDOM INTERNATIONAL

In response to Truth Emergency conference outcomes, the Media Freedom Foundation and Project Censored launched an effort to both become a repository of independent news and information as well as a producer of content in what are called Validated Independent News stories vetted by college and university professors and students around the world. As corporate media continue their entertainment agenda and the PR industry—working for governments and corporations—increasingly dominates the content, we have the socio-cultural opening to transform how the public receives their news.

Project Censored believes that corporate media is increasingly irrelevant to democracy and working people in the world, and that we need to tell our own news stories from the bottom up. What better project in support of media democracy than for universities and colleges worldwide to support truth telling by validating news stories from independent news sources?

Only 5 percent of college students under thirty read a daily newspaper. Most get all their news from corporate television and increasingly from the Internet. One of the biggest problems with independent media sources on the Internet is a perception of inconsistent reliability. The public is often suspicious of the truthfulness and accuracy of news postings from non-corporate media sources. Over the past ten years, in hundreds of presentations all over the US, Project Censored staff has frequently been asked, "what are the best sources for news and whom do we trust?"

The goal of this effort is to encourage young people to use independent media as their primary sources of news and information and to learn about trustworthy news sources through the Project Censored International News Research Affiliate Program. There are currently thirty affiliate colleges and there are plans to expand college and university participation tenfold this next year. Through these institutions of higher learning, validated independent news stories can be researched by students and scholars, then written, produced and disseminated via the web. In addition to the production of validated independent news content, on any given day at the Media Freedom Foundation website, one can view enough independent news stories from RSS feeds to fill nearly fifty written pages, more than even the largest US newspapers.[29]

THE HOPE FOR REAL INFORMATION CHANGE

Recently, the US Senate Judiciary Committee began considering a truth and reconciliation commission, as has been done in countries with troubled pasts to seek knowledge and healing over controversial or even illegal and catastrophic issues. Vermont Senator Patrick Leahy "wants Congress to convene an independent, blue-ribbon commission to poke into some of the dark secrets and possible government wrongdoing of the Bush years: the alleged torture of prisoners held at Guantánamo Bay, controversial warrantless wiretapping, and the politicization of the hiring and firing of federal prosecutors." According to a recent Gallup Poll, six in ten Americans agree.[30] Despite such public outcry and even high-ranking mention in the Senate, it is doubtful there is political will to follow through in light of the continuing economic meltdown emanating from Wall Street echoing through Main Street. Further, President Obama has already remarked that he wants to look forward and not backward while tackling the country's problems, insinuating that he is not interested in pursuing Bush administration crimes. Only a massive public groundswell can possibly change this, which requires an even more informed and empowered populace. After all, the facts are on their side.[31]

It is up to the people to unite and oppose the common oppressors manifested in a militarist and unresponsive government along with their corporate media lapdogs and PR propagandists. Only then, when the public forms and controls its own information resources, will it become armed with the power that knowledge gives to move forward, not under reformist mindsets, but to create a new and truly vibrant democratic society that promises as well as delivers liberty, peace, and prosperity to all.

PETER PHILLIPS is a professor of sociology at Sonoma State University and director of the Media Freedom Foundation and Project Censored.

MICKEY HUFF is an associate professor of history and social science at Diablo Valley College and associate director of the Media Freedom Foundation and Project Censored.

Notes

1. US General Tommy Franks, quoted in the *San Francisco Chronicle*, March 23, 2002, online at http://www.globalsecurity.org/org/news/2002/020323-attack01.htm.
2. Peter Phillips and Andrew Roth, *Censored 2009* (New York: Seven Stories Press, 2008), pp. 19–25. This story is the number one censored story of the year at Project Censored for this year, archived online at http://www.projectcensored.org/top-stories/articles/1-over-one-million-iraqi-deaths-caused-by-us-occupation. For the earlier casualty numbers see http://www.countercurrents.org/iraq-polya070207.htm.
3. Mass killings from Rwanda to Darfur, from Cambodia to Viet Nam, have ranged from the hundreds of thousands to several millions, with Iraq now an easy rival in between. Watch AlterNet.org columnist Joshua Holland's speak at Project Censored's "Modern Media Censorship Lecture Series" from September 25, 2008, at http://www.projectcensored.org/lectures/lecture092508/. His article about the over one million dead in Iraq can be seen at http://www.alternet.org/images/home/splash/6words_splash.php. For more on the refugees see Dahr Jamail's "Iraq: Not Our Country to Return To" at http://ipsnews.net/news.asp?idnews=41430.
4. Various theories exist on the problem of the subject, from historian Rick Shenkman's *Just How Stupid Are We* to historian and cultural critic Thomas Frank's *What's the Matter with Kansas*, but few examine its effects on the peace community. For more on the issue of American historical amnesia, see Gore Vidal on *Democracy Now!* at http://www.democracynow.org/2004/5/21/gore_vidal_on_the_united_states. See also, *In These Times* at http://www.inthesetimes.com/article/3099/the_united_states_of_amnesia, and for a broader academic look at the issue of how Americans have become arguably the least informed, most entertained people in the modern world, reference the now classic work from the late New York University media scholar Neil Postman, *Amusing Ourselves to Death: Public Discourse in the Age of Show Business* (New York: Viking Adult, 1985). This article hopes to shine more light on the impact of all

of the aforementioned on the peace movement in general and what can be done about it. For another view of this written at the outset of the US invasion of Iraq in 2003, see Felix Kolb and Alicia Swords, "Do Peace Movements Matter?" *Commondreams.org,* May 12, 2003, online at http://www.commondreams.org/views03/ 0512-08.htm.

5. For the Institute of Medicine study on lack of health care related deaths see http://www.iom.edu/?id=19175, also see the study done by Peter Phillips at Sonoma State University at http://www.projectcensored.org/articles/story/practices-in-health-care/ and cited in Michael Moore's 2007 film, *Sicko.* For a broader look at the Truth Emergency movement and its many facets from election fraud to 9/11, from torture to the fiscal crisis, see http://truthemergency.us/ as well as the essay on Truth Emergency by Peter Phillips and David Kubiak at http://www.projectcensored.org/ articles/story/truth-emergency-us/.

6. For more on the NCMR study, see Peter Phillips and Andy Roth, eds., *Censored 2009* (New York: Seven Stories Press, 2008), chapter 11, "Truth Emergency Meets Media Reform," pp. 281-295. For more on the NCMR, see http://freepress.net.

7. In addition to the Media Reform study in chapter 11 of *Censored 2009* cited above, see Peter Phillips, *Censored 2007* (New York: Seven Stories Press, 2006), pp. 307–341. "The Global Dominance Group and US Corporate Media" by Peter Phillips, Bridget Thornton, and Lew Brown is online at http://www.projectcensored.org/articles/story/ the-global-dominance-group/.

8. C. Wright Mills. *The Power Elite* (New York: Oxford University Press, 2000, reissue).

9. Peter Phillips, "Barack Obama Administration Continues US Military Dominance," http://www.projectcensored.org/articles/story/http-wwwprojectcensoredorg-articles-story-barack-obama-administration-c/.

10. Diane Farsetta, Center for Media Democracy, studies on Pentagon propaganda online at http://www.prwatch.org/pentagonpundits and http://www.prwatch.org/node/8180. Zachary Roth, "Lawmaker On Withdrawn IG Report: 'The American People Have Been Misled,'" May 6, 2009, http://tpmmuckraker.talkingpointsmemo.com/2009/05/lawmaker_on_withdrawn_ig_report_the_american_peopl.php.

11. Peter Phillips, *Censored 1999* (New York: Seven Stories Press, 1999). For Operation Tailwind and CNN, see chapter 5, pp. 158–163, and http://www.putnampit.com/ppeditorialjuly18-1998.html. Glenn Greenwald, "The Pulitzer-winning investigation that dare not be uttered on TV," April 21, 2009, online at http://www.salon.com/opinion/greenwald/2009/04/21/pulitzer/. See previous endnote for the link to Diane Farsetta's piece.

12. Norman Soloman, "The Military-Industrial-Media Complex: Why war is covered from the warriors' perspective," *Extra!* July/August 2005, published by Fairness and Accuracy in Reporting (FAIR), http://www.fair.org/index.php?page=2627.

13. Ibid.

14. Quoted by Norman Soloman at http://www.globalpolicy.org/empire/media/ 2005/07militarymedia.html. Originally published in Chris Hedges, *War Is a Force That Gives Us Meaning* (Cambridge: Public Affairs, Perseus Group, 2002). This phenomenon goes back to journalist Louis O'Sullivan coining the phrase "Manifest Destiny" in 1845 in the New York papers on the eve of the Mexican-American War. The Hearst newspapers in New York on the run-up to the Spanish-American War also willingly spread false claims of the sinking of the U.S.S. Maine. Edward Bernays and George Creel further used a compliant press to rouse support for US entrance in WWI and the same happened after Pearl Harbor in WWII. Each time, each source was not interested in independent, factual reporting; rather, they were interested in being useful tools of the powerful to fulfill establishment policies. For an overview of

propaganda history and US war policy, as well as a deeper look at media myth-making through the events of 9/11, see Mickey Huff and Paul Rea, chapter 14 in *Censored 2009*, "Deconstructing Deceit: 9/11, the Media, and Myth Information," pp. 341–364, or the expanded version online at http://www.projectcensored.org/articles/story/ deconstructing-deceit/.

15. I. F. Stone, *In a Time of Torment: 1961–1967* (New York: Random House, 1967), p. 317.

16. For an overview study of Iraq War propaganda, see John Stauber and Sheldon Rampton, *Weapons of Mass Deception: The Uses of Propaganda in Bush's War on Iraq* (New York: Tarcher Penguin, 2003), and their follow up *Best War Ever: Lies, Damned Lies, and the Mess in Iraq* (New York: Penguin, 2006). For reports on the continuation of war policy under President Barack Obama, see Center for Media Democracy's John Stauber, "How Obama Took Over the Peace Movement," http://www .prwatch.org/node/8297, and Peter Phillips, "Barack Obama Administration Continues US Military Dominance," http://www.projectcensored.org/articles/story/ http-wwwprojectcensoredorg-articles-story-barack-obama-administration-c/.

17. Peter Phillips, *Censored 2008* (New York: Seven Stories Press, 2007), pp. 35–44. Online at http://www.projectcensored.org/top-stories/articles/1-no-habeas-corpus-for-any-person/ and http://www.projectcensored.org/top-stories/articles/2-bush-moves -toward-martial-law/.

18. See *Censored 2008*, chapter 1, story 6, pp. 55–59. Also online at http://www.projectcensored.org/top-stories/articles/6-operation-falcon-raids/. The stories mentioned here are only a few examples. For a complete up to date list of current censored stories, see Peter Phillips and Mickey Huff, eds., *Censored 2010*, chapter 1 of this volume for the latest list of Project Censored's most important stories missed or distorted by corporate mainstream news for 2008 and 2009. Also see the Media Freedom Foundation PNN website for year round validated independent news stories online at http://mediafreedom.pnn.com/5174-independent-news-sources.

19. Online at http://www.atlanticfreepress.com/news/1/2473-corporate-media-turned-out-for-jena-but-not-for-anti-war-heres-why.html.

20. Linda Milazzo, "Corporate Media Turned Out for Jena, but Not for Anti-War. Here's Why." *Atlantic Free Press*, September 23, 2007, online at http://www.atlanticfreepress.com/news/1/2473-corporate-media-turned-out-for-jena-but-not-for-anti-war-heres-why.html.

21. Andrew L. Roth, Zoe Huffman, Jeff Huling, Kevin Stolle, and Jocelyn Thomas, "Covering War's Victims: A Content Analysis of Iraq and Afghanistan War Photographs in the *New York Times* and *San Francisco Chronicle*," in *Censored 2008* (New York: Seven Stories Press, 2007), pp. 253–271.

22. Jeffrey M. Jones, "In U.S., More Optimism About Iraq, Less About Afghanistan: New high of 42% say war in Afghanistan a mistake," March 18, 2009. See the Gallup Poll results online at http://www.gallup.com/poll/116920/Optimism-Iraq-Less-Afghanistan.aspx.

23. For more on the Winter Soldiers, see *Censored 2009*, chapter 1, story 9, pp. 58–62 and online at http://www.projectcensored.org/top-stories/articles/9-iraq-and-afghanistan-vets-testify/; see also chapter 12, pp. 297-319. See the KPFA radio and Corp Watch website for the coverage at http://www.warcomeshome.org/wintersoldier2008.

24. Peter Phillips, "Barack Obama Administration Continues US Military Dominance," http://www.projectcensored.org/articles/story/http-wwwprojectcensoredorg-articles-story-barack-obama-administration-c/.

25. Edward Herman and Noam Chomsky, *Manufacturing Consent: The Political Economy of the Mass Media* (New York: Pantheon Books, 1988, 2002). For an introduction of

the Propaganda Model, see chapter 1 of the work, or see a retrospective by Edward Herman online at http://www.chomsky.info/onchomsky/20031209.htm.

26. Peter Phillips, *Censored 2008*, see chapter 7, "Left Progressive Media Inside the Propaganda Model," pp. 233–251, http://www.projectcensored.org/articles/story/left -progressive-media-inside-the-propaganda-model/.

27. Coauthor Peter Phillips, interviewed Carmon Aponte while visiting the Patare Community TV and radio station in a trip to Venezuela for a book fair in 2008. The station was one of thirty-four locally controlled community television stations and four hundred radio stations now in the barrios throughout Venezuela.

28. Coauthor Peter Phillips, attended the major journalism conference in Cuba in 2008. About his experiences there, Phillips remarked, "During my five days in Havana, I met with dozens of journalists, communication studies faculty and students, union representatives and politicians. The underlying theme of my visit was to determine the state of media freedom in Cuba and to build a better understanding between media democracy activists in the US and those in Cuba.

"I toured the two main radio stations in Havana, Radio Rebelde and Radio Havana. Both have Internet access to multiple global news sources including CNN, Reuters, Associated Press and BBC with several newscasters pulling stories for public broadcast. Over ninety municipalities in Cuba have their own locally-run radio stations, and journalists report local news from every province.

"During the course of several hours in each station, I was interviewed on the air about media consolidation and censorship in the US and was able to ask journalists about censorship in Cuba as well. Of the dozens I interviewed, all said that they have complete freedom to write or broadcast any stories they choose. This was a far cry from the Stalinist media system so often depicted by US interests."

29. For more details see the Project Censored website at http://projectcensored.org/; for independent media feeds see Media Freedom Foundation at http://mediafreedom .pnn.com/5174-independent-news-sources; and for more on the Project Censored International Affiliates Program, see http://projectcensored.org/project-censored- international-affilates-program. For more on how to become the media, see David Mathison's work at http://bethemedia.com.

30. Alex Kingsbury, "Why Sen. Patrick Leahy Wants a "Truth Commission," *U.S. News and World Report*, March 4, 2009, http://www.usnews.com/articles/news/politics/ 2009/03/04/why-sen-patrick-leahy-wants-a-truth-commission.html.

31. Naomi Wolf, "Do the Secret Bush Memos Amount to Treason? Top Constitutional Scholar Says Yes," *Alternet.org*, March 25, 2009, http://www.alternet.org/rights/ 133273/do_the_secret_bush_memos_amount_to_treason_top_constitutional_scholar_ says_yes/.

Note: All online sources were accessed and viewed between March 25 and 31, 2009, and then reviewed and revised between May 13 and 15, 2009.

CHAPTER 6

Lying About War
Deliberate Propaganda and Spin by the Pentagon

by Diane Farsetta, Sheldon Rampton, Daniel Haack, and John Stauber
of the Center for Media and Democracy

Public diplomacy is a catch-all term for the various ways in which the
United States promotes itself to international audiences (as opposed to
"regular" diplomacy, which targets foreign governments). These include
international media, such as the Voice of America, cultural and educational exchanges, such as the Fulbright Program, and a wide range of
information activities, including foreign press centers, speaking events
and publications. As the University of Southern California's Center on
Public Diplomacy notes, the term "was developed partly to distance overseas governmental information activities from the term propaganda,
which had acquired pejorative connotations."

In the United States, public diplomacy's legislative history also
involves propaganda. The Smith-Mundt Act of 1948, which provided a
legal framework for public diplomacy activities, forbids the government
from disseminating within the United States information intended for
foreign audiences. Other legislation, such as appropriations bills, theo-
retically reinforces the ban on using taxpayer money for "publicity or
propaganda purposes."

From 2002 to 2008, the Defense Department secretly cultivated more
than seventy retired military officers who frequently serve as media commentators. Initially, the goal was to use them as "message force
multipliers," to bolster the Bush administration's Iraq War sell job. That
went so well that the covert program to shape US public opinion—an
illegal effort, by any reasonable reading of the law—was expanded to
spin everything from then-Defense Secretary Rumsfeld's job performance to US military operations in Afghanistan to the Guantánamo Bay
detention center to warrantless wiretapping.

On April 20, 2009, David Barstow of the *New York Times* wrote
"Behind TV Analysts, Pentagon's Hidden Hand," a stunning exposé of
the Bush administration's most powerful propaganda weapon used to

sell and manage the war on Iraq. This involved the embedding of military propagandists directly into the TV networks as on-air commentators. We and others have long criticized the widespread TV network practice of hiring former military officials to serve as analysts, but even in our most cynical moments we did not anticipate how bad it was. Barstow painstakingly documented how these analysts, most of them military industry consultants and lobbyists, were directly chosen, managed, coordinated and given their talking points by the Pentagon's ministers of propaganda.

Thanks to the two-year investigation by the *New York Times,* we today know that Victoria Clarke, then the assistant secretary of defense for public affairs, launched the Pentagon military analyst program in early 2002. These supposedly independent military analysts were in fact a coordinated team of pro-war propagandists, personally recruited by Secretary of Defense Donald Rumsfeld, and acting under Clarke's tutelage and development.

One former participant, NBC military analyst Kenneth Allard, has called the effort "psyops on steroids." As Barstow reports, "Internal Pentagon documents repeatedly refer to the military analysts as 'message force multipliers' or 'surrogates' who could be counted on to deliver administration 'themes and messages' to millions of Americans 'in the form of their own opinions.' . . . Don Meyer, an aide to Ms. Clarke, said a strategic decision was made in 2002 to make the analysts the main focus of the public relations push to construct a case for war."

Clarke and her senior aide, Brent T. Krueger, eventually signed up more than seventy-five retired military officers who penned newspaper op-ed columns and appeared on television and radio news shows as military analysts. The Pentagon held weekly meetings with the military analysts, which continued until April 20, 2008, when the *New York Times* ran Barstow's story. The program proved so successful that it was expanded to issues besides the Iraq War. "Other branches of the administration also began to make use of the analysts. Mr. Gonzales, then the attorney general, met with them soon after news leaked that the government was wiretapping terrorism suspects in the United States without warrants, Pentagon records show. When David H. Petraeus was appointed the commanding general in Iraq in January 2007, one of his early acts was to meet with the analysts."

The use of these analysts was a glaring violation of journalistic standards. As the code of ethics of the Society of Professional Journalists explains, journalists are supposed to

> ➤ Avoid conflicts of interest, real or perceived.
> ➤ Remain free of associations and activities that may compromise integrity or damage credibility.
> ➤ Refuse gifts, favors, fees, free travel, and special treatment, and shun secondary employment, political involvement, public office, and service in community organizations if they compromise journalistic integrity.
> ➤ Disclose unavoidable conflicts.
> ➤ Be vigilant and courageous about holding those with power accountable.
> ➤ Deny favored treatment to advertisers and special interests and resist their pressure to influence news coverage.
> ➤ Be wary of sources offering information for favors or money.

The networks using these analysts as journalists shamelessly failed to vet their experts and ignored the obvious conflicts of hiring a person with financial relationships to companies profiting from war to be an on-air analyst of war. They acted as if war was a football game and their military commentators were former coaches and players familiar with the rules and strategies. The TV networks even paid these "analysts" for their propaganda, enabling them to present themselves as "third party experts" while parroting White House talking points to sell the war.

Since the 1920s there have been laws passed to stop the government from doing what Barstow has exposed. It is actually illegal in the United States for the government to propagandize its own citizens. As Barstow's report demonstrates, these laws have been repeatedly violated, are not enforced and are clearly inadequate. The US Congress therefore needs to investigate this and the rest of the Bush propaganda campaign that sold the war in Iraq.

The Iraq war would likely never have been possible had the mainstream news media done its job. Instead, it has repeated the Big Lies that sold the war. This war would never have been possible without the millions of dollars spent by the Bush administration on sophisticated and deceptive public relations techniques such as the Pentagon military analyst program that David Barstow has exposed. It should come as no surprise to anyone that Victoria Clarke, who designed and oversaw this

Pentagon propaganda machine, now works as a commentator for TV network news. She may have changed jobs and employers since leaving the Pentagon, but her work remains the same.

In April 2008, shortly after the *New York Times* first reported on the Pentagon's pundits—an in-depth exposé that recently won the *Times*'s David Barstow his second Pulitzer Prize—the Pentagon suspended the program. In January 2009, the Defense Department Inspector General's office released a report claiming "there was an 'insufficient basis' to conclude that the program had violated laws." Representative Paul Hodes, one of the program's many Congressional critics, called the Inspector General's report "a whitewash."

Now, it seems as though the Pentagon agrees. On May 5, 2009, the Defense Department Inspector General's office announced that it was withdrawing its report on the Pentagon pundit program, even removing the file from its website.

"Shortly after publishing the report . . . we became aware of inaccuracies in the data," states the "withdrawal memo" (PDF) from the Inspector General's office. The office's internal review of the report—which it has "refused to release," according to the *Times*—"concluded that the report did not meet accepted quality standards." The report relied on "insufficient or inconclusive" evidence, the memo admits. In addition, "former senior [Defense Department] officials who devised and managed" the Pentagon pundit program, including Victoria Clarke and Lawrence Di Rita, "refused our requests for an interview."

While the Inspector General's "highly unusual" about-face is welcome, it gets us no closer to accountability. "Additional investigative work will not be undertaken," the withdrawal memo states, because the Pentagon pundit program "has been terminated and responsible senior officials"—such as Allison Barber—"are no longer employed by the Department."

Of course, accountability for the Pentagon pundit program was never likely to come from the Defense Department itself. Now it's up to Congress to demand—and the Government Accountability Office and the Federal Communications Commission to carry out—real investigations into the elaborate propaganda campaign.

There is a long history of various administrations seeking to propagandize the American people. The Bush administration, and the Clinton administration before it, funded video news releases (VNRs) that television stations across the United States aired as independent "reports" during their news programming. Not surprisingly, the VNRs portrayed government actions and policies in a favorable light. One on educational assistance under No Child Left Behind concluded, "This is a program that gets an A-plus."

Congress' investigative arm, the Government Accountability Office (GAO), repeatedly ruled that government VNRs are illegal covert propaganda unless their source is made clear to viewers. The Bush administration rejected the GAO's rulings, substituting their own intent-based standard. They argued that government VNRs are permissible, whether disclosed or not, as long as the intent behind them is to inform, not to persuade.

The Department of Defense has also relied on intent to dismiss concerns about propaganda blowback. The Department's 2003 Information Operations Roadmap admits, "Information intended for foreign audiences, including public diplomacy and PSYOP [psychological operations], increasingly is consumed by our domestic audience and vice-versa." However, it argues that, "the distinction between foreign and domestic audiences becomes more a question of USG [US government] intent rather than information dissemination practices."

The 8,000 pages of Pentagon pundit documents, which the *New York Times* obtained through a Freedom of Information Act request (backed up by lawsuits) and the Department of Defense later made public, reveal the daily operations of the program.

The morning of June 20, 2006, an email message circulated amongst US Defense Department officials. "Jed Babbin, one of our military analysts, is hosting the Michael Medved nationally syndicated radio show this afternoon. He would like to see if General [George W.] Casey would be available for a phone interview," the Pentagon staffer wrote. "This would be a softball interview and the show is 8th or 9th in the nation."

Why would the Pentagon help set up a radio interview? And how did they know that the interview would be "softball"?

From early 2002 to April 2008, the Department of Defense offered talking points, organized trips to places such as Iraq and Guantánamo Bay, and gave private briefings to a legion of retired military officers working as media pundits. The Pentagon's military analyst program, a covert effort to promote a positive image of the Bush administration's wartime performance, was a multi-level campaign involving quite a few colorful characters.

One Pentagon pundit arguably steals the spotlight: Jed Babbin. A former Pentagon official himself, the retired Air Force officer served as a deputy undersecretary of defense with the George H. W. Bush administration. Since then he has kept busy authoring books, serving as a contributing editor to the conservative monthly American Spectator, frequently filling in for right-wing radio hosts such as Laura Ingraham and Hugh Hewitt, and appearing as a military pundit on cable television.

Babbin repeatedly appears in the Pentagon pundit documents, usually either emailing his American Spectator articles to Pentagon officials or using his special access to arrange interviews with high-ranking government and military officers for his articles and radio guest host gigs.

In February 2006, Babbin emailed Pentagon legal advisor Thomas Hemingway. "I'm subbing for Hugh Hewitt again tomorrow and want to bash the UN report," he wrote, referring to an inquiry into conditions at Guantánamo Bay that led the United Nations to call for the detention center to be closed. "I asked for [US Army Major General] Jay Hood and got the answer that the military isn't going out on that now. Can you do it? Please call asap." Babbin didn't just use Pentagon public affairs staffers as his radio bookers. He also asked them for their thoughts on what he should say, as a pundit.

"I just got a call from Jed Babbin," wrote one Pentagon public affairs officer in October 2006. "He is going to be on [the CNBC show] Kudlow [& Company] tonight and want [sic] to be prepared if they ask him about the [Al-Qaeda] threat to Saudi oil fields. . . . Anything we could share with him??"

The Pentagon was also more than proactive. "[Fox News's] Hannity and Colmes is having Jed Babbin on today to talk about North Korea," emailed Pentagon public affairs staffer Dallas Lawrence to Ruff and Whitman in February 2005. "We are getting Jed a one pager on the status of forces in the Korean Peninsula (the message being, we still have a massive deterrent there for [North Korea]). We will also put him into touch with State for talking points on the 6 party talks."

In a phone interview, Babbin defended his communications with the Pentagon. "I am a journalist," he told me. "I have information that's given to me by sources of all sorts. Private information is what you normally do in Washington. You get confidential sources and you rely on them. I'm not compromised. I can't speak for anybody else other than myself, but I have no relationship with defense contractors, I have no contracts with the Pentagon. There's no conflict there."

But Babbin's contacts with the Pentagon are still problematic, according to Kelly McBride, ethics group leader at the Poynter Institute for media studies. "When you hire a former general [as a media commentator], you're hiring him for his expertise and his ability to independently analyze what's going on," she explained. "If you're assuming because he's retired he has a measure of independence and then you find out, no, he's actually been to all these trainings where he's received talking points, that's a problem. You have promised your audience that you're going to deliver them independent analysis—not a mouthpiece for the Pentagon."

That raises the question of whether the responsibility to ensure the integrity and independence of military analysts lies with the pundits themselves or with the media outlets that hired them. In this case, says McBride, it's the latter.

"The journalists had the obligation to figure out if their sources were independent," she said. "Each show decided how they were going to use these people, and at that point, somebody should've been having a conversation about what they're bringing to the product and how that works, and then finally, there should be an overall standard that says when we hire people, here is what we should ask of them."

In his defense, Babbin said that "everyone I wrote for and so forth knew I was talking to people in the Pentagon." Babbin also went on government-funded trips to Iraq and Guantánamo Bay, but said he doesn't believe that any of the media outlets he writes or appears on-air for have policies against such activity. So, Babbin concludes that he had no conflicts of interest.

Do the media outlets that Babbin appeared on feel the same way? Salem Radio Network, which produces both "The Hugh Hewitt Show" and "The Michael Medved Show," radio programs that Babbin appeared on while participating in the Pentagon's pundit program, refused comment. Phone calls to the American Spectator and WMET of Washington, DC were not returned.

Todd Meyer, a producer for Greg Garrison's show on Indianapolis radio station WIBC, one of Babbin's more frequent stomping grounds, said, "I'm not sure if Jed mentioned he was a part of [the Department of Defense's military analyst program]. He might at some point. He said over the years, though, that he's been part of many, many briefings at the Pentagon, most when he was actually working there under Bush."

Meyer added that Babbin was never presented on the show as an independent analyst. "Jed Babbin is the editor of Human Events, he wrote for *National Review*, he wrote for *American Spectator*. He's conservative," stressed Meyer. "We're a conservative talk show. Mr. Babbin's been on our show many, many times over the years and he comes from a conservative background. He was privy to a number of briefings. We took advantage of hearing what was in those briefings."

But is being conservative synonymous with being a mouthpiece for the Pentagon?

Babbin contends that he was nothing of the sort. "If they were buying my loyalty, they got a pretty bad bargain. If they thought they were buying my reporting, they really had a very poor investment. Look at my stories, look at what I've written. I've been very highly critical at times of the president and a lot of the people who conduct the war."

Judging by the Pentagon pundit documents, the Department of Defense sees Babbin as an ardent supporter. "Babbin will do us well," Pentagon PR staffer Bryan Whitman wrote in a March 2005 email. In June 2005, Larry Di Rita told fellow Pentagon public affairs officers, "We really should try to help [Babbin secure guests for his radio hosting gigs]. . . . He is consistently solid and helpful." Another message, this one from Thomas Hemingway to Eric Ruff in June 2006, reads: "I'm sure all your folks are familiar with the tremendous support we've received from Jed." And that's in addition to the aforementioned "softball interview" comment.

While Jed Babbin was only one of some seventy-five retired military officers that the Department of Defense used as their so-called "message force multipliers" and "surrogates," and while he wasn't seeking defense contracts like some of his fellow pundits, his case is representative of the breakdown of transparency and accountability consequent to the Pentagon's covert program. Babbin's experience also shows that someone could consistently parrot the administration's talking points while believing himself to be independent and even, at times, critical of the official narrative.

But the pundits weren't just selling government talking points. As Robert Bevelacqua, William Cowan and Carlton Sherwood enjoyed high-level Pentagon access through the analyst program, their WVC3 Group sought "contracts worth tens of millions to supply body armor and counterintelligence services in Iraq," reported Barstow. Cowan admitted to "push[ing] hard" on a WVC3 contract during a Pentagon-funded trip to Iraq.

Then there's Pentagon pundit Robert H. Scales Jr. The military firm he cofounded in 2003, Colgen, has an interesting range of clients, from the Central Intelligence Agency and US Special Operations Command to Pfizer, Syracuse University, Fox News, and National Public Radio.

Of the twenty-seven Pentagon pundits named publicly to date, six are registered as federal lobbyists. That's in addition to the less formal—and less transparent—boardroom to war-room influence peddling described above. (There are "more than seventy-five retired officers" who took part in the Pentagon program overall, according to Barstow.)

The Pentagon pundits' lobbying disclosure forms help chart what can only be called a military-industrial-media complex. They also make clear that war is very good for at least some types of business.

Fox News analyst Timur J. Eads works for the military contractor Blackbird Technologies. His job title there, "vice-president of government relations," is often used to describe someone who crafts lobbying strategies but may not take part in lobbying meetings. So, it's not surprising that Eads isn't listed on Blackbird's lobbying disclosure forms. (In 2007 and 2008, Blackbird lobbied Congress on "communications technologies" and the National Guard on "information systems.")

From 2001 to 2003, Eads was in the lobbying trenches for EMC Corporation, a multinational "information infrastructure" company. Eads helped lobby Congress and a long list of federal agencies—including the Air Force, Army, Marine Corps, Navy and Coast Guard—for "funding for data storage infrastructure." EMC's annual report (PDF) for 2003 lists the Air Force Materiel Command and Pentagon Renovation and Construction Program Office among its US government clients.

Prior to EMC, Eads lobbied for the major defense contractor Science Applications International Corporation (SAIC). In 1999 and 2000, he was on SAIC's million-dollar-plus lobbying team, influencing federal spending on the armed services, foreign operations, national security and Veterans Administration, among many other appropriations bills.

A January 2009 public diplomacy conference was organized in Washington, DC to critically reconsider Smith-Mundt. Many presenters supported changing the Act, specifically removing or watering down its restriction on domestic dissemination. Among the reasons given were that the restriction, which effectively divides the world into US residents and everyone else, is outdated in the global information age, that it hampers public diplomacy efforts, that it suggests to foreign audiences that US government-provided information is suspect, since it can't be shared with US residents, that it denies US residents useful information, and that it keeps US residents from accessing information necessary to evaluate work done overseas in their name and with their tax dollars. On the other side, there were conference attendees who argued that the Smith-Mundt restriction doesn't impact work in the field, and that it helps insulate sensitive international work from domestic political pressures.

It was an informed, in-depth debate, led by people with extensive State Department and military experience. But until Rep. Hodes spoke—during the last session of the day—no one mentioned that, until just nine months ago, there had been an active covert campaign to influence US public opinion: the Pentagon's pundit program.

"Let me posit what I believe should be the rule," said outgoing Undersecretary of State for Public Diplomacy and Public Affairs James Glassman, a keynote speaker at the conference. Domestic dissemination should be permissible, he suggested, "if the intent of the work involving domestic audiences is to influence foreign audiences." According to Glassman the government's motivation behind engaging US residents is key. "The reasonable way to judge whether the State Department should be prohibited from disseminating a film, or a television program, or a speech, or a magazine, is the intention of the department," he declared. While "traditional American concerns about government involvement—not merely in influence, but in information—are deeply rooted and appropriate . . . intent should be our guide. If our target is foreign audiences, as it must be in public diplomacy, then we should be able to engage domestic individuals and groups in this effort."

Glassman's emphasis on intent is nothing new. In other words, it doesn't matter whether material designed to influence foreign audiences—including, in the case of military information operations and psychological operations campaigns, material that may be misleading—is conveyed to US residents as "news." All that matters is that the responsible government officials' hearts are pure.

We know that the conveniently slippery standard of intent has already resulted in fake TV news that would make Soviet-era propagandists proud. As professor Marc Lynch noted at the conference, "Who knows what evil lurks in the minds of men? The Shadow knows, but State Department lawyers don't, which makes it very difficult to build a regulatory foundation on questions of intent, particularly when . . . intent can be multi-faceted and highly complex."

The State Department—and the US Information Agency, before it was folded into State—used to be responsible for public diplomacy. In 1999, then-President Clinton tasked numerous federal agencies with "influenc[ing] foreign audiences." He established an International Public Information group, comprised of officials from the State, Defense, Justice, Commerce, and Treasury departments, along with the FBI and CIA. Post-9/11, the Pentagon's budget ballooned and then-Defense Secretary Donald Rumsfeld proclaimed that communications must be "a central component of every aspect of this struggle." As a result, the US military has become increasingly involved in public diplomacy.

On the question of Smith-Mundt, its ban on domestic dissemination has clearly been rendered moot by Google. Instead of using that as an excuse to burn down firewalls, the US government should follow strict media ethics standards, regardless of whether its intended audience is in Iowa or Islamabad. All public diplomacy communications and activities should be clearly attributed. Information operations and psychological operations, which require a lack of transparency, should be kept completely separate from public diplomacy and public affairs. Lastly, the military's role in public diplomacy should be decreased and perhaps ended.

Instead of loosening propaganda restrictions by relying on intent, why not adjust to the global information era by ensuring clear attribution of all government communications? Truth is an obvious second standard, but public diplomacy by definition deals with issues in which the US government is an interested party. It's therefore naive to claim that a standard of "truth"—which must transcend, or at least fairly acknowledge, competing interests—could be upheld.

Today, the broadcast and cable networks are steadfastly refusing to cover or otherwise address the Pentagon military analyst program, with very few exceptions. In this case, though, the pundits' undeclared financial interests are only part of a larger and much more serious problem. These officers participated in a covert government program designed to shape US public opinion—an illegal program, and one that relied on the willingness of major media to play along, without asking too many questions. And that's exactly what happened. The media outlets that featured the Pentagon's pundits need to address both aspects of this debacle: that they failed to identify or disclose conflicts of interest, and that they helped propagandize US news audiences.

Increasingly, news audiences are realizing the many ways in which interested parties skew media coverage. Media outlets need to wake up to that reality and work to strengthen their safeguards in defense of the public interest. Their only alternative is to start composing their next weak and belated mea culpa in a desperate attempt to protect their ever-dwindling credibility.

DIANE FARSETTA is the Center for Media and Democracy's senior researcher.

Searchable versions of the Pentagon pundit documents available at http://www.prwatch.org/pentagonpundits.

CHAPTER 7

Fear & Favor
Fairness and Accuracy in Reporting

by Peter Hart

FINANCIAL WOES ACCELERATE CORPORATE PRESSURE IN THE NEWSROOM

The broad downturn in the US economy has hit the media industry especially hard, as corporate owners who gambled on debt-financed expansions have seen their business models head south on the back of shrinking subscription and advertising revenue. In any economic climate, there are pressures on working journalists, but the current problems in the industry seem likely to exacerbate those unfortunate trends.

Services that obliterate the line between journalism and advertising might see a brighter future; as John Reinan reported in the online news site MinnPost on August 8, 2008, "The dark cloud over the traditional media business looks like a silver lining" to a company like ARANet, which specializes in "free print and Web content that carries client messages wrapped in consumer lifestyle articles." The company's clients include sixty-five of the top 100 US newspapers, where sometimes disclosure (or lack thereof) can be an issue: "Where the online articles typically are identified as sponsored content, the print articles merely carry an 'ARA' designation, similar to the 'AP' identifier that runs with Associated Press articles."

Pressure from owners, advertisers, and government officials is an ever-present part of the corporate media landscape. 2008 brought the dramatic example of government propaganda efforts to sell Iraq War policies via a select group of retired military officers who, unbeknownst to viewers, were receiving special briefings and talking points from the Pentagon (as was reported in the *New York Times* on April 20, 2008). The most revealing aspect of the arrangement, however, may have been the near-total silence from the broadcast and cable outlets who put the Pentagon pundits on the air —suggesting that becoming conduits for a propaganda campaign ("message force multipliers" was the term) was not something the outlets felt they needed to explain to the public.

A survey of reporters conducted by the Project for Excellence in Journalism on March 17, 2008 found that large majorities of print and television reporters believe that financial pressures on their news organizations have increased; about a quarter say owners and advertisers exert either a great deal or a fair amount of influence in their newsrooms. Nearly half of Internet-based reporters (who, in the PEJ study, are mostly employed by those same print and TV outlets) see such influence—which might temper the enthusiasm of those who look to the Internet to save journalism.

ADVERTISER INFLUENCE

"From increasing demand for editorial credits and ads disguised as editorial content to calls for cover presence, advertisers are ratcheting up pressure on magazines for treatments that blur church-state lines, according to editors, publishers and media buyers," reported *AdWeek*.

While the magazines in question are less "newsy"—*Harper's Bazaar*, *Parents*, and *Life & Style* were mentioned prominently—these trends are worrisome. The economic climate seems to put even more pressure on corporate news media to go the extra mile for advertisers. It was no surprise, then, to see Fox News Channel host Bill O'Reilly announce on January 31, 2008 that, "One of the sponsors here is Liberty Mutual, and I'm very impressed by their new ad." After the ad aired, O'Reilly declared, "For encouraging kindness and generosity in America, the Liberty Mutual people are patriots."

A *New York Times* magazine profile of syndicated talker Rush Limbaugh reported that the host has a "new option" for some advertisers: "At a much higher rate, he will weave a product into his monologue." (To a caller who said he took two showers after voting for Hillary Clinton as part of Limbaugh's Operation Chaos, Limbaugh responded, "If you had followed my advice and gotten a Rinnai tankless water heater, you wouldn't have needed to take two showers. And I'll tell you why . . .")

Along the same lines, Forbes.com reported on April 17, 2008 that "many papers remain hampered by insufficient communication between the editors and writers generating content and those on the business side charged with selling it to advertisers." Of course, that lack of communication is exactly the way things are supposed to work at an ethical media outlet, but "the newspaper industry's increasingly grim financial outlook leaves editors with little choice but to work across the aisle." According to *Forbes* reporter Louis Hau, editorial staffers at the Gannett-owned *Des Moines Register* are increasingly involved in projects coordinated with the advertising department; a sports editor, for example, "confers with advertising to determine what they can do together" before coverage of high-profile events. The changes "wouldn't have happened 10 years ago," according to the paper's editor.

According to FolioMag.com, at one magazine industry event there was discussion of the need "to blow up the church-state boundary between advertising and editorial." A *PR Week* survey from June 23, 2008 showed that boundary is not so difficult to overcome. The magazine found 19 percent of marketers admitted to having "bought advertising in return for a news story about their company or product," and 10 percent said they "have had an implicit/nonverbal agreement with a reporter or editor that advertising will result in favorable coverage." Eight percent had "either paid for or provided a gift to an editor in exchange for a news story about their company."

Some examples are remarkably straightforward. At the Las Vegas Fox affiliate KVVU, sitting at the morning show desk with the anchors are McDonald's iced coffees (which are actually undrinkable props). The station's news director, Adam P. Bradshaw, called the arrangement a "nontraditional revenue source," according to the *Las Vegas Sun*. Bradshaw seemed to think the incident bolstered the journalistic credentials of his station's news staff; according to a July 22, 2008 article in the *New York Times*, "There was a healthy dose of skepticism, and I'm pleased there was—it means they're being journalists." The *Times* report also revealed that KVVU parent company Meredith was accepting product placements on its local morning shows in other markets, and that McDonald's has struck similar deals with local Fox stations in Chicago (WFLD) and Seattle (KCPQ), as well as Univision 41 in New York City.

PAY-TO-PLAY

McDonald's isn't the only corporate entity looking to place itself in the news. In Dallas, local station NBC 5 had an arrangement to feature sources from the local Children's Medical Center in its weekly "Children's Health Check" report, which airs on the station's morning newscast. The deal, according to former Dallas Morning News TV reporter Ed Bark, was arranged by a local advertising agency and costs the hospital somewhere between $250,000 and $300,000. "This is a sponsorship. They don't control editorial content," news director Susan Tully explained. "They give us resources and story ideas, but we decide what we're going to cover, how we're going to cover it." Such assurances are hard to swallow, given that the station is relying solely on sources from the hospital footing the bill.

According to a March 28, 2008 report in the *Charleston Gazette*, West Virginia's Division of Natural Resources (DNR) pays $90,000 to local TV station WCHS to produce "West Virginia Wildlife" segments on its newscast. "While the station does acknowledge the sponsorship, there is no indication during the news broadcast that 'West Virginia Wildlife' is any different from other news segments," the paper reported. "But unlike other advertisers, who might sponsor the station's weather coverage every night, DNR dictates its own coverage."

The contract between the station and the government agency also requires that the station cover two events of the agency's choosing. "I don't think I have any issues with the segment at all," said station news director Matt Snyder. "The DNR wanted a news station to show it in the best light possible."

POWER AND PR

"The Infinite Mind" radio show was heard across the country for years—until 2008, when the host's deep conflicts of interest came to light. As reported by Slate.com on May 9, 2008, a panel Dr. Fred Goodwin convened on his show to discuss Prozac comprised a curious bunch, and failed to include important disclosures: "All four of the experts on the show, including Goodwin, have financial ties to the makers of antidepressants. Also unmentioned were the 'unrestricted grants' that Infinite Mind has received from drug makers, including Eli Lilly, the manufacturer of the antidepressant Prozac." Slate reported that the Prozac show "may stand in a class by itself for concealing bias. In addition to the show's unrestricted grants from Lilly, the host, Goodwin, is on the board of directors of Center for Medicine in the Public Interest, an industry-funded front, or "Astroturf" group, which receives a majority of its funding from drug companies."

"The Infinite Mind" story was picked up by the *New York Times* months later, and the paper reported that—as was uncovered by investigations by Sen. Charles Grassley (R-IA)—Goodwin "earned at least $1.3 million between 2000 and 2007 giving marketing lectures for drug makers, income not mentioned on the program." The *Times* noted that "Goodwin's radio programs have often touched on subjects important to the commercial interests of the companies for which he consults." Though Slate.com reported difficulties in getting comments from Goodwin or others related to the program, the *Times* had more luck:

> In an interview, Dr. Goodwin said that Bill Lichtenstein, the program's producer, knew of his consulting activities but that neither he nor Mr. Lichtenstein thought that "getting money from drug companies could be an issue. In retrospect, that should have been disclosed." But Mr. Lichtenstein said that he was unaware of Dr. Goodwin's financial ties to drug makers and that he called Dr. Goodwin earlier this year and asked him point-blank if he was receiving funding from pharmaceutical companies, directly or indirectly, and the answer was, No.

NPR announced that the show would be pulled from their satellite service.

And problems of disclosure were seen elsewhere. In a segment about the government's action to rescue mortgage giants Freddie Mac and Fannie Mae, CNBC turned to former Clinton administration official Howard Glaser for comment. Viewers heard Glaser call the government action a "message of confidence" and a "good move." What they did not hear, though, was any acknowledgment that Glaser was a paid consultant for the very same mortgage companies. According to *Politico*, Glaser became "something of a media go-to guy," appearing in the Associated Press, the *New York Times, Congressional Quarterly*, and *CBS Evening News*.

Such arrangements are not unusual. As the St. Louis weekly the *Pitch* reported on July 28, 2008, telecom analyst Jeff Kagan's name is familiar in reports about wireless companies like Sprint; he's been cited dozens of times over the past two years, and about half of those cites appeared in the local *Kansas City Star*. What was not known to readers, or apparently to the *Star* reporter who kept dialing him up, was that Kagan was a paid consultant to several large corporations, including Sprint. The *Star's* Jason Gertzen explained that while he is "usually pretty careful" about checking sources' conflicts of interest, he wasn't sure he had done so with Kagan. Checking Kagan's past wouldn't have been so hard; his role as a paid corporate pundit had been reported by the *New York Post* in 2006.

Some of the changes in the media industry have made it easier for corporate flacks to sneak into the news. As Adam Weinstein reported in *Mother Jones*, when the Florida-based Tallahassee Democrat looked for local voices to "fill out the paper's local coverage," they turned to Stacey Getz, who was publishing a popular local blog. The paper began printing some of her blog entries in its Metro section. In one instance, she wrote about proposals to build a Wal-Mart, which had engendered local opposition, leading her to ponder why "the mere mention of [Wal-Mart] turns some otherwise reasonable people into illogical lunatics." Unbeknownst to readers of the paper, Getz was actually a PR flack who had recently worked on behalf of a local Wal-Mart.

In Boston, local CN8 TV anchor Barry Nolan learned a different kind of lesson: be careful what you say about other powerful media figures. According to a May 6, 2002 report from *Extra!*, when Nolan learned that Fox's Bill O'Reilly was set to receive the Governors Award at the New England Emmy awards, Nolan thought the intemperate, factually challenged cable loudmouth wasn't exactly the kind of person whose record deserved celebrating. He decided to protest by passing out a document with quotes from O'Reilly's sexual harassment lawsuit. But he apparently drew more attention than his Comcast employers liked; as Nolan later wrote in *Think Progress*, "I got fired from my job on a news and information network for reporting demonstrably true things in a room full of news people."

From time to time we get a peek behind the corporate media curtain, thanks to anecdotes shared by those in a position to know how the news business works. Some are remarkably candid, if lacking in specifics— as when former CBS anchor Dan Rather declared, "It is a fact that corporate overlords working in secret collusion with the powers in Washington are intruding far too often in far too many newsrooms" (*New York Daily News*, February 27, 2008).

More often the pressures are described as being subtle. Writing about NBC correspondent Richard Engel's work in Baghdad, the *Washington Post's* Howard Kurtz reported that there was some unspecified pressure on the network: "Three years into the Iraq war, Richard Engel was hold-ing down the fort as NBC's Baghdad bureau chief when a top producer in New York, M. L. Flynn, told him there was 'tremendous pressure' in the newsroom to lighten up his coverage. 'It was all about getting good-news stories out there,' Engel says. 'There was a collective impression that all the journalists were getting it wrong. It quickly spread to the blo-gosphere and the world of punditry. It seemed orchestrated.'"

Writing in the December 2008 issue of *Harper's*, lawyer Scott Hor-ton explained that there was pressure at both PBS's flagship news program and CNN to go easy on torture commentary: "I myself was twice warned by PBS producers, in advance of appearances on the *News Hour with Jim Lehrer*, that I could use the word 'torture' in the abstract but that I was to refrain from applying it to the administration's policies. And after an interview with CNN in which I spoke of the administra-tion's torture policy, I was told by the producer, 'That's okay for CNN International, but we can't use it on the domestic feed.'"

Former *Dateline NBC* correspondent John Hockenberry wrote a lengthy piece for MIT's *Technology Review* about his years at the network. A package on suffering in the early days of the Iraq War got a wary recep-tion from a network "standards" executive, who worried that the Baghdad-based reporter might have a "point of view." The piece never aired, and Hockenberry took it as a lesson: "Empathy for the civilians did not fit into the narrative of shock and awe."

Years prior, Hockenberry wrote that he learned similar lessons in the wake of the September 11 attacks, when NBC stymied his efforts to report on the bin Laden family; it did not help matters that GE, NBC's parent company, had business connections to the Bin Laden Group. Hocken-berry expressed frustration that the network's "entertainment programs often took on issues that would never fly on *Dateline*." But it's not as if other news/entertainment considerations weren't at work:

> Sometimes entertainment actually drove selection of news sto-ries. Since *Dateline* was the lead-in to the hit series *Law & Order* on Friday nights, it was understood that on Fridays we did crime. . . . In 2003, I was told that a story on the emergence from prison of a former member of the Weather Underground, whose son had graduated from Yale University and won a Rhodes Scholarship, would not fly unless it dovetailed with a

storyline on a then-struggling, soon-to-be-canceled, and now-forgotten Sunday-night drama called *American Dreams*, which was set in the 1960s. I was told that the Weather Underground story might be viable if *American Dreams* did an episode on "protesters or something."

PETER HART is the activism director at FAIR. He writes for FAIR's magazine *Extra!* and is also a co-host and producer of FAIR's syndicated radio show CounterSpin.

Index On Censorship: 2008-2009

by Jo Glanville

Defamation has been a recurring theme for Index this year. It casts a universal chill on free speech, is the most common tool for policing and punishing dissent in authoritarian regimes, and is one of the most significant obstacles to freedom of expression in democracies. As a magazine/website based in the UK, Index on Censorship has to battle the world's most notorious libel laws on its own doorstep. Over the past year, English libel law has been singled out as singularly hostile to free speech and overly friendly to claimants. Thanks to "libel tourism," which allows plaintiffs from overseas to bring their cases to courts in England, the UK has virtually become an international tribunal for defamation. The rest of the world, however, is at last beginning to take notice. In 2008, the UN Human Rights Committee declared that English libel law discourages "critical media reporting on matters of serious public interest, adversely affecting the ability of scholars and journalists to publish their work." New York, Illinois and Florida have passed laws protecting their residents from English libel suits and there is now a bill before Congress that would allow US judges to block libel judgments that would be unconstitutional. In the UK, the House of Commons Select Committee on Culture, Media and Sport conducted an inquiry into libel and privacy in 2009. Index on Censorship has also held its own inquiry into the impact of libel in the UK with English PEN. We've even dedicated an entire issue of Index on Censorship's magazine to the subject, looking at the state of defamation around the world.

While there is a strong and welcome move for reform, there is also remarkable reluctance to make significant changes. This is partly because of an endemic mistrust of the press—and the fear that tipping the law in favour of free expression would unleash the media from all restraint. It is also because defamation laws remain a useful tool for the powerful to protect their interests. The fundamental role of the press as a watchdog seems to be forgotten when it comes to discussing libel. Moreover, defamation does not just affect journalists; it affects writers, even writers of fiction, book publishers, websites, and bloggers. Since the Internet revolution, there has as yet been no attempt in the UK to bring libel law up to date. While no libel action can be brought once a year has passed following the publication of an article in the print media, the same rule does not apply to online publication. A libel action can be brought at any time.

While there needs to be recourse for those whose good name and livelihood have been unjustly damaged, defamation suits should not be a vehicle for intimidation or censorship. The author Salman Rushdie's case in 2008 pointed one way forward. Following the publication of a book by a former policeman who had made false allegations about Rushdie, the writer was happy to accept a declaration of falsity in court and no damages. Should there be binding arbitration before any case comes to court? It might be one way of taking the financial fangs out of libel.

This is an area of free speech where it is difficult for liberal democracies to cast the first stone at authoritarian regimes, partly because most still have criminal defamation on their books. In the most extreme cases, criminal defamation legislation is a blatant means of controlling the media. In Sudan, for example, the police have a habit of detaining journalists and then releasing them before the case comes to trial. In Senegal, there are roughly twenty criminal defamation prosecutions a year, although few journalists in fact receive prison sentences. In both cases, the threat is enough to inhibit freedom of expression and promote a culture of self-censorship. In the UK, a number of peers in the House of Lords have been calling for its repeal, along with seditious libel. It's even still extant in a number of states in the US. If democracies were to repeal criminal defamation, it would be a significant global step forward for free speech.

But there are also more philosophical questions to be asked about reputation. Should corporations be entitled to a reputation? Australia, illiberal in so many other areas of free speech, has actually changed the law and made it possible only for corporations with fewer than ten employees, or that are not-for-profit, to sue. And what about the most volatile subject of defamation—religion—which currently has the UN Human Rights Council campaigning in its name? Should it be more difficult for public officials to bring libel actions (as it is in the States)? These are questions that need to be asked if, in the end, we're aiming for a law that is not based on archaic notions of honor, and if we truly want to push the boundaries of free speech.

"LIBEL LIBEL"

Free expression advocates have long argued that existing legal frameworks do not support an appropriate balance between the protection of reputation and the fundamental right to freedom of expression. In our first issue in spring 1972, Index on Censorship reported on the case of a Lebanese journalist who was imprisoned for libelling King Faisal of Saudi Arabia. Since then, libel has made a regular appearance in "Index Index," our chronicle of free expression violations around the world. Here, in "Libel Libel," we record libel cases around the world that occured from 2008 to 2009. Libel/defamation is a criminal offense in many countries, with prison sentences, sanctions, and heavy fines making the act of damaging someone's reputation a costly and dangerous business. Criminal libel remains on the books of many western European countries, sending a message that these outdated laws are acceptable. But even when libel is a civil offence, it has a serious impact on free expression simply because of the financial costs involved.

Azerbaijan

The trial of journalist Faramaz Novruzoglu, an advisor for *Nota* newspaper, and Ilham Tumas, the editor-in-chief of *24 Saat* newspaper, was heard in the Binagadi District Court on December 30, 2008. The chairman of the Adalat Party, Ilyas Ismayilov, lodged a lawsuit for insult and libel against the two media workers in relation to an article published in *24 Saat* on May 28, 2008. The judge postponed the next hearing for an indefinite period of time after sending the article in question for an expert opinion to determine whether it was written by Novruzoglu. In the article, Ismayilov is accused of having ties to separatists and working for Russia (IRFS).

Belarus

On March 27, 2008, secret security agents carried out raids on the homes of thirteen journalists, the radio stations Radio Racyja and European Radio for Belarus, and the satellite TV station Belsat. Agents seized equipment from Radio Racyja and interrogated one of its journalists. The authorities said the raids were to investigate alleged links between the media organizations and and three activists with the NGO Third Way who fled the country in 2005 after being accused of defamation when they posted satirical cartoons of President Lukashenko online. The journalists believe the raids were revenge for impartial reporting of a major opposition demonstration on March 25 (RSF).

Canada

Radio journalist Rafe Mair and Vancouver radio station CKNW were cleared on charges of defamation in the Supreme Court on June 27, 2008. Activist Kari Simpson sued Mair after he compared her to racist and violent historical figures on his radio program. Mair's comments were ruled to be fair comment. The case was thought to be likely to set a precedent in the way defamation cases are tried in the country (Canadian Journalists for Free Expression).

Chad

Radio FM Liberte was taken off air on January 17, 2008. The police detained its director, Djekourninga Kaoutar Lazare, on allegations of defamation after the station broadcast a petition brought against a minister by the Chadian Association for the Defence of the Rights of Consumers. The petition protested against administrative fees for the acquisition of government documents. The closure of the radio station also stemmed from critical reports of the government's treatment of wounded soldiers from non-Zaghawa ethnic groups and for interviewing opposition supporters and members (CPJ).

China

China Xu Dawen, the widow of renowned film director Xie Jin, announced that she was suing two bloggers for saying her husband died while spending the night with a prostitute. Xu demanded Song Zude and Liu Xinda delete articles about Xie's death from their blogs on major Chinese portal websites, and pay 500,000 yuan (US$73,000) for psychological injury. The Jing'an District People's Court in Shanghai lodged the case on February 23, 2009 (China Economic Net).

Egypt

On January 20, 2009, the al Zohor court of misdemeanors fined Mohammed Mabrouk 2,500 Egyptian pounds (US$450). The Trust

Chemicals Company filed a lawsuit after Mabrouk accused the company of throwing hazardous substances into the lake at al Manzlah and into the Suez Canal on his blog, Hakika Masriyah. Mabrouk also alleged that working conditions in the company are so hard that workers staged a sit-in against sackings and demanded copies of their contracts. Compensation was also awarded to the Trust Chemicals Company in a libel case filed by the company in June 2008 (Arabic Network for Human Rights).

Ethiopia

Amare Aregawi, editor for weekly newspaper the *Reporter*, was released on bail on August 28, 2008 after being arrested on August 22 in connection with a libel case lodged by the Dashen brewery in Gondar. The lawsuit was filed following the publication of an article about two former brewery employees quoted as saying they were wrongfully dismissed. After being arrested at the Addis Ababa headquarters of the Media and Communications Centre, which owns the *Reporter*, Aregawi was relocated to a prison in Gondar (RSF).

France

Vittorio de Filippis, former managing editor of the daily *Libération*, was arrested at his home on November 28, 2008 in connection with one of the many libel cases brought by the founder of the company Free against the newspaper. Under the country's 1881 press law, de Filippis was technically considered to be the author of the offending articles because he was editor at the time of the publication. He was informed he was under investigation and released after questioning and a body search (RSF).

Germany

The president of the German Football Federation (DFB) launched libel cases in two separate courts against Jens Weinrich in July 2008. The lawsuit followed the investigative freelance journalist's reference to Theo Zwanziger as an "incredible demagogue" on his blog. The courts ruled in Weinrich's favor. On November 14, DFB issued a press release said to contain a number of factual errors attacking the journalist for his remarks (IFJ).

Ghana

On February 27, 2009, a high court exonerated Western Publications Limited, publishers of the Accra-based privately owned *Daily Guide* newspaper, on libel charges brought against it by the country's foreign minister. The court awarded 1,000 cedis (US$717) to each of the defendants. In April 2004, Alhaji Mohammed Mumuni brought charges of defamation against managing editor Gina Blay, former deputy editor Ebenezer Ato Sam, and Western Publications Limited in connection with an article stemming from an interim audit report that claimed that Mumuni had engaged in criminal misconduct between 1997 and 2001 when he was at the Ministry of Mobilization and Social Welfare (MFWA).

Greece

On June 5, 2008, the European Court of Human Rights found the Greek government guilty of violation of freedom of expression for having convicted the daily *I Avgi* and its editor, Konstantinos Karis, of libel in 2003. Kyriako Velopoulos, who was elected in 2008 as a parliamentary representative of Popular Orthodox Alert, sued *I Avgi* for mentioning his alleged role in organizing a far right rally in Thessalonika. The European Court ordered the government to pay Karis and the newspaper's owners, I Avgi Publishing and Press Agency SA, E60,000 (US$81,573) in damages (newswatch.in).

India

BV Seetaram, chairman and chief editor of Chitra Publications, whose primary publication is the Mangalore-based newspaper *Karavali*, was arrested in the district of Udupi, Karnataka on January 5, 2009. Seetaram's detention relates to defamation charges filed in March 2007, when he and his wife were arrested for stirring up religious animosity. Seetaram lodged a complaint with the Press Council of India in December 2008, alleging that there was an active campaign by some political forces in the state to hamper distribution of *Karavali*. It was reported that the editor did not petition to be released on bail because he had reason to believe that some of those responsible for sabotaging the newspaper's circulation intended to cause him harm (IFJ).

Indonesia

The Supreme Court overturned the libel case against *Time* magazine on April 16, 2009. The magazine filed an appeal on February 21, 2008, calling for a September 2007 ruling to be overturned. At the end of the lengthy lawsuit, the magazine had been ordered to pay libel damages of US$106 million to former president Haji Muhammad Suharto, now deceased, following the publication of an article in 1999 accusing his family of theft of over US$15 million from the country (Index from April of 2007, IHT, *New York Times*, RSF).

Iraq

On November 4, 2008, a criminal court in Sulaymania found Shwan Dawdi, editor-in-chief of Kirkuk-based newspaper *Hawal*, guilty on three defamation charges filed by retired judge Kemal Mustafa, former head of the Sulaymania courthouse. Dawdi was jailed the same day and fined 300,000 Iraqi dinars (US$264) for publishing articles in 2004 on various problems in the court. He was charged and tried under an obsolete statute. A new, more liberal law, which took effect in October 2008, eliminates prison terms for offences such as defamation. Press freedom organizations petitioned the Kurdistan Regional Government's minister of justice, urging the court of appeals to hear the editor's case immediately. Dawdi's conviction was subsequently overturned (CPJ).

Kazakhstan

On January 16, 2009, the Medeus district court of Almaty ordered local newspaper *Taszhargan* to issue a retraction for an article published in April 2008. Senator Romin Madinov sued the newspaper and journalist Almas Kusherbayev for libel following an article in which Kusherbayev speculated that the rising price of bread and grain was caused by the fact that producers could secure a better price abroad. The article mentioned Madinov, who heads a company that controls a major part of the grain market. On February 26, 2009, it was reported that the city court had increased the amount Kusherbayev was required to pay in compensation for moral damages from 3 million tenge (US$20,130) to 30 million tenge (US$200,000) (IHT, Media Legal Defence Initiative, interfax Kazakhstan).

Morocco

Rachid Niny, the publisher of the newspaper *al Massae*, was fined 600,000 (US$72,937) by a Casablanca court on December 1, 2008 for allegedly libelling Mohammed Ziane, the head of the Rabat bar association (RSF).

Nicaragua

Jaime Chamorro Cardenal, editor of *La Prensa*, and Eduardo Enriquez, the paper's managing director, were convicted of libelling five women linked to the government party on April 22, 2008. They were ordered to pay 27,000 cordobas (US$1,381) and to publish the verdict immediately and without comment (Iapa).

Nigeria

During a raid on the head office of the *Leadership* newspaper in Abuja on May 6, 2008, deputy editor Danladi Ndayebo was arrested and detained for six hours in connection with a defamatory article about Senator Isa Mohammed. Police ordered Ndayebo to have the newspaper's former political editor, Saidu Usman Sarki, who was said to have written the offending article, report to them, and presented a list of sixteen senior editorial staff that they claimed were wanted for criminal defamation (allAfrica.com).

Philippines

On February 24, 2009, the Court of Appeals in Manila turned down a reconsideration motion filed by presidential spouse Jose Miguel "Mike" Arroyo to stop the hearing of the class suit filed against him by thirty-six journalists together with the Center for Media Freedom and Responsibility, the Philippine Center for Investigative Journalism and the *Daily Tribune*. The Court of Appeals affirmed its September 22 ruling to allow the Makati regional trial court to continue hearing the 12.5 million peso (US$261,000) class suit filed against Arroyo on December 28, 2006 in response to the eleven libel suits he had filed against forty-six journalists and media practitioners (CMFR).

Russia

The State Duma voted 339–1 on April 25, 2008 to tighten media rules on slander and libel. Redefining the offenses as "dissemination of deliberately false information," the new legislation allows authorities to shut down media outlets (*Chicago Tribune*).

South Africa

The Supreme Court of Appeal ruled on March 17, 2009 that Sunday newspaper *City Press* must pay defamation damages to Congress of the People President Terror Lekota and Kwazulu-Natal premier Sibusiso Ndebele. The charges relate to an article published on August 7, 2005 that claimed that Lekota and Ndebele had supplied confidential information to an agent who was purporting to be a journalist. The High Court in Johannesburg upheld the defamation claims made by Lekota and Ndebele and awarded them 150,000 rand (US$15,913) and 112,500 rand (US$11,935) respectively (iol.co.za).

Taiwan

On February 15, 2009, Shih-Mingthe, who initiated a campaign in 2006 calling on then-President Chen Shui-bian to step down, expressed his intentions to press defamation charges against former presidential adviser Ellen Huang, Tainan City Councillor Wang Ting-yu, Chtonic lead vocalist Freddy Lim, Control Yuan member Chien Lin Huichien, and magazine *Scoop Weekly* for accusing him of appropriating funds from the campaign. Shih said he would seek NT$10 million (US$296,348) in damages from each of the four individuals and NT$20 million (US$592,696) from the magazine, as well as a half-page apology in four major newspapers (*Taipei Times*).

Thailand

It was reported on December 2, 2008 that journalist Nonghart Harnavilai, who faced a libel suit filed by Tesco Lotus, Tesco's Thai subsidiary, in March, reached an agreement to settle the case with the retail giant. Nonghart and Tesco Lotus came to an agreement before a judge on the wording of a clarification to be published in the newspaper *Bangkokbiznews*. Tesco Lotus had filed a 103 million baht (US$3 million) libel suit against Nonghart after a January 2008 *Bangkokbiznews* article stated that the global retailer did not "love" Thailand (Seapa).

Turkey

It was reported on October 16, 2008, that a court ordered the blocking of the *Vatan* newspaper's website. The move followed a complaint filed by writer and creationist Adnan Oktar, who claimed that he was defamed on the readers' comments section of the site. Oktar was also said to be responsible for blocking access to the website of British evolutionist Richard Dawkins over defamation charges in September 2008 (*Guardian*).

United Kingdom

On May 15, 2008, the Crown Prosecution Service and West Midlands Police formally apologised to the producers of *Undercover Mosque*, a Channel 4 documentary highlighting inflammatory speech in UK mosques. The filmmakers sued the Crown Prosecution Service and West Midlands Police for defamation after they alleged that the documentary had been edited to misrepresent the various speakers. The CPS and police are also expected to pay up to £1,000,000 (US$1,446,736) in costs and damages (BBC).

United States

The New York State Legislature passed a law on May 1, 2008, protecting American journalists from defamation lawsuits brought against them overseas. The Libel Terrorism Protection Act, known as "Rachel's Law," was introduced after Rachel Ehrenfeld was successfully sued for libel in the UK by Khalid bin Mahfouz, a Saudi businessman she alleged had financed terrorism. The law provides for New York courts to assume jurisdiction over anyone who brings a defamation lawsuit anywhere against a New York resident, and disallow such decisions' enforcement unless it can be demonstrated that foreign law offers the same freedom of speech guarantees offered by the US Constitution (*Times* [UK]).

JO GLANVILLE is editor for the Index on Censorship in London, England.

CHAPTER 9

The Hyperrealilty of a Failing Corporate Media System

by Andrew Hobbs and Peter Phillips

Hyperreality is the inability to distinguish between what is real and what is not. Corporate media, Fox in particular, offers news that creates a hyperreality of real world problems and issues. Consumers of corporate television news—especially those whose understandings are framed primarily from that medium alone—are embedded in a state of excited delirium and knowinglessness.

Corporate media hasn't acted as a cohesive, protective "fourth estate" in several decades, instead gilding lilies such as the Iraq War, torture, and the true extent of Hurricane Katrina's devastation. Contemporary corporate news is best seen in a post-modern context of hyperreality. The news from US networks is based on the presentations of partially factual stories framed inside socio-emotional story lines that juxtapose "evil" with patriotism and Christian fervor. There are multiple examples of this, but we will examine two distinct cases.

The bias towards hyperreality inherent in modern media is so rampant, consumers only need turn on the TV to be exposed to the spin. Two notorious, controversial modern figures will be examined here to explain what we mean by a hyperreality of knowinglessness. News coverage of Venezuelan President Hugo Chávez and right-wing radio personality Rush Limbaugh are unique examples, primarily because of their perceived opposing views and their unapparent similarities. But they are similar in that both should have little operable relevance to American policy, at least domestically, as one is an entertainer and the other is the leader of another country. They both are media personalities as well: Limbaugh claims an audience of 20 million a week,[1] while Chávez hosts a telecast every Sunday through which he speaks to millions of people of Venezuela. Further, they are both strongly ideological in their pursuit of their beliefs, which seem diametrically opposed to each other.

Unfortunately, they both have ill-gotten relevance, ironically at least partially gleaned from the massive amount of attention turned to them by their press adversaries. This allows an opportunity for analysis: what is the public consequence of attention, be it positive or negative?

THE EVILNESS OF HUGO CHÁVEZ

Big business would be foolish to ignore the threat posed to their supply side paradigm in Venezuela, since the longer reaches of Chávez's influence may well extend to far wealthier economies. Should the people's revolution in Venezuela gain footholds elsewhere, it will be difficult for those same economic models to be argued against here in the US. If a country with resources like Venezuela's is able to offer programs and facilities of a certain quality, why can't the US, with its greater resource pool, repeat the success here? Since Chávez's social advances for the people in Venezuela run so drastically contrary to those avowed to the captains of industry in the US, any action Chávez takes is systematically vilified by the US corporate media.

Fox News, one of the largest media outlets in the US, has been the epicenter for demonizing Chávez. The station features such luminaries as Glenn Beck, who once called Cindy Sheehan a "tragedy slut" and discussed murdering Michael Moore[2] on his program. Fox attack pieces on Chávez are uniform and systematic to the point of redundancy. In examining transcripts from Fox News regarding Chávez, we find a continued use of emotionally negative descriptive terms like authoritarian, strongman, socialist, cruel, sinister, radical, militant, and dictator. Chávez has repeatedly over the past decade been democratically elected by a vast majority of the people in Venezuela. However, the US corporate slant on Chávez is always the same predictable negative opposition filled with emotional slanders.

After Chávez used licensing laws to shut down RCTV in Caracas, possibly because the RCTV directors were heavily involved in the conspiracy to overthrow Chávez during the coup of 2002, Fox covered the incident as if censorship had been his motivation, pushing headlines such as "Protests in Venezuela Turn Ugly."[3] The first sections of Fox's coverage were full of rubber bullets and tear gas; as the story dwindled, Fox continued to report unsubstantiated estimates of mass protesters and increasing authoritarianism. This is the essential structure to most any news on Chávez found in the US corporate media.

Unfortunately, Fox's coverage never really examines the origins of the protests—as in, who are the people participating? Are they the same individuals who so violently opposed Chávez a few years prior? A poll in Venezuela conducted after the closing of RCTV actually indicated a broad ambivalence towards the closing, with some 70 percent of those polled opposed to shutting down the station; however, most people indicated it was because their favorite soap operas and other programming were being cancelled.[4]

Fox News and Glenn Beck seem adamant about tying Obama's administration to socialism. Chávez provides a convenient straw man through which to beat up on progressivism, socialism, and President Obama as well. In February, 2009, in a TV piece entitled "Would You Vote for Hugo Chávez?,"[5] Beck claimed that the US is "on a highway to socialism" as a result of our move to "nationali[ze] our banks." He then proposed that, with one more bank bailout, America could be ready for a Chávez presidency. Chávez has become, for Fox, a symbol of evil. The resulting emotional knowinglessness is being used to undermine the Obama presidency. Fox completely ignores the facts of the enormous bailouts—which had been supported by the previous Bush administration—such as those for Bear Stearns and AIG. It uses hyperreal slander to describe Chávez, linking these feelings to Obama in a purely emotional manner without using logic or facts.

Led by President Hugo Chávez, the United Socialist Party of Venezuela (PSUV) gained over one and half million voters in the most recent elections on November 23, 2008. Before the election of Hugo Chávez as president in 1998, college attendance was primarily for the rich in Venezuela. Today, over 1,800,000 students attend college, three times the rate ten years ago.

For the lowest-income two thirds of people in Venezuela, Hugo Chávez means health care, jobs, food, and security in neighborhoods where in many cases nothing but absolute poverty existed ten years ago. With unemployment below a US level, sharing the wealth has taken real meaning in Venezuela. Despite a 50 percent increase in the prices of food last year, local Mercals offer government subsidized cooking oil, corn meal, meat, and powered milk at a 30 to 50 percent discount. Additionally, there are now 3,500 local communal banks with a $1.6 billion dollar budget offering neighborhood-based micro-financing loans for home improvements, small businesses, and personal emergencies.

In Venezuela, the corporate media are still owned by the elites. The five major TV networks, and nine of ten of the major newspapers, maintain an effort to undermine Chávez and the socialist revolution. Despite the corporate media bias and the continuing financial support to anti-Chávez opposition institutions from USAID and National Endowment for Democracy ($20 million annually, paid for by US taxpayers), two-thirds of the people in Venezuela continue to support President Hugo Chávez and the United Socialist Party of Venezuela.

Fox has no bounds to its obsession with Chávez. They have run stories about his rocky divorce and child custody struggles as well as his vocal contribution to an album by artists "engaged in the Bolivarian Revolution." Barack Obama's greeting of Chávez at the Organization of American States meeting, and its potential diplomatic consequences, warranted Fox commentary from Karl Rove; John Bolton, former US ambassador to the UN; *and* Beck.[6]

There is an abundant source of negative Chávez news found on the Associated Press (AP) wires as well. AP's stories are often close to Fox's assertion that Venezuela is a socialist petro-fiefdom.

Chávez isn't without political moves; as any leader democratically elected multiple times would have to be heavy-handed to some degree. Unfortunately, only half the story is reported in the US. Again, the best example of partial reporting is the coverage of Chávez's not renewing the broadcast license of RCTV in 2006, by exercising the Law on the Social Responsibility of Radio and Television. US reporting on this was completely myopic in nature.[7] Had producers and executives of an American media outlet conspired against the US Government, they most certainly would have been dealt with in far stricter terms than those applied at RCTV. RCTV was allowed to broadcast for the remainder of their licensing period.

After the Constitutional Reforms of 2007, US corporate media outlets began claiming Chávez had inserted language into the constitution that could make him "President for life." Again, this was a case of the truth being stretched. The changes had only included a reform that would have allowed a possible third term for Chávez. Other nations that do not have term limits at all include Germany, the UK, and Australia, yet none of these are labeled in the US media as "dictatorships." That 2007 reform was ironically defeated, but a newer bill, removing term limits altogether, was passed in February of 2009.

The US corporate media doesn't likely pose much difficulty to Chávez and his democratically elected agenda—he's been winning elections since 1998. Moreover, what Chávez does in Venezuela has very little impact on policies and circumstances in the US. But the ongoing demonization of Chávez allows for the perpetuation of a deeply embedded emotional hyperreality inside American public consciousness. A hyper-real Chávez is continually available for comparison with other contemporary issues. US corporate media ignores many contemporary dictators. King Abdullah of Saudi Arabia, who sits on the throne of an autocratic dictatorship under which women have essentially no rights, holds a perennial place on the "Parade's World's Worst Dictator" list,[8] as does Hu Jintao, China's President. Searches for each leader on Fox's website returns a total of 806 and 888 results, respectively, from their entire database. The same search for Chávez—the democratically elected leader of a country with just three million more people than Saudi Arabia, but a fraction of China's population—yields 2,743 pages. Saudi Arabia, home of Osama Bin Laden and fifteen of the alleged nineteen 9/11 hijackers, is portrayed as an ally to the US.

THE GLORY OF RUSH LIMBAUGH

Rush Limbaugh has found himself in a position of far more influence than anybody except himself could ever believe. Anointed "boss" by both the press and the right-wing lawmakers who apologize to him after contradicting his ideology, Limbaugh has taken his continued popularity as mandate and continues to push his agenda.

Limbaugh has sharpened his attack since the 2008 election, as seen during a June 4, 2009 interview with Fox's Sean Hannity.[9] Hannity treated Limbaugh as something of a moral and constitutional authority, allowing him to conduct himself in an almost pastoral way, delivering dogmatic sermons on Americanism. Limbaugh maintained the position that Barack Obama's efforts to restore the bruised economy are tantamount to socialism and fascism. Limbaugh joked, "Fidel Castro and I (Hugo Chávez), if we're not careful, are going to end up to the right of Obama" in reference (though the context was not related) to General Motors becoming "Government Motors." Limbaugh went on to say, "You can keep a chart here of who's nationalizing more, Obama or Chávez . . . it's probably neck and neck."

Rush Limbaugh was in the middle of a storm of exchanges between the Democrat and Republican leadership during the early spring of 2009. White House chief of staff Rahm Emanuel[10] claimed that the radio host is "the voice and the intellectual force and energy behind the Republican Party." Republican National Committee Chairman Michael Steele says he has reached out to Rush Limbaugh to tell him he meant no offense when he referred to the popular conservative radio host as an "entertainer" whose show can be "incendiary." "My intent was not to go after Rush—I have enormous respect for Rush Limbaugh," Steele said. "I was maybe a little bit inarticulate. . . There was no attempt on my part to diminish his voice or his leadership."

Crooner Pat Boone[11] waxes poetic in a tribute piece: "Rush Limbaugh is a patriot. Pure and simple, a patriot. I see him in the select company of other patriots like Paul Revere, Thomas Paine and Ben Franklin. Thankfully, he hasn't been asked to make a dying proclamation like Nathan Hale—"'I regret that I have but one life to give for my country'— but I suspect he would, if it came to that."

Conservative activist Phyllis Schlafly[12] further holds Rush to be a model citizen: "One secret to Limbaugh's success is that he is not intimidated into appeasing the organized pressure groups that frighten so many others into platitudinous mush. He takes them all on: the radical feminists, the wacky environmentalists, the open-borders crowd, and even President George W. Bush's deviation from conservatism."

Rush Limbaugh is a man of Christian values—although which congregation he attends remains a question—and believes that America is a nation founded upon Christian principals.

Born in 1951 to a prominent Missouri family, young Rush was a Boy Scout but never earned a single merit badge. Perhaps to placate his parents, Limbaugh enrolled for two semesters and a summer at Southern Missouri State University; His mother told biographer Paul Colford that he had "flunked everything,"[13] unable to pass even a modern ballroom dancing class. His career during the 1970s was primarily spent as a music station DJ, moving from station to station before taking a stint as director of promotions for the Kansas City Royals in 1979. Returning to the airwaves in 1984, it wasn't until the Reagan administration repealed the fairness doctrine that Rush was able to hit his full stride.

How and when was it that he gained this fluency, which he purports to possess, and how does it display itself? Consider Limbaugh's May 14, 2008, commentary from his radio program concerning the Great Depression and his choice of adversaries to defame.[14] "The straw man," a favorite tactic of Rush's, is deployed. He Google searches some terms trying to uncover popular hits explaining the Great Depression; his search yields, predictably, an academic paper titled "The Main Causes of the Great Depression" published in 1996. Rush systematically disassembles the paper like an angry professor, not so much refuting it as ridiculing it, finally concluding that it should be checked for plagiarism against the works of Karl Marx. He goes on to claim the author, Paul Gusmorino, is "exactly wrong" after saying, "I didn't end up in college and have my mind polluted and brainwashed by a bunch of Marxist professors." Unfortunately for Rush, neither had the piece's author Gusmorino. Gusmorino, who is currently a Program Manager for Microsoft, was in tenth grade when he wrote the piece in 1996—hardly a Marxist political economy professor.

Rush Limbaugh inside the corporate media is a caricature of patriotism and Christian values. That he lacks factual understandings of socio-political circumstances doesn't matter in a hyperreal corporate media system. Just the fact that he is openly discussed by both political parties sets forth an emotion-based parody of specific issues and creates an excited delirium of knowinglessness.

WHAT'S THE SCORE HERE?

Michael Savage found himself banned from the UK[15] after his tone was "allegedly fostering extremism or hatred," citing his claim that the

"Qur'an . . . is a 'book of hate.'" Yet in the US there are no such challenges of hate speakers like Limbaugh in the corporate media. The US as a society has seen an undeniable upswing in domestic extremism since the change of administrations. Individuals associated with right-wing groups or following traditionally right-leaning causes, such as gun control or abortion, have emerged in patterns of hate-based excited deliriums.

On the night of Obama's inauguration, "self-proclaimed white supremacist" Keith Luke was arrested following an apparent multiple rape-homicide, which left two dead and a third severely injured and raped; all his victims were black. He had been planning to end the spree with a massacre at a local synagogue's "Bingo Night."

Three Pittsburgh Police officers paid with their lives for Richard Poplawski's paranoid fear that the Obama administration was going to take his guns.

Dr. George Tiller, survivor of multiple attempts on his life already, was gunned down in his own church, serving as an usher for the Sunday, May 31, 2009 service.

Just ten days later, eighty-eight-year old white supremacist, James von Brunn, took the life of a security guard and injured others after he opened fire at the US Holocaust Museum in Washington, DC. These are but the outliers that reflect a disturbing trend. Already, some are questioning the role the media may be playing.[16] Perhaps it is not fair to blame corporate media for right-wing extremism, but an expanding knowinglessness is undoubtedly a contributing factor.

Without a context of factual understanding, Glenn Beck is able to say on national Fox television news that the shooting at the Holocaust Museum was openly supported by 9/11 truth people. Beck claimed[17] that 9/11 truth proponents see James von Brunn as a "hero." Beck's statement is completely without factual merit and represents a hyperreal emotional slamming of a group already slanderously pre-labeled by the corporate media as conspiracy theorists. Beck continued his diatribe by further equating 9/11 truth with white supremacy and al-Qaeda, claiming that they all want to "destroy the country" (See Chapter Ten for an update on 9/11 issues).

Our cultural decline will continue as long as the spin that incites it is present. The consumer body itself will eventually decide that these messages are meaningless. The ongoing decline of confidence in US corporate media is already evidence of such a reversal of belief. This becomes apparent when news—as entertainment media—follows the same paradigm as any media, which is highly cyclical and repetitious in nature: it loses appeal and the carrier eventually fails.

Meanwhile, many Americans are deeply imbedded in a state of excited delirium of knowinglessness. Reversing this tendency is a vital part of building media democracy. Only a vibrant independent news media based in rational factually-researched news can alleviate our crisis of hyperreality.

ANDREW HOBBS is a philosophy major at Sonoma State University. Research assistance on this chapter was provided by SSU students Ian Marlowe and Kevin Gonzalez.

Notes

1. "Limbaugh's Audience Size? It's Largely Up in the Air," *Washington Post*, March 7, 2009.
2. *The Glenn Beck Program*, August 15, 2005 and May 17, 2005, respectively.
3. See http://www.foxnews.com/story/0,2933,275912,00.html.
4. "Venezuela Replaces Opposition TV with State Network," Reuters, May 28, 2007.
5. See http://www.foxnews.com/story/0,2933,494065,00.html
6. Fox News Contributors, "By Greeting Hugo Chávez, Is President Obama Slighting US Allies?" April 21, 2009.
7. "Coup Co-Conspirators as Free-Speech Martyrs," FAIR, May 25, 2007.
8. See http://www.parade.com/dictators/2009/
9. Fox News, "Rush Limbaugh on Hannity," June 4, 2009.
10. "Steele to Rush: I'm Sorry," *Politico*, March 2, 2009.
11. See http://www.worldnetdaily.com/index.php?fa=PAGE.view&pageId=70559.
12. See http://www.wnd.com/index.php?fa=PAGE.view&pageId=71100.
13. Paul D. Colford, *The Rush Limbaugh Story: Talent On Loan From God: An Unauthorized Biography* (New York: St. Martin's Press, 1993).
14. See www.rushlimbaugh.com/home/daily/site_051408/content/01125111.guest.html
15. See http://www.cbc.ca/world/story/2009/05/05/britain-banned-list050.html
16. Errol Louis, "Connect the Dots of Hatred . . ." *New York Daily News*, June 14, 2009.
17. See http://www.youtube.com/watch?v=lUTATYaIZYI&feature=related.

Analysis of Project Censored: Are We a Left-Leaning, Conspiracy-Oriented Organization?

by Peter Phillips and Mickey Huff

> *Where justice is denied, where poverty is enforced, where ignorance prevails, and where any one class is made to feel that society is an organized conspiracy to oppress, rob and degrade them, neither persons nor property will be safe.*

—Frederick Douglass

Critics of Project Censored often declare that we are a left-leaning organization. This is an interesting claim, given that over 200 faculty and students from multiple disciplines and political orientations work with Project Censored each year. Over 1,500 students have been trained in media research techniques since we began in 1976, and it would be hard to find a more mainstream, mostly Californian college student body.

Critical thinking and fact finding are not left leaning, they are the basis of democracy, and we proudly stand for the maximization of informed participatory democracy at the lowest possible level in society. To this end, Project Censored supports social justice and media democracy in action.

The second most often announced complaint is that we cover news stories that are really not "censored." But our definition of censorship has been quite clear all along. Any interference with the free flow of information is censorship. Even if the interference is structural or not deliberate, it has the same impact of creating a lack of public awareness on critical issues. This means that when the *New York Times* chooses to cover the updates on celebrity deaths, marriages, or divorces, and ignores the ACLU's release of military autopsy reports proving that the US was torturing prisoners to death in Iraq and Afghanistan (Censored Story #7, 2007), that is censorship. It is censorship even if most of the *New York Times* journalists didn't know about the ACLU report; they certainly should have—it was an AP release! The ACLU report was only covered in a dozen or so newspapers (not the *Times*) and went widely unnoticed. For a story this important to go virtually unreported implies a degree of overt censorship.

Further, if journalists ignore topics related to 9/11, election fraud, electromagnetic weapons, contrail irregularities, and so on because they might be labeled "conspiracy theorists," that is censorship as well. Any decision to cover up, ignore, avoid, steer away from, or simply fail to investigate—even if the investigation is not fruitful—is censorship because it implies a willful choice to not cover a particular story. Ignoring important news stories, no matter the reason, is not commensurate with the principles of a free press.

CONSPIRACY THEORIES

Those who think we at Project Censored are "left leaning" and who dispute our definition of censorship also accuse us of reporting on and perpetuating conspiracy theories—as though this were a bad thing. Allow us to explain our position on this topic.

Conspiracies tend to be actions by small groups of individuals rather than massive collective plots by governments and corporations. However, small groups can be dangerous, especially when the individuals have significant power in huge public and private bureaucracies. But it is very unlikely that conspiracies can be interlinked in a macro way, bridging the gaps between dozens of corporations and government bureaucracies. There are just too many opportunities for leaks and exposures.

Nonetheless, corporate boards of directors do meet in closed rooms to plan how best to maximize profit. If they knowingly make plans that hurt others, violate laws, undermine ethics, or show favoritism to friends, they are involved in a conspiracy. Conspiracies exist everywhere, and yes, people do sit in rooms and conspire all the time. They may not congregate at the end of dark piers, in abandoned warehouses under lights with no shades, smoking cigars in trenchcoats and looking askance, but conspirators do exist. Micro-plots may well be the answer to some of the famous conspiracies theories floating in our circles of cynicism on the Internet. However, without accurate, thorough investigations, we can only stew in our distrust. Critical thinking and accurate, transparent investigative research are needed to counter the emotional fraud and propaganda of speculative ideas, fear mongering, and groupthink.

The first thing that critics of investigations on 9/11, election fraud, and any other issues do is to link all the questions—including some of the most hairbrained ideas—together in a crazy hodgepodge of irrationality that undermines legitimate investigations. There is often a series of logical fallacies used by critics of controversial issues, including ad hominem attacks, red herring and straw person distractions, and false dilemmas. Because many people are taken in by these irrationalities, some journalists are fearful of being labeled conspiracy theorists. To protect their careers many—especially those in corporate media—will steer their inquiries to "safer" stories.

For example, in 2007, Project Censored covered research into the events of 9/11 by Brigham Young University physics professor Steven E. Jones. Dr. Jones concluded that the official explanation for the collapse of the World Trade Center (WTC) buildings was implausible according to laws of physics. Jones called for an independent, international scientific investigation "guided not by politicized notions and constraints but rather by observations and calculations." Jones specifically investigated the collapse of WTC 7, a forty-seven-story building that was not hit by planes, yet dropped in its own "footprint" in the same manner as a controlled demolition late in the afternoon on September 11, 2001. WTC 7 collapsed in 6.6 seconds, just .6 of a second longer than it would take an object dropped from the roof to hit the ground. "Where is the delay that must be expected due to conservation of momentum, one of the foundational laws of physics?" Jones asked. "That is, as upper-falling floors strike lower floors—and intact steel support columns—the fall must be significantly impeded by the impacted mass," he explained. "How do the upper floors fall so quickly, then, and still conserve momentum in the collapsing buildings?" The paradox, he says, "is easily resolved by the explosive demolition hypothesis, whereby explosives quickly removed lower-floor material, including steel support columns, and allow near free-fall-speed collapses."

To support his theory, Jones and eight other scientists conducted chemical research on the dust from the World Trade centers. Their research results were published in a peer-reviewed scientific journal. The *Open Chemical Physics Journal*, Volume 2, 2009, included their research article, "Active Thermitic Material Discovered in Dust from the 9/11 World Trade Center Catastrophe." In the abstract the authors write, "We have discovered distinctive red/gray chips in all the samples. These red/gray chips show marked similarities in all four samples. The properties of these chips were analyzed using optical microscopy, scanning electron microscopy (SEM), X-ray energy dispersive spectroscopy (XEDS), and differential scanning calorimetry (DSC). The red portion of these chips is found to be an unreacted thermitic material and highly energetic." Thermite is a pyrotechnic composition of a metal powder and a metal oxide, which produces an aluminothermic reaction known as a thermite reaction and is used in controlled demolitions of buildings.

Additionally, architect Richard Gage, AIA, founder of Architects and Engineers for 9/11 Truth, has to date amassed over 700 scientific professionals in the fields of architecture, engineering, and physics who have signed a petition calling for a new investigation of the events of 9/11 in New York. Gage's and Jones' empirical research suggesting the possibility of controlled demolition have moved thousands of others to question the events of 9/11, but most in the media have either ignored their hard data, marginalized their significance, or outright attacked them. Again, this is not the role of a free press. If bias is unacceptable, these views should be heard and vetted fairly in an open society regardless of their ultimate outcomes and without contingency upon their popularity.[1]

In the case of Gage and Jones, there are scientific, factual arguments that establish the clear possibility of controlled demolition of the World Trade Center buildings on September 11, 2001, and there is zero coverage in the corporate media in the US. This is top down corporate censorship pure and simple. Even if other scientists can be found to disagree with the study, the policy of ignoring the topic inside the corporate media is absolute. It seems unlikely that corporate journalists are unaware of the research, as it is listed on hundreds of websites worldwide. Perhaps the mainstream science journalists leave their critical thinking skills at home and give the scientific method the day off. Or maybe the real conspiracy exists within the boardrooms of the corporate mainstream media.

We asked a faculty physicist at Sonoma State University what she thought about the new research from Dr. Jones in the *Open Chemical Physics Journal*. She had been critical of Jones when he spoke on our campus in 2006. At that time she said she didn't need to read Jones' research because she had read a *Popular Mechanics* article on the issue, a nonacademic report that has been debunked in scholarly circles. She went on to imply that she "just knew" Jones was wrong. So when presented with a peer-reviewed release in an academic chemical journal, her response was that it was not one of the most prestigious journals, without going into any detail. In other words, if one doesn't like what a scientific journal says, one can dismiss it a priori. No debate, no open discussion required. These are hardly principles of the academy and they are not tenets of a free press. In fact, these tactics and practices of attack and avoidance are enemies of free thought in any democratic society.

PROJECT CENSORED AS LEFT LEANING

According to the editor of the *Pasadena Weekly*, Project Censored suffers from a "perceived extreme left-leaning bent that editors . . . have assumed over the years in selecting, writing, and publishing its stories . . . more than anything it has been the Project's perceived long leftward lean that has done the most damage to its overall credibility. Although the group never explicitly takes a political stance, a majority of the stories Project Censored highlights have a leftist political slant, criticizing big business, economic inequality, damage to the environment, the Pentagon, and misdeeds of conservative politicians, among other progressive issues."[2]

Why stories about the powerful in government and big business or about environmental and inequality issues are left leaning is beyond our understanding. It seems that this is just good journalism—the journalism that is missing in the corporate media—and could just as well be middle-leaning-journalism, right-leaning-journalism or crazy California journalism. We are holding those in powerful positions in society accountable for their decisions and actions, which we believe is what a free press is supposed to do. Nonetheless, to address the accusation we decided to examine the key stories Project Censored covered over the past sixteen years during both the George W. Bush and the William Jefferson Clinton administrations. Perhaps we would detect the bias in our records.

But after examining our censored news stories from both the Bush and Clinton administrations, we found very evident similarities. Both administrations lied to support military aggression, supported policies that resulted in hundreds of thousands of civilian deaths, spied on Americans, undermined civil liberties and violated international treaties, supported global arms sales/distribution and private mercenaries, ignored environmental issues, lobbied for unsafe industrial practices, allowed big banks and Wall Street unregulated freedoms, and encouraged media consolidation and repression of open journalism.

Following are some of the stories Project Censored covered under the Clinton and Bush presidencies; you may decide for yourself whether a bias toward the Left is expressed. All stories are archived online at http://projectcensored.org under the archives link catalogued by year.[3]

ARMS SALES/SUPPORT AND CONSEQUENCES

Under Clinton

Turkey Destroys Kurdish Villages with US Weapons
Censored 2000, Story #5

Source: Kevin McKiernan, "Turkey's War on the Kurds," The Bulletin of Atomic Scientists, March/April, 1999.

In 1995, the Clinton administration recognized that the Turkish government used American arms in domestic military operations where human rights abuses occurred. In fact, Turkey has forcibly evacuated, leveled and burned more than 3,000 Kurdish villages in the past decade. Most of the atrocities, which have cost over 40,000 lives, took place during Clinton's first term in office. As an ally of the US through NATO, Turkey receives US weapons from dozens of companies, including Hughes, Boeing, Raytheon, and General Dynamics. Despite a horrifying report of violent abuse by Amnesty International, the State Department passed arms deals with Turkey. The war in Turkey represents the greatest use of US weapons in combat anywhere in the world today.

Under Bush

US Aid to Israel Fuels Repressive Occupation in Palestine
Censored 2004, Story #24

Sources: John Steinbach, "Palestine in the Crosshairs: US Policy and the struggle for Nationhood," *Covert Action Quarterly,* Spring 2002, No. 72; Matt Bowles, "US Aid Lifeblood of the Occupation," *Left Turn,* March 4, 2002; Bob Wing, "Israel Erecting 'Great Wall' Around Palestine," *Wartimes,* April 2003.

US aid to Israel over the course of its fifty-four years of nationhood has fueled the illegal occupation of Palestinian land superceding Palestinian rights to self-government.During the last twenty-five years US aid to Israel has been about 60 percent military aid and 40 percent economic aid. There is a new plan to phase out all economic aid by 2008 in order to have all the aid going to military. Israel receives about $3 billion a year in direct aid and $3 billion a year in indirect aid in the form of special loans and grants. Under the Arms Export Control Act the US can only supply weapons that are used "for legitimate self defense." The US Foreign Assistance Act prohibits military assistance to any country "which engages in a consistent pattern of gross violations of internationally recognized human rights." The Proxmire Amendment bans military assistance to any government that refuses to sign the Nuclear Non-Proliferation Treaty and to allow inspections of its nuclear facilities. All three of these laws are currently being broken with aid to Israel.

PREWAR INTELLIGENCE USED TO JUSTIFY MILITARY AGGRESSION

Under Clinton

Evidence Indicates No Pre-war Genocide in Kosovo
Censored 2000, Story #12

Sources: Mark Cook, "William Walker: 'Man With a Mission,'" *Covert Action Quarterly*, Spring/Summer 1999; *The Progressive Review*, "My Multinational Entity, Right or Wrong," June 1999; Pablo Ordaz , "Spanish Police and Forensic Experts Have Not Found Proof of Genocide in the North of Kosovo," *El Pais*, September 23, 1999.

According to the *New York Times,* the "turning point" to NATO's decision to go to war against Yugoslavia occurred on January 20, 1999 when US diplomat William Walker led a group of news reporters to discover a so-called Serb massacre of some forty-five Albanians in Racak, Kosovo. This story made international headlines and was later used to justify the NATO bombings.

The day before the "massacre," Serb police had a firefight with Kosovo Liberation Army (KLA) rebels that was covered by an Associated Press (AP) film crew. At the end of day, the village was deserted. Then, the next day, the village had been reoccupied by the KLA, and it was the KLA who initially led foreign visitors to the alleged massacre site. William Walker arrived at noon with additional journalists and expressed his outrage at a "genocidal massacre" to the world press.

Walker's story remains shrouded with doubt. "What is disturbing," remarks war correspondent Renaud Girard, "is that the pictures filmed by the AP journalists radically contradict Walker's accusations." Challenges to Walker's massacre story were published in *Le Monde* and *Le Figaro*: "During the night, could the UCK (KLA) have gathered the bodies, in fact killed by Serb bullets, to set up a scene of cold-blooded massacre?" (*Le Figaro*). Belarussian and Finnish forensic experts were later unable to verify that a massacre had actually occurred at Racak.

Under Bush

US Illegally Removes Pages from Iraq UN Report
Censored 2004, Story #3

Source: Michael I. Niman, "What Bush didn't want you to know about Iraq," *The Humanist* and *ArtVoice*, March/April 2003.

Throughout the winter of 2002, the Bush administration publicly accused Iraqi weapons declarations of being incomplete. The almost unbelievable reality of this situation is that it was the United States itself that had removed over 8,000 pages of the 11,800 page original report given by Iraq to the UN. This came as no surprise to Europeans, however, as Iraq had made extra copies of the complete weapons declaration report and unofficially distributed them to journalists throughout Europe. The Berlin newspaper *Die Tageszetung* broke the story on December 19, 2002, in an article by Andreas Zumach.

According to Niman, "The missing pages implicated twenty-four US-based corporations and the successive Ronald Reagan and George Bush Sr. administration in connection with the illegal supplying of Saddam Hussein government with myriad weapons of mass destruction and the training to use them." Groups documented in the original report that were supporting Iraq's weapons programs prior to Iraq's 1990 invasion of Kuwait included Eastman Kodak, Dupont, Honeywell, Rockwell, Sperry, Hewlett-Packard, and Bechtel; US government agencies such as the Department of Energy, Department of Agriculture, and Department of Defense; and nuclear weapons labs such as Lawrence-Livermore, Los Alamos, and Sandia.

Beginning in 1983, the US was involved in eighty shipments of biological and chemical components, including strains of botulism toxin, anthrax, gangrene bacteria, West Nile fever virus, and Dengue fever virus. These shipments continued even after Iraq used chemical weapons against Iran in 1984.

CIVILIAN DEATHS IN IRAQ

Under Clinton

US Weapons of Mass Destruction Linked to the Deaths of a Half-Million Children

Censored 1999, Story #5

Sources: Dennis Bernstein, "Made in America," *San Francisco Bay Guardian*, February 25, 1998; Bill Blum, "Punishing Saddam or the Iraqis," *I.F. Magazine*, March/April 1998; Most Rev. Dr. Robert M. Bowman, Lt. Col., USAF (Ret.), "Our Continuing War Against Iraq," *Space and Security News*, May 1998.

For the past seven years, the United States has supported sanctions against Iraq that have taken the lives of more Iraqi citizens than did the war itself. The sanctions imposed on Iraq are causing shortages of food, medical supplies, and medicines. Since the war ended, more than half a million children under the age of five have died. UNICEF reports that 150 children are dying every day.

The Iraqi people are being punished for their leader's reticence to comply fully with US-supported UN demands "to search every structure in Iraq for weapons of mass destruction." Ironically, 1994 US Senate findings uncovered evidence that US firms supplied at least some of the very biological material that the UN inspection teams are now seeking.

A 1994 US Senate panel report indicated that between 1985 and 1989, US firms supplied microorganisms needed for the production of Iraq's chemical and biological warfare. The Senate panel wrote, "It was later learned that these microorganisms exported by the United States were identical to those the United Nations inspectors found and removed from the Iraqi biological warfare program.

Under Bush

Over One Million Iraqi Deaths Caused by US Occupation
Censored 2009, Story #1

Sources: Michael Schwartz, "Is the United States Killing 10,000 Iraqis Every Month? Or Is It More?" *After Downing Street*, July 6, 2007; Joshua Holland, "Iraq death toll rivals Rwanda genocide, Cambodian killing fields," AlterNet, September 17, 2007; Luke Baker, "Iraq conflict has killed a million, says survey," Reuters (via AlterNet), January 7, 2008; Maki al-Nazzal and Dahr Jamail, "Iraq: Not our country to Return to," Inter Press Service, March 3, 2008.

Over one million Iraqis have met violent deaths as a result of the 2003 invasion, according to a study conducted by the prestigious British polling group Opinion Research Business (ORB). ORB's research covered fifteen of Iraq's eighteen provinces. Those not covered include two of Iraq's more volatile regions—Kerbala and Anbar—and the northern province of Arbil, where local authorities refused them a permit to work. In face-to-face interviews with 2,414 adults, the poll found that more than one in five respondents had had at least one death in their household as a result of the conflict, as opposed to natural causes.

Authors Joshua Holland and Michael Schwartz point out that the dominant narrative on Iraq—that most of the violence against Iraqis is being perpetrated by Iraqis themselves and is not our responsibility—is ill conceived. Interviewers from the Lancet report of October 2006 (Censored 2006, #2) asked Iraqi respondents how their loved ones died. Of deaths for which families were certain of the perpetrator, 56 percent were attributable to US forces or their allies. Schwartz suggests that if a low pro rata share of half the unattributed deaths were caused by US forces, a total of approximately 80 percent of Iraqi deaths are directly US perpetrated.

ADMINISTRATIVE SUPPORT FOR BIG BANKS AND STOCK BROKERS

Under Clinton

New Mega-Merged Banking Behemoths = Big Risk
Censored 1997, Story #6

Source: Jake Lewis, "The Making of the Banking Behemoths," *Multinational Monitor*, June 1996.

Nineteen ninety-five was a record year of bank mergers. Chase Manhattan and Chemical banks combined to create the nation's largest bank, with $300 billion in assets—while on the West Coast, the merger of First Interstate and Wells Fargo created a new giant with over $100 billion in assets. The massive consolidation of the nation's banking resources has resulted in 71.5 percent of US banking assets being controlled by the 100 largest banking organizations, representing less than 1 percent of the total banks in the nation.

The trend toward bigger banks is creating a system whereby giant banking institutions are taking on "too big to fail" status. Indeed, a failure of any one of these new giants would have a devastating effect on the nation's financial health. And with the Federal Reserve capping the amount that financial institutions have to pay into the government's bank insurance fund at $25 billion, just 1.25 percent of deposits are now insured. Consequently, any bailout of one of these new megabanks would come directly from the pockets of taxpayers.

Studies have also found that banks in concentrated markets tend to charge higher rates for certain types of loans, and tend to offer lower interest rates on certain types of deposits than do banks in less concentrated markets. A 1995 study by the US Public Interest Research Group and the Center for Study of Responsive Law showed that fees on checking and savings accounts increased at twice the rate of inflation from 1993 to 1995 as bank mergers moved forward.

Under Bush

Little Known Stock Fraud Could Weaken US Economy
Censored 2006, Story #18

Sources: David Hendricks, "Naked Short Selling Is A Plague For Businesses And Investors," *San Antonio Express News*, March 2, 2005; Karl Thiel, "Who's Behind Naked Shorting?" TheMotleyFool.com, March 30, 2005; Stockgate Today Series, "SEC's Donaldson Addresses Liquidity Fraud," *Financial Wire*, September 20, 2004; and Dave Patch, "Dateline NBC Cancelled and Attorney Accuses DTCC of Cheap Thuggery," April 7, 2005.

While the balance of supply and demand is a fairly well known principle of economic health, a related and similar relationship exists between liquidity—the availability of liquid, spendable assets such as cash, stocks and bonds—and security—the stability, endurance and trustworthiness of more long-term financial mechanisms.

The scandal, coined "Stockgate" by the *Financial Wire*, involves the abuse of a practice called "short selling." As opposed to a traditional approach to investing in which stocks are researched and bought on the hope they will rise over the "long" term, going "short" involves a bet that a stock is about to go down in value. In a short sale, an investor sells stock that he or she technically doesn't own. The investor borrows these shares of stock from their broker, who in turn may likely borrow the shares himself from a financial clearinghouse like a brokerage firm or hedge fund. Hoping that the price of the stock will drop, the investor is obligated to eventually "close" the short by buying back the sold shares at a hopefully lower price, thus making a profit from the fall of the stock. When the time runs out for "covering" the short and the price hasn't dropped, the investor is forced to buy back the shares at a loss and take a financial hit. The short sale of stocks is a risky bet, usually not recommended except for speculation or hedging to protect long-term financial positions with short-term offsets. As short selling is a sale of stocks not owned, but loaned, it is an example of buying on margin—a category of practices whose abuses stand out clearly in many people's minds as a significant factor in the Stock Market Crash of 1929 which ushered in the Great Depression.

Naked shorting is an illegal abuse of short selling in which investors short sell stock that they have no intention or ability to ever cover. When allowed to occur, naked shorting drives the stock value of a company down by creating more stock shares flowing around the market than actual shares of stock that the company can back with their current earnings. Companies, their shareholders, and indeed the entire economy are hurt financially by naked shorting, as it reduces the money available to support economic growth.

Additional References: David Sedore, "Hedge Fund Assets Frozen," March 4, 2005, and "Hedge Fund Virtually Bare," March 12, 2005, *The Palm Beach Post*; "First American Scientific Corp. Takes Counter Measures to Stop 'Naked Shorting' of its Stock," PrimeZone Media Network, December 17, 2004.

NATIONAL SECURITY/GOVERNMENT SECRECY

Under Clinton

Little Known Federal Law Paves The Way for National Identification Card

Censored 1998, Story #8

Sources: Cyndee Parker, "National ID Card is Now Federal Law and Georgia Wants to Help Lead the Way," *Witwigo*, May/June 1997; Mainstream media coverage: *New York Times*, September 8, 1996, section 6; page 58, column 1; related article in the *San Francisco Chronicle*, September 19, 1996, page A1.

In September 1996, President Clinton signed the Illegal Immigration Reform and Responsibility Act of 1996. Buried on approximately page 650 was a section that creates a framework for establishing a national ID card for the American public. This legislation was slipped through without fanfare or publicity.

This law has various aspects: it establishes a "Machine Readable Document Pilot Program" requiring employers to swipe a prospective employee's driver's license through a special reader linked to the federal government's Social Security Administration. The federal government would have the discretion to approve or disapprove the applicant for employment. In this case, the driver's license becomes a "national ID card."

The author of the national ID law, Dianne Feinstein (D-CA), stated in a Capitol Hill magazine that it was her intention to see Congress immediately implement a national ID system whereby every American would be required to carry a card with a "magnetic strip on it on which the bearer's unique voice, retina pattern, or fingerprint is digitally encoded." Congressman Dick Armey (R-TX), among others, has strongly denounced the new law, calling it "an abomination, and wholly at odds with the American tradition of individual freedom."

Under Bush

Bush Administration Moves to Eliminate Open Government

Censored 2006, Story #1

Source: Karen Lightfoot, "New Report Details Bush Administration Secrecy," Committee on Government Reform, September 14, 2004, http://www.commondreams.org/cgi-bin/newsprint.cgi?file=/news2004/0914-05.htm.

The Freedom of Information Act (FOIA) gives citizens the ability to file a request for specific information from a government agency and provides recourse in federal court if that agency fails to comply with FOIA requirements. Over the last two decades, beginning with Reagan, this law has become increasingly diluted and circumvented by each succeeding administration.

Under the Bush administration, agencies make extensive and arbitrary use of FOIA exemptions (such as those for classified information, privileged attorney-client documents and certain information compiled for law enforcement purposes) often inappropriately or with inadequate justification. Recent evidence shows agencies making frivolous (and sometimes ludicrous) exemption claims, abusing the deliberative process privilege, abusing the law enforcement exemption, and withholding data on telephone service outages.

The Bush administration also engages in an aggressive policy of questioning, challenging and denying FOIA requesters' eligibility for fee waivers, using a variety of tactics. Measures include narrowing the definition of "representative of news media," claiming information would not contribute to public understanding.

The Bush administration has also obtained unprecedented authority to conduct government operations in secret, with little or no judicial oversight. Under expanded law enforcement authority in the USA PATRIOT Act, the Justice Department can more easily use secret orders to obtain library and other private records, obtain "sneak-and-peek" warrants to conduct secret searches, and conduct secret wiretaps.

HOMELAND SECURITY AND GOVERNMENT SPYING

Under Clinton

Exposing the Global Surveillance System
Censored 1998, Story #4

Source: Nicky Hager, "Secret Power: Exposing the Global Surveillance System," *Covert Action Quarterly* (CAQ), Winter 1996/1997.

For over forty years, New Zealand's largest intelligence agency, the Government Communications Security Bureau (GCSB), has been helping its Western allies to spy on countries throughout the Pacific region. Neither the public nor the majority of New Zealand's top elected officials had knowledge of these activities. These procedures have operated since 1948 under a secret, Cold War-era intelligence alliance between the United States, Great Britain, Canada, Australia, and New Zealand—the UKUSA agreement. But in the late 1980s, the US prompted New Zealand to join a new and highly secret global intelligence system. The US National Security Agency (NSA) is one of the world's biggest, most closely held intelligence projects. Unlike many of the Cold War electronic spy systems, ECHELON is designed primarily to gather electronic transmissions from nonmilitary targets: governments, organizations, businesses, and individuals in virtually every country.

The system works by indiscriminately intercepting very large quantities of communications and using computers to identify and extract messages of interest from the mass of unwanted ones. Computers at each secret station in the ECHELON network automatically search millions of messages for pre-programmed key words. For each message containing one of those key words, the computer automatically notes time and place of origin and interception, and gives the message a four-digit code for future reference.

Under Bush

Homeland Security Threatens Civil Liberty
Censored 2004, Story #2

Sources: Alex Jones, "Secret Patriot II Destroys Remaining US Liberty," *Global Outlook*, Volume 4; Frank Morales, "Homeland Defense: Pentagon Declares War on America," *Global Outlook*, Winter 2003; Charles Lewis and Adam Mayle, "Justice Department Drafts Sweeping Expansion of Terrorism Act," Center for Public Integrity, http://publicintegrity.org.

The Department of Homeland Security (DHS) represents the most extensive restructuring of the US government since 1947—the year the Department of War was combined with the army, navy, marines, coast guard, and air force to create the Department of Defense. The new Department of Homeland Security combines over one hundred separate entities of the executive branch, including the Secret Service, the coast guard, and the border patrol, among others. The DHS employs over 170,000 federal workers and commands a total annual budget of $37 billion.

One DHS mandate largely ignored by the press requires the FBI, CIA, state, and local governments to share intelligence reports with the department upon command, without explanation. Civil rights activists claim that this endangers the rights and freedoms of law-abiding Americans by blurring the lines between foreign and domestic spying (as occurred during the COINTELPRO plan of the 1960s and 1970s). According to the ACLU, the Department of Homeland Security will be "100 percent secret and 0 percent accountable."

As part of Homeland Security, the USA PATRIOT Act of 2001 allows the government increased and unprecedented access to the lives of American citizens and represents an unrestrained imposition on our civil liberties. Wiretaps, previously confined to one phone, can now follow a person from place to place at the behest of government agents and people can now be detained on the vague suspicion that they might be a terrorist—or assisting one. Detainees can also be denied the right to legal representation (or the right of private counsel when they are allowed to meet with their attorneys).

PRIVATE MERCENARY COMPANIES USED AROUND THE WORLD

Under Clinton

Mercenary Armies in Service to Global Corporations
Censored 1999, Story #16

Sources: Pratap Chatterjee, "Mercenary Armies & Mineral Wealth," *Covert Action Quarterly*, Fall 1997, No. 62; Pratap Chatterjee, "Guarding the Multinationals," *Multinational Monitor*, March 1998.

In many countries, multinational corporations have paid directly for private policing services from the local army; or have hired outside security companies to harass nationals who protest against the environmental impact of their operations. The firms involved represent a growing number of new corporate security operations around the world, linking former intelligence officers, standing armies, and local death squads.

One of these security companies is Defense Systems Limited (DSL). DSL is run by two ex-Special Air Service commandos out of London offices, across the street from Buckingham Palace. Their clients include petrochemical companies, multinational banks, embassies, nongovernmental organizations, and national and international organizations. One of DSL's biggest contracts is with Mark Heathcote, a former MI6 (British equivalent of the CIA) officer who ran operations in Argentina during the Falklands War. Heathcote is now the chief of security for British Petroleum (BP). In 1996, DSL sent a group of British personnel to train Colombian police on BP-owned rigs. Training included lethal-weapons handling, sniper fire, and close quarter combat.

Another firm, Executive Outcomes, also offers mercenary armies to multinationals. Executive Outcomes fielded a private mercenary army in Angola in 1993 and offers high-tech security forces to corporations all over the world. In Nigeria, the Anglo-Dutch multinational Shell Corporation has been accused of causing major pollution in the Niger Delta for the last thirty-eight years. Shell directly employs an elite detachment of Nigerian police to protect its own interests. Numerous demonstrators have been beaten and executed because of Shell operations in Nigeria.

Under Bush

Behind Blackwater Inc.
Censored 2008, Story #7

Source: Jeremy Scahill, "Our Mercenaries in Iraq: Blackwater Inc and Bush's Undeclared Surge," *Democracy Now!* January 26, 2007, http://www.democracynow.org/article.pl?sid =07/01/26/1559232.

The company that most embodies the privatization of the military industrial complex—a primary part of the Project for a New American Century and the neoconservative revolution—is the private security firm Blackwater (now called Xe). Blackwater is the most powerful mercenary firm in the world, with 20,000 soldiers, the world's largest private military base, a fleet of twenty aircraft, including helicopter gunships, and a private intelligence division. The firm is also manufacturing its own surveillance blimps and target systems.

Blackwater is headed by a right-wing Christian-supremacist and ex-Navy Seal named Erik Prince, whose family has had deep neo-conservative connections. Bush's latest call for voluntary civilian military corps to accommodate the "surge" will add to over half a billion dollars in federal contracts with Blackwater, allowing Prince to create a private army to defend Christendom around the world against Muslims and others.

One of the last things Dick Cheney did before leaving office as Defense Secretary under George H. W. Bush was to commission a Halliburton study on how to privatize the military bureaucracy. That study effectively created the groundwork for a continuing war profiteer bonanza.

ADMINISTRATION SUPPORT FOR THE CHEMICAL INDUSTRY

Under Clinton

Clinton Administration Lobbied for Retention of Toxic Chemicals in Children's Toys

Censored 1999, Story #9

Source: Charlie Gray, "Out of the Mouths of Babes," *Multinational Monitor*, June 1998.

The Clinton administration and the Commerce Department have lobbied on behalf of US toy and chemical manufacturers against proposed new European Union (EU) restrictions, which would prevent children's exposure to toxic chemicals released by polyvinyl chloride (PVC) toys such as teething rings. Documents obtained under the Freedom of Information Act (FOIA) suggesting that the US government lobbied at the behest of toymaker Mattel and chemical manufacturer Exxon may help explain the European Commission's rejection of the proposed emergency ban. A cable from Vernon Weaver, the US Representative to the EU in Brussels, sent "heartfelt thanks" to Washington and US missions in Europe for "making contact" with member state representatives of the EU Product Safety Emergencies Committee. "We are told by Exxon Chemical Europe Inc. that the input was very effective and the weigh-in was invaluable."

Health authorities in several European countries, including Austria, Belgium, Denmark, Germany, and the Netherlands, have recommended a ban on PVC toys, such as teething rings and bath toys. The Spanish government requested action by the EU in March 1998. PVC, or polyvinyl chloride (also known as vinyl), is a common plastic that frequently contains toxic additives. *The Front* reports that no major US retailers have taken precautionary action, chiefly because the US Consumer Product Safety Commission (CPSC), which is responsible for toy safety regulations, has yet to take action.

Under Bush

Chemical Industry is EPA's Primary Research Partner
Censored 2007, Story #15

Sources: Jeff Ruch, "Chemical Industry Is Now EPA's Main Research Partner," *Public Employees for Environmental Responsibility*, October 5, 2005; Jeff Ruch, "EPA Becoming Arm of Corporate R&D," *Public Employees for Environmental Responsibility*, October 6, 2005.

The US Environmental Protection Agency (EPA) research program is increasingly relying on corporate joint ventures, according to agency documents obtained by Public Employees for Environmental Responsibility (PEER). The American Chemical Council (ACC) is now EPA's leading research partner and the EPA is diverting funds from basic health and environmental research towards research that addresses regulatory concerns of corporate funders.

Since the beginning of Bush's first term in office, there has been a significant increase in cooperative research and development agreements (CRADAs) with individual corporations or industry associations. During Bush's first four years, EPA entered into fifty-seven corporate CRADAs, compared to thirty-four such agreements during Clinton's second term.

EPA scientists claim that corporations are influencing the agency's research agenda through financial inducements. One EPA scientist wrote, "Many of us in the labs feel like we work for contracts." In April 2005, EPA's Science Advisory Board warned that the agency was no longer funding credible public health research. It noted, for example, that the EPA was falling behind on issues such as intercontinental pollution transport and nanotechnology.

ATTACKS ON JOURNALISTS

Under Clinton

Did the US Deliberately Bomb the Chinese Embassy in Belgrade?
Censored 2001, Story #4

Sources: Joel Bleifuss, "A Tragic Mistake?" *In These Times*, December 12, 1999; Seth Ackerman, "Mission Implausible," June 26, 2000, http://inthesetimes.com; Yoichi Shimatsu, "Reports Showing US Deliberately Bombed Chinese Embassy Deliberately Ignored by US Media," *Pacific News*, October 20, 1999; Action Report, "NY Times on Chinese Embassy

Bombing: Nothing to Report," *Fairness & Accuracy in Reporting*, February 9, 2000, http://www.fair.org/activism/china-response2.html.

Elements within the CIA may have deliberately targeted the Chinese embassy in Belgrade, without NATO approval, because it was serving as a rebroadcast station for the Yugoslavian army.

The *London Observer* and Copenhagen's *Politiken* reported that, according to senior US and European military sources, NATO knew very well where the Chinese embassy was located and listed it as a "strictly prohibited target" at the beginning of the war. The *Observer* stated that the CIA and its British equivalent, M16, had been listening to communications from the Chinese embassy routinely since it moved to its new site in 1996. The Chinese embassy was taken off the prohibited target list after NATO detected it sending Yugoslavian army signals to forces in the field. "Nearly everyone involved in NATO air operations (radio) signals command knows that the bombing was deliberate," said Jens Holsoe, lead investigative reporter on the news team reporting on the story for *Politiken*.

President Clinton called the bombing a "tragic mistake" and said it was the result of a mix-up. NATO claimed that they were using old maps and got the address wrong. However, Observer reporters quoted a Naples-based flight controller who said the NATO maps that were used during the campaign had correctly identified the Chinese embassy.

A French Ministry of Defense report stated that the flight that targeted the Chinese embassy was not under NATO command, but rather an independent US bombing raid. In July 1999, CIA director George Tenet testified before Congress that of the 900 sites struck by NATO during the bombing campaign, the only one targeted by the CIA was the Chinese embassy.

Under Bush

Journalists Face Unprecedented Dangers to Life and Livelihood
Censored 2006, Story #7

Sources: Steve Weissman, "Dead Messengers: How the US Military Threatens Journalists," *Truthout*, February 28, 2005; http://www.truthout.org/docs_2005/022405A.shtml; Dahr Jamail, "Media Repression in 'Liberated' Land," Inter Press Service, November 18, 2004, http://www.ipsnews.net/interna.asp?idnews=26333.

According to the International Federation of Journalists (IFJ), 2004 was the deadliest year for reporters since 1980, when records began to be kept.

Over a twelve-month span, 129 media workers were killed and forty-nine of those deaths occurred in the Iraqi conflict. According to independent journalist Dahr Jamail, journalists are increasingly being detained and threatened by the US-installed interim government in Iraq. When the only safety for a reporter is being embedded with the US military, the reported stories tend to have a positive spin. Non-embedded reporters suffer the great risk of being identified as enemy targets by the military.

The most blatant attack on journalists occurred the morning of April 8, 2004, when the Third Infantry fired on the Palestine Hotel in Baghdad, killing cameramen Jose Couso and Taras Protsyuk and injuring three others. The hotel served as headquarters for some 100 reporters and other media workers. The Pentagon officials knew that the Palestine Hotel was full of journalists and had assured the Associated Press that the US would not target the building.

ENVIRONMENTAL ISSUES

Under Clinton

Clinton Administration Retreats on Ozone Crisis
Censored 1995, Story #5

Source: David Moberg, "Full of holes: Clinton's retreat on the ozone crisis," *In These Times*, January 24, 1994.

The ozone hole over Antarctica has continued to grow every year since its discovery in 1985 and damage to the ozone layer over heavily populated areas of the Northern Hemisphere also has been increasing rapidly. Scientists recorded all-time low levels of ozone over the United States in 1993.

The ultraviolet rays that penetrate a weakened ozone layer have been linked to increased cataracts, skin cancer, genetic damage and infectious diseases among humans—as well as reduced plant growth. Meanwhile, the Clinton administration has been moving backward on protecting the stratospheric ozone layer. This ominous precedent will encourage other industrial countries to stall on their own CFC phase-outs and puts the administration in a far weaker position to argue for an accelerated phase-out of CFCs in the developing countries where CFC production is soaring.

DuPont, the giant chemical firm that developed the first industrial CFC, had planned to halt CFC production at the end of 1994. Yet in late

1993, EPA asked DuPont to keep making CFCs until 1996. The EPA defended its decision as a "consumer protection" measure that will make it easier for car owners to recharge their old air conditioners, which use CFCs as a cooling agent.

Under Bush

Bush Administration Manipulates Science and Censors Scientists
Censored 2005, Story #3

Sources: Robert F. Kennedy Jr., "The Junk Science of George W. Bush," *The Nation*, March 8, 2004; "Censoring Scientific Information," *Censorship News: The National Coalition Against Censorship Newsletter*, Fall 2003, #91; Sunny Lewis, "Ranking Scientists Warn Bush Science Policy Lacks Integrity," Environment News Service and Oneworld.net, February 20, 2004; Committee on Government Reform - Minority Staff, "Politics And Science In The Bush Administration," Office of US Representative Henry A. Waxman, August 2003, updated November 13, 2003.

Critics charge that the Bush administration is purging, censoring, and manipulating scientific information in order to push forward its pro-business, anti-environmental agenda. In Washington, D.C. more than sixty of the nation's top scientists, including twenty Nobel laureates, leading medical experts, and former federal agency directors, issued a statement on February 18, 2004 accusing the Bush administration of deliberately distorting scientific results for political ends and calling for regulatory and legislative action to restore scientific integrity to federal policymaking.

Under the current administration, the Environmental Protection Agency (EPA) has blacklisted qualified scientists who pose a threat to its pro-business ideology. When a team of biologists working for the EPA indicated that there had been a violation of the "Endangered Species Act" by the Army Corps of Engineers, the group was replaced with a "corporate-friendly" panel.

MEDIA DEREGULATION

Under Clinton

Telecommunications Deregulation: Closing Up America's "Marketplace of Ideas"
Censored 1996, Story #1

Source: Ralph Nader, James Love, and Andrew Saindon, "Federal Telecommunications Legislation," Consumer Project on Technology, July 14, 1995.

The Telecommunications Deregulation Bill eliminates virtually all regulation of the United States communication industry. As tends to be the case with most anti-consumer legislation, the bill stealthily moved under the guise of "encouraging competition"—but will, in reality, have the opposite effect of creating huge new concentrations of media power.

The most troubling aspect of the bill allows easing—and outright elimination—of current anti-trust regulations. In what the *New York Times* described as "a dazzling display of political influence," the nation's broadcast networks scored big in the House version of the bill by successfully getting the limits on ownership eased so that any individual company can control television stations serving up to 50 percent of the country. The Senate version of the bill provides for a more modest 35 percent coverage.

The legislation also dismantles current regulations, which limit the number of radio stations that can be owned by a single company. Currently no one single company can own more than forty stations. It also would lift the current FCC ban on joint ownership of a broadcast radio or TV license and a newspaper in the same market—allowing a single company to have 100 percent control over the three primary sources of news in a community.

Under Bush

FCC Moves to Privatize Airwaves

Censored 2003, Story #1

Sources: Jeremy Rifkin, "Global Media Giants Lobby to Privatize Entire Broadcast System," *Guardian*, April 28, 2001 and in *Media File*, Autumn 2001 volume 20, #4; Brendan L. Koerner, "Losing Signal," *Mother Jones*, Sept/October 2001; Dorothy Kidd, "Legal Project to Challenge Media Monopoly," *Media File*, May/June 2001.

For almost seventy years, the Federal Communications Commission (FCC) has administered and regulated the broadcast spectrum as an electronic "commons" on behalf of the American people. The FCC issues licenses to broadcasters that allow them, for a fee, to use, but not own, one or more specific radio or TV frequencies. Thus, the public has retained the ability to regulate, as well as influence, access to broadcast communications.

Several years ago, the Progress and Freedom Foundation, in their report "The Telecom Revolution: An American Opportunity," recommended a complete privatization of the radio frequencies, whereby broadcasters with existing licenses would eventually gain complete ownership of their respective frequencies. They could thereafter develop them in markets of their choosing, or sell and trade them to other companies. The few non-allocated bands of the radio frequency spectrum would be sold off, as electronic real estate, to the highest bidders. With nothing then to regulate, the FCC would eventually be abolished. The reasoning behind this radical plan was that government control of the airwaves has led to inefficiencies. In private hands, the frequencies would be exchanged in the marketplace, and the forces of free-market supply and demand would foster the most creative (and, of course, most profitable) use of these electronic "properties."

This privatization proposal was considered too ambitious by the Clinton administration. However, in February 2001, within months after a more "pro-business" president took office, thirty-seven leading US economists requested, in a joint letter, that the FCC allow broadcasters to lease, in secondary markets, the frequencies they currently use under their FCC license. Their thinking was that with this groundwork in place, full national privatization would follow, and eventually nations would be encouraged to sell off their frequencies to global media enterprises.

VIOLATIONS OF INTERNATIONAL TREATIES

Under Clinton

Planned Weapons in Space Violate International Treaty
Censored 2000, Story #8

Sources: Karl Grossman, "US Violates World Law to Militarize Space," *Earth Island Journal*, Winter/Spring 1999; Bruce K. Gagnon, "Pyramids to The Heavens Space," *Toward Freedom*, September/ October 1999.

The Outer Space Treaty of 1967 bans the deployment of space weapons of mass destruction. Recently the US Congress ignored further need of such a treaty, and approved the development of the US Military's Space Command Weapons program. This sudden shift of viewpoint coincides with the complete absence of any foreign government competition, and with the increase in the ability of the US to effectively use satellite surveillance in military campaigns. The proposed system is designed to extend control of space far beyond the outer boundaries of the Earth's atmosphere. To prevent deployment of any adversarial country's satellites, the Pentagon is well along in its research and development of an anti-satellite weapons program. The reemergence of a "Star Wars" weapon system is echoed in the words of General Joseph Ashly, commander-in-chief of the US Space Command: "It's politically sensitive but its going to happen . . . we are going to fight from space and we are going to fight into space." Concerned with the possibility of nuclear contamination of the atmosphere from satellite breakup, the European Space Agency has urged the US to utilize solar power to fuel space-military command modules.

Under Bush

Treaty Busting By the United States
Censored 2004, Story #7

Sources: Marylia Kelly and Nicole Deller, "Rule of power or rule of law?" *Connections*, June 2002; John B. Anderson, "Unsigning the ICC," *The Nation*, April 2002; Eamon Martin, "US Invasion Proposal Shocks the Netherlands," *Ashville Global Report*, June 20-26, 2002; John Valleau, "Nuclear Nightmare," *Global Outlook*, Summer 2002.

The United States is a signatory to nine multilateral treaties that it has either blatantly violated or gradually subverted. The Bush administration is now outright rejecting a number of those treaties, and in doing so places global security in jeopardy as other nations feel entitled to do the same. The rejected treaties include: the Comprehensive Test Ban Treaty (CTBT), the Treaty Banning Antipersonnel Mines, the Rome Statute of the International Criminal Court (ICC), a protocol to create a compliance regime for the Biological Weapons Convention (BWC), the Kyoto Protocol on global warming, and the Anti-Ballistic Missile Treaty (ABM). The US is also not complying with the nuclear Non-Proliferation Treaty (NPT), the Chemical Weapons Commission (CWC), the BWC, and the UN framework Convention on Climate Change.

The ABM Treaty alone is a crucial factor in national security; letting Bush get away with facilitating its demise will destroy the balance of powers carefully crafted in our Constitution. The Bush administration has no legitimate excuse for nullifying the ABM Treaty since the events that have threatened the security of the United States have not involved ballistic missiles, and none of them are in any way related to the subject matter of the ABM Treaty. Bush's withdrawal violates the US Constitution, international law, and Article XV of the ABM Treaty itself. The Bush administration says it needs to get rid of the ABM Treaty so it can test the SPY radar on the Aegis cruisers against Intercontinental Ballistic Missiles (ICBM) and so that it can build a new test facility at Fort Greely, Alaska. In addition, some conservatives have willingly dismissed the ABM Treaty because it stands as the major obstacle towards development of a "Star Wars" missile defense system. Discarding treaty constraints and putting weapons in space is nothing short of pursuing absolute military superiority.

The Nuclear Non-Proliferation Treaty is crucial to global security because it bars the spread of nuclear weapons. The US is currently in noncompliance with the NPT requirements, as demonstrated in the January 2002 US Nuclear Posture Review. Moreover, critics charge that the National Ignition Facility (NIF) under construction at Livermore lab violates the Comprehensive Test Ban Treaty (CTBT), which the US signed in 1996 but has not ratified. The CTBT bans nuclear explosions, and its language does not contain any "exceptions allowing laboratory thermonuclear explosions."

SOME THINGS NEVER CHANGE: POWER OF ELITES INSIDE THE TRILATERAL COMMISSION

Under President Jimmy Carter

Jimmy Carter and the Trilateral Commission
Censored 1977, Story #1

Sources: Michael Crozier, Samuel P. Huntington, Joji Watanuki, *The Crisis of Democracy: Report on the Governability of Democracies to the Trilateral Commission* (New York: New York University Press, 1975); *The Review of the News*, August 18, 1976; Gar Smith, *The Berkeley Barb*, July 30, 1976; Gary Allen, "Carter Brings Forth a Cabinet," *American Opinion*, February 1977; W.E. Barnes, Political Analyst, *San Francisco Examiner*, December 12, 1976; *In These Times*, February 2, 1977; Noam Chomsky, "Trilateral's RX for Crisis: Governability Yes, Democracy No," *Seven Days*, February 14, 1977.

In the election year of 1976, Jimmy Carter ran a successful campaign for the presidency based on his image as an antiestablishment, peanut-farming, ex-governor of the state of Georgia. Yet, since the fall of 1973, Carter had been associated with David Rockefeller and other members of an international power elite through his association with the Trilateral Commission, one of Rockefeller's many policy-making organizations. According to the Italian publication Europa, as cited in *The Review of The News*, Rockefeller and Zbigniew Brzezinski, a founding director of the Trilateral Commission (TLC), had agreed on Carter's potential as our next president as far back as 1970. Supportive of Carter's close relationship with this little-known power elite is the fact that many members of his administration have been drawn from the membership rolls of the TLC. These include Cyrus Vance, secretary of state; Brzezinski, national security adviser; W. Michael Blumenthal, secretary of treasury; Harold Brown, secretary for East Asian and Pacific affairs; Warren Christopher, deputy secretary of state; Richard N. Cooper, under secretary of state for economic affairs; Andrew Young, US ambassador to the United Nations; and C. Fred Bergsten, assistant secretary of the treasury for international economic affairs. Carter's personal choice for vice president, Walter Mondale, is also a member of the TLC.

Under President Barack Obama

Obama's Trilateral Commission Team
Censored 2010, Story # 22

Source: Patrick Wood, "Obama: Trilateral Commission Endgame," *The August Review*, January 30, 2009, http://www.augustreview.com/news_commentary/trilateral_commission/obama%3a_trilateral_commission_endgame_20090127110/.

Barack Obama has appointed no less than eleven members of the Trilateral Commission to top-level and key positions in his Administration. During Obama's presidential campaign Zbigniew Brzezinski, co-founder of the Trilateral Commission with David Rockefeller in 1973, was Obama's principal foreign policy advisor.

According to official Trilateral Commission membership lists, there are only eighty-seven members from the United States (the other 337 members are from other regions). Thus, in less than two weeks since his inauguration, Obama's appointments encompass more than 12 percent of Commission's entire US membership.

CONCLUSION

*No experiment can be more interesting than that we are now trying,
and which we trust will end in establishing the fact, that man may
be governed by reason and truth. Our first object should therefore be,
to leave open to him all avenues of the truth. The most effectual hith-
erto found, is the freedom of the press. It is, therefore, the first shut up
by those who fear the investigation of their actions.*

—Thomas Jefferson, 1804

Media scholar and FreePress.net founder Robert McChesney wrote in
his book *Rich Media, Poor Democracy,* "A media system set up to serve
the needs of Wall Street and Madison Avenue cannot and does not serve
the needs of the preponderance of the population . . .What types of
important stories get almost no coverage in the commercial news media?
The historical standard is that there is no coverage when the political
and economic elites are in agreement."[4]

Reflecting upon the aforementioned examples of censored topics and stories, the bias of Project Censored seems to be quite simple: we promote protection of First Amendment rights in support of a truly free press, one that holds those in power, elected by the people or appointed, accountable. Investigating controversial and difficult subjects that impact society should not earn journalists and scholars the label "conspiracy theorist." Labeling is a tactic of suppression and censorship.

Furthermore, supporting the US Constitution should not be distorted as an ideological bias of Left or Right. It is merely patriotic duty to enforce the rule of law, in so far as the law is based upon the true notions of liberty and justice for all. Without media freedom, not only can democracy not thrive, it simply cannot exist.

PETER PHILLIPS is professor of sociology at Sonoma State University, director of Project Censored, and president of the Media Freedom Foundation.

MICKEY HUFF is associate professor of history at Diablo Valley College, associate director of Project Censored and the Media Freedom Foundation, and the Project Censored College and University Affiliates Coordinator for Media Freedom International (http://mediafreedominternational.org).

Elliot van Patten and Frances A. Capell provided research and editing assistance for this article.

Notes

1. Niels H. Harrit, Jeffrey Farrer, Steven E. Jones, Kevin R. Ryan, Frank M. Legge, Daniel Farnsworth, Gregg Roberts, James R. Gourley, Bradley R. Larsen, "Active Thermitic Material Discovered in Dust from the 9/11 World Trade Center Catastrophe," *The Open Chemical Physics Journal*, Volume 2, pp. 7–31, http://www.bentham-open.org/pages/content.php?TOCPJ/2009/00000002/00000001/7TOCPJ.SGM. For more detailed, scientific discussion on these issues, including possibilities of controlled demolition, see Richard Gage and Architects and Engineers for 9/11 Truth online at http://AE911Truth.org.

   Then-President George W. Bush said to the UN in November, 2001, "Let us never tolerate outrageous conspiracy theories concerning the attacks of September the 11; malicious lies that attempt to shift the blame away from the terrorists, themselves, away from the guilty." Apparently, even though the eventual official story of the 9/11 Commission itself was a conspiracy theory, the press seemed to follow Bush's lead by not looking closely at the many problems associated with the events of 9/11 (which can be viewed at http://www.projectcensored.org/articles/story/unanswered-questions-of-9-11-july-2005/). Even most "left-leaning" journalists refuse to honestly and openly investigate the events of 9/11 as was noted by Peter Phillips in the study "Left Progressive Media Inside the Propaganda Model," online at http://www.projectcensored.org/articles/story/left-progressive-media-inside-the-propaganda-model/. For more fact-based information regarding the many research problems associated with the official government theories on 9/11, see http://911truth.org.

We in a free society should be entitled to robust debate in the press. As Thomas Jefferson stated in his 1801 inaugural address, "If there be any among us who would wish to dissolve this Union, or to change its republican form, let them stand undisturbed as monuments of the safety with which error of opinion may be tolerated, where reason is left free to combat it." This is a crucial component of media democracy.

2. Uhrich, Kevin, "Uncovering Project Censored," *Pasadena Weekly*, May 18, 2006.

3. All the stories in this chapter were published by Project Censored as part of the Top 25 Censored Stories for each year between 1976 and 2009. Included here are only brief summaries of each story example. For more details on each, please see the Project Censored website. The stories are accessible online at http://www.projectcensored.org/top-stories/publications/. There, the stories are catalogued by year in their Top 25 rankings. A subject archive is available online as well at http://ringnebula.com/. All other sources not in endnotes here are in the actual text of this article with more available online in the Project archives.

4. Thomas Jefferson quote from *The Jeffersonian Cyclopedia*, p. 637. Robert McChesney, *Rich Media, Poor Democracy: Communication Politics in Dubious Times* (New York: The New Press, 1999), p. xiii, xviii.

CHAPTER II

Election 2008
Vanishing Votes, Disappearing Democracy and Media Misdirection

by Brad Friedman

And *You* Lose Your Vote! And *You* Lose Your Vote! And *You* Lose Your Vote! It's one thing when millions of voiceless Americans are disenfranchised in one form or another—as we saw in the presidential elections of both 2000 and 2004—but it's another matter altogether when *Oprah's* vote gets "lost." Now that's a real problem. That's what happened in November of 2008, when one of the country's most well-known celebrities attempted to cast her vote for the Democratic Party phenomenon, whom she'd famously endorsed, and who would eventually become president—with or without Oprah's vote.

Who knows if Oprah Winfrey's vote was actually counted for Barack Obama? She doesn't. She can't. Nobody can. Oprah cast her vote, during the early voting period, presumably for Obama, on a 100 percent unverifiable Direct Recording Electronic (DRE, usually touchscreen) voting machine.

"When I voted yesterday electronically, the first vote that you vote for on the ballot is the presidential candidate," she explained on TV,[1] breathlessly detailing her personal freakout upon discovering her selection for Obama had *disappeared* by the time she arrived at the e-ballot's final "review screen." Naturally, as most voters do, she blamed *herself*.

"It was my first time doing electronic, so I didn't mark the X strong enough, or I held down too long," she explained over audience gasps and screams. "Because then when I went back to check it, it had not recorded my presidential vote."

Unfortunately, Oprah not alone in 2008. An untold number of legal American voters saw their votes simply disappear into the ether on electronic voting systems. Others *didn't* see it disappear. Millions of them, whether they saw the selection properly registered on the "review screen" or not, have no idea whether their vote was actually counted accurately, or even at all.

It's 100 percent physically and scientifically impossible to know if *any* vote, for *any* candidate or initiative on *any* ballot, cast during *any* actual election, has ever been recorded accurately by a DRE voting machine. That's just one of the "voting industry's" dirtiest little anti-democratic secrets. Until the human eye is capable of seeing electrons inside a computer, there remains no way to verify that the data was recorded accurately, much less recorded *at all.*

Incredibly enough, jurisdictions across the country continued to use these machines in 2008 anyway. Even more incredibly, the corporate media barely bothered to notice.

In Oprah's case, while the report of her alarming tale gained enough interest to knock out my web server at BradBlog.com for several hours, and was noteworthy enough to merit a momentary blip on the crawl of the nation's cable news outlets, it otherwise quickly disappeared. Just like her vote. The nation's corporate media did little to find out how many *other* voters faced similar fates, even though the same model of voting machine that failed for her was used to cast and record millions of votes across the country. In Chicago (Cook County, IL), the machine Oprah would have used[2] was a Sequoia AVC Edge, the same system used in eleven states, including the swing states of Nevada, Missouri and Virginia.

Even Oprah didn't bother to revisit the topic. Had she done so, her star power might have helped reform the nation's entire dangerously imperiled, now-almost-wholly corporatized and privatized system of "public" elections.

Sequoia was not the only private e-voting company whose mission-critical systems failed during the critical moment of their mission in 2008. All four of the major e-voting vendors—ES&S, Diebold (now calling themselves Premier), Sequoia, and Hart Intercivic—saw similar failures, similarly under- or mis-reported, on their DRE systems in state after state. And it wasn't just touchscreen/DREs that failed either. Optical scan systems, which allow voters to ink their selections on paper ballots, also failed to tabulate votes accurately, and sometimes not at all.

How many other legal American votes were lost and/or changed without the voters' knowledge in 2008? Because none of them were Oprah's, nobody actually knows.

FIRST WORST IN THE NATION

In 2008 the country saw a record voter turnout throughout one of the longest and most riveting Democratic Party primary contests in US history. Long declared by the punditry to be the party favorite, Sen. Hillary Clinton was knocked for a loop when she faced an upset defeat from Illinois's upstart freshman Senator Barack Obama in Iowa's fully transparent—if often confusing, to those of us from outside the Hawkeye State—caucuses on Thursday, January 3.

The turnout in Iowa was unprecedented. Caucus-goer Kathy Barger told CNN that the room she was in was packed to the brim with a line out the door at her caucus site in Walnut, Iowa. "I don't know how they are going to be able to fit everybody in the room, much less count the votes," she said.[3]

Yet within hours, the results, transparently recorded as citizens stood to cast their votes and bear witness to the counting first-hand across the state, were in. Clinton was soundly defeated, coming in third behind Obama and former North Carolina Senator John Edwards.

The same pundits who had pronounced her the Democratic Party's *de facto* nominee months, if not years before—including those on the right who, oddly enough, seemed to be rooting for Hillary—quickly declared her bid for the presidency was all but over, unless, just five days later on Tuesday, January 8 in New Hampshire's "First in the Nation" primary, she was able to become the new "comeback kid."

Buoyed by his Iowa win, Obama surged in the pre-election New Hampshire polls.[4] Rasmussen had him 8 points ahead of Clinton. CNN and Marist each favored Obama by 7 in their post-Iowa, pre–New Hampshire samplings. CBS predicted Obama by 5, and Zogby showed him up by an astounding 13 points. In all, the final average of dozens of independent pre-election polls predicted a +8.3 spread in Obama's favor just prior to Election Day.

When New Hampshire voters headed to the polls on Tuesday to cast their votes *on paper ballots*, Hillary was on the ropes. Yet when the unofficial results of the election were tabulated—80 percent of them by Diebold's AccuVote optical-scan system—Hillary Clinton would be declared the *winner* of the contest by 2.6 points over Obama, who quickly announced his concession before 11pm ET, before even a single Diebold-tabulated ballot had been checked for accuracy by any human being.

NBC's Tim Russert quickly announced the results as "the most stunning upset in the history of politics." Pundits and pollsters from across the corporate media and, disappointingly, even in the progressive blogosphere, turned tortured backflips trying to determine how they had "gone wrong" in their pre-election predictions.

Was it Clinton's widely-reported, tearful moment at a town hall event over the weekend? Notoriously independent Granite State voters loathe to allow "hicks" from Iowa to make up their minds for them? Mischievous Republicans voting for Hillary, believing her either more "conservative" than Obama, or otherwise easier to defeat in November? Could racism and the so-called "Bradley Effect"[5]—where poll respondents answer one way to appear "politically correct," only to vote another way when in the privacy of the voting booth—have played a part?

There were plenty of reverse-engineered explanations for the apparent remarkable come-from-behind victory for New York's junior Senator. The trouble is, none of the explanations were actually verifiable; all were just best-guesses from the same "experts" who'd presumably gotten it so wrong in the first place (twice, if you count their wrong calls in Iowa, as well.)

All the while, as pollsters and pundits naval-gazed and second-

guessed to determine how their polls and predictions could have been so terribly wrong, not one of them stopped to wonder if the reported election results were actually *right*. Not one.

Eighty percent of New Hampshire's ballots were tabulated on Diebold AccuVote optical-scan systems. The other 20 percent are counted by hand, at the precincts, on Election Night, in one of the very few states where a tradition of citizen-overseen hand-counting still takes place.

Adding to the anomaly of New Hampshire's reported results was the fact that where ballots were hand-counted, mostly in rural areas, Obama had won. In the more populated areas, where Diebold counted the votes, Clinton was reported the victor. A comparison of the hand-counted results versus the Diebold-counted results revealed they were virtually flipped, almost exactly opposite percentages of votes for Clinton and Obama. Overall, Clinton received an approximate 7 point bump (+4.5 for her, -2.5 for Obama) where machines tabulated instead of humans.

Blogger Ben Moseley analyzed the data from each town in New Hampshire in the days following the election. He noted that "the results were somewhat surprising:

"[M]ore statistics from the data show that Obama in non-Diebold towns is garnering 38.7% of the vote to Clinton's 36.2%. The results in Diebold towns show the exact opposite: Clinton with 40.7% of the vote and Obama with 36.2%. Not only are the positions swapped but the informal statistics have the second place candidate holding 36.2% in both cases, which could easily be a pure coincidence. . . . All the other numbers [are] almost exact for every candidate, even Edwards who received 17% of the vote in Diebold towns compared to 17.6% in non-Diebold towns. That still doesn't make up for the extra 2% vote Clinton is receiving when she leads in certain towns compared to when Obama has the lead."

There could be perfectly legitimate reasons for Obama's popularity in the more rural areas where they hand-counted, and Clinton's winning in the more metropolitan areas where Diebold counted the vote. I just don't know what they are. Neither did the Wednesday morning quarterback pundits when they tried to explain them. They were, frankly, just guessing, rather than bothering to make sure the results were truly *accurate*.

In towns where machines were used to count, the Diebold AccuVote systems used were the very same make and model (down to the firmware) seen used to flip the results of a mock election in Leon County, Florida, in HBO's Emmy-nominated 2006 documentary *Hacking*

Democracy.[6] The climax of the landmark film features a first-of-its-kind, "live" video-taped experiment, in which a computer expert exploits the flaws of the machines' sensitive memory cards which are inserted into op-scan systems to store scanned ballot results.

In the experiment,[7] eight paper ballots were cast in a mock election. Voters answered one simple YES or NO question: "Can the votes on this Diebold system be hacked using the memory card?"

On camera, all eight ballots are seen as they are run through the Diebold optical-scan machine. Six voters voted "NO"; two voters voted "YES."

Yet, when the results of the tabulation were printed by the Diebold AccuVote, they were reported as a horrifying seven "YES"; one "NO."

The results of the mock election—held on the very same make and model of electronic tabulating system used in New Hampshire's 2008 Primary—had been entirely *flipped*. Only a manual hand-count would have revealed that fact. The computer expert had hacked the memory card used in the AccuVote system and exploited a programming flaw in Diebold's operating system to "invisibly" reverse the results of the election.

Back in New Hampshire, where the announced results of the primary had produced another sea change in the 2008 presidential race, not a single paper ballot from among the 80 percent tallied by Diebold had been checked to assure the machines had accurately counted them. That happened even though the results of the primary[8] in December of 2005, as documented in the 2006 film, had caused reverberations across the nation at the time—at least among election officials, election vendors, and those in the election integrity community. The shocking discovery that a race could be flipped with little possibility of detection vis-a-vis a simple memory card exploit led Leon County, Florida to immediately dump their Diebold op-scan system. However, no changes were made in New Hampshire, nor in most other states that also used them. This same vulnerable system would be used in the "First in the Nation" primary in January of 2008.

To make matters worse, LHS Associates, the company that exclusively sold the machines and maintained and programmed the Diebold voting systems and their memory cards in New Hampshire (and most of New England), had a disturbing, and even criminal, history.

Its director of sales and marketing, Ken Hajjar, the company owner's childhood friend, had previously been sentenced to twelve months in prison after pleading guilty to a narcotics felony. Hajjar had also come by the Brad Blog some years ago to post a profane rant in comments, resulting in Connecticut's Secretary of State banning him from working on their voting systems. He was angry that we'd posted photos after our visit to Diebold headquarters in Allen, TX showing voting machines sitting out in the open on their loading dock, unguarded and easily tampered with, before shipment to customers.

Moreover, Hajjar had previously admitted, on air, that he and other employees frequently swapped out Diebold memory cards—the same type used by to hack the mock election in Leon County—in the middle of elections in Connecticut, where that is illegal. He told the stunned host of *Talk Nation Radio*: "I don't pay attention to every little law." This was the outfit running the crucial New Hampshire election on Diebold's hackable voting machines.

Not only pre-election polls predicted a tidy Obama win over Clinton. Same-day exit polls had predicted similarly. Pollster John Zogby, who predicted a 13-point Obama rout in the days before the race, told me via email later that week, "The actual exit poll had Obama up by 3—41 percent to 38 percent." He characterized many of the reverse-engineered explanations for Clinton's upset as "preposterous," noting in particular that there was "no evidence that race was an issue."

MSNBC's Chris Matthew was also flummoxed[9] about the full 10-point swing from independent pre-election polls to the final, mostly Diebold-reported results, and also reported on same day exit polls he'd been looking at on Tuesday afternoon indicating a "significant victory" for Obama.

On Thursday's *Hardball*, following Tuesday's primary, Matthews peppered his pollster guests to explain why "even our own exit polls, taken as people came out of voting, showed [Obama] ahead."

"What's going on here?" he wondered aloud. Raw data from NBC's exit polls, commissioned and shared by a consortium of corporate news outlets, has never been released to the public (it never is, even data from 2004, despite demands from statisticians and citizens across the nation who noted the infamous discrepancies indicating a John Kerry win over George W. Bush in state after state).

Virtually alone in the mainstream media, willing to note the disparity he'd seen with his own eyes in his company's own internal exit data, Matthews asked questions during one show and promised viewers he would not revisit the topic after that day. He kept his promise. The exit polls were not discussed again and concerns about the *results* themselves almost as little. Obama never said a public word questioning any of it.

"It's ludicrous," Rep. Dennis Kucinich's senior campaign representative David Bright told me. "New Hampshire has the privilege of being the first in the nation. This election brings in 3 billion dollars to the economy, so you'd think a measly 70k would be part of the cost of doing business," he told me the week following the election.

Bright was complaining about the $69,900 that New Hampshire was billing Kucinich for a complete hand count of paper ballots in the Democratic race. As a candidate in the contest, the Ohio Congressman had standing to request such a count. "If Obama had done it, it would have been $2,000," Bright noted, referring to state law allowing a candidate, in a close election, as Obama was, to pay just $2,000 total for a complete hand count. The amount would have been a pittance, at the time, to the Illinois senator. Instead, with a campaign war chest low on funds, Kucinich paid $27,000 for a partial count.

Hailing from the Buckeye State, home of 2004's infamous election failures, Kucinich was particularly sensitive to voting machine concerns. "Ever since the 2000 election—and even before—the American people have been losing faith in the belief that their votes were actually counted," he said when announcing his demand for a hand count. "This recount isn't about who won 39 percent or 36 percent or even 1 percent. It's about establishing whether 100 percent of the voters had 100 percent of their votes counted exactly the way they cast them. . . . It is about the integrity of the election process."

On the Republican side, where John McCain was reported to have won handily, an obscure candidate, Albert Howard, a Michigan chauffer, also demanded a hand count after noting that he'd seen as many as 187 votes reported for himself on C-SPAN on election night, but only forty-four votes in the final reported tally.

"My real concern is the controversial Diebold Electronic Scanning machines . . . used for 81 percent of the vote counting in New Hampshire," he echoed Kucinich when announcing his own call for a hand count. "I believe it is better to take action now in the first primary than later."

Howard's recount was largely funded by supporters of Republican candidate Ron Paul. They had long been suspicious of electronic voting systems after watching the collapse of Diebold optical-scanners used in the

2007 summer GOP Iowa straw poll. That first contest of the 2008 presidential election ended up requiring a hand count of thousands of ballots.

Paul supporters were further outraged when they witnessed, on video tape, Mitt Romney supporters literally "stuffing" the Sequoia touch-screen voting systems, voting again and again and again in the December 2007 GOP straw poll in Tampa, Florida.

Romney would "win" that contest, tallying 893 votes to Paul's 534 (his supporters vowed to only vote once each). The documented multiple voting by Romney supporters resulted in the local GOP chairman threatening "bodily harm" to Paul supporters if they didn't cease their public complaints.

Albert Howard paid just less than $60,000 to see all ballots on the Republican side hand counted.

"I'm very concerned that this is not a fully transparent process that is happening there," said voting rights attorney John Bonifaz, legal director of VoterAction.org, a non-partisan organization that had successfully challenged the use of electronic voting systems in many states. He had traveled to Concord to witness the "recount" after becoming concerned about the Diebold tabulation in New Hampshire.

The sensitive memory cards containing the programming and tabulation from the Diebold op-scanners, he'd learned after speaking with the New Hampshire secretary of state and assistant secretary of state and their deputy attorney general, were "missing in action" just one week after the contested race. He was told by secretary of state William Gardner that his office doesn't get involved in tracking what happens to memory cards, but he believed some had already been returned to LHS Associates and may have already been erased.

"When you have a private company counting 80 percent of the votes, and you later learn that the memory cards are unaccounted for, you have a serious question about the transparency and accountability in that process," Bonifaz told me.

Federal law requires the retention of all election-related materials for twenty-two months following federal elections. But whether memory cards are used in DRE or optical-scan systems anywhere in the country, those cards are routinely erased for re-use shortly after elections, making any later forensic investigation—in order to determine if a Leon County-style attack, or mere failure, may have occurred—completely impossible. Lawsuits, Bonifaz noted, are likely needed to enforce the retention of those materials.

Partisan and nonpartisan election integrity advocates from around the country descended on New Hampshire's capitol to oversee, and document on video, every step of both the Democratic and Republican hand counts—at least those parts they were allowed to tape. Howard, in filing for his hand count, had demanded to examine the memory cards from the voting systems and other related materials, such as voting machine poll-tapes, poll books and unvoted ballots. He was told, however, that he would not be allowed to do so. Only the hand counting of voted paper ballots would be included in the state's "recount."

This became a major issue for the assembled election integrity advocates. Examination of the memory cards and end-of-day poll tapes might offer clues to whether the precinct-based scanners showed anomalies or different numbers than those reported by state tallies. Unvoted ballots needed counting to make certain they were accounted for, and not somehow used to stuff ballot boxes or replace legitimate votes. The chain of custody for ballots as they were transported to the state capital to be hand-counted needed to be secure and verified.

Videos and photographs made their way onto the Internet—though rarely into mainstream press accounts—revealing the shoddy condition of cardboard boxes of ballots which election integrity advocates were able to reach directly into, even with so-called "security seals" still intact. The "security seals" themselves were, as seen on video, easily peeled off and restored without leaving a trace of tampering behind. The boxes of ballots were transported from towns across the state back to Concord by two state employees who called themselves Butch and Hoppy. There was virtually no oversight during that transport, and boxes were sometimes left in the open in the counting room at night during the several weeks of hand counting.

New Hampshire's Secretary of State Gardner is officially a Democrat, though by the 2008 primary he'd been in office for sixteen terms, approved time and again by the Republican-majority legislature for most of those years. Despite his experience, he seemed wholly unprepared to handle the new generation of election integrity advocates who—wizened since the days of 2004—came armed with video cameras and demanding both answers and transparency in every step of the process. His consistent deer-in-the-headlights expression caught on camera by citizen activists only heightened concern about what quickly revealed itself as an horrifically sloppy process—at least to those bothering to pay attention. Stories in the mainstream press, however, painted a very different picture.

"We requested that unvoted ballots be counted, but they're not being counted," Manny Krasner, Kucinich's local attorney overseeing the counting complained in frustration when I spoke with him following a front page story in the *Concord Monitor*[10] quoting some of the Brad Blog's critical coverage of the hand count. The paper described Krasner, however, as saying only that he "hadn't seen anything suspicious."

The paper quoted Gardner in response to advocates on the ground, complaining about a lack of transparency. They wrote: "'If this isn't transparent . . .' Gardner said, raising his eyebrows and gesturing to the tables of counters and observers. 'What could we do to make it more transparent!'"

The *Union Leader* editorialized[11] on New Hampshire's behalf with the rosiest of scenarios: "Whatever the recount's results, Gardner has opened the process to observers so there can be no question about the integrity of the count. Doubters on both sides should let this settle the issue. If they question Gardner's integrity, then we'll know for sure not to trust anything else they have to say."

Problems of all sorts were discovered during Kucinich's partial count. In addition to hundreds of ballots discovered miscounted by the Diebold machines, public records requests for trouble reports from Election Day indicated problems such as "Printout indicated 550 'blank voted' ballots which indicated that bad pens were used" in the town of Stratham, "Corrupt Count" in the town of Lebanon, "P/U [pickup] 3rd Bad Machine per John S." (likely a reference to LHS's John Silvestro) in Manchester.

"If it wasn't 550 ballots, but just 55 or so in some places, would they even have seen it and known to recount ALL of the ballots on Election Night?" BlackBoxVoting.org's Bev Harris wondered after reviewing the trouble reports.

In the actual hand count, in ward after ward, the Diebold op-scans had been found to have miscounted enormous numbers of ballots for almost all candidates. In Nashua's Ward 5, for example, Hillary Clinton had received 1,030 votes according to Diebold, but according to the hand-tally, she received just 959, an error rate of 7.4 percent. John Edwards had also been over-tallied by Diebold at the same precinct. His actual results were 7.42 percent lower upon manual examination, while Barack Obama gained just 5 votes at that ward (a .73 percent error rate).

Secretary of State Gardner and the friendly local papers downplayed the problems. They had good reason (billions of them, in fact) to paint that rosy scenario in hopes of retaining their "First in the Nation" status. Where Clinton might have lost thirty votes in one precinct, but gained twenty-nine votes in another, Gardner and the newspaper would report: "Minor discrepancies in recount, Clinton's tally off by just 1 vote."

The *Eagle-Tribune* opined,[12] on Martin Luther King Day of all days, that "It doesn't matter" that machines failed to count every vote. The Democratic Party hand count was part of a "conspiracy theory" and "destructive to Americans' confidence in the democratic process." They said Kucinich had "abused" the state's recount law and "corroded public confidence in the electoral process . . . without a care for the damage he is doing to the country."

The *Eagle-Tribune* didn't mention Republican Albert Howard's similar demand, which also found tally problems across the board for all candidates. But by the time he received his full count, following Kucinich's partial count, the media had moved on to the next contests between the revitalized Clinton and the upstart sensation Obama.

As Kucinich's counting funds ran out, he lodged a letter of complaint with Secretary of State Gardner, charging "significant percentage variances in four voting districts" in one county alone, and detailed miscounts of 10.6 percent here, 4.9 percent there, 7.5 percent over there. And that was just in the few areas he could afford to have counted. He requested Gardner use his "constitutional authority to order a complete and accurate recount of all ballots in the New Hampshire Democratic Presidential Primary election."

Instead, the next day, the *Nashua Telegraph* reported[13] Gardner as saying Kucinich was "satisfied at the integrity of the recount, and it has concluded. . . . The recount revealed no evidence of irregularities in cities and towns that used electronic voting machines."

The federal Help America Vote Act (HAVA) of 2002, passed in the wake of the Florida 2000 election debacle, allocated nearly $4 billion for states to "upgrade" their voting equipment to electronic systems. The legislation also specified a *maximum* allowable error rate of 0.0002 percent for those systems. That the results tallied by Diebold's AccuVote systems in New Hampshire—the same model that was set to be used in upcoming elections in the days and months ahead in dozens of states across the country in the landmark 2008 presidential election—*far* exceeded that maximum allowable rate by magnitude simply didn't matter. The state's local media didn't want to report it, for fear of making "First in the Nation" New Hampshire look bad; the national media were more interested in making all-new predictions, based on all-new pre-election polls, whether or not they would be right or wrong again, for the unprecedented horse race galloping full speed ahead towards November.

When the Brad Blog and a handful of other independent, alternative media outlets and election integrity-focused sites covered the goings-on in the Granite State, we were derided, not just by the expected sources, but even from supposedly progressive outlets typically more sympathetic to issues of transparency and questions of election integrity.

Concerns about what had happened in New Hampshire needed to be painted as little more than stuff and nonsense by some, whether in preemptive defensiveness of Hillary Clinton, or the Democratic Party in general, or the state of New Hampshire, or out of the oft-heard, if wholly unsubstantiated concern that voters might withdraw from the process should their confidence in its legitimacy be questioned in any way. Scrutinization of the process, in the wake of Tim Russert's "most stunning upset in the history of politics," was denounced as "conspiracy theory" bunk; "fringe elements were marginalized for allegedly suggesting "Hillary Clinton had stolen the New Hampshire Primary." Never mind there were no such suggestions from serious critics of the New Hampshire process. Had the election in fact been "stolen" there were any number of potential "suspects"—including known election gamers, such as Karl Rove—who would have had a keen interest in seeing Clinton revive her bid for the Democratic nomination.

Even on Daily Kos, one of the most popular progressive-leaning websites, someone writing pseudonymously under the name of "DHinMI" the day after the election posted a front page article[14] headlined, "Enough with the 'Diebold Hacked the NH Primary' Lunacy." The writer misdirected readers in attempting to "debunk" concerns by stating "New Hampshire has no touchscreen voting. None." Since paper ballots are used in New Hampshire, the pseudonymous writer argued, nobody would be foolish enough to hack the tabulators. "The incentive for hacking them is not very great," the writer argued, because the culprit would be discovered if they did. "If Tuesday's results really were the likely result of malfeasance, the Obama and Edwards campaigns would be raising holy hell. They would be seeking a recount, and investigation of the voting, and they would be doing it because they saw the irregularities in the vote results."

"DHinMI" had a short memory, already having forgotten the 2004 "irregularities in the vote results" in Ohio (and elsewhere) when John

Kerry (and his running mate John Edwards) failed to either "seek a recount" or "raise holy hell" of any sort.

Other usually progressive sites deferred to the Daily Kos's "debunking"[15] of concerns about New Hampshire results before a single Diebold-counted ballot had been examined to assure *any* of them had been tabulated accurately. "There aren't any serious irregularities in the results of Tuesday's Democratic primary," the Daily Kos writer pronounced in no uncertain terms. "New Hampshire has an excellent reputation for running clean elections."

What "DHinMI" *didn't* announce to readers is that he was Dana Houle, until only recently the Chief of Staff for New Hampshire's Democratic US Congressman Paul Hodes.

As the dust settled and the primary cycle moved on to other states, New Hampshire's reputation as "First in the Nation" would remain largely intact. The Granite State could look forward to doing it all over again in four years, and to seeing "billions of dollars" (as Kucinich's representative had complained) once again pour into the state's coffers in support of the kickoff of the 2012 presidential primary campaign.

Whether "paper or plastic," it doesn't matter. Without full transparency and citizen oversight of every aspect of elections, legitimate questions will persist, and democracy will remain in peril.

AMERICA FLIPS OUT, MEDIA BARELY NOTICES, PARTIES BARELY CARE

While concerns about electronically tabulating paper ballots on oft-failing, insecure optical-scan systems would go underappreciated and underinvestigated by the mainstream media, electronic touchscreen voting systems (DREs) would be of moderately passing notice to the nation's news outlets in the weeks and months following New Hampshire.

Failure after failure in primary after primary and state after state plagued the 2008 election. Where Oprah Winfrey's problem received a modest moment of coverage, similar occurrences across the country on virtually every make and model of machinery from every vendor would receive little more than a blip of coverage, quickly downplayed as nothing but a "calibration issue" that could be handled with a quick maintenance procedure by election officials or employees of voting machine vendors.

Never mind that study after study by states such as Ohio, California, Colorado and others, and academic institutions such as Princeton and the University of California, had found virtually every electronic system highly vulnerable to error and/or manipulation, particularly if sensitive memory cartridges were accessed while in election-ready mode. Yet the solution to touchscreen "vote-flipping" across the nation would be a quick, hands-on technical adjustment—or so argued the bulk of officials and vendors, whose careers and company solvency depended on minimizing such failures as little more than "glitches," "hiccups," "snags," and "snafus," as they were almost always downplayed in the media.

Whether marginalized or not, the failures were extraordinarily widespread in 2008, just as they were in 2004 (and in 2006), after which little was done before all would all be repeated again in the next presidential election.

Some progress, one could argue, had been made in the intervening four years. At least reported occurrences of failures and vote flips were not as immediately dismissed as "conspiracy theories" that never actually happened, as they'd been frequently characterized in 2004. By 2008 enough citizens had become aware of known, documented problems with DRE voting, so reports were taken somewhat more seriously. And it didn't hurt that many grassroots outlets such as Video the Vote had sprung up to document polling place problems, nearly instantaneously, by citizens armed with video cameras.

There were many notable failures on touchscreen systems even before early voting for the General Election kicked off. For example, in Horry County, South Carolina, in the Republican presidential primary held entirely on ES&S iVotronc touchscreen voting systems just days after the New Hampshire election, *all* machines in the county failed to fire up at all when the polls opened at 7:00 am.

As CNN reported[16] that afternoon, "Workers have been giving out paper ballots but at least one precinct has run out of envelopes to seal them in (not a sign of turnout—they had just 23 such ballots on hand)." Untold numbers of voters were sent away unable to vote at all, local news outlets reported. "Everyone is being turned away," concerned voter Steve Rabe complained to News 13, "There are no paper ballots. We were just turned away along with many of our neighbors. We were told to check back later . . . in the rain. This is a crisis."

Tom Reynold wrote in, "I voted by paper ballot at the Socastee library and saw them run out of those while I was there at 10 a.m. I went to the

Forestbrook precinct with a neighbor, picked up some paper ballots there and took them to the Socastee library. They told me they had 'turned away' 20 voters in the time I was gone! Turned away?! That's not supposed to happen according to the Horry county elections commission."

"All over the county," it had been reported by evening, voters used scraps of paper, notebook paper, and even paper towels as ballots before officials were able to get most of the unverifiable touchscreens working around noon. The county would be forced to hand-count thousands of pieces of paper to determine results of the election that night.

Before the Democratic primary in the same state the following week, CNN's *Lou Dobbs Tonight* would report on the meltdown and discuss the matter as an illustration of problems inherent in "paperless electronic voting machines." CNN's Kitty Pilgrim neglected to note in her report, however, that even if South Carolina's DREs had "paper trail" printers, they would have been of no use since the machines failed to fire up at all, so they couldn't have printed out so-called "voter-verifiable paper audit trails" featured on certain DRE models.

Given the disaster the week before, Democrats, in advance of their primary the next Saturday, instructed voters to print out sample ballots at home before going to the polls, just in case the massive failure of the Republican primary was repeated. The machines "worked" the following week, even though it would still be 100 percent impossible to know if *any* machine succeeded in recording *anybody's* vote accurately.

Three days later, in Palm Beach County, Florida's primary (yes, ground zero for the 2000 presidential paper ballot battle, prompting the hasty move to e-voting systems), Rush Limbaugh himself encountered problems with his touchscreen vote "when the screen seemed to freeze or 'stick' on the list of presidential candidates." The *Palm Beach Post* blog[17] reported Limbaugh's description to listeners on his widely-syndicated radio show.

"I hit 'next' and it didn't go there," Limbaugh explained, before he then hit the 'back' button and "got my candidate page again with the vote already recorded there."

"So I said 'hmmmmm, I wonder if this is going to count twice.'" He unclicked his candidate, selected it again and hit "Next" a second time, and saw his selection properly on the review screen. "I don't know if I voted twice," Limbaugh told listeners. "Probably not," he guessed, not knowing for certain, of course, if his vote would count even once.

The following week, in New Jersey, on the February 5 "Super Tuesday," Democratic Governor John Corzine "was unable to vote . . . at his designated polling site in Hoboken because the voting machines were not working," as AP reported.[18] He was delayed for forty-five minutes when the AVC Advantage DRE systems, made by Sequoia, failed to start up, making it impossible to vote—not unlike what had happened to voters in South Carolina two weeks earlier. "The big question is, why did this polling place not have any provisional ballots?" ABC 7 asked[19] that day, noting "lots of people were obviously turned away" during the pre-work morning crush at the polls.

That same day, over at Daily Kos—the same site which pooh-poohed concerns about New Hampshire, and even purged users and diaries raising concerns about the 2004 election years earlier—a report[20] was posted from a diarist noting her husband's selection "reset" from Obama to Clinton, several times, on New Jersey's touchscreen machines before he was able to push "the vote button" without it flipping back to Clinton.

The couple's experience would become commonplace, repeated again and again, at polling place after polling place, in state after state, as the election 'glitched,' 'hiccupped,' 'snagged,' and 'snafud' towards November 3.

As early voting began in October, so too did nearly nonstop reports through Election Day of votes flipping and/or disappearing on DRE voting machines. As in previous years, the flips were almost always from Democratic candidates to others. A few examples:

➤ In Jackson County, WV, Virginia Matheney told the *Sunday Gazette-Mail:*[21] "When I touched the screen for Barack Obama, the check mark moved from his box to the box indicating a vote for John McCain." Others in the same precinct reported identical experiences on their ES&S iVotronics DREs. Who knows how many others didn't notice, or didn't report it.

➤ In Putham County, WV, Martha Louise Harrington reported a similar problem with the same machines: "I was very cautious to put my fingernail in the middle of the square. I hit it in the square to vote for Obama. Immediately, it went to McCain."

➤ In Nashville (Davidson County), TN, Patricia Earnhardt—ironically, the executive producer of *Uncounted: The New Math of American Elections,* a documentary film focused on the dangers of touchscreen voting—saw her own ES&S iVotronic vote flip from Obama to Green Party candidate Cynthia McKinney: "I touched 'Obama' for president & nothing lit up. I touched 2 or 3 more times & still nothing lit up. I called the poll worker back over to tell him I was having a problem. He said I just needed to touch it more lightly. I tried it 2 or 3 more times more lightly with the poll worker watching & still nothing lit up. The poll worker then touched it for me twice—nothing lit up. The third time he touched the Obama button, the Cynthia McKinney space lit up!" she emailed me, as reported on the Brad Blog at the time.

➤ (In yet another irony, akin to Earnhardt's—one that would momentarily light up the Internet with headlines such as "Election Integrity Journalist Sees Own Votes Flipped"—four of twelve of my own votes would be misprinted by the e-voting system in Los Angeles County during California's June 2008 state primary.)

➤ On Hilton Head Island (Beaufort County), SC, Nancy Roe discovered that races were missing on the review screen of her ES&S iVotronic touchscreen: "I'm real political, so I checked the ballot. If I had only given it a quick glance and punched 'vote,' I never would've known," she told the *Island Packet*.[22] She solved the problem by voting with a paper ballot.

➤ In Berkeley County, WV, again on the ES&S iVotronic, Roger Bolozier told poll workers when he tried to vote "straight Democratic ticket. But it switched my vote to Republican candidates five different times." He was "concerned about a lot of people who might not notice or people who might be intimidated."

➤ In Palo Pinto County, TX, residents reported the by then too-familiar tale of problems with the ES&S iVotronic. Lona Jones told the *Mineral Wells Index*:[23] "When I cast an early vote at Palo Pinto County Courthouse, my vote was switched from Democrat to Republican right in front of my face—twice!" Teresa Crosier, an alternate election judge and office manager of the Palo Pinto County Democratic Headquarters had the same problem when she tried to vote straight party Democratic "and it came up straight party, Republican party."

➤ Back in WV, the problems on the ES&S systems continued, as the *Sunday Gazette-Mail* reported[24] in late October, in at least six different counties (Jackson, Putnam, Berkeley, Ohio, Monongalia, and Greenbrier). And just one day after she'd held a press conference to discuss problems with ES&S vote-flipping in the state, West Virginia's Secretary of State Betty Ireland actually presented an "award of merit" to ES&S vice-President Gary Greenhalgh, "a pioneer in the use of technology in the election process." As ES&S's vice president of sales, *Wired* reported,[25] Greenhalgh "helped the company win a $17 million contract to supply machines to West Virginia in 2005 and was the company's point person for dealing with election officials." It was the perfect illustration of our e-voting vendor/election official logrolling nightmare in a nutshell.

➤ To the credit of Adams County, CO's clerk and recorder Karen Long, a Diebold touchscreen system that had flipped votes from a Democratic candidate to a Republican was removed from service and quarantined, rather than allowed to be dangerously "recalibrated" in the middle of the election. But only after it happened to the Democratic state representative who had tried to vote for herself, only to see it flipped to her opponent. "I always just trusted the machines, and it opened my eyes," state Rep. Mary Hodge told the *Colorado Independent*.[26]

Had anyone bothered to pay attention to Dan Rather's breathtaking investigative HDNet report, "The Trouble with Touch Screens," in the summer of 2006, they might have expected these problems, particularly from ES&S machines. Rather detailed nearly non-existent quality control in the Filipino sweatshop where many of them were built. Election officials may not have noticed Rather's exposé, however, since not a single mainstream media outlet bothered to note, much less offer follow-up reportage on his award-worthy investigative report.

Even had those officials bothered to notice, most of them were, by then, so deeply in denial and/or millions of dollars into their commitment to the machines and private vendors who sold and serviced them, that dumping them for another likely-as-unreliable system was no longer an option—not if they wished to hold an election that year and continue their careers in the election industry thereafter.

DEMOCRATS NOWHERE TO BE FOUND

The Democratic Party—clearly with much to lose from the now-familiar pattern of e-voting systems adversely affecting attempted votes for their own candidates—was also in denial.

Just prior to the general election, Pennsylvania's Democratic Secretary of the Commonwealth Pedro A. Cortes fought tooth and nail—even in court—against providing "emergency paper ballots" at polling places. Only a federal court challenge from voting rights advocates and the NAACP forced the state to offer at least a few paper ballots at the precincts, in case of machine failures. Earlier in the year, just before the make-or-break Pennsylvania primary, election reform journalist Jake Soboroff asked officials[27] if they had concerns about DRE systems used virtually across the entire state. Democratic Governor Ed Rendell dismissed Soboroff, admitting he "didn't know enough about it to answer" before pointing to state and federal approval of the machines (the same ones found insecure, inaccurate, and hackable by one state test after another by then).

Philadelphia Mayor Michael Nutter summed up the thinking of so many elected officials on the issue of voting machines by telling Soboroff, "I just got elected on them last year," so how bad could they be?

Subsequently and predictably there were *major* problems on Election Day in Pennsylvania, particularly in Philadelphia, that April. All the while, Democrats, including the Obama campaign, had long been singing their familiar 2004 refrain: "If anything goes wrong at the polls this year, we'll have thousands of attorneys on the ground, ready to take care of it." Apparently, as in 2004, they were just kidding.

The day before the 2008 general election, the Brad Blog reported on hundreds of incidents called into Obama's election protection hotline in Nevada as detailed in their incident report database, code-named "Atlas Voter Protection." In one incident after another during the state's early voting period, machines failed to turn on, candidate names were reported missing and so-called "voter-verifiable paper audit trail" printers failed to work on the state's Sequoia DRE systems.

The Obama/DNC attorneys declined to demand any of the failed systems be removed from service, or that voters be given paper ballots to record votes instead. Rather, the entire matter was kept quiet, the information never shared with the public.

Earlier in the year, citizen journalist Michael Richardson and I had broken the story of the illegal certification and use of Nevada's Sequoia DRE "paper trail" system in 2004 by then Secretary of State Dean Heller (now a US Congressman, elected on his own machines in 2006.) Heller publicly lied about machine failures as they were being tested by the US Election Assistance Commission's woeful certification process. He also lied about them being federally certified when he first used them in 2004, in violation of state law. The EAC, responsible for overseeing all such certification and testing of e-voting systems at the federal level, not only looked the other way, but actually colluded in helping Heller use the uncertified machines illegally. When notified, neither the new Democratic secretary of state nor the mainstream media in Nevada batted an eyelash. (Our complete investigative report was published as a chapter in Mark Crispin Miller's 2008 *Loser Take All*, a compilation of similar election failures). Heller's illegally certified machines would fail again during the 2008 cycle, as neither Obama nor the Democrats nor the mainstream media seemed to care.

There was, of course, reason for *everyone* to be concerned, particularly about voting machines made by Sequoia Voting Systems, Inc. The company had been on the verge of bankruptcy and hostile takeover all year, and—though they had told federal investigators that they had divested from Smartmatic, their Venezuelan-owned, Hugo Chávez–tied parent company, in late 2006, after a hue and cry from Republicans—all of their systems' intellectual property rights had secretly remained under the ownership of the Venezuelan firm.

In May of 2008, the Brad Blog reported the exclusive story of Sequoia's lie to federal investigators, including company CEO Jack Blaine's admission on a company-wide phone call that they didn't own the IP rights to their own products—Smartmatic still did. We also detailed his lies-by-omission to Chicago officials—who'd just purchased the company's touchscreens (the ones to be used by Oprah)—concerned that the divestiture had been "a sham transaction designed to fool regulators." It was, indeed. But again, the corporate media failed to notice, and Sequoia was able to invoke claims of IP violations while arguing against independent examinations of their machines in a New Jersey court case after their touchscreens misreported vote totals on Super Tuesday, and in DC, where thousands of "phantom votes" appeared on the city's optical-scan systems in their September primary.

PAY NO ATTENTION TO THE MAN BEHIND THE CURTAIN

While many Democrats were ultimately satisfied with the outcome of the 2008 elections, they were a mess nonetheless. Rather than the machinery of American democracy improving since 2002's Help America Vote Act, democracy continued to disappear as corporate control solidified and citizens became farther removed from the ability to oversee their own elections.

The media, however, happily distracted the American people from the those issues. While offering wall-to-wall coverage of the GOP's "ACORN Voter Fraud" hoax, real cases of disenfranchising voter registration fraud, revealed by the arrest of the head of the company hired by California's GOP to register voters, was barely reported. (Had I not, myself, during an appearance on Fox News, noted the arrest, it seems unlikely the cable "news" channel would have reported it at all.)

While evidence-free allegations of Democratic "voter fraud" made headlines, the well-documented case of Ann Coulter's *actual* voter fraud in Florida was almost entirely ignored.

The story of record turnout would eclipse stories of illegally purged voter rolls in state after state, as the same private voting machine companies who'd performed so abysmally with voting machines were given state contracts to computerize voter rolls.

While Republicans fought for photo ID requirements at polls, nuns, veterans, minorities, students, and the elderly who had no state-issued ID were turned away, disenfranchised, robbed of their rights.

While the media obsessed over Norm Coleman's challenge to Al Franken's victory in Minnesota's razor-thin US Senate Race—featuring the most transparent, painstakingly accurate post-election recount in the history of the nation (thankfully, they had paper ballots *and* bothered to count them!)—few noticed when a citizen transparency project discovered hundreds of ballots deleted without notice by Diebold's optical-scan system in Humboldt County, CA. The company admitted the problem had been known since 2004.

While easily debunked Republican conspiracy theories of Franken ballots appearing "mysteriously" in an election director's car were echoed again and again, the corporate media took little notice of a small plane crash killing the GOP's top IT guru, Mike Connell, after he'd allegedly been threatened by Karl Rove weeks earlier when subpoenaed to testify about GOP election fraud in 2004. (See Chapter 1 for details on the Brad Blog's Project Censored Award-winning coverage of the Connell story.)

California's investigation of Humboldt's deleted ballots revealed that Diebold/Premiere's audit log system was in violation of federal voting system standards. E-voting audit logs had been pointed to by vendors for years as insurance that any mischief could easily be spotted by reviewing the supposedly indestructible logs. As the state investigation revealed, however, Diebold's audit log system allowed deletion of ballots without notice; misdated and mis-timestamped entries, and featured a "clear" button allowing complete deletion of all audit log records with a single mouse click.

A Diebold/Premier spokesman admitted,[28] during a CA Secretary of State hearing in March of 2009, that the flaws in the Diebold GEMS audit log exist in every version of its tabulation software—the same software used in thirty-one states across the nation and, yes, in the state of New Hampshire, where our 2008 nightmares began.

But in the end, the story that would continue to be the most under-reported was the quiet, nearly-complete takeover of our public democracy by private corporations, paving the way for so many of those nightmares. VotersUnite.org's Ellen Theisen warned in a critical, if largely ignored, August 2008 report that "Vendors are Undermining the Structure of US Elections."

As we approached the 2008 general election, the structure of elections in the United States—once reliant on local representatives accountable to the public—had become almost wholly dependent on large corporations, which are not accountable to the public. Most local officials charged with running elections are now unable to administer elections without the equipment, services, and trade secret software of a small number of corporations.

Our dependence on vendor support has left our election structure vulnerable to corporate decisions that are not in the public interest, corporate profiteering, and claims of trade secrecy for information that is essential to public oversight of elections.

Theisen adds ominously, "If the vendors withdrew their support for elections now, our election structure would collapse."

In Humboldt County, California , after the discovery that Diebold/Premier's system deleted ballots without notice in March of 2009, the company quietly sent two letters to the county, unilaterally "terminating" them.

"Premier has chosen to terminate the County's right to use Premier's GEMS software upon certification of your upcoming May 2009 election," one letter stated. Humboldt would no longer be allowed to use the voting system, which the county had already decided to abandon following discovery of the ballot deletions.

The second letter gave Humboldt ninety days to uninstall the company's voter registration software, which the county had no problems with. The vindictive letter informed that the company was "terminating its relationship with the County" in all regards, sending Humboldt scrambling for another voter registration system—likely from another private vendor—even as they were trying to ensure accuracy and accessibility for all voters in their May 2009 state special election.

In 2010, a national census year, elections across the nation will help determine the political balance of power for the next decade as Congressional districts are redrawn and reapportioned to match new census numbers. Those in power after the crucial 2010 elections will draw the boundaries set to affect elections and power in this nation for at least the next ten years. Those elections will be almost wholly run by four private for-profit companies, accountable to virtually no one.

Unless the media do their job by stepping up to report these matters, helping to force election officials, elected officials and law enforcement to do *their* jobs, the citizens—the rightful owners of those elections—will be able to do little about it.

Is anybody paying attention to the man behind the curtain yet?

Notes

1. Friedman, Brad, "Video: Oprah Sees Own Presidential Vote Dropped By Touch-Screen Voting Machine," October 21, 2008, http://www.bradblog.com/?p=6603.
2. http://verifiedvoting.org/verifier/map.php?state=Illinois&county=Cook&ec=allall&year=2008.
3. See http://www.cnn.com/2008/POLITICS/01/03/iowa.caucuses/index.html.
4. Real Clear Politics, January 8, 2008, http://www.realclearpolitics.com/epolls/2008/president/nh/new_hampshire_democratic_primary-194.html.
5. Wikipedia, "Bradley Effect," http://en.wikipedia.org/wiki/Bradley_effect.
6. See http://hackingdemocracy.com/.
7. Susan Pynchon, "Around the States: The Harri Hursti Hack and its Importance to our Nation," Florida Fair Elections Coalition, January 21, 2006, http://www.votetrustusa.org/index.php?option=com_content&task=view&id=820&Itemid=113.
8. "Latest Investigations from Black Box Voting," December 13, 2005, http://www.bbvforums.org/cgi-bin/forums/board-auth.cgi?file=/1954/15595.html.

9. Brad Friedman and Chris Matthews, "Raw EXIT POLL Data 'Indicated Significant Victory' for Obama in NH," January 10, 2008, http://www.bradblog.com/?p=5535.

10. Dorgan, Lauren, "One Ballot at a Time," January 18, 2008, *Concord Monitor*, http://www.concordmonitor.com/apps/pbcs.dll/article?AID=/20080118/FRONT-PAGE/801180340.

11. "The recount: Kucinich goes for answers," NewHampshire.com, January 21, 2008, http://www.unionleader.com/article.aspx?headline=The+recount%3A+Kucinich+goes+for+answers&articleId=8813e51e-89a1-4cc1-a917-f39324575beb.

12. "Our view: Recount won't change New Hampshire result," *The Eagle-Tribune* online, January 21, 2008, http://www.eagletribune.com/puopinion/local_story_021103319?keyword=topstory+page=1.

13. Kevin Landrigan, "Paul Backers Paid for GOP Recount," *Nashua Telegraph*, January 24, 2008, http://www.nashuatelegraph.com/apps/pbcs.dll/article?AID=/20080124/NEWS08/143908662/-1/news08.

14. Dana Houle, "Enough With the 'Diebold Hacked the NH Primary' Lunacy," Daily Kos, January, 9, 2008, http://www.dailykos.com/storyonly/2008/1/10/02623/2264/85/434176.

15. Josh Marshall, "Enough," Talking Points Memo, January 10, 2008, http://www.talkingpointsmemo.com/archives/063292.php.

16. "South Carolina primary plagued by bad voting machines, snow," CNNPolitics.com, January 19, 2008, http://www.cnn.com/2008/POLITICS/01/19/south.carolina.gop/index.html?iref=newssearch.

17. "Rush Limbaugh has Trouble Voting," PlanBeachPost.com, January 29, 2008, http://www.postonpolitics.com/2008/01/rush-limbaugh-has-trouble-voting/.

18. "Corzine can't vote because of poll problems," Associated Press, February 05, 2008, http://www.nj.com/news/index.ssf/2008/02/corzine_cant_vote_because_of_p.html.

19. "McCain, Hillary Win in NJ, Polling Problems Earlier in the Day," ABC, Feburary 6, 2008, http://abclocal.go.com/wabc/story?section=news/politics&id=5936011.

20. "Trying to Vote for Obama, Machine Resets to Clinton in NJ," Daily Kos, February 5, 2008, http://www.dailykos.com/storyonly/2008/2/5/123158/7065/255/450294.

21. Paul Nyden, "Some early W.Va. Voters Angry over Switched Votes," WVGazette.com, October 18, 2008, http://wvgazette.com/News/200810170676.

22. Renee Dudley, "Machine Ballots Omit Candidates' Names," *Island Packet*, October 22, 2008, , http://www.islandpacket.com/news/local/story/645376.html.

23. See http://www.mineralwellsindex.com/local/local_story_298161535.html.

24. Paul Nyden, "Voting Machine Complaints Continue," WVGazette.com, October 27, 2008, http://wvgazette.com/News/200810270020?page=1&build=cache.

25. Kim Zetter, "W. Virginia Gives E-Voting VP an Award While Machines Malfunction," Wired.com, http://www.wired.com/threatlevel/2008/10/w-virginia-give/.

26. Ernest Luning, "Adams County 'Quarantines' Machine that Switched Candidate's Vote," *The Colorado Independent*, October 29, 2009, http://coloradoindependent.com/13187/adams-county-quarantines-machine-that-switched-candidates-vote.

27. "PA Officials: No Trouble With Touchscreens," Why Tuesday?, April 17, 2008, http://www.whytuesday.org/2008/04/17/pa-officials-no-trouble-with-touchscreens/.

28. Kim Zetter, "Diebold Admits Systemic Audit Log Failure; State Vows Inquiry," Wired.com, March 17, 2009, http://www.wired.com/threatlevel/2009/03/diebold-admits/.

Expanding Investigative Research for Independent Media and Human Betterment

by Peter Phillips

Investigative research is the use of social science research methods to conduct data collection and analysis of important socio-economic issues for broad public dissemination—much like in-depth investigative reporting. Investigative research, in a college/university setting, focuses on releasing valuable information through independent media for public consumption in addition to, or instead of, academic journals or presentations at scholarly conferences. Investigative research is a democracy building process that addresses the socio-structural circumstances of who decides, who wins and who loses in society. Public investigative research in the social sciences asks the questions: Who are the people with the most power? Who makes the important decisions that affect our lives? How did these socio-political elites acquire their positions? What advantages do these individuals share and what impacts do these advantages have over others in society?

In a capitalist society, the economic winner is invariably advantaged, honored, and encouraged. From little league to academics, American society encourages competition. The winners are rewarded with honor, fame, and advantages in future competitions. Success is seldom solely based on individual effort. Many structural advantages involving race, class, and gender are in place in society that creates unequal results among various groups of people.

For example, racial inequality remains problematic in the US. People of color continue to experience disproportionately high rates of poverty, unemployment, police profiling, repressive incarceration and school segregation.

According to a new UCLA civil rights report, "Reviving the Goal of an Integrated Society: A 21st Century Challenge," by Gary Orfield, schools in the US are currently 44 percent non-white, and minorities are rapidly

emerging as the majority of public school students. Latinos and Blacks are the two largest minority groups.[1] However, Black and Latino students attend schools more segregated today than during the civil rights era. Over fifty years after the US Supreme Court case *Brown v. Board of Education*, schools remain separate and not equal. Orfield's study shows that public schools in the Western states, including California, suffer from the most severe segregation in the US, rather than schools in the southern states, as many people believe.

This new form of segregation is primarily based on how urban areas are geographically organized—as Cornel West so passionately describes—into vanilla suburbs and chocolate cities.

Schools remain highly unequal in terms of money, qualified teachers, and up to date curricula. Unequal education leads to diminished access to colleges and future jobs. Non-white schools are segregated by levels of income as well as by race. These "chocolate" low-income public schools are where most of the nation's dropouts occur, leading to large numbers of virtually unemployable young people of color struggling to survive in a troubled economy.

Diminished opportunity for students of color invariably creates greater privileges for whites. White privilege is a challenging concept for many whites. Whites like to think of themselves as hardworking individuals whose achievements are deserved due to personal efforts. In many cases this is partly true; hard work in college often pays off in many ways. Nonetheless, many whites find it difficult to accept that geographically—and structurally—based racism remains a significant barrier for many students of color. Whites often think that racism is in the past, and we that need not address it today. Yet inequality stares at us daily from the barrios, ghettos, and from behind prison walls. Inequality continues in privileged universities as well.

A multi-ethnic and culturally diverse experience on university campuses is strongly valued in the US and is considered an important aspect of a college education.[2] Higher education racial balance along with class equity is an ongoing subject of social justice research in many academic disciplines. Since the civil rights movement and 1960s campus unrest, much progress has been made on increasing minority and low-income access to colleges in the US. Public universities, and to a degree private universities, across the country annually assess their progress toward building socio-economic and racial equity. It is rare to see a public university that has effectively reversed this trend and deliberately tried to increase student wealth and maintain a non-diverse student population.

Project Censored students and faculty conducted an investigative research study on inequality in the California State University system in late 2008.[3] The study described how Sonoma State University (SSU) had recently achieved the status of having the whitest, and likely richest, student population of any public university in the state of California. The investigative research showed that beginning in the early 1990s, the SSU administration specifically sought to market the campus as a public Ivy institution, offering an Ivy League experience at a state college price. Part of this public Ivy packaging was to advertise SSU as being in a destination wine country location with attractive physical and cultural amenities. These marketing efforts were principally designed to attract upper-income students to a *Falcon Crest*–like campus.

To achieve the desired outcome of becoming a wine-country public Ivy, SSU's administration implemented special admissions screening processes that used higher SAT-GPA indexes than the rest of the California State University (CSU) system. According to Lani Guinier and Gerald Torres in *The Miner's Canary*, high SAT scores correlate directly to both race and income with little relationship to actual success in college.[4]

SSU also conducted recruitment at predominately white upper-income public and private high schools throughout the west coast and

Hawaii. Consequently, SSU freshmen students with family incomes over $150,000 increased by 59 percent between 1994 and 2007, and freshmen students from families with incomes below $50,000 declined by 21 percent. The campus remained over three-quarters white during this fifteen-year period, while the rest of the CSU campuses significantly increased ethnic diversity.

The study was published on the SSU Faculty Senate website, the statewide faculty union affirmative action website, and at Project Censored's Investigative research site. The SSU student newspaper, *Star*, covered the story on the front page, and the local regional newspaper, *Press Democrat*, featured the story on their front page as well. The online news site *InsideHighered.com* covered the story nationally, and the authors were interviewed on two local talk radio stations as well as the much larger regional Pacifica station KPFA in Berkeley.[5]

While the SSU university administration denied that they had deliberately tried to recruit richer students, they were unable to deny the facts in the report and are now taking significant steps to correct the situation. An SSU President's emergency task force on diversity was created in the spring of 2009. While we cannot claim full credit for this apparent reversal in policy at SSU, we certainly raised the level of discussion and awareness of the issue by releasing our investigative research study.

The data gathered from the study also supported the writing of a 700-word research informed opinion article entitled, "A Black President Doesn't Mean Racism is gone in America."[6] The article was published on over fifty websites, including *Truthout*, Global Research, and the national black online newspaper *SF Bay View*. Several international websites translated and posted the article as well.

The opinion piece stressed that our society has reached a point where a majority of the population has elected a black President of the United States. This presidency is a hugely symbolic achievement for race relations in the US. However, we must not ignore the continuing disadvantages for people of color and the resulting advantages gained by whites. Institutional policies and *de facto* segregation contribute to continuing inequalities that require ongoing review, discussion and redress. Efforts against racism must continue if we are to truly attain the civil rights goal of equal opportunity for all. These efforts cannot be realized unless investigative research, such as the studies listed above, are available not only for academics inside specific disciplines, but also for a far boarder democratic public policy process that is inclusive of citizen level activism for human betterment.

THE ROLE OF PUBLIC UNIVERSITIES IN BUILDING MEDIA DEMOCRACY AND TRANSPARENCY OF THE POWERFUL

Public colleges and universities have a role to play in building media democracy and the full transparency of what the powerful are doing society. Universities are institutions founded on scientific factual research and on sharing the results of this research with others, both within specific disciplines and outside the academy. As the corporate media continues on the path of entertainment, declining support for investigative reporting and instead engaging in watered down news reporting, an opportunity for colleges and universities is emerging to take a role in validating independent news and doing investigative research for publication in independent media news sources worldwide (see chapter 5 for more on this topic).

Often college professors do not think about the research they are doing in terms of its public benefit. Most professors are trained to write for academic journals in a style that is factual, but often too complex for mass public reading.

The role of universities in supporting public education is receiving new attention, as evidenced by disciplines being more receptive to action research, liberation sociology, applied anthropology, comparative historical analysis, qualitative methods, community service involvement, and experiential learning. Certainly some aspects of these research styles have at their base an understanding and assumption that the research being done is for human betterment and democracy building, rather than just theory/discipline expansion.

Investigative research asks the questions, why do inequalities persist in society, and who are the beneficiaries of these inequalities? More specifically, investigative research identifies key deciders. Rarely do the powerful claim that they are the primary decision-makers, as in George W. Bush's famous quote, "I am the decider."[7] However when we examine and identify the individuals behind significant decisions inside powerful institutions in society, a different level of public awareness can emerge that pulls the covers off those people behind the bureaucratic curtains and exposes their self interest and unequal rewards.

INVESTIGATIVE RESEARCH ONLINE: HEALTH CARE

Practices in Health Care and Disability Insurance: Delay, Diminish, Deny, and Blame

by Peter Phillips and Bridget Thornton: Sociology 436 class, Spring 2007, with David Abbott, Brandon Beccio, Daniela Bravo, Laura Buck, Chris Castro, Andrew Kent, Chris Morello, Brian Murphy, Debra Sedeno, Kimberly Soho, and Yuri Wittman.
(http://www.projectcensored.org/articles/story/practices-in-health-care/)

This study examined the historical circumstances that brought about our private health and disability insurance system in the US. We looked at the organizational structures of private for-profit and non-profit insurance companies that dominate the health care industry and the strategies these firms use to delay, diminish, and deny payment for health care and disability benefits for people across the country. We discussed the impact of delays and denials on patients and disabled individuals, and the ways insurance companies deliberately create psychological doubt and self-blame among those who are legitimately entitled to benefits. We summarized the results of twenty extensive interviews with people who have experienced major difficulties in receiving payments of benefits and for heath care service they expected from their insurance providers. We further examined the general lack of regulation, enforcement of existing laws, government motivation to meet the health and disability needs of all Americans, and the socio-economic power of the health insurance industry to dominate health care policy.

In order to understand how insurance companies strategize to maximize profits and limit payouts for benefits, we examined the evolution of the industry and the socio-economic power base of the top health insurance companies in the US. The power of the companies to set national policies contrasts with the personal difficulties of the individuals interviewed, demonstrating a system-wide process of profit taking at the expense of fulfilling promises, and of diverting money intended to pay for necessary health care goods and services.

Investigative Research Methods Used:

➤ Literature review on history of private health insurance in the US

➤ Literature review of problems with health insurance companies for patients

➤ Data collection of the names of the people on the Boards of Directors from the top nine health and disability insurance companies in the US. Presidential campaign donations by the top companies and their directors

➤ Qualitative interviews with twenty families who had experienced problems with health insurance coverage

➤ Profits for top nine companies for 2006: $38 billion

Health Care Study Conclusions:
Each person interviewed for this study had insurance at the onset of his or her malady. They paid monthly premiums through employer sponsored plans or had purchased individual/family policies directly from insurance companies. The people in this study believed they would receive the benefits they were promised in the event of an accident, disease, or illness. The management practices of the health or disability insurance company delayed, diminished, and denied payment for expected benefits.

Health and disability insurance companies are for-profit entities, despite some organizations operating under tax-exempt status. Customer care and quality of service falls to second place under this profit-driven model of health care. These practices are part of a growing structural arrangement between private business and government that is unlikely to be undone without extensive government re-regulation. As a health care regulator, the state is working for the benefit of capital expansion instead of health care for every person. In fact, the state is motivated to extensively regulate individual behavior and ignore corporate malfeasance.

Private insurance has a structural motivation to delay, diminish, and deny payment for promised benefits, in order to maintain profit margins. They use these profits to propagandize the American public and influence voters through scare tactics of socialized medicine and long delays of service that supposedly occur in single-payer systems. Using corporate media and massive political donations to both parties, private health insurance companies have increased profits and maintained their influence in the system. The state complies with this arrangement and individuals within both systems use this compliance for revolving door career advancement.

The people in this study never anticipated the ways in which their lives would be changed by an inadequate and profit-driven system. They had health and disability insurance to protect them from insolvency and provide them with a minimum level of care and comfort. However, the companies with which the participants dealt managed to compound pain, trauma, and suffering instead of relieving it.

Adequate health care for everyone is a human right, acknowledged by the world in the 1948 United Nation's Declaration of Human Rights. Most Americans pay higher combined taxes, health and disability insurance premiums, co-payments, and various health-related expenses than citizens in common pool, single-payer systems, yet those countries allow all their citizens equal access to services. When the American people collectively decide that health care and basic social security is a right that belongs to everyone, the health and disability system can be changed to provide necessary benefits for all.

In addition to publishing the full study online, the following 730-word op-ed was published in October 2007 on some thirty websites, including www.calnurses.org, www.usatoday.com, www.information-clearinghouse.info, www.consumerfedofca.org, and dozens of newspapers nationwide.

Why the US Lacks Full Health Care

by Peter Phillips and Bridget Thornton

Health and disability insurance companies are systematically cheating the American public. Michael Moore's top-grossing movie *Sicko* is one example of the growing concern surrounding health care in the US.

The number of Americans without health insurance reached forty-seven million at last count, or 16 percent of the population. The cost of health insurance is rising two to three times faster than inflation and is the number one cause of personal bankruptcy in the country. We pay more and get less medical care than the rest of the industrialized world. The total per capita health care cost in the US exceeds the health care expense per person in all other full care countries.

The Institute of Medicine estimates that as many as eighteen thousand Americans die prematurely each year because they do not have health insurance. This figure does not include those who die prematurely each year because their insurers delay, diminish, or deny payment for promised benefits. Reports about people who die unnecessarily from services denied or delayed by insurance companies seldom receive broad coverage in the corporate media. Lack of media coverage has led to a nation of people uninformed about how national health and disability policies are controlled by the private insurance industry and how government regulators are powerless to do anything about it.

If industrialized countries around the world offer health care as a basic right, why is full health care not a right in the US? Private insurance companies are motivated to make as much money as possible and do so by systematically delaying, diminishing, and denying payment for promised services, and blaming individuals for their own misfortune.

On the boards of directors of the nine largest insurance companies are one hundred thirteen people. These directors are some of the richest people in the world. They hold one hundred fifty past and/or present positions with major financial or investment institutions in the US, including such major firms such as J. P. Morgan, Citigroup, Lord Abbett, Bank of America, and Merrill Lynch. Additionally, these board members have connections to some of the largest corporations in the world including General Motors, IBM, Ford, Microsoft, and Coca-Cola. The combined affiliations among the one hundred thirteen health insurance directors represented revenue of over 2.5 trillion dollars 2006.

As some of the richest, most powerful people in America, health care executives dominate health policy with their campaign donations and active lobbying efforts. They spend millions to keep themselves in the health insurance delivery business despite overwhelming evidence that we would all be better off without them. They use these profits to propagandize the American public and influence voters through scare tactics of "socialized medicine" and long delays of service that supposedly occur in single-payer systems.

The single-payer advocacy group, Physicians for a National Health Program, reports that private insurance corporations spend an enormous amount of money on business-oriented expenses rather than health-related investments. A 2003 study in the *New England Journal of Medicine* estimates that spending for administrative costs associated with health care amount to over $320 billion per year or about 31 percent of health care costs in the US overall. The administrative costs in the Canadian national health care system amount to 16.7 percent or about half of the administrative overhead in the US.

Countries with common pool or single-payer health care systems provide similar levels of service to every person. In such countries, it is the responsibility of society as a whole to provide health care for each individual.

People in the US have a choice. We can continue with a high-cost, profit-driven, private insurance health care system leaving millions to languish without care, and millions more to face the frustrations of systematic delays, diminished care, and denials of promised benefits. Alternatively, we can build a common pool health care system that provides necessary health care goods to everyone—for less than what we are now paying.

Let's find and support the politicians who will provide health care for all outside of corporate fat-cat control.

INVESTIGATIVE RESEARCH ONLINE: GLOBAL DOMINANCE GROUP

The Global Dominance Group: 9/11 Pre-Warnings & Election Irregularities in Context

by Peter Phillips, Bridget Thornton, Celeste Vogler and Lew Brown
(http://www.projectcensored.org/articles/story/the-global-dominance-group/)

The leadership class in the US is now (as of 2006) dominated by a neoconservative group of people with the shared goal of asserting US military power worldwide. This global dominance group, in cooperation with major military contractors, has become a powerful force in world military unilateralism and US political processes. This research study is an attempt to identify the general parameters of those who are the key actors supporting a global dominance agenda and how collectively this group has benefited from the events of September 11, 2001, and irregularities in the 2004 presidential election. This study examines how interlocking public private partnerships, including the corporate media, public relations firms, military contractors, policy elites, and government officials, jointly support a US military global domination agenda. We asked the traditional sociological questions regarding who wins, who decides, and who facilitates action inside the most powerful military-industrial complex in the world.

Investigative Research Methods Used:

➤ Literature review on power elite and military industrial complex in the US

➤ Literature review on history neo-conservatives in the US

➤ Data collection of the names of the people on the board of directors from the top ten defense contractors in the US and post-9/11 profits

➤ Data collection of the names of the directors of the leading policy institutes promoting a military dominance agenda

➤ Interlocks with military defense contractors and corporate media in the US

➤ Database of the 236 individuals who advocated for and benefited from the continuing expansion of US military dominance of the world

In addition to publishing this investigative research study on line, the database portions of the study, with a somewhat different analysis, were included as chapters in the books *9/11 and American Empire* (2007) and *Impeach the President: the Case against Bush and Cheney* (2006).[8]

In addition to publishing the full study online, the following 710-word op-ed was published in February of 2006 on some thirty websites, including Commondreams, 911forum.org.uk, granma.cubaweb, democraticunderground, and dozens of newspapers nationwide.

Is US Military Dominance of the World a Good Idea?

by Peter Phillips

The leadership class in the US is now dominated by a neo-conservative group of some two hundred people who have the shared goal of asserting US military power worldwide. This global dominance group, in cooperation with major military contractors, has become a powerful force in military unilateralism and US political processes.

A long thread of sociological research documents the existence of a dominant ruling class in the US, which sets policy and determines national political priorities. C. Wright Mills, in his 1956 book on the power elite, documented how World War II solidified a trinity of power in the US that comprised corporate, military, and government elites in a centralized power structure working in unison through "higher circles" of contact and agreement.

Neo-conservatives promoting the US military control of the world are now in dominant policy positions within these higher circles of the US. *Adbusters* magazine summed up neo-conservatism as "the belief that Democracy, however flawed, was best defended by an ignorant public pumped on nationalism and religion. Only a militantly nationalist state could deter human aggression . . . Such nationalism requires an external threat and if one cannot be found it must be manufactured."

In 1992, during Bush the First's administration, Dick Cheney supported Lewis Libby and Paul Wolfowitz in producing the *Defense Planning Guidance* report, which advocated US military dominance around the globe in a "new order." The report called for the United States to grow in military superiority and to prevent new rivals from rising up to challenge us on the world stage.

At the end of Clinton's administration, global dominance advocates founded the Project for a New American Century (PNAC). Among the PNAC founders were eight people affiliated with the number-one defense contractor Lockheed Martin, and seven others associated with the number-three defense contractor Northrop Grumman. Of the twenty-five founders of PNAC twelve were later appointed to high-level positions in the George W. Bush administration.

In September 2000, PNAC produced a seventy-six-page report entitled *Rebuilding America's Defenses: Strategy, Forces and Resources for a New Century*. The report, similar to the 1992 *Defense Planning Guidance* report, called for the protection of the American homeland, the ability to wage simultaneous theater wars, perform global constabulary roles, and the control of space and cyberspace. It claimed that the 1990s were a decade of defense neglect and that the US must increase military spending to preserve American geopolitical leadership as the world's superpower. The report also recognized that: "the process of transformation . . . is likely to be a long one, absent some catastrophic and catalyzing event such as a new Pearl Harbor." The events of September 11, 2001, presented exactly the catastrophe that the authors of *Rebuilding America's Defenses* theorized were needed to accelerate a global dominance agenda. The resulting permanent war on terror has led to massive government defense spending, the invasions of two countries, the threatening of three others, and the rapid acceleration of the neo-conservative plans for military control of the world.

The US now spends as much for defense as the rest of the world combined. The Pentagon's budget for buying new weapons rose from $61 billion in 2001 to over $80 billion in 2004. Lockheed Martin's sales rose by over 30 percent at the same time, with tens of billions of dollars on the books for future purchases. From 2000 to 2004, Lockheed Martins stock value rose 300 percent. Northrup-Grumann saw similar growth with DoD contracts rising from $3.2 billion in 2001 to $11.1 billion in 2004. Halliburton, with Dick Cheney as former CEO, had defense contracts totaling $427 million in 2001. By 2003, they had $4.3 billion in defense contracts, of which approximately a third were sole source agreements.

At the beginning of 2006 the global dominance group's agenda is well established within higher circle policy councils and cunningly operationalized inside the US government. They work hand in hand with defense contractors promoting deployment of US forces in over 700 bases worldwide.

There is an important difference between self-defense from external threats, and the belief in the total military control of the world. When asked, most working people in the US have serious doubts about the moral and practical acceptability of financing world domination.

ADDITIONAL INVESTIGATIVE RESEARCH COMPLETED WITH PROJECT CENSORED

Deconstructing Deceit: 9/11, The Media, and Myth Information

by Mickey Huff and Dr. Paul W. Rea, with online revision research assistance from Project Censored intern Frances Capell (2008).
(http://www.projectcensored.org/articles/story/deconstructing-deceit/)

This investigative report addresses the ongoing phenomena of media myth making and the events of September 11, 2001. Corporate mainstream media have resurrected powerful myths from America's past to shape public perception in the present. Through the prism of 9/11 as case study, one can see how the corporate mass media are in fact involved in more myth-making than news reporting. This amounts to a form of censorship. Professors Huff and Rea examine central historic

American myths that corporate media, and even much of the alternative independent media, have extended into the post-9/11 era, especially regarding the events of 9/11 themselves. This analysis looks at how media myth-making surrounding the events of 9/11, exploiting the strong emotions these events aroused, has prevented a dispassionate inquiry of its causes or of those responsible.

US Media Bias, Human Rights, and the Hamas Government in Gaza

By Janeen Rashmawi, Nelson Calderon, Sarah Maddox, Christina Long, Andrew Hobbs, and Peter Phillips (2008).
(http://www.projectcensored.org/articles/story/us-media-bias-human-rights-and-the-hamas-government-in-gaza/)

This investigative study was a content analysis of mainstream corporate news coverage of Hamas since the general elections in Palestine in January of 2006.

ONGOING INVESTIGATIVE RESEARCH STUDY SPRING 2009

In the spring of 2009 seventeen students in the investigative research class at Sonoma state University conducted a study of the number of law enforcement related deaths that occurred in 2007 and will compare those deaths to an earlier database from 1997. Students used electronic newspaper databases to collect all the newspaper stories in the US that describe a police shooting or law enforcement related death. Additionally, students conducted in-depth interviews with fifteen families who had lost a loved one in a law enforcement related death in the San Francisco Bay area. Students also interviewed fifteen police officers regarding procedural training and law enforcement related deaths.

CONCLUSION

Undergraduate students at Somona State University completed the data collection for each of the studies listed above. Students used various social science research methods to address contemporary issues. The data collected is permanently available for further research, and the studies produced were published for public reading. Shorter op-eds were created and widely distributed through the Internet linking back to the original study online.

A study we produced in 2007, on the current capabilities of the US military use of electromagnetic (EMF) devices to harass, intimidate, and kill individuals, as well as the continuing possibilities of violations of human rights by the testing and deployment of these weapons, resulted in over 250,000 downloads in the first year after posting.[9]

We strongly believe that investigative research can be widely applied in colleges and universities throughout the US. Having students as researchers on important social justice, human rights, and inequality issues serves the dual purpose of training students and expanding knowledge for human betterment. Investigative research builds and inspires media and democracy activism, demonstrating the possibilities of using independent media for public education and democracy building from the bottom up.

Notes

1. G. Orfield, *Reviving the Goal of an Integrated Society: A 21st Century Challenge* (Los Angeles, CA: The Civil Rights Project/Proyecto Derechos Civiles at UCLA), http://www.fairhousingforall.org/news/reviving-goal-integrated-society.

2. Lee Bollinger, "Why Diversity Matters," *Educational Digest*, Vol. 73 Issue 2, 2007, p. 26-29; M. J. Chang, N. Denson, K. Misa, and V. Saenz, "The Educational Benefits of Sustaining Cross-Racial Interaction among Undergraduates," *The Journal of Higher Education*, 77.3, 2007, p. 430-455; S. Hu, and G.D. Kuh, "Diversity Experiences and College Student Learning and Personal Development" *Journal of College Student Development*, 44.3, 2003, p. 320-334.

3. Peter Phillips, "Building a Public Ivy-Sonoma State University, 1994-2007: A Study of Student Racial Diversity and Family Income at SSU Compared to Other California State Universities," Research by Nelson Calderon, Sarah Maddox, Carmela Rocha, and the Spring 2008 Investigative Sociology Class at Sonoma State University: Ashley Aldern, Reham Ariqat, Elizabeth Bourne, Nate Bradley, Niki Brunkhurst, Meredith Carey, Lea Carre, Kimberly Copperberg, Erica Elkington, Erin Garnett, Keri Kirby, Tara Loch, Lisa McKee, Particia Ochoa, Phillip Parfitt, Kelsey Percich, Nina Reynoso, Juana Som, Miasha Terry, Ruby Virelas, Nicholas Vos, Daniel Wyatt, http://www.project-censored.org/articles/story/building-a-public-ivy/.

4. Lani Guinier and Gerald Torres, *The Miner's Canary* (Cambridge: Harvard University Press, 2007).

5. David Moltz, "Not So White Noise About Diversity," February 25, 2009, http://www.insidehighered.com/news/2009/02/25/sonoma; *Flashpoints Radio Show*, http://aud1.kpfa.org/data/20090410-Fri1700.mp3; Guy Kovner, "Is SSU too white and wealthy?" March 23, 2009, http://www.pressdemocrat.com/article/20090323/NEWS/903230309.

6. Peter Phillips, "A Black President Doesn't Mean Racism is gone in America," April 15, 2009, http://dailycensored.com/2009/04/15/a-black-president-doesn%E2%80%99t-mean-racism-is-gone-in-america/.
7. George Bush video, "I am the Decider!" YouTube.com, January 22, 2007, www.youtube.com/watch?v=E2ZviT4Qdv4.
8. David Ray Griffin and Peter Dale Scott, eds., *9/11 and American Empire: Intellectuals Speak Out* (Olive Branch Press, 2007); Dennis Loo and Peter Phillips, eds., *Impeach the President: the Case Against Bush and Cheney* (New York: Seven Stories Press, 2006).
9. Peter Phillips, Lew Brown and Bridget Thornton, "A Study of the History of US Intelligence Community Human Rights Violations and Continuing Research," http://www.projectcensored.org/articles/story/us-intelligence-community-human-rights-violations/.

CHAPTER 13

No "Pretty Woman"
Human Trafficking and Domestic Prostitution Reconsidered

by Aashika N. Damodar

> *When I learned about what human trafficking was, it gave me an*
> *identity I longed for . . . not as a criminal but as someone who was*
> *horribly wronged. In our society, we need the term trafficking to heal.*
> *It has helped me.*
>
> —Michelle

Consider the following: a young woman of ten, fifteen, or perhaps older is feigned affection from an older man. He befriends her, offers to give her a comforting shoulder in the struggle through her teenage years, and promises her a better life with him. She believes him and accepts his offer. But what happens when this man forces her to engage in numerous sex acts per day with customers, takes all of her earnings, and beats and threatens her if she tries to leave? One might see this as a relatively common, even benign, situation in the world of street prostitution.

This is a dangerous misrepresentation of prostitution in America. While I do not aim to generalize for all of the sex industry in the US, those familiar with the issue of human trafficking might recognize this behavior as that of a pimp engaged in trafficking. Each day thousands of US-based pimps engage in these very behaviors. Most Americans look abroad when they hear the term "human trafficking," but pimps are trafficking women and girls in US cities and suburbs. According to a recent University of Pennsylvania study, an estimated 200,000 American children are at high risk for trafficking and commercial sexual exploitation each year.

The formal definition of human trafficking according to the Trafficking Victims Protection Act (TVPA) is,

> Sex trafficking in which a commercial sex act is induced by force, fraud, or coercion, or in which the person induced to perform such an act has not attained 18 years of age; or

the recruitment, harboring, transportation, provision, or obtaining of a person for labor or services, through the use of force, fraud or coercion for the purpose of subjection to involuntary servitude, peonage, debt bondage or slavery.[1]

Based on the TVPA definition, pimps are defined as sex traffickers because they use beatings, sexual assault, gang rape, lies, false promises, deception, and threats to force and coerce women and children to engage in commercial sex acts. Like international sex traffickers, pimps are US-based sex traffickers that use the same tactics against people for the purpose of subjection to involuntary servitude and sex slavery. Indeed, judges and juries in numerous federal US district courts have convicted pimps of sex trafficking (See *United States v. Pipkins, United States v. Brice, United States v. Curtis*), and many states have prosecuted pimps using state anti-trafficking laws.

This chapter aims to explore the world of the "domestically trafficked," or US citizens who are trafficked into the sex industry by pimps. As a result of our society's current understanding of human trafficking as an issue of immigration, the prominence of prostitution in America has been grossly underestimated, and is perhaps one of the largest human rights abuses occurring in our cities today. This issue is further complicated by the glamorization of the pimping phenomenon in hip-hop culture. Very little of what is written about human trafficking prepared me for the chaos of "everyday street prostitution," a concept I have observed and learned about through various non-profit organizations serving sexually exploited women. This essay attempts to explore some of these issues.

In contemporary discussions of human rights, the term modern day slavery and human trafficking are often used synonymously.[2] Even more problematic are the estimates for the number of trafficking victims in the world. The United Nations Office on Drugs and Crime says 2.5 million people throughout the world are at any given time recruited, entrapped, transported, and exploited—a process called human trafficking.[3] Dr. Kevin Bales, author of *Disposable People and Ending Slavery*, estimates 27 million people are enslaved today.

The concept of human trafficking has made itself visible in relation to the larger spectrum of urgent social and political problems such as immigration and prostitution. Many countries and international bodies such as the United Nations and non-governmental organizations have put the combat of human trafficking on their agendas. The issue of trafficking is referred to as human trade, trafficking in human beings, trafficking in persons, alien smuggling, illegal immigrant smuggling, trade of human beings, human commodity trafficking, and modern day slavery. Because of differing contexts, trafficking discourse also occupies different perspectives and understandings of morality, criminality, human rights, public order, fair labor, and gender.[4] Human trafficking discourse looks at these boundaries and points out differences between urgent social and political problems.

It is necessary to define boundaries because the issue of human trafficking unfortunately exists in a realm where anecdotal evidence is relied upon to express the true nature of a given situation. Most discussions of trafficking rely on widely circulated stories about typical trafficking case—for example, the story of the young woman affected by poverty and under false pretenses of employment abroad. Stories like these raise questions for practitioners of human rights and anti-trafficking and perpetuate assumptions about the types of people who fall victim to trafficking. Are they migrants, criminals, or prostitutes? Into what category of human rights victims do they belong? Once those who have been trafficked are placed into categories, language begins to play an incredible role in labeling people, so that debates on human trafficking may be based on taken-for-granted ideas of what it means to be a prostitute or an immigrant, making it difficult to accurately gauge how to help those who have been enslaved. The discourse of trafficking now must be analyzed in terms of the conditions under which those stories have definite truth. It is from this place of truth that my inquiries into domestic sex trafficking begin.

I AM NOT A "PRETTY WOMAN"

The 1990 romantic comedy film *Pretty Woman* is centered on a prostitute named Vivian Ward who is hired by a wealthy businessman named Edward Lewis. Vivian becomes his escort during his week-long business trip; as the days pass, the two develop a relationship. Producer Laura Ziskin originally intended *Pretty Woman* to be a commentary on prostitution issues in Los Angeles. Due to its controversial subject mater, the movie was heavily edited and changed into a comedy, portraying a woman's life as a prostitute without violence or physical abuse.

This chapter is titled "No Pretty Woman" so that readers may see the other side of the story from the point of view of a woman who has had a very different experience with prostitution. The subsequent paragraphs describe the story of a domestic sex trafficking case. For anonymity, I will refer to the subject as "Michelle." Stories of sexual exploitation, violence, and prostitution are commonplace. What makes Michelle's story integral to this discussion is the way the term trafficking has come to play an integral role in her identity. After having been out of the life of prostitution for several years, she expressed her frustration with the stereotype of the "pretty woman," saying, "it's just not as glamorous as it seems." She identifies herself as a survivor of trafficking. Her subjectivity provides us with an insightful understanding of trafficking while highlighting the problem of human trafficking discourse.

MICHELLE

Michelle's story is one of domestic sex trafficking by a local pimp. She was forced onto the streets at the age fourteen. While she was a runaway she met a man who would later become her pimp. At first, he offered to take care of her and be a loving boyfriend. Her pimp relocated her to another state, where she would be groomed by other women who were under her pimp's control. They made her learn the tricks of the streets so she could contribute to the "household." Michelle never kept any of her income and was constantly malnourished, and beaten and raped if she did not meet her monetary quota. Eventually she was rescued by a trafficking organization that was able to establish a case. She says, "I am not a prostitute. I never was a prostitute. I was sexually abused for someone else's gain. Trafficking is a term I could use to heal."

Prostitution is a social practice that has generated controversy, confusion, scorn, pity, fascination, myths, and theories—not just in current debates, but for thousands of years. Most of what the world "knows" about prostitution comes not from we who have lived it, but from self-proclaimed "experts" who have rationalized, justified, politicized, glamorized, and occasionally condemned the buying and selling of women (mostly) as interchangeable market items. Economists use the term "alienable" to describe this quality of exchangeability. When your car or computer, for example, becomes less functional, it can be replaced by another.

Discussions of capitalism can help us understand the idea of alien-ability. Elizabeth Bernstein of Columbia University, in "Desire, Demand and the Commerce of Sex," looks at how feminists and other scholars have debated what is "really" purchased in the prostitution exchange and transaction: is it a relationship of domination? Is it love, addiction, pleasure? Can sex be a service like any other?[5] Bernstein writes, "In the late 20th century, however, with the shift from a production based to a consumption-based economy, the focus of moral critique and political reform is gradually being displaced: The prostitute is normalized as either "victim" or "sex-worker," while attention and sanction is directed away from labor practices and toward consumer behavior."[6]

Women who have been domestically trafficked inhabit themes of alienability, of being reduced to no value except as a commodity to be traded. Rubin's discussion of trafficking as a facet of capitalism says that women such as Michelle and others have been "transacted" for a monetary value, leaving them no leeway to realize their self-worth within this system.

Theresa, another survivor of trafficking, describes how this feels:

> One afternoon they took me. I was instructed towards his business partners and said to them, "I have something very special planned for you all today." They pulled out several pieces of rope, tied me to a bed and several men used me. They never cared just how badly they hurt me, I was just a pawn in their business. . . . Nick said, "You HAVE no rights here . . . I OWN you!"

Survivors also talk about issues of abandonment (both physical and social) by their families. In telling their stories, many of them talk about perception of relationship fissure—a severance of ties with adult caregivers, resulting from feelings of abandonment. Michelle spoke of "being abandoned or left behind" by parental figures during childhood. There seem to be two types of abandonment, the literal and symbolic—both of which are equally true experiences of the feeling.

Literal experiences of alienability and abandonment usually begin in the home. Michelle described her biological mother as an intravenous heroin addict and her father as an alcoholic. She remembers her mother "shooting up and passing out . . . she fell flat on her stomach . . . she was pregnant with my little sister at the time . . . when eventually put in foster care, things were rarely different. Her foster mom said that I would end up the same way and one day she pulled a gun on us and kicked my sister and I out." Another survivor explained that she had also been in foster care; she was molested by her foster mother's son and became pregnant. She was put in a detention center, but by ninetten she was "aged-out" of the system.

Symbolic abandonment includes the feeling of familial rejection. As children, the women felt the emotional absence of their parents. Parents were either unwilling or unable to provide for their basic emotional and physical needs. Many of the issues include parental failure to protect children against sexual abuse, parental unavailability due to drug addiction and mental illness. Sexual victimization is quite common and mothers tell their children to just let it go. Bad things happen and you have to forget about them. Michelle said, "it was easy for me to turn a trick because I could just take myself out—like with my dad. It was like I took myself out of the situation and just focused on something else, and it was like I wasn't even there." Ideas of abandonment circulated around themes of parental unavailability, domestic violence, drug addiction, and verbal degradation.

A home ridden with violence prompted Michelle to run away. While on the streets she met a man who offered to take care of her. "He said, 'girl, I can take care of you, buy you everything you want, just be with me' . . . I didn't know he was a pimp at the time." Michelle continued,

> the guy takes control of the relationship really fast. He is going to take care of her, he buys her things and then after awhile he is going to say "you owe me, you have to help me" . . . it was always like "you owe me. What did you think, that was all for free?" The girls don't want to lose the relationship. They have run away from home, or are in some desperate situation like I was. They don't want to steal, shoplift or sell drugs—that's a dangerous road. A lot of girls sometimes rationalized for themselves and say, "at least when I do this, I am the only person getting hurt."

In her book *The Prostitution of Sexuality*, Kathleen Barry reports that 80 to 95 percent of all prostitution is pimp controlled.[7] Several anti-trafficking organizations have used the term "pimp-controlled" to describe and recognize this form of prostitution as sex trafficking. As stated above, the TVPA defines one form of human trafficking as "sex trafficking in which a commercial sex act is induced by force, fraud or coercion, or in which the person induced to perform such an act has not attained 18 years of age." Under this definition, there are several organizations around the US that identify US citizens under pimp control as victims of trafficking, and define pimps as sex traffickers.

Using physical and psychological force, fraud and coercion, pimps wield complete control over one or more women or girls. They use charisma, charm and business savvy to maintain pimp-prostitute relationships. Often times there are emotional attachments. Pimping strategies are often employed with young girls, typically runaways who are new to the streets; these tactics involve manipulation and deceit. Pimps wear masks of concern, offer assistance and provide necessities for survival. The generosity doesn't last long before they demand "favors"—and by then the women have no choice. Typically, a pimp establishes nightly quotas of $500–$1000 that the women and girls under his control must earn through commercial sex acts in order to eat or sleep. He keeps all of the money. Often, women and girls under a pimp's control will not self-identify as victims of trafficking or seek help on their own, and—like victims of domestic violence—they may not leave their exploitative situations for a number of reasons, such as fear, violence, threats, and self-blame. Recognizing prostitution-involved women as embedded within unique social and an environmental context is vital for understanding how this is a setting for a newly conceptualized form of trafficking.

CONSTRUCTION OF "VICTIMHOOD"

There aren't enough organizations in the US that view citizens who were under pimp control as victims of sex trafficking. Because the narratives of those on the street vary to a wide degree, it is difficult to find one single story that can describe trafficking in its entirety. The politics of victimhood forces us to ask the question "who can claim to be a victim?" Organizations such as Polaris Project and others have positioned themselves as experts in the field and believe that anyone who has suffered physically or psychologically due to force, fraud or coercion can claim to be a victim. But the category of the "trafficked victim" is essentially constructed by governing bodies, NGOs, and the wider trafficking discourse.

NGOs and government agencies have formed the concept of the "ideal" trafficking victim by interviewing people and configuring narratives that parallel their idea of human trafficking discourse. Stories that don't fit into the trafficking category are perceived as sexual exploitation or typical "prostitution narratives." It's as if the traffick does not exist until an NGO or government recognizes it. In the case of international trafficking, the issue blends with the highly problematic nature of international migration. Domestic sex trafficking has a whole different set of issues stemming from current stereotypes associated with the streets, poverty, and prostitution.

As I have pointed out, the unique aspects of domestic sex trafficking are rarely discussed in the anti-trafficking movement, which has more of an international focus. This is partly because the ambivalence, ambiguities, and paradoxes of working in the sex industry in the US are difficult to convey in a structural analysis that casts them as victims of the political economy. The experiences of domestic victims bring new issues to the dynamics of an age-old phenomenon that are difficult to understand due to the US's history, culture, politics, and economies.

These ambivalences and paradoxes are often most visible in the context of social services for victims. Anthropologists often use the phrase "structural violence" to describe a form of violence which corresponds with the systematic ways that a social structure or institution can hurt people.[8] Examples of structural violence range from institutionalized values to more abstract phenomena like elitism, classism, racism, or sexism. A classic example in anthropology is Petra Kelly's piece *In Fighting for Hope* (1999), where she discusses how people in developing countries suffer from a myriad of health issues; however the cost of our inaction is worse than trying to solve it. It is argued that structural violence differs from other types of violence because power relations within structural violence are not readily visible, but are embedded within social systems and hierarchies we live in. It is often the case that in structural violence, there is no single identified source—though the consequences are readily visible.

Listening to survivors of domestic sex trafficking, we learn that structural violence begins with life on the street and continues into the recovery process. The mechanisms by which structural violence operates are found in the state and its institutions. The entry point of this discussion can begin with the TVPA. The definition of "severe forms of trafficking in persons" includes both US citizens and foreign nationals.

The recognition of these two forms reflects an understanding that human trafficking is not limited to non-citizens, therefore more than just an immigration issue. Despite the broad and inclusive definition that includes internal trafficking, the majority of anti-trafficking efforts in the US since the TVPA passage have focused almost exclusively on non-citizen victims. This lack of parity is reflected in only counting the number of foreign victims, or service grant requirements, which mandate that grantees, such as several anti-trafficking NGOs, only serve foreign victims. For example, the TVPA has mandated $15 million annually for the Department of Health and Human Services and Department of Justice to serve foreign national victims. There are no explicit legal benefits to deeming oneself as a domestic sex trafficking victim.

It is often assumed that US citizen trafficking victims do not require specialized support services and can easily access government benefits simply by virtue of being citizens. This unfortunately does not reflect the reality of service-providers, which are often unattainable, frequently exposing domestic sex trafficking victims to further violence, or what can be deemed as secondary victimization. One of the common issues found with victims of trafficking (both foreign nationals and US citizens) is a lack of personal identification documents. Document confiscation is a common tactic traffickers use to maintain control over victims. Traffickers understand that to qualify for any government benefits or services, one must have a birth certificate, social security card, or some form of identification. Without these documents, they render victims helpless to any forms of aid.

Many domestic sex trafficking survivors and servicing agencies and organizations claim that the majority of women and children preyed on by pimps have gone though unthinkable levels of abuse, rape, threats, daily monetary quotas, trauma, gaps in schooling, unstable families and much more. "As a result of the crimes perpetrated upon them, these victims often haven't developed the life skills needed to navigate their way to a healthy level of functioning in society."[9] Victims of sex trafficking also encounter stigma and victim-blaming attitudes when they try to return to healthy functioning. For example, victims are often blamed for their own abuse and trauma. Michelle says,

> The hardest question people ask me is why would I stay? Why didn't I get out? Part of it was pimp control physically and men-

tally. Pimps, like batterers, intentionally keep women isolated from the rest of the world (except the rest in his stable) which reinforces the idea that there is no going back . . .

The answer to the question "why didn't she just leave?" now so well understood in the context of spousal abuse and domestic violence, is still not comprehended when we think of domestic sex trafficking, although victims experience comparable cycles of physical and emotional abuse, trauma bonding to the abuser (Stockholm Syndrome), and feelings of self-blame.

Another formidable hindrance to accessing help are the victims' criminal histories. Many domestic sex trafficking victims who have been "in the life" of prostitution due to the violence, threats, and deception of a pimp have criminal histories that hinder their ability to receive services. Many institutions designed to serve them do not recognize them as victims, often because of past solicitation charges from being in the sex industry, truancy charges, or outstanding bench warrants on their criminal background check. The majority of victims have faced these charges despite the force or coercion by their pimps using violence, lies, and threats. Michelle for example, missed several court dates because her pimp forced her to work. Victims also fear detection and arrest if they go to government offices, may be mistreated by civil servants because of the stigma of their criminal history, and may actually become ineligible for certain state benefits because of past criminal convictions.

Domestic sex trafficking victims are also frequently ineligible for welfare and other government benefits that are often assumed to be readily available. An example includes the Temporary Assistance for Needy Families (TANF), the nation's welfare system. Unfortunately, this is rarely an option for most US citizens of trafficking because it is only available to survivors with children. It also requires participation in jobs that victims of trafficking, with their current levels of trauma, are ill-equipped to handle within the program's timeframe without significant support.

Housing is also an immediate problem for survivors of domestic sex trafficking. Most homeless youth shelters are often reluctant to accept sex trafficking victims, or "former prostitutes," into their shelter community due to criminal history, stigma issues, safety, cultural misunderstandings, and a "general lack of fit." There are some "Open Door" shelters, where anyone needing temporary shelter can go. However, these shelters are unsafe and are a prime recruiting location for pimps. Some of these shelters also have waiting lists, which render them an unstable solution. To find permanent housing means victims must have some form of credit history, savings, or "clean" background check. Without some of these essential needs, survivors remain victimized by structural violence.

Structural violence is also found in State Victims' Compensation Fund. Most states' crime victim compensation programs do not cover the crime of trafficking. State Victims' Compensation funds generally reimburse only for medical bills incurred as a direct result of covered crimes. However, many domestic sex trafficking victims are not eligible for these compensation funds because they are not understood as victims of a crime. Women are seen as offenders and criminal history renders them ineligible.

Survivors always say that the reason why people backslide to pimps and perpetuate the debate of "choice" out on the streets is that the social services aren't there. Rejection in emergency rooms and county hospitals and lack of financial resources clearly serves as an inducement for women to go back to pimps. Women who are trafficked into the US are eligible for monthly cash assistance for a period of eight months following T-visa and certification, or for funds from the Matching Grant Program that can provide, in lieu of cash assistance, upfront funds for rental support and transportation.[10] However, none of these benefits are available to American-born women who are trafficked.

Individual agency is constrained by popular perceptions (of the streets). Women continue to be marginalized due to popular perception that street prostitution is a choice; many people don't recognize that pimp control is behind some cases. Popular view of street prostitution does not create grounds to understand the situation as "victimization"; rather, the women are seen as perpetrators of a crime.

Antagonistic relations between the police and members of the black community also contribute to officers' contempt or indifference to girls and women of color on the street; a situation that repels women seeking help from law enforcement. As a result, black women in the sex trade become invisible persons in their community. Prominent prostitution researcher Melissa Farley writes, "You cannot understand the issue until you understand how race, sex and class come together to hurt a person at the same time. . . . People are chosen in prostitution because of extreme imbalance of power. The most vulnerable are made available for constant sexual access."[11] Lessons in history demonstrate that racial, ethnic, and class differences between girls and women and their customers are part and parcel of what makes buying sex acceptable. Shrage writes, "Every black woman was, by definition, a slut according to this racist mythology; therefore to assault her and exploit her sexually was not reprehensible."[12]

Primo Levi describes this as "useless violence" or violence perpetrated against those already exploited. He wrote, "Consider that you were going to kill them all . . . what's the point of humiliation and the cruelties? To make it possible for them to do what they were doing. In other words: the victim must be degraded, so that the murderer will be less burdened by guilt. This is an explanation not devoid of logic but it shouts to heaven: it is the sole usefulness of useless violence."[13] This explanation can be used to understand the otherwise inexplicable violence experienced by trafficking victims on the streets.

As mentioned, there are only a handful of anti-trafficking organizations that serve and specialize in cases of domestic sex trafficking. As a result, many victims receive no specialized case management or have no access to services. They often lack knowledge of benefits available to them, and lack the ability to navigate through the benefit system, just like non-citizens from other countries. Rachel Lloyd of GEMS in New York sums up the situation quite well: "you don't have to be from another country to feel like you have no options in this country."

PIMPING AND POPULAR CULTURE

I don't know what you heard about me / But a bitch can't get a dol-lar out of me / No Cadillac, no perms, you can't see / That I'm a motherfucking P-I-M-P

—50 Cent, lyrics from Hot 100–charted song, "P.I.M.P."

Behind these lyrics lie violent stories—the stories of women who are domestically trafficked by violent pimps. As I have explained, survivors and anti-trafficking organizations today say that the "pretty woman" conception can be a misnomer. Structural violence is one of our critical entry points into this discussion on servicing victims of trafficking; however, popular culture is another which is much more pervasive, elusive, and entrenched in our everyday lives.

From its birth, provocative rhythms, and flamboyant lyrics and images have made the hip hop lifestyle a provocative fixture in the landscape of American and youth culture. Author of *Black Noise* Tricia Rose writes that the "noisy element of contemporary American popular culture . . . draws a great deal of attention to itself."[14] Increased media attention on hip hop and rap culture seems to be fixated on its content of lurid fantasies of cop killing, pimping and working hos, drug addictions, and glamorous cars.[15] These celebratory and inflammatory aspects of hip hop culture have brought them into the limelight of debates about the position of popular music and youth culture and gender politics. How do we address this positive fixture that includes vivid images of pimps, prostitution, and commodified sex with the framework of anti-trafficking?

Rose emphasizes that rap music brings together several complex social, cultural, and political issues into American society. According to Rose, hip hop music is black cultural expression that prioritizes black voices from the margins of urban America.[16] Hip hop music also serves as both a hegemonic (successful corporate commodity) and counter-hegemonic ("street" subculture) phenomena respectively. By taking these together and discussing them alongside different rap and hip hop songs and cultural practices, I hope to attempt a broadening of our knowledge of the pimping phenomenon, women's roles, and the representation of both as they are engaged in the ever-growing and popular industry of hip hop. This is by no means an effort to defame hip hop and rap culture as a whole. I aim to express the vivid pervasiveness of "domestic sex trafficking" within several socio-cultural institutions such as artists, music, and Internet. This new gender politics holds up the pimp as a desirable identity while subordinating women as disposable and exchangeable commodities.

In contemporary society, several scholars have looked at important evidence on the role of industry, organizational structure, and markets in the creation of cultural goods. Rappers developed "tropes of artistic legitimacy to cope with the threat of corporate incursion into the market reflected by the 'hustler' character."[17] Eithne Quinn describes the "hustler," "mack," or "pimp" to mean one who is a persuader, trickster, and rapper.[18] She argues that semantic shifts make sense of the contemporarily perceived equivalencies between pimps and rap artists. In the lyrics of major rap songs, we see shared vernacular and oral narratives that exemplify the meaning of pimping. The large-scale shift toward hardcore rap lyrics after 1988 may have been promoted by rap artists who sought to reconfigure their previous anti-commerciality to a status of "corporate artists." They felt pressure to craft an identity suitable (and saleable) in the mainstream recording industry while "keepin' it real."

Despite the surface-level tension that exaggerated violence in hardcore rap provokes between reality and art, it still manages to represent "a religion and ideology of authenticity."[19] This hardcore identity is embodied in the phrase "being real"—especially in other phrases and jargon such as "real niggaz for life" and "stayin' real." Other examples of cultural goods exemplifying the pimp or hustler character include popular rap artist Snoop Dogg, who in 2006 was named "America's Most Lovable Pimp" by *Rolling Stone* magazine. Snoop was a pimp before beginning his rap career, and was an apprentice of Bishop Don Magic Juan, the father of the Player's Ball and "teacher" in the "art of pimping."[20]

Within pimp poetics lays the articulation of roles and performativity though language. Taking the misogyny, drugs, and violence as a given to these lyrics, we ought to draw out the ways in which these texts address political ambiguities and the ways in which they comment on the negotiation of power. In this regard I do not focus solely on the "real-life pimps," but the ways in which the emblematic black pimps are at a privilege within their own cultural commercial production and marketing.

Ain't no way I can control my P.I.
See why women hit the strip and wanna be my bitch (bitch)
Break them heels off and make me rich . . .

Ain't no shame in my game
I needs bitches to increase my dividends
I'm livin in shit that looks like i'm makin the killin in
I'm a plan maker
I'm the man that can break a school girl down to be in the grand
    shaker
In a strip club somewhere near you I makes it happen . . .

They don't keep nothin dough
They bring it straight to daddy
You catch them stealin dawg
You beat that ass badly

    —"Can't Stop Pimping," lyrics by Lil John, East Side Boys

The pimp has long been associated with the ladies man, prostitute-manager, and gangster lifestyle. These lyrics capture the themes and iconography of what we might consider the pimp culture in hip hop and gangster rap. Quinn argues that the subcultural pimp can act as an "aristocrat who is admired and recognized to the point of acute purchase placed on reputation and appearance."[21] In addition to this "hardcore identity" is the idea of "street credibility" closely associated with the phenomenon of pimping. In early rap, lyrics were created heavily based on inspiration from the local environment (street cred), and producers rewarded this for its authentic artistic value. In contrast, the major label-dominated market for rap music today features lyrics that mix up "street credibility" with the hustler or pimp protagonist.[22] In an analysis of several hip hop and rap songs, references are made to the kind of pimping and prostitution with which anti-trafficking organizations are consistently confronted. For example, breaking down women to "make me rich," needing "bitches to increase my dividends," "don't keep nothing dough . . . straight to daddy," and "beat that ass badly" are all part of the domestic trafficking experience.

The subculture of pimping as embedded within the larger socio-cultural phenomenon of hip-hop is inherent with power and playful vernacular and imagery. It makes available a variety of roles that a participant may embody—one of as a practitioner or consumer of popular culture to the other extreme of actual pimping. An example of such includes the Players Ball, an annual gathering of pimps held in major cities through out the US. This party has been a long-standing tradition, often held in November to celebrate the birthday of Bishop Don Magic Juan, a famous pimp who has trained such people as Snoop Dogg. At these events, awards such as "Pimp of the Year" and "Best Attendance" are given to individual pimps. Many attend these balls, and they dress like the iconic pimps. As a subculture, many youth invest in these heavily stylized signs of group identity as reflected in music. They signify ways of "talking, walking, which all coalesce in complex and over determined ways around the fantasized desire of wanting to be pimps . . . the pimp constitutes an icon of upward mobility for black working-class males . . . with heightened style politics."[23] Imagine the conspicuous popularity of the Zoot suit as synonymous.

The pimp figure as produced within hip hop culture can be read as a symbol of diasporic black stylization. In the pimp narratives and musical lyrics, the style assumes occupational imperatives. For example, Ice-T has conveyed that pimpin' is a cool lifestyle that also has nothing to do with prostitution. This semantic shift results from a turn to the pimp as entrepreneurial and smart. Quinn argues that the pimp "lifestylization in rap" is an emblem for problematic within modern capitalism.[24] On one hand the pimp figure captures the tension between the cult of consumerism and individualism and deep employment frustrations. She says that pimps "selling pussy" is a highly stylized form of entrepreneurialship that acts as a response to diminishing opportunities for blue-collar men.[25]

"Who's the pimp" as an issue between the literal and the figurative is a power play between vernacular and practice. Male "blackness" in this context has been constructed through types of performance and imagery. The pimp imagery fits into certain contemporary paradigms of popularity and culture. We must be as wary of embracing the figurative pimp as are of embracing the literal pimp, because the acceptance of either one is the acceptance of the methods by which pimps exploit, abuse and traffick people.

Lyrics about pimping in hip hop and rap music are predicated on self-referencing as well. Many of the lyrics in the appendix exemplify the embodiment of pimp storytelling, and not all of them are necessarily pimping themselves. This identification slip between a real pimp persona and rapper is not uncommon. There is an ease with which rappers can play with the pimp figure. Quinn points that this is because there are a set of equivalencies between the player (pimp) and the rapper, such as the "smooth talk, fame, big bank roles, women, cars, and outfits."[26] This creates a slippery slope of identities and configurations that make categories problematic.

This slippery slope on which hip hop culture rests is not unique to American society. We can also refer to Teresa Caldeira's work on hip hop in São Paulo, Brazil as an example of the ways in which hip hop acts as a political tool used to critique the everyday issues of racism, corruption and classism. Male rappers use this medium to express feelings of marginality while living on the periphery of poverty, drugs, and misery. By doing so, they project a set of behaviors that have allowed for their survival in the periphery. However, Caldeira suggests that black favelas are isolated from general Brazilian society and therefore hip hop serves not as a medium of integration, but of self-enclosure and self-determination. For example, "In the song *Fim de Semana no Parque*" ("Weekend in the park"), a poor black boy can only dream of the life inside the walls where upper class children enjoy their heated swimming pools and go-karts."[27] Caldeira notes, however, "rappers such as Racionais MC's

Mano Brown do not try to negotiate social inclusion, but rather locate their identities in the *periferia* (periphery), in a realm wholly distinct from that of the denizens of elite neighborhoods and gated condominiums." Members of hip-hip use this medium to reflect on the conditions of life outside the city. Caldeira concludes that this may be more injurious than helpful to achieving social mobility and better conditions. NGOs like Polaris Project who look closely at pimping may agree with Caldeira's claims that the pimp and hip hop subculture may actually impede on the social mobility it aims to achieve. Additionally, current debates on gender and identity politics in hip hop culture serve as a smokescreen, hindering our understanding of the violence and suffering that occurs in the practice of pimping. By servicing victims of domestic sex trafficking who have suffered violence by pimps, they implicitly place themselves within a new black gender and identity politics with some legitimacy.

Dr. Sharpley-Whiting's book entitled *Pimps Up, Hos Down: Hip Hop's Hold on Young Black Women* also offers insight as to how hip hop is a locus for gender politics among the youth to be negotiated and renegotiated. She addresses the male-dominated aspect of hip hop and the various ways in which young black women connect with that culture. She argues that the "pimps up" mutation of pimp culture is a commentary on hip hop's commercial success that is predicated on the sexualization of young black women. Overexposed young black female flesh "pimped out" and "played" in videos, television, film, rap lyrics, fashion, and on the Internet is indispensable to the mass-media engineered appeal of hip hop culture and is helping to shape a new black gender politics.[28] This insight reveals one of the major hindrances to organization's contextualizing trafficking within the realm of hip hop and pimping glamorization.

Sharpley-Whiting discusses the large sex trade surrounding hip hop, including strip clubs, pornography, and sex tourism. She never uses the term trafficking in the book, but when viewed through the lens of the "sex trafficking" paradigm, her book alludes to several examples where glamorization of pimping will pose problems for advocating this discourse. The "pimped out" woman constitutes the normal state of affairs in the hip hop world, making it possible for forms of gendered violence to be ignored.

Europe's brothel, and in Brazil in particular, has become place where one can fuck, tan and eat. Sex tourism and prostitution in Brazil is on the rise as Brazilian women and girls look for a way out of dire poverty. . . . Brazil is identified as the land of the bikini wax, samba, and sensuality. In Brazil, large parties are thrown by moguls such as Sean "Puffy" Combs during Carnival and the Brazilian fascination with all things Americana, especially mass produced and globally exported black commodities such as music and music videos provide cultural currency for hip hop generation black men that gives them a Brazilian ghetto tour pass that includes discounts on women.[29]

In 2004, the African American community spent $4.6 billion on travel, lodging, and transportation. While the Caribbean and Africa have long been heavily marketed as tourism options, there are lots of partnerships between the Brazilian government and African America media moguls like Essence magazine.[30]

There are also online interest groups such as "African American Men & Brazilian Women" where they provide "do and don't tips" for those who may be involved in trafficking. "Bgcaliber 1" offers these tips:

Though it may be tough . . . try to see her a few times in Brazil b4 bringing her back.

If you do eventually get her here, do not trust her to visit other girlfriends living here by herself. KEEP HER AWAY FROM OTHER BRAZILIAN GIRLS HERE IN THE STATES . . . with limited English and no papers yet, where is the first place she'll think about going. You got it . . . the STRIP CLUB!

In further exploring the intricacies of the new black gender politics, understanding the complex space of identities and stereotypes are crucial. Gendered relations reflected historical identities and stereotypes that survivors of domestic trafficking have come to define as posing a hindrance to their recovery. For example, the "jezebel stereotype" of black women, which refers to the bad black girl, a hypersexual female who yearns for sexual encounters, is one of the most problematic. Scholars believe that the jezebel image originated with slave owners who were looking for an excuse to hide their interest in female slaves. Jewel Suel wrote, "the masters, who privately coerced their female slaves, offering them harsh alternatives if they were unwilling to submit to their sexual whims, publicly attributed these liaisons to the hypersexuality of the female slave, who was purported to be the seducer."[31] Michelle mentions,

> The stereotypes rule you. They destroy your self-esteem and self image. It is difficult not to internalize the differences. If you're acting in that manner, it kind of doubles the impact on you. You have to do esteemable things and recognize that self-esteem is only the reputation you have with yourself. People assume the jezebel.

Based on community interviews, it seems that many endorse the jezebel typecasting, attributed to the fact that this image of women has permeated all sections of society through popular media. The corresponding music video for many songs contains images of young women laying their bodies on the pimp, fighting, and seeking attention of the pimp out of a large group of women, and more often than not, barely clothed. Hip hop and rap music portray these women as "jezebels," perhaps one of the most pivotal reasons why it is so difficult to conceptualize the violence and potential trafficking that can occur behind it. Stereotypes created by the images seen in music videos, magazines, and television influence power dynamics, ideas of agency, and one's conceptualization of victimhood in this context.

Professor Michael Silverstein at the University of Chicago commented on the scandal where MSNBC anchor David Shuster was suspended after suggesting that the Clinton campaign was "pimping out" first daughter Chelsea. Professor Silverstein's response was "To say that someone is pimping is really an extraordinarily negative description . . . It takes a lot of work to use it so ironically that it becomes positive."[32] I firmly believe this is one of the core issues that our generation will face as we try to address pimping as a form of sex trafficking. Pimping involves a lot of work and special tactics that have been experimented and built on over the years. This is complicated by the fact that pimping's prevalence in popular culture and the media perpetuate it as a positive identity and subculture.

Hip hop music, media images, magazines, videos, and products collectively serve a small set of material culture that represents a relatively unexplored subculture in anthropology. These anthropological subjects, such as the rap artists themselves, their lyrics, and their videos, provide an entry point for understanding group-specific beliefs and practices. We in the movement against commercial sexual exploitation must understand this as we navigate human rights and trafficking discourse.

CONCLUSION: PROBLEMATIZING THE "TRAFFICKING" SUBJECT

In a piece titled, "Soft Glove, Punishing Fist," Wendy Chapkis writes that the TVPA was drafted to specifically exempt a small class of abused and exploited migrants.

She discusses how sex workers within this context can be both victims and criminals because of the agency/choice debates, and can suffer at the hands of the state.[33] Organizations that currently serve victims of domestic sex trafficking are working to end this state of being both a victim and criminal. While it is well understood that women who have been domestically trafficked are seen as criminals of prostitution in wider society, in the eyes of a handful of anti-trafficking organizations, they are viewed as victims. Under their care, women are allowed to speak their life narratives, construct new identities, and slowly remove themselves from the label of "criminals" to attain the status of one who is "trafficked and deserving of rights."

As the stories show, victims of trafficking are not a clearly defined category. The notion of victim has appealed to both activist and scholars in an attempt to distinguish trafficking women form illegal migrants or prostitutes.The anti-trafficking movement ought to look at the vast diversity of narratives that speak to suffering and exploitation within the trafficking context. As long as pimps continue to operate with relative impunity in the US, women and young children under their control will never be viewed as victims of trafficking. Passing stronger laws that acknowledge pimp control and reduce secondary victimization of prostitutes is critical if we are to move forward in our quest to end this formidable human rights abuse at home. If mainstream prostitution cases in the news and images of glamorized pimps in popular culture cause us to lose sight of women like Michelle and others, the suffering of those who did not willingly choose prostitution will live in the shadows, their voices forever silenced.

Notes

1. Public Law: Trafficking Victims Protection Act of 2000.
2. According to the *Oxford English Dictionary*, the term "traffic" or "traffick" was in use soon after 1500 to refer to the transportation of merchandise or saleable commodities for the purpose of trade; trade between distant communities. Eventually it came to be associated with the sinister or evil connotation of commerce, where one deals and bargains in something which should not be made the subject of trade. Because modern day trafficking includes false debt bondage and involuntary servitude, organizations such as Polaris Project, Free the Slaves, and others have combined these concepts as modern-day slavery.
3. United Nations Office on Drugs and Crime, "UNODC Launches Global Initiative to Fight Human Trafficking," 2007,http://www.unodc.org/unodc/en/press/releases/2007-03-26.html.
4. Kelly L. and Regan L., "Stopping Traffic: Exploring the Extent of, and Response to, Trafficking in Women for Sexual Exploitation in the UK," *Police Research Series*, Paper 125 (London: Stationary Office, 2000), p 37.
5. Ibid.
6. Ibid., 105.
7. Kathleen Barry, *The Prostitution of Sexuality* (New York: New York University Press, 1995), 50.
8. A. Kleinman, V. Das and M. Lock, "Introduction," *Social Suffering* (Berkeley: University of California Press, 1997), ix–xxvii.
9. Polaris Project.
10. See www.ojp.gov/ovc/help/tip.html.
11. Presentation, "Trafficking for Prostitution: Making the Connections," August, 2007.
12. Laurie Shrage, *Moral Dilemmas of Feminism: Prostitution, Adultery and Abortion* (New York: Routledge, 1994), 56.
13. Primo Levi, *The Drowned and the Saved* (New York: Vintage International, 1989), 125–126.
14. Tricia Rose, *Black Noise: Rap Music and Black Culture in Contemporary America"* (Connecticut: Wesleyan University Press, 1994), 1.
15. I use the terms hip hop and rap synonymously, but in general, "hip hop" is a more expansive term than rap. It can include particular styles of language, music, dress, and dance. Rap strictly refers to a particular method of musical production.
16. Tricia Rose, *Black Noise: Rap Music and Black Culture in Contemporary America* (Connecticut: Wesleyan University Press, 1994), 6.
17. Jennifer Lena, "Social Context and Musical Content of Rap Music, 1979–199," *Social Forces*, 2006, Vol. 85, Number 1, 489.
18. Ethine Quinn, "Who's the Mack: The Performativity and Politics of the Pimp Figure in Gangsta Rap," *Journal of American Studies*, 34, UK Cambridge University Press, 2000, 115.
19. Jennifer Lena, "Social Context and Musical Content of Rap Music, 1979-1995," *Social Forces*, 2006, Vol. 85, Number 1, 489.
20. See http://www.thebishop.us/.
21. Quinn, 131.
22. To supplement this research, Professor Denise Herd in the Department of Public Health has found a dramatic six-fold increase in references to illegal drug use in rap music since 1979, the year of Sugar Hill Gang's "Rapper's Delight" hit the charts. In the study, they find that illegal drug use is becoming increasing linked during this time period of wealth, glamour, and social standing, marking a significant change form ear-

lier years when rap music was more likely to depict the dangers of drug abuse. Professor Herd says that "Rap is inherently powerful . . . they are role models and trendsetters, and their music serves as the CNN for our nation's young people providing them with a way to stay current. But we have to ask ourselves whether there are other kinds of messages rap music could deliver" (Herd, April 2008). Messaging is a problem that Polaris' campaigns consistently confront as they try to raise questions and assumptions about the ever powerful hip-hop phenomena with regards to pimping glamorization.

23. Quinn, 123.
24. Ibid., 125.
25. Ibid., 125.
26. Ibid., 126.
27. Teresa P. Caldeira, "Hip-Hop, Periphery, and Spatial Segregation in Sao Paulo," 2004, http://www.cccb.org/en/edicio_digital?idg=10357.
28. Tracy Sharpley-Whiting, *Pimps Up Hos Down Hip Hop's Hold on Young Black Women* (New York: New York University Press, 2007), 11–12.
29. Ibid., 44–45.
30. Ibid., 46.
31. Jewel K. Suel, *From Mammy to Miss America and Beyond: Cultural Images and the Shaping of US Social Policy* (New York: Routledge, 1993), 37.
32. *Culture Matters*, February 2008, http://culturematters.wordpress.com/category/media.
33. Wendy Chapkis, "Soft Glove, Punishing Fist: The Trafficking Victims Protection Act of 2000," *Regulating Sex: The Politics of Intimacy and Identity*, E. Bernstein and L. Schaffner, eds. (New York: Routledge, 2005), 51–66.

Water as Commodity or Commons?
Issues from the 2009 World Water Forum

by Andrew L. Roth

From March 16 to 22, 2009, the World Water Council (WWC) presented the fifth World Water Forum in Istanbul, Turkey. Boasting participation by over 33,000 people from around the globe, the WWC heralded the Forum as "the world's biggest ever water-related event." Nonetheless, as detailed in Chapter 1, the World Water Forum, and its competing People's Water Forum, ranks prominently among 2008 to 2009's most underreported news stories.

The dearth of US coverage should surprise even the most jaundiced critics of America's corporate media. At least four episodes from the forum not only fit conventional definitions of newsworthiness, but also contrasted sharply with the forum's declared theme, "Bridging Divides for Water." Thus, most Americans probably do not know that:

➤ Turkish police forces shot water cannons to disperse protesters outside the forum. Water cannons, they subsequently explained, were more cost-effective than tear gas.

➤ Though the forum's official program heralded "more diverse participation mechanisms," in Istanbul the World Water Council refused to allow the president of the United Nations General Assembly a public audience. President Miguel D'Escoto Brockmann has been an outspoken critic of water privatization.

➤ At the forum's inaugural event, two activists representing International Rivers unfurled a banner reading "No Risky Dams" in peaceful protest. Ann Kathrin Schneider and Payal Parekh were immediately detained, arrested and subsequently deported after being charged with "manipulating the public opinion."[1]

Turkish police disperse demonstrators with water cannons outside the World Water Forum, Istanbul, March 18, 2009. BULENT KILIC/STRINGER/GETTY IMAGES

Of course, since its inception in 1996, the World Water Forum has constituted an ongoing attempt to manipulate public opinion, specifically regarding the desirability, if not the inevitability, of privatized water as both a commodity, and, in the words of the World Water Council's president, Loïc Fauchon, "a strategic resource." Though President Fauchon has publicly advocated that the "human right to water should be formally, constitutionally recognized in every country across the globe," his business interests—including his long-standing affiliation with Eaux de Marsielle, the subsidiary of two multinational French water corporations—undermine his claim's credibility.

▶ Finally, many Americans would be surprised to learn that in Istanbul, the United States joined China and several other countries in opposing a declaration of the right to water. Instead, the Forum concluded that access to water was a "basic need."

As Maude Barlow, a senior advisor to the president of the UN General Assembly noted, the distinction between a *right* and a *basic need* is not simply semantic: "[Y]ou cannot trade or sell a human right or deny it to someone on the basis of an inability to pay."[2]

This chapter aims to remedy the corporate media's inadequate coverage of the World Water Forum by examining:

➤ the significance of water control as a means of power;

➤ the history, organization, and aims of the World Water Council;

➤ the significance of Turkey as the host site of the fifth World Water Forum; and

➤ what concerned citizens can do to support alternatives to the WWC and its utilitarian belief in water as nothing more than a commodity and strategic resource.

These four themes' significance stems in part from the fact that, on one hand, according to World Health Organization figures, 1.4 billion people worldwide lack access to clean drinking water and 2.6 billion lack access to sanitation and on the other hand, the battle over privatization of water hinges on different conceptions of *accountability*. Advocates of water privatization—including the majority of invited participants in the World Water Forum—ultimately place their faith in markets, and they understand accountability as a matter of *corporate* entities' responsibilities to their *shareholders*. In this view, water is a *commodity*.

By contrast, advocates of water as a basic human right seek recognition of water as a *public trust*, so that accountability for its management, delivery, and use ultimately resides in local *communities*. In this view, water is not a *commodity*, but a *commons*, belonging to and equally shared

by all. In *Water Wars*, Vandana Shiva writes, "Water is a commons because it is the ecological basis of all life and because its sustainability and equitable allocation depends on cooperation among community members."[3]

UNDER WHAT CONDITIONS IS WATER CONTROL A SOURCE OF POWER?

When World Water Council President Fauchon describes water as a "strategic resource," he is, to some extent, correct. As Donald Worster and other scholars of water control demonstrate, in arid environments control of water is a source of both economic wealth and political power.[4] Thus, in *Rivers of Empire* Worster argues:

> Control over water has again and again provided an effective means of consolidating power in human groups—led, that is, to the assertion by some people of power over others. Sometimes that outcome was unforeseen, a result no one really sought but that dire necessity seemed to require. In other places and times, the concentration of power within human society that comes from controlling water was a deliberate goal of ambitious individuals, one they pursued even in the face of protest and resistance.

To explain how water control contributes to the consolidation of power, Worster develops the concept of *hydraulic society*, which he defines as "a social order based on the intensive, large-scale manipulation of water and its products in an arid setting."[5]

Worster then identifies three distinct modes of hydraulic society, defining each mode in terms of its (1) *scale* of water works, (2) managerial *authority*, and (3) *goals*. He characterizes the most developed form of hydraulic society, the "capitalist-state mode," in terms of:

➤ large scale, technologically advanced water works
➤ controlled by an "iron-triangle" of bureaucratic planners, elected officials and corporate agriculture
➤ with the aim of "rational, calculating, unlimited accumulation of private wealth"

This social order is flawed for two fundamental and intertwined reasons, Worster argues. First, the consolidation of power that occurs in the capitalist-state mode of water control is counter democratic. Though the iron triangle of elites must contend with one another, overall their rule is resistant to traditional democratic checks and balances. "Democracy cannot survive," Worster writes, "where technical expertise, accumulated capital, or their combination is allowed to command."[6] Second, hydraulic societies risk "environmental vulnerabilities," including the problems of water quantity, water quality, and the degradation of ecological communities.

For Worster, hydraulic society's twin threats to democracy and the environment suggest what a sustainable alternative to the capitalist-state mode of water control must look like:

> [T]he promotion of democracy, defined as the dispersal of power into as many hands as possible, is a direct and necessary, though perhaps not sufficient, means to achieve ecological stability. . . . [D]espite so much rhetoric to the contrary, one cannot have life both ways—cannot maximize wealth and empire and maximize freedom and democracy too.

Worster's point about the ultimate incompatibility of wealth and empire on one hand and freedom and democracy on the other is essential to understanding the World Water Forum and the ambitions of those who created it.

WHAT IS THE WORLD WATER COUNCIL?

Who established the World Water Council? According to the WWC's website, the council "was established in 1996 in response to increasing concern from the global community about world water issues." The passive construction—"was established"—proves significant here. A subsequent page elaborates only somewhat, revealing that the council was established "on the initiative of renowned water specialists and international organizations."

Suez and Veolia, two of the world's largest private water corporations, are accurately described as "water specialists" and "international organizations." It is not clear from the WWC's website whether Suez and

Veolia created the World Water Council, but a look beneath the surface of the council's webpage reveals the extent to which these two corporations constitute the prime movers of the WWC.[7] The council's president, Löic Fauchon, is also president of Groupe des Eaux de Marseille, which Veolia and a Suez subsidiary jointly own. Compagnie Générale des Eaux, a subsidiary of Veolia, has employed the WWC's alternate president, Charles-Louis de Maud'huy, since 1978.

Moreover, the WWC's Board of Governors is composed primarily of individuals and institutions that fit closely with Worster's model of the bureaucratic planners who constitute one third of the ruling iron triangle. The council's board members represent countries, corporations and organizations that actively promote and/or stand to benefit financially from water privatization.[8]

Among the board of governors, even Green Cross International (GCI)—an environmental education organization, and the lone board member that *appears* to represent civil society—advocates private financing and management of water according to market principles. GCI's founding president and honorary board member, Mikhail Gorbachev, has publicly stated that corporations are "the only institutions" with the intellectual and financial potential to solve the world's water problems.[9]

The World Water Council has risen to prominence partly by filling a vacuum in governance. In 1947, when the United Nations passed the Universal Declaration of Human Rights, it did not include water as a human right. World leaders did not perceive a human rights dimension to water at the time. As an unintended consequence, water policy today has shifted from "the UN and governments toward institutions and organizations that favor the private water companies and the commodification of water."[10]

However, as Aldo Leopold observed in his famous land ethics essay, ethical criteria evolve over time.[11] Leopold advocated an evolving land ethic that would counter a strictly utilitarian conception of land as property by enlarging "the boundaries of the community to include soils, waters, plants, and animals, or collectively: the land." In this view,

> a system of conservation based solely on economic self-interest
> is hopelessly lopsided. It tends to ignore, and thus eventually
> eliminate, many elements in the land community that lack com-

mercial value, but that are (as far as we know) essential to its healthy functioning.

Building on Leopold's ethical vision, Sandra Postel and others advocate the development of a water ethic:

> Instead of asking how we can further control and manipulate rivers, lakes, and streams to meet our ever-growing demands, we would ask instead how we can best satisfy human needs while accommodating the ecological requirements of freshwater ecosystems. It would lead us, as well, to deeper questions of human values, in particular how to narrow the wide gap between the haves and have-nots while remaining within the bounds of what a healthy ecosystem can sustain.[12]

Despite Leopold and Postel's eloquence, not to mention the concerted efforts of local communities and the global justice movement, the World Water Council and its supporters continue to promote a market-based, utilitarian approach to the world's water crisis. Perhaps no nation in the world today more clearly exemplifies the extremes of treating water as commodity than Turkey, the host nation of the fifth World Water Forum.

WHY MEET IN TURKEY?

Under the leadership of the ruling Justice and Development Party (AKP), the government of Turkey is currently undertaking what may be "the most sweeping water privatization program in the world."[13] The government not only wants to privatize the nation's drinking water supply and delivery systems, but also the water itself. Such a transformation would be unprecedented in modern history, since the proposal entails the sale of not only the rights to *use of* the water, which has been commonplace since water was first treated as a commodity, but in fact the *water itself*. The conventional legal distinction between rights to use of the water and ownership of the water itself would be overturned by Energy and Natural Resources Minister Hilmi Güler's plan to sell at least a dozen rivers, including the Euphrates and Tigris, to private companies for up to forty-nine years.[14]

Officials estimated that privatizing the nation's water would generate

$3 billion in revenues for the government. Notably, in addition to opposition from Turkish agriculturalists, two articles of the national constitution (articles 43 and 168) reserve control of natural resources and their operating rights to the state. As of the March 2009, the Turkish government has not succeeded in modifying articles 43 and 168 of its constitution to implement sales of the nation's rivers and lakes. Nonetheless, one can imagine that the World Water Council looked favorably on Turkey as a host nation for its 2009 forum, given the AKP's audacious proposal to sell the nation's water to private corporations.

In addition to the Turkish government's evident support for the World Water Council's privatization agenda, at least four of the ten forum sponsors listed in the Istanbul 2009 program are Turkish-based multinational corporations with vested interests in water privatization:

CENGIZ HOLDING, a conglomerate of twelve companies, established in 1987, is currently constructing four major dams with hydroelectric power plants, as well as two additional dams and three irrigation canals in Turkey;

NUROL, a construction conglomerate founded in the 1966, includes dams and hydroelectric power plants, irrigation and drainage systems, and water supply and sewage systems among its infrastructure projects;

BM HOLDING A.S., established in 1972, is now building at least six large-scale dams and/or hydropower plants in Turkey; and

ENERJISA, an electricity provider established in 1996, aims to control ten percent of the Turkish market by 2015; Enerjisa is owned jointly by the Sabanci Group, one of Turkey's leading industrial and financial conglomerates, and Verbund, an Austrian-based hydropower producer.

A fifth sponsor of the 2009 World Water Forum, GRUNDFOS, is a Danish multinational that produces water pumps and pumping systems. Each of these five sponsors clearly has business interests in alignment with the World Water Council's agenda.

Finally, Turkey is strategically situated relative to Iraq, Iran, Syria, and Israel, four Middle Eastern states that loom large in contemporary global politics. One recent example will serve to illustrate this point. In April

2009, Iraq's Water Resources Minister, Abdul-Latif Jamal Rasheed, accused Turkey and Iran of contributing to Iraq's growing water shortages. Minister Rasheed blamed dams and reservoirs on the Tigris and Euphrates, both of which originate in Turkey, and called for Iraq to receive a "sufficient and fair share of water" from the rivers.[15]

Of course, the 2009 World Water Forum brought together not only a global elite ambitious to consolidate its members' wealth and power by promoting water privatization as the only viable response to the world's water crisis, but also activists intent on challenging this agenda. Those who would concentrate wealth and power by privatizing water met with protest, resistance, and a positive alternative vision in Istanbul.

At the meeting's conclusion, Maude Barlow spoke on behalf of the alternative People's Water Forum, telling *Democracy Now!*'s Amy Goodman, "It's no longer about the World Water Forum . . . [N]ow it's about us and our vision. The World Water Forum is bankrupt. They're bankrupt of ideas. They're bankrupt of money, frankly. And they have nothing to offer but what's failed . . . It's been a transfer of power."

Advocates of water as a human right will aim to consolidate that transfer of power during the December 2009 United Nations Climate Change Conference in Copenhagen, Denmark. Many expect water issues, includ-

Activists at the opening ceremony of the Forum, subsequently arrested for "manipulating public opinion." MUSTAFA OZER/GETTY IMAGES

ing the ongoing public-private debate, to feature prominently in Copenhagen, when the world's leaders gather to update the 1997 Kyoto Protocol.

WHAT CAN YOU DO?

If you are reading a chapter about water in *Censored 2010*, chances are you already cast a wary eye on bottled water, take shorter showers, and avoid pouring your used motor oil down the storm drain. So what else can you do to link arms with members of the global justice movement who gathered in Istanbul to resist the privatization of water and to promote the establishment of water as a basic human right? Here are six activities to engage you in the global effort for water justice.

Inform yourself about local and global water issues. In addition to the books cited in this chapter, each of which is worth reading, independent film makers have now produced a number of excellent documentaries on water issues, including:

➤ *Flow* (directed by Irena Salina, 2008), http://www.flowthefilm.com.

➤ *Thirst* (Alan Snitow & Deborah Kaufman, 2004), http://www.pbs.org/pov/thirst/ and http://www.bullfrogfilms.com/catalog/thirst.html.

➤ *Dead in the Water* (Neil Docherty, 2004), http://www.cbc.ca/fifth/deadinthewater/index.html.

➤ *The Dammed* (Franny Armstrong, 2003; originally titled *Drowned Out*), http://www.pbs.org/wnet/wideangle/shows/dammed/index.html and http://www.spannerfilms.net/?lid=16.

➤ *Cadillac Desert* (Jon Else, 1997), http://web.archive.org/web/20030212083841/www.kteh.org/cadillacdesert/home.html.

Become watershed literate. A watershed encompasses all the land surface that collects and drains water to a single exit point.[16] After exploring the length of the Colorado River in 1890, John Wesley Powell encouraged the US Congress to organize the settlement of the American West on the basis of watersheds, a recommendation Congress ignored.[17] More than one hundred years later, advocates of ecologically sustainable communities are adapting and extending Powell's vision. The Occidental Arts and Ecology Water Institute is one of the leaders in promoting watershed literacy. See http://oaecwater.org.

Harvest rainwater. Turn water scarcity into abundance by learning how to design and implement simple water harvesting systems for the home and yard. As an example of rainwater harvesting's potential, Brad Lancaster calculates that the average annual rainfall for the desert city of Tucson (population approaching 1 million) exceeds the city's current municipal water use, suggesting that, at least, all residential outdoor water needs could be met by rainwater harvesting, reducing the city's pumping of groundwater and reliance on imported Colorado River water.[18] See http://www.harvestingrainwater.com. And for an immediate and consciousness-changing start, place a bucket in your shower to catch the water flow while you wait for the warm water. Carry the bucket to the yard to water flowers or vegetables.

Advocate for a clean water trust. In the US, urge your congressional representatives to create a clean water trust fund. Food & Water Watch, a nonprofit consumer organization, challenges corporate control and abuse of food and water. See http://www.foodandwaterwatch .org/water/trust-fund.

Call for water as a basic human right. Join the grassroots movement for water democracy by urging the United Nations to establish a covenant on the right to water. See http://www.blueplanetproject.net and http://www.article31.org.

Demand better coverage of water issues from corporate media, and support independent media that do provide informative, useful reports. Submit letters to the editor and opinion pieces on water issues, local and global. Give kudos when journalists and news organizations provide good coverage. Keep them honest when they fail to do so.

ANDREW L. ROTH has taught sociology courses focused on water issues at UCLA, Pomona College, and Sonoma State University. He was associate director of Project Censored from 2006–2008. He now lives in Tucson, Arizona, where he harvests rainwater and continues to advocate for water justice.

Notes

1. For Ann Kathrin Schneider's account see http://www.alternet.org/bloggers/schneider/132725/why_i_was_deported_from_turkey/.

2. Maude Barlow, "Making Water a Human Right," in *Water Consciousness: How We All Have to Change to Protect Our Most Critical Resource*, edited by Tara Lohan (San Francisco: Alternet Books, 2008), p. 181.

3. Vandana Shiva, *Water Wars: Privatization, Pollution, and Profit* (Cambridge, MA: South End Press, 2002), p. 24.

4. Donald Worster, *Rivers of Empire: Water, Aridity and the Growth of the American West* (New York: Oxford University Press, 1985). See also Marc Reisner, *Cadillac Desert: The American West and Its Disappearing Water*, revised edition (New York: Penguin, 1993).

5. Worster extends Karl Wittfogel's original conception "hydraulic society" as a distinct type of social order. Wittfogel (1896–1988) drew on Karl Marx, Max Weber and the emerging Frankfurt School to understand the relationships among nature, technology, and society. Wittfogel raised the profound question that Worster's study pursues: "How, in the remaking of nature, do we remake ourselves?" (p. 30).

6. Alan Snitow and Deborah Kaufman reiterate Worster's point: "The concept of democracy itself is being challenged by multinational corporations that see Americans not as citizens, but merely as customers. They don't see government as something of, by, and for the people, but as a market to be entered for profit." Snitow and Kaufman, "The New Corporate Threat to Our Water," in *Water Consciousness*, op cit, p. 45.

7. Jeff Conant's award-winning Alternet reports emphasized the corporate foundations of the World Water Council's leadership.

8. Unfortunately, the WWC website lists the Board of Governors membership for April 2006. Though dated, the available roll call nonetheless provides a clear picture of the Council's driving interests.

9. Barlow, "Making Water a Human Right," *Water Consciousness*, op cit, p. 181.

10. Ibid, p. 179.

11. Aldo Leopold, "The Land Ethic," pp. 201-226 in *Sand County Almanac* (New York: Oxford University Press, 1989).

12. Sandra L. Postel, "Why We Need a Water Ethic," in *Water Consciousness*, op cit, p. 188. See also Sandra Postel, *Last Oasis: Facing Water Scarcity* (New York: W. W. Norton, 1992).

13. See, for example, Olivier Hoedeman and Orsan Senalp's "Turkey Plans to Sell Rivers and Lakes to Corporations," AlterNet, April 23, 2008, http:/www.alternet.org/story/83304/. This story should probably have been awarded a Project Censored prize in 2007-2008.

14. See http://www.globalwaterintel.com/archive/8/9/general/the-puzzle-of-turkish-river-privatisation.html.

15. "Blackwater bowing out; Va. Firm will protect US diplomats in Iraq," *Arizona Daily Star*, April 2, 2009: A2. Notably the information on the Iraqi minister's complaint against Turkey and Iran was effectively buried at the end of the headline story about the private security firm, Blackwater.

16. Brock Dolman, "Watershed Literacy: Restoring Community and Nature," in *Water Consciousness*, op cit, p. 101.

17. See Worster, *Rivers of Empire*, op cit, pp. 138–143.

18. Brad Lancaster, *Rainwater Harvesting for Drylands and Beyond* (Tucson: Rainsource Press, 2008), pp. 18–19.

Lesbian and Gay Standpoint Films

by James Joseph Dean

This chapter examines independent American cinema's representations of homosexuality from 1980 to 2000. I examine lesbian and gay standpoint films, which are films that focus on lesbian and gay characters' lives from the point of view of a lesbian and gay subculture. Specifically, I argue that the development of lesbian and gay standpoint films in the late 1980s and 1990s is a response to the shift toward normalizing images of homosexuality in mainstream Hollywood films of the 1980s and 1990s.[1] Mainstream Hollywood films that normalize gay identity, however, almost always isolate the gay or lesbian from a larger lesbian and gay subculture. Consequently, gay standpoint films can be seen as a challenge to mainstream films that exclude subcultural depictions.

To research these themes I analyzed fifty-eight films appearing between 1960 and 2000. Of the twenty-two films viewed that appeared between 1970 and 1989, seventeen adopted a narrative of homosexual stigmatization. In the 1990s, only four films exhibited a stigmatizing narrative, while the remaining fell into affirming images of homosexuality. Of the thirty-one films I viewed in the 1990s, twelve represent mainstream Hollywood film, nine films fall into the lesbian and gay standpoint category, and another nine represent Queer Cinema.[2]

Following a Weberian tradition that analyzes social phenomenon through ideal types, I examine gay and lesbian standpoint films as an ideal type that follows particular patterns in its narrative representation of homosexual identity and normative heterosexuality. I use the following five concepts to analyze sexual identity and normative heterosexuality: (1) the presentation of sexual identities as centered or decentered; (2) the depiction of gay or lesbian subcultures; (3) how the norm of heterosexuality operates within the narrative; (4) the presentation of gender identities; and (5) critique, if any, of normative heterosexuality and normative gender conventions.

Recent scholarship has noted a visible shift occurring in mainstream Hollywood depictions of gay and lesbian characters in the 1980s and

1990s. A shift away from stigmatized representations of homosexuality is evidenced in recent mainstream Hollywood films that have been made since the 1990s, where a preponderance of normal and good portrayals of homosexual characters has appeared.[3] This shift in depiction, although uneven and still evidencing stigmatizing depictions at times, follows the dominant logic of normative heterosexuality that makes homosexuality into a minority identity while maintaining heterosexuality as the normative identity of the majority. However, this normalizing trend argues for a newfound respect and view of the homosexual as a normal individual, deserving of recognition and tolerance, if not equality.

Mainstream Hollywood films which normalize gay identity, however, almost always isolate the gay or lesbian character from a larger gay/lesbian subculture. And it is exactly this feature, a gay/lesbian subculture, that gay and lesbian standpoint films of the 1980s and 1990s make integral to their depictions of gay and lesbian life. Subcultural settings challenge the norm of heterosexuality, undermining it as the right and only way in which to be sexual. Furthermore, if mainstream films were to portray gay and lesbian subcultures as legitimate forms of social life, they would be arguing not only for tolerance for gays and lesbians, but also for equality and social recognition of their relationships and lives. Subcultural depictions question and challenge cultural norms that privilege heterosexual families (e.g., norms of monogamy and marriage) and their sexual and gender conventions (e.g., masculine men and feminine women and the norm of compulsory heterosexuality). This notwithstanding, gay and lesbian standpoint films present their own limitations in their depiction of homosexual identity. Chiefly, these films make gay and lesbian identity into a uniform and essentialist identity, where the main characters' lives revolve around their homosexuality.

GAY AND LESBIAN STANDPOINT FILMS (1980s–1990s)

By the 1980s, a change in the social status of homosexuals in the United States had occurred. After the Stonewall Riots of 1969, the 1970s and 1980s witnessed an efflorescence of gay and lesbian organizing. Prior to Stonewall, there were about fifty lesbian and gay groups in the US.[4] Within five years after the riots, over a thousand different groups had formed, ranging from political and legal organizations to social clubs and newspapers. The '70s and '80s represent the rise of lesbian and gay liberation movements as well as political and legal organizations, such as the National Gay and Lesbian Task Force, the Human Rights Campaign, and Lambda Legal Defense. Legal changes range from the development of domestic partner benefits to the passage of gay adoption laws and the spread of anti-discrimination ordinances across the country. In other words, it is during this time that gays and lesbians emerge as a distinct and ethnic-like interest group.

Not surprisingly, it is also during this time that gay and lesbian standpoint films start to emerge. Gay standpoint films represent the development and entrenchment of gay and lesbian life as an affirmative basis of identity, community, and politics. Beginning in the 1970s, and well entrenched by the 1980s, gay enclaves became a hallmark of urban centers across the US, often marking out their territorial space with rainbow flags. A gay and, to a lesser extent, lesbian subculture established itself around this network of businesses, restaurants, churches and bars.[5] Like gay and lesbian literature, gay and lesbian standpoint films indicate the development and influence of a gay and lesbian perspective and voice in the cultural realm.

In the afterward to the revised edition of the *Celluloid Closet*, Vito Russo (1987) states, "Gay visibility has never really been an issue in the movies. Gays have always been visible. It's *how* they have been visible that has remained offensive for almost a century."[6] Appearing in 1988, Harvey Fierstein's *Torch Song Trilogy* is an excellent example of a film that still exhibits some of the residual elements of stigma and pollution of mainstream depictions of homosexuality that Russo refers to while at the same time carving out an affirming narrative that centers on the experiences of a strongly identified gay man.

I illustrate the logic of gay and lesbian standpoint films by discussing films that are unambiguous in their standpoint logic (i.e., *Torch Song Trilogy*, *Jeffrey*, and *Bar Girls*) and then consider films during this period, the late 1980s to 2000, that situate gays and lesbians from both a multiple standpoint position and a queer, decentered one (i.e., *The Broken Hearts Club*, *Watermelon Woman*, and *Go Fish*).[7]

In *Torch Song Trilogy*, the main character, Arnold, played by Fierstein, displays a clearly essentialist gay identity. The film, like all gay/lesbian standpoint films, argues for the need of making homosexuality an affirmative basis of identity and community. It is important to note that this film does not depict the impact of the AIDS epidemic on gays; it's a pre-

AIDS film but it does clearly show the marginalized status of homosexuals and homosexuality in the late '70s and early '80s, making it a narrative focus and problem for Fierstein's character.

The opening scene shows Arnold at age five playing with a doll and putting on his mother's makeup. It seems that Arnold is not only predestined to be gay, but also a female impersonator, because of his predilection for "girls'" clothes and cosmetics. Arnold's character is endearing and commendable: he is a feminine gay man who works as a drag queen, struggling to find love and respect in a homophobic world.

Arnold's gay identity is portrayed in strong essentialist terms. Arnold sees the world through his experience as a gay man. For example, his work, friends, and social problems are gay-related. There is also a rigid gender binary depicted in the film. Homosexuality is marked as feminine and inferior, reinforcing the privileged statuses of heterosexuality and masculinity. Let me illustrate each of these points by drawing on Arnold's relationships with the two other main characters in his life: his bisexual lover, Ed (Brian Kerwin), and his mother (Anne Bancroft).

The film begins with Arnold becoming involved with Ed. Ed is a closeted bisexual school teacher who is too afraid to commit to being gay or thus too afraid to be in an open relationship with Arnold. Arnold and Ed have been dating for a couple of months. Although Arnold has agreed to an open, nonmongamous relationship, he has done it to please Ed. It's Arnold's birthday and Ed won't pick up the phone or return his calls, so Arnold goes over to Ed's apartment and finds him making dinner for someone else. But it's not another man that Ed has been seeing behind Arnold's back; it's a woman. Arnold storms out of Ed's apartment after Ed greets the woman, Laurel, with a kiss. The following dialogue is from the scene where Ed chases after Arnold, trying to justify his relationship with Laurel.

> ED: I am not like you. Being gay is what you are. It's what you like. It's what you're comfortable with. I want more. I can't be happy living in a ghetto of gay bars, restaurants.
>
> ARNOLD: We've never done that.
>
> ED: I need to be proud of who I am.

ARNOLD: How can sleeping with a woman make you proud of yourself if you know you'd rather be with a man? How are you ever gonna get any respect from anyone if you're not going to respect yourself?

ED: And where's your self-respect?

ARNOLD: You want to see my self-respect? Here! (Yelling at Ed and slamming the elevator door in his face). Here's my self-respect.

This scene illustrates well the logic of a gay standpoint film. First of all, it shows that Ed marks Arnold as the essentially gay one between the two of them. Like Ed says to Arnold, "Being gay is what you are." Arnold's entire identity is reduced to his homosexuality. Ed's essentialist logic reinscribes a binary distinction between bisexuals (himself) and gay men (Arnold), marking the latter as polluted types who live on the margins of society. Ed, a school teacher who passes as heterosexual at his institution and in public life in general, cannot imagine himself as a gay man. Homosexuality is still too polluted for him. Ed also pathologizes the gay enclave as a place where only marginalized gay men like Arnold can be happy. As Ed states, "I can't be happy living in a ghetto of gay bars, restaurants." Although Arnold corrects Ed, telling him, "We've never done that," Ed's point is clear; he cannot identify with such a polluted identity. The closet's repressive normative heterosexuality is too strong and overwhelming.

Second, the film replays the battle between the polluting logic of the closet and the liberatory coming out logic of homosexual emancipation. Arnold's tale is an allegorical one. He is the intrepid gay man who must overcome the barriers of a noncommittal bisexual lover (Ed), the death of his second lover to gay bashers (Allan), as well as the homophobic disapproval of his lifestyle by his mother. However, following the logic of a gay standpoint film, we know that Arnold will overcome these barriers: Ed will come out; his mother will come around; and gay identity will be made into a positive personal and social standpoint. Although essentializing homosexuality as a unitary social category of identity, the film argues for homosexuality to be seen as the moral equivalent of heterosexuality. Arnold has accepted and normalized his homosexual identity, and it is up to Ed and his mother to eventually come around to his understanding.

Third, the film depicts a gay subcultural lifeworld. The subcultural context situates the centrality of Arnold's homosexuality and difference. From his work as a female impersonator who sings tragic torch songs, hence the film's title, as well as Arnold's metaphor for gay oppression, to his friends and every other major obstacle he faces in life, a gay subcultural existence is central.

The next two films, *Bar Girls* (1994) and *Jeffrey* (1995), both feature protagonists who already out of the closet, thus the identity work of coming out is absent. Moreover, the audience is assumed to have normalized gay and lesbian identity and to be able to empathize with the conflicts the main characters face in their lives. While showing a diversity of gender styles among the characters, both films still essentialize homosexual identity. That is, homosexuality acts as the organizing principle on which these characters' lives revolve. These films portray characters that see the world through a gay prism. Their work, friends, social engagements, the type of discrimination faced as well as their leisure and volunteer activity are almost always gay-related.

In *Bar Girls*, Loretta, the lead character, is an animated cartoonist of a character named Rhonda. Rhonda solves relationship problems and is Loretta's alter ego. As Loretta becomes involved with Rachel, she has Rhonda become involved with a woman as well. In short, her personal life as a lesbian is mirrored in her professional life as an animated cartoonist. Similarly, while the title character Jeffrey does not incorporate his personal life into his career, he is still a waiter and aspiring actor, both industries that the film presents and our culture stereotypically marks as having high concentrations of gay men, since both industries are aestheticizing, service-orientated occupations coded as feminine. Both Loretta and Jeffrey then have work occupations in which their homosexuality is either a topic of focus or an industry stereotyped and portrayed as having a gay constituency.

Moreover, both *Bar Girls* and *Jeffrey* situate their protagonists within the gay and lesbian subcultures of Los Angeles and New York City, respectively. Not only does a subcultural context reinforce the centrality of the main characters' homosexuality, but it also signals a shift in narrative focus and depicts a general feature of gay/lesbian standpoint films. These characters do not focus on coming out or the problems heterosexuals have with homosexuality, but rather the focus is on their daily lives within the context of the gay and lesbian community. This is an important and central move of gay and lesbian standpoint films which make the target and focus of its narrative gay and lesbian audiences, not heterosexual ones. For example, *Bar Girls* focuses on Loretta's relationship problems, such as the threat of a predatory lesbian, issues of fidelity, and monogamy while the title character Jeffrey deals with the quandaries of dating an HIV positive man. Both narratives focus on problems situated within gay subcultural life.

Another important feature to take account of in gay and lesbian standpoint films is how the norm of heterosexuality is presented. While random acts of homophobic violence against gays and lesbians are portrayed, these films fail to depict a larger society structurally and socially organized around the norm of heterosexuality. For example, in *Jeffrey*, Jeffrey himself is a victim of gay bashing. However, this is the only scene which shows the oppression of gays. Moreover, even though the film deals with the fears that Jeffrey has with dating Steve because of his HIV positive status, the AIDS epidemic is not presented as a form of oppression. Indeed, only random acts of violence gesture to gay oppression and the norm of heterosexuality. The film *Jeffrey* consequently does not present a culture patterned or system structured around the norm of heterosexuality.

Similarly, even when films like *Jeffrey and Bar Girls* offer a critique of normative heterosexuality, it is often diluted. In *Bar Girls*, Loretta is told she cannot have her animated character Rhonda have a lesbian relationship, as it will lose ratings and sponsors. Loretta says that this fear of bad rating is the patriarchy at work, not compulsory heterosexuality or homophobia. Her character uses patriarchy as a coded, indirect way to criticize normative heterosexuality. As a result, gay and lesbian standpoint films, like *Jeffrey* and *Bar Girls*, often elide or completely omit depicting the coercive power of normative heterosexuality, thus missing the chance to provide a critique of its hegemonic power and subvert its normalizing force. Further, the status of heterosexuality is privileged through this elision or omission as well as by the very depiction of subordinate gay characters. In short, the depiction of heteronormativity is often a good measuring stick for whether an accompanying critique will be leveled against it. Often times if heteronormativity is absent, then critique is as well.

Moreover, lesbian and gay standpoint films unwittingly reinforce heteronormativity through reproducing a clear gender binary. As queer theorists have explicated for us, heterosexuality's dominance is reinforced through the establishment of binary gender roles and identities. That is, rigid constructions of gender as male/female and masculine/feminine set up a logic of oppositional binaries and hierarchies which privilege, valorize, and reinforce the norm of heterosexuality. For example, in *Jeffrey*, two of the characters, Patrick Stewart's Sterling and Michael Weiss's Steve, are clearly marked as stereotypical gays, which entails a feminizing of their talk, dress, comportment, style, as well as their characters' emphasis on pleasure, elegance, surfaces, and consumerism in general. The lead character, Jeffery, presents a more complicated coding. While Jeffrey is very conventionally masculine (in talk, dress, and comportment), he is still coded as feminine in subtle ways. He is afraid to have sex because of HIV/AIDS, and this fear creates a character who is indecisive, passive, and weak-willed. His psyche and personality are subtly coded as "feminine." As a result, one can see that the gender binary and its accompanying hierarchy of heterosexual privilege subtly and not so subtly still mark the homosexual male as feminine, leaving the absent, unmarked heterosexual male as masculine. In short, the gender binary of masculine/feminine is reproduced in the maintenance of the heterosexual/homosexual binary, thereby privileging heterosexuality and masculinity once again. Similarly, *Bar Girls* marks Loretta, her girlfriend Rachel, and Loretta's sexually experimental straight friend—Veronica, who pursues a butch—as feminine lesbians (all of whom have long hair, wear conventionally feminine clothes, and could pass as straight), while marking the predatory lesbian JD, and the southern lesbian Tracey, as the more masculine butch dykes. Loretta warns Veronica against pursuing Tracey, saying, "Tracey is not a femme. She drives a Harley. She's learned in the ways of dykeness." Although the statement is meant to be humorous on one level, it still marks Tracey and butch lesbians as more dangerous, even polluted. In short, *Bar Girls*, while showing a diversity of gender styles among its lesbian characters, reinforces a rigid binary that privileges feminine gender norms for women and normative heterosexuality once again.

While all standpoint films make gay and lesbian identity an affirmative basis of self and community, there is an interesting transition from *Torch Song Trilogy*, which I consider to be part of the shift from polluted to normalized representations of gays, to gay/lesbian standpoint films of the 1990s and beyond. In *Torch Song Trilogy*, the binary divide between individuals who have and have not come to terms with their homosexuality is the dominant logic of the film, marking Arnold as the good "out" gay while Ed is the bad closeted gay. The film's logic argues for coming out and establishing an affirmative gay identity. In the previous standpoint films there was also a binary between the good and bad gay; however, this good/bad binary distinction was not one that argued for the bad gay to come out and affirm his or her homosexual identity. Rather, the later gay/lesbian standpoint films have already normalized homosexuality and are beyond the narrative of coming out. The new binary focuses on distinctions or problems within the gay and lesbian subcultural life. This binary, in fact, turns out to be moral and ethical distinctions which gays and lesbians make, justly and unjustly, about other gays and lesbians within the community. For example, the narrative focus of *Jeffrey* is the title character's fear and wrongly prejudiced binary between having sex or not having sex with an HIV positive gay men. The coming out narrative here is one where Jeffrey learns to overcome his fear of sex with HIV positive men. Similarly, *Bar Girls* shows how its protagonists, Loretta and Rachel, wrongly draw binaries between predatory lesbians and non-monogamy when insecurity and trust are really at the heart of their polluting distinctions. Furthermore, although the latter standpoint films, *Broken Hearts Club*, *Watermelon Woman*, and *Go Fish*, start to decenter gay and lesbian identity through depicting multiple-standpoint identities (such as Cheryl Dunye's autobiographical portrayal as a black lesbian filmmaker) or portraying sexuality as fluid for a single character, they nonetheless also focus on the binary distinctions that are by about gays and lesbians within the community, making these very distinctions narrative problems for their characters to resolve (such as race and interracial relations or the policing of identity).

> There is not a single film in the cinema canon that paints a portrait of a gay man that any of us would aspire to be. What are our options: noble suffering AIDS victims, the friends of noble suffering AIDS victims, compulsive sex addicts, common street hustlers, and the most recent edition to the lot, stylish confidantes to lovelorn women.
>
> —Howie, gay psychology graduate student in *Broken Hearts Club*

The above quote demonstrates well the intent of *Broken Hearts Club* (2000), which not only attempts to provide a portrait of a gay man that one could aspire to, but also starts the process of critiquing the gay community from within. The film depicts a complicated, multidimensional view of the gay ghetto, acknowledging its affirming and non-affirming qualities. First, the film offers a series of gay characters who face a variegated set of problems, from being a "player" and having meaningless sex to the problems involved in long term relationships to coming out to oneself, family, and the larger gay community. The protagonist of the story, Dennis, is an attractive twenty-eight-year-old gay white man living a public gay life in West Hollywood, California. He has a well developed gay personal and social life, with a host of gay friends with whom he both works and plays during his leisure time. However, according to Dennis, his overwhelming problem is his life in the gay ghetto. For him, gay ghetto life has led to a pattern of having meaningless sex, emotional detachment, and a stultifying gay identity. Towards the end of film Dennis directly says this, remarking to Kevin, a recently out gay man he befriended and regrettably had sex with, "I'm twenty-eight years old and the only thing I'm good at is being gay . . . And I'm OK with it. I didn't get to be gay for twenty-five years. I figure I got some catching up to do. [pause] But I need to move on. I need to make my life into something else instead of just my friends and the parties. That's the only way I'll have something to give back to someone. Do you see that? [He's looking at Kevin.] Tell me you see that."

Dennis and *Broken Hearts Club* offer a much different critique of gay identity and the gay enclave than Ed in *Torch Song Trilogy*. In *Torch Song Trilogy*, Ed is unable to commit to Arnold because a gay identity is too stigmatizing for him, saying, "I can't be happy living in a ghetto of gay bars, restaurants." From one perspective, one might say that Dennis is too happy living in the ghetto. He has come to accept his gay identity without a sense of inferiority, and for Dennis, the gay ghetto is a source of not only friendship and fun but also financial and social support (he works as a waiter in a gay restaurant).

Broken Hearts Club's standpoint logic argues for working through the trials and tribulations of contemporary gay life, whether it's Howie (Matt McGrath), who resolves to accept that he is not the most straight-acting or attractive member of the group, or Cole (Dean Cain), the unabashed sexual agent who learns to be less callous towards men and develops a stronger ethic of care towards his friends and "tricks." While *Broken Hearts Club* depicts the gay ghetto of West Hollywood, *Watermelon Woman* presents the lesbian and gay community of Philadelphia.

The protagonist of *Watermelon Woman* (1997), a black lesbian, provides an intersectional or multiple standpoint from which to depict and critique lesbian life. The lead character of the film, Cheryl (an autobiographical portrayal by writer and director Cheryl Dunye), provides a critique of not only the centered, unmarked status of whiteness within the gay community, but her character also creates a faux documentary that focuses on portraying the missing history of black actresses in 1920s and 1930s Hollywood films.

In the film, Cheryl is an aspiring filmmaker who is making a documentary about a black actress who played a number of mammy roles in 1920s Hollywood film. Cheryl hopes to discover the actual name and identity of the Watermelon Woman, which was the only credit given to the black actress who played the roles. The film's narrative is told from three separate but overlapping axes of identity. On one hand, Cheryl's character is reclaiming and writing the lost and hidden history of black women on film who played mammies, maids, and servants in an overtly racist film industry. At the same time, Cheryl's documentary film of the Watermelon Women uncovers a history of black lesbian life, excavating not only images of black women on the screen, but black lesbian life during the early part of the century. The actress who played the Watermelon Woman turns out to have had a lesbian relationship with the woman director who employed her in several films. Cheryl's documentary uncovers a lesbian subculture and the Watermelon Woman's cult following among the "tom butches" of Philadelphia of the time. The film creates a history of black women on film, an unknown black lesbian life past, and explores how issues of race and racism continue to affect the character's own lesbian relationship in the present.

Cheryl ends the film with the statement that she has not only found a story and history of black actresses on film but also a story of hope and inspiration. Thus, she tells us that her documentary of the Watermelon Woman was her own creation, but that "Sometimes you have to create your own history. The *Watermelon Woman* is fiction."

While some film scholars have noted the centering of whiteness in depictions of gay and lesbian images in both Hollywood as well as standpoint films, both filmic movements continue to reinforce not only whiteness, but gay men as the dominant face of filmic images of homosexuality.

While on one hand multiple standpoint representations are valuable in terms of diversifying the image of homosexuals and homosexuality, providing a situated critique and elaborating a multicultural world of difference within gay/lesbian communities, they also end up at times simply substituting a multiple standpoint for a previous unitary one. For example, instead of the image of white gay men, we have the image of lesbians or, with Dunye, a black lesbian. All of these images are needed, and at their best they provide valuable standpoints from which to critique heteronormative society. *Go Fish* (1994), the last film I shall discuss as a standpoint film, is more of a hybrid between a lesbian standpoint film and Queer Cinema. What I mean is that *Go Fish* assumes the logic of a standpoint film (witness its essentialist lesbian identities, and the fact that the narrative is told from standpoint of lesbian subculture), but it also makes the queer critique, arguing for understanding sexuality as fluid and decentered. Moreover, it argues against the coercive subcultural norms that inform any identity politic.

Go Fish is firmly rooted in an urban lesbian subculture and its narrative is told from this standpoint. The film's main characters are all lesbians. Gay men and heterosexuals do not even figure as peripheral characters in the film. *Go Fish* addresses a lesbian audience first and foremost. It offers a conventional romantic love narrative of two women falling in love, while at the same time contesting and decentering lesbian identity, normative heterosexuality, and other lesbian subcultural norms.

Go Fish presents us with the representation of the "lesbian who sleeps with men." Daria is the subversive, queer lesbian of the pack. Her subversiveness is represented through her sexual "promiscuity." In the film, we consistently see her, and only her, with a different woman or "trick." Moreover, Daria's voluminous number of "tricks" includes men. In a dream like sequence, which allows the film to make this scene hyperbolic, fantasy-like, we see Daria walking late at night and then suddenly get carried away by a gang of dykes. This diverse bevy of lesbians act as judge and jury in Daria's crime of disloyalty to the lesbian nation. Daria is charged with the crime of sleeping with a man and claming to be an "authentic" dyke. How does she plead? Guilty, but her plead is that it was just sex. That is, Daria claims that she can and should be seen as a "real" lesbian since she actively chooses to make her life with other women, not men. And thus, she is as much a lesbian as anyone else. She argues that lesbian identity does not entail the exclusion of male lovers, specifically with regards to casual sex. Daria's lesbian identity is obviously not rigid, stable, or discrete. She does primarily desire women but still wants to be able to have (casual) sex with men if she chooses to. Basically, Daria wants to have her cake and eat it too, meaning she wants to retain her lesbian identity and community identification but still have sex with whomever she chooses to.

Consequently, Daria's character argues for a decentered lesbian sexuality. This point is made explicit in the fantasy trial scene where she is tried for sleeping with a man. This scene has an excess of similarities with Salem witch trials. Not only does the scene argue for opening up lesbian identity, but it highlights the importance of not reinscribing the same mistakes of a male-dominated culture that disavowed and killed women for their differences. I do not think that the similarities between Daria's trial and Salem witch trials are accidental; the scene is meant to be didactic shoring up that lesbians need to be careful of the coercive norms that their subculture creates and to avoid repressing differences amongst themselves. The dialogue from this trial scene elucidates these points:

PACK OF LESBIANS: What do you think you're doing? It makes me sick.

DARIA: Does it make you sick, or does it just scare you?

P: Just don't call yourself something that you're not.

D: If you're talking about me calling myself a lesbian, it's what I am.

P: My definition of a lesbian does not involve men in any way. How are we suppose to establish some kind of identity if lesbians are going around having sex with men?

D: Maybe we need to . . . [she gets cut off].

P: Go out and get some dick.

D: We're not talking life commitment here, we're talking about sex.

Here we see that "sleeping with a man" is a violation of normative lesbian subcultural norms. Lesbians who sleep with men constitute the abject outside of this normative injunction. However, Daria pleads that casual sex with a man should not be seen as invalidating her lesbian identity. Rather, she thinks it should be seen as one sex act, among others. Therefore, it does not invalidate her lesbian identity but makes sexuality messier and more complicated for herself and her fellow lesbians. For Daria, lesbianism is her primary identification, and she wants to retain her lesbian identity but still be able to acknowledge the fluidity of her sexual desires. In short, Daria's character makes the case for a decentered lesbian identity that eschews the notion of authenticity. Her character argues for recognizing differences among lesbians. Daria does not want to have to subscribe to a lesbian subculture that disavows her because of its need to police boundaries and enforce loyalty. Her point is that desire is not circumscribed by (lesbian or any) identification, but is only part of its constitution. However, her character highlights the importance of retaining identity categories like lesbian, while at the same time highlighting how desire escapes normative (lesbian) identity codes.

In conclusion, I would argue that gay and lesbian standpoint films are emblematic of the larger political landscape in which we find ourselves today. While filmic visibility is important in creating representations of ourselves that we find pleasurable and entertaining, it is important that we keep a critical eye to the images we consume on the screen. Moreover, if, as I argued, we understand lesbian and gay standpoint films as a response to the repressive social logic of normative heterosexuality in mainstream Hollywood films, then gay standpoint films provide an important corrective to mainstream films, which exclude gay subcultural depictions.

JAMES DEAN, PHD, is an assistant professor of sociology at Sonoma State University. He teaches Sociology of Sexualities, Gender, Race and Ethnicity, Culture and Social Theory. His research and teaching focus on the sociology of sexualities, particularly the sociology of heterosexualities.

Notes

1. Suzanna Walters, *All the Rage: The Story of Gay Visibility in America* (Chicago, IL: University of Chicago Press, 2001); Steven Seidman, *Beyond the Closet: the Transformation of Gay and Lesbian Life* (New York, NY: Routledge, 2002).
2. For a discussion of Queer Cinema see James Joseph Dean, "Gays and Queers: From the Centering to the Decentering of Homosexuality in American Film," *Sexualities* 10: 363–386, 2007.
3. Joshua Gamson, "Sweating in the Spotlight: Lesbian, Gay and Queer Encounters with Media and Popular Culture," in Diane Richardson and Steven Seidman (eds.) *Handbook of Lesbian and Gay Studies* (Thousand Oaks, CA: Sage Publications, 2002).

4. Barry Adam, *The Rise of a Gay and Lesbian Movement* (New York, NY: Twayne Publishers, 1995); John D'Emilio, *Sexual Politics, Sexual Communities: the Making of a Homosexual Minority in the United States, 1940–1970* (Chicago, IL: University of Chicago Press, 1983); Steven Epstein, "Gay and Lesbian Movements in the United States: Dilemmas of Identity, Diversity, and Political Strategy," in Adam, Duyvendak and Krouwel (eds.) *The Global Emergence of Gay and Lesbian Politics: National Imprints of a Worldwide Movement* (Philadelphia, PA: Temple University Press, 1999).
5. Martin Levine, "Gay Ghetto," in M. Levine (ed), *Gay Men: The Sociology of Male Homosexuality* (New York, NY: Harper & Row, 1979).
6. Vito Russo, *The Celluloid Closet: Homosexuality in the Movies*, 2nd edition (New York, NY: Harper and Row, 1987).
7. The following films are discussed in this essay: *Bar Girls*, 1994, Dir. Marita Giovanni, Orion Classics; *Broken Hearts Club*, 2000, Dir. Greg Berlanti, Sony Pictures Entertainment; *Go Fish*, 1994, Dir. Rose Troche, Evergreen Entertainment; *Jeffrey*, 1995, Dir. Christopher Ashley, Orion Classics; *Torch Song Trilogy*, 1988, Dir. Paul Bogart, New Line Cinema; *Watermelon Woman*, 1997, Dir. Cheryl Dunye, First Run Feature.

Acknowledgments

by Peter Phillips

Project Censored is managed through the Department of Sociology in the School of Social Sciences at Sonoma State University, in cooperation with Media Freedom Foundation Inc., a 501-C-3 nonprofit fund-raising organization. We are an investigative research and media analysis project dedicated to journalistic integrity and the freedom of information throughout the United States.

History professor Mickey Huff from Diablo Valley College has been associate director of Project Censored since 2008 and is coeditor of this year's book. Dr. Ben Frymer from the Sonoma State University Liberal Studies program will step in as director of Project Censored at the start of the 2009–2010 research year.

As this is my last year as director of Project Censored, I want to personally thank those close friends and intimates who have counseled and supported me through many years of Project Censored work. Most important is my wife, Mary M. Lia, who as my trusted friend and life-partner provides daily consultative support. The men in the Green Oaks Breakfast Group—Noel Byrne, Bob Butler, Bob Klose, Derrick West, Colin Godwin, Peter Tracy, and Bill Simon—are personal advisors and confidants who help with difficult decisions. Special thanks also to Carl Jensen, founder of Project Censored and director for twenty years. His continued advice and support are critical to the Project. Trish Boreta and Kate Sims are Project Censored coordinators and associate administrators. Their dedication and enthusiasm are greatly appreciated. And a special thank you to the directors of Media Freedom Foundation, who provide the policy and planning support to Project Censored.

Big thanks go to the people at Seven Stories Press. They are not just a publishing house, but have also become close friends, who help edit our annual book in record time and serve as advisors in the annual release process of the "Most Censored Stories." Publisher Dan Simon is dedicated to building democracy in America through knowledge and literature. He deserves full credit for assembling an excellent support crew, including Jon Gilbert, Veronica Liu, Anna Lui, Theresa Noll, Tara Parmiter, Lars Reilly, Ruth Weiner, and Crystal Yakacki.

Thanks also to Jim Nichols, Nan Fulle, Bill Mockler, and the sales staff at Consortium Book Sales and Distribution, who will see to it that every independent bookstore, chain store, and wholesaler in the US is aware of *Censored 2010*. Thanks to Publishers Group Canada, our distributors up north, as well as Turnaround Publisher Services Ltd. in the UK and Europe, and Palgrave Macmillan in Australia.

We especially thank Novi Mondi Media in Italy for translating and distributing the Censored yearbooks in Italian and for coordinating the Project Censored Italy visit in the summer of 2008. Ernesto Carmona translates Project Censored stories into Spanish for ARGENPRESS.info and our Spanish language publisher in Switzerland Timeli Editions Suiza and Pedidos in Venezuela.

Joel Challender and his team in Japan have been coordinating the Japanese language translation of the Censored stories, which can be seen on the Project Censored website.

A big acknowledgement to Jodi Solomon Speakers Bureau in Boston for their long time support in arranging speaking engagements at various colleges and universities nationwide. Proceeds from these appearances are a continuing financial supplement to Project Censored.

Thank you to Dahr Jamail, who wrote the introduction to the *Censored 2010* edition. His continuing political journalism work on the Middle East and his efforts in support of global peace and human rights is extremely important.

Thanks also to the authors of the most censored stories for 2010; without their often-unsupported efforts as investigative news reporters and writers, the stories presented in *Censored* would not be revealed.

Our guest writers this year include Andrew Roth, Peter Hart, Ben Frymer, James Dean, Frances A. Capell, Brad Friedman, Andrew Hobbs, Sarah Maddox, Geoff Davidian, Aashika N. Damodar, Jo Glanville, Diane Farsetta, Sheldon Rampton, Daniel Haack, John Stauber, and the wonderful team at *Yes! Magazine* led by Sarah van Gelder.

This year's book features the cartoons of Khalil Bendib. We welcome his brilliant and satirical work to our 2010 edition.

Our national judges, some of whom have been involved with the Project for thirty-three years, are among the top experts in the country concerned with First Amendment freedoms and media principles. We are honored to have them as the final voice in ranking the Top 25 censored stories. We welcome a new national judge to our roster: the national copresident of the Action Coalition for Media Education, Rob Williams.

We are sad to announce the passing of two of our national judges this year: Dr. Tom Lough, professor emeritus of sociology at Kent State University, and Judith Krug, formerly with Office for Intellectual Freedom, American Library Association. Both had been longtime friends and supporters of Project Censored.

Important thanks go to our financial supporters, including: the Sonoma State University Instructionally Related Activity Fund, the School of Social Sciences at Sonoma State University, the Wallace Global Fund, Quitiplas Foundation, Caipirinha Foundation, Elizabeth Sherif, Michael Kieschnick at Credo Mobile, Mark Swedlund & Deborah Dobish, Lynn & Leonard Riepenhoff, and the thousands of individuals who purchase books and send us financial gifts each year. You are our financial base, the important few who continue to give year after year to this important student-run media research project.

This year we had over 130 faculty/community evaluators from two dozen universities and colleges assisting with our story assessment process. These expert volunteers read and rated the nominated stories for national importance, accuracy, and credibility. In April, they participated with over 150 students from several colleges in selecting the final Top 25 stories for 2008-2009.

Most of all, we need to recognize the Sonoma State University students in the Spring 2009 Media Censorship class and the Fall 2008 Sociology of Media class, who worked thousands of hours nominating and researching some 300 under-published news stories. Additionally, we recognize the expanding number of students in affiliate colleges and universities around the world working in conjunction with Media Freedom International. Students are the principle writers of the Censored news synopses posted on our websites, and are the base research for the final selection of the Top 25 most important censored stories of the year. Additionally, over sixty students served as interns for the project, working on various teams, including public relations, web design, news story research, office support, events/fund-raising, book/chapter research and writing, and broadcast production. Student education is the most important aspect of Project Censored, and we could not do this work without the dedication and effort of our student interns.

Adam Armstrong is the web coordinator for the Project Censored websites, including: www.projectcensored.org, the PNN Daily News site at: http://mediafreedom.pnn.com/5174-independent-news-sources, the Project Censored daily blog at http://dailycensored.com, and the Media

Freedom International validated news at http://www.mediafreedom-international.org/. Mark Blair from Bairworks is our web consultant.

Lastly, I want to thank our readers and supporters from all over the United States and the world. Hundreds of you nominated stories for consideration as the censored news story of the year. Thank you very much!

PROJECT CENSORED STAFF

Peter Phillips, PhD, director (director emeritus, July 1, 2009)
Mickey Huff, associate director
Ben Frymer, associate director (director, effective July 1, 2009
Carl Jensen, PhD, director emeritus and project advisor
Tricia Boreta, coordinator/editor
Katie Sims, finance/production coordinator
Adam Armstrong, webmaster
Sarah Maddox, research assistant
Ashley McLoud, office staff
Robyn Swan, office staff

BOARD OF DIRECTORS MEDIA FREEDOM FOUNDATION

May 9, 2009, Media Freedom Foundation Board of Directors (B) and PC Staff (S): left to right: Cynthia Boaz-B, Dennis Bernstein-B, Adam Armstrong-S-Web, Mary Lia-B, Peter Phillips-B, Ben Frymer-B, Trish Boreta-S, Carl Jensen-B, Kate Sims-S, Gary Evans-B, Mickey Huff-B, Miguel Molina-B, Bill Simon-B, Board members not shown: Noel Byrne, Judith Volkart, and David Mathison.

FALL 2008 & SPRING 2009 INTERNS AND COMMUNITY VOLUNTEERS

Courtney Callejas, Mathew Leatherman, Ian Marlowe, Jennifer Donahue, Chris McManus, Kevin Gonzales, Sean Richards, Kyle Kelly, Taylor Minnick, April Rudolph, Ashley McLoud, Jordan Harvey, Francis Capell, Jenna Tantilo, Kristin Luhnow, Carena Gilbert, Sarah Vortman, Vincente Ramirez, Rebecca Newsome, Allison Murray, Melissa Willenborg, Gina McIntyre, Michael Seramin, Emma Smales, Andy Hobbs, Carmela Rocha, Wesley Lacher, Robyn Swan, Sarah Maddox, Brad Moreno, Krista Lettko, Bill Gibbons, Dan Bluthardt Jr., Leora Johnson, Kerry Headley, Karene Schelert, Rob Hunter and Lizbeth Malmsted

STUDENT RESEARCHERS IN SOCIOLOGY OF MEDIA CLASS, FALL 2008

Faculty: Mickey Huff
Staff: Tricia Boreta

Chris McManus, Ryan Larkin, Jayson Reed, Lizbeth Malmsted, Krisden Kidd, Carlos Maldonado, Ian Bridges, Edward Martin, Michael Seramin, Caitlin Morgan, Ronni Poole, Jennifer Donahue, Stephanie Smith, Chelsea Davis, Alan Grady, Rob Hunter, Natalie Dale, Allison Murray, Jennifer Gibson, Elizabeth Vortman, Anthony Del Monte

STUDENT RESEARCHERS IN SOCIOLOGY OF MEDIA CENSORSHIP, SPRING 2009

Faculty: Peter Phillips
Staff: Tricia Boreta

Aimee Drew, Erin Galbraith, Alan Grady, Curtis Harrison, Ashleigh Hvinden, Ben Kaufman, Victoria Masucci, Chris McManus, Malana Men, Melissa Robinson, April Rudolph, Caitlin Ruxton, Rosemary Scott, Christine Wilson

PROJECT CENSORED 2008–2009 BROADCAST SUPPORT TEAM

COORDINATOR: Kate Sims, INTERNS: Krista Lettko, Kyle Kelly, Kevin Winters, Josh Travers, Sean Richards, Brad Moreno, Paul Sarran, Melissa Curtin BROADCAST PARTNERS: KPFA—Flashpoints Team: Dennis Bernstein, Miguel Gavilon Molina, Miguel A. Molina Jr., Nora Borrows-Friedman

SSU PROJECT CENSORED RESEARCH GROUP 2009

SOUTHWEST MINNESOTA STATE UNIVERSITY:
Justice and the Media, Spring 2009
Faculty: William Du Bois
Samantha Barowsky, Demarco Butts, Shannon Clark, Justin Hanson, Rena Hawkins, John Herrera, Michael Jans, Valerie Janssen, Trudy Kaiser, Ann Kopitzke, Matthew Lapakko, Kristofer Lee, Alexander Rott, Brittany Sandager, Amie Shirkey, Samantha Stout

DEPAUW UNIVERSITY:
Media Culture & Society, Spring 2009
Faculty: Kevin Howley
Gail Allison, Melissa Bock, Gwendolyn Brack, Laura Brinlee, Morgan Burke, Leslie Gaber, Hallie Fischer, Elizabeth Geiler, Bernadette Gorman, Jean Gossett, Kim Heiniger, Paige Henderson, Randall Heyde, Daryl Mowrey, William Roberts, Scott O'Neil, Taylor Prodromos, Ross Robinson, Ava Roebuck, Anne Sexton, Michael Shropshire

NIAGARA UNIVERSITY
Investigation and Reporting for the Media, Spring 2009
Faculty: Brian Murphy
Genna Mitchell, Kevin Hooks, Jared Hoyt, Jake Scott

ST. CLOUD STATE UNIVERSITY
Change Agent Skills, Spring 2009
Faculty: Julie Andrzejewski
Danielle Ammerman, Jordan Angelle, Courtney Bergstrom, Jessica Bjerk, Brittany Goedtke, Britten Johnson, Stephanie Menke, Lucas Ped-

ersen, Jill Schaeppi, Nicholas Sieben, Amber Taveirne, Melinda Xiong, Janelle Anderson, Abby Buesgens, Hannah Durbin, Moses Ehlers, Mitchell Fennell, Rebecca Jordan, Bryce Mackey, Amber Michel, Alyssa Paulson, Zachary Stoe, Alicia Wegman, Bee Yang, Wanjiru Mugo

DREXEL UNIVERSITY
Critical Reasoning, Spring 2009
Faculty: Bryan Sacks
Binoy Bhatt, Anthony Cronce, Ameer Desai, Anthony Fittipaldi, Greg Guerin, Ankit Harpaldas, Dyna Hin, Kevin Homer, Jeanette Huynh, Ali Ince, Annmary Ittan, Ben John, Drew Kurtz, Angeline Mombrun, Erin O'Connell, Keyur Patel, Rupali Patel, Gregory Pierce, Ruchi Sondhi, Wing Lung Suen, Wing Lung, Brian Thoman, Sean Treston, Andrew Walsh, Chloe Yeung

SUNY POTSDAM
Rhetoric of Social Movements, Fall 2008
Faculty: Dr. Christina M. Knopf
Lorraine Angona, Robert Bice, Nicole Briggs, Mark Burtick, Nick Carelli, Reagan Fierle, Chris Franke, Andy Gardner, Chris Green, Rachel Jenack, Christopher Jerome, Sarah Johnson, Andrea McCarthy, Maureen McCullough, Allison Pepe, Billy Richards, Rachel Richman, Jacey Rourke, Lisa Scanlon, Nick Steblenko, Frances Stevens, Devin Taft, David Tiedeman

CALIFORNIA STATE UNIVERSITY NORTHRIDGE
Linda Bowen, Assistant Professor Communications Studies
Project Leader: Josselle Sison

Student Chaper of the Society of Professional Journalists
Salena Barcenas, Richard Casteneda, Dessiraee Eleby, Marilyn Garcia, Jamie Garrison, Anthony Graham, Natalie Jaurequi, Crystal Kelly, Briaune Knighton, April Lowder, Kristin MacQueen, Jeremiah McDaniel, Harriet Miranda, Satoru Narue, Alonso Tacanga, Travis Van Noty

PROJECT CENSORED 2008-09 NATIONAL JUDGES

ROBIN ANDERSEN, associate professor and chair, Department of Communication and Media Studies, Fordham University; director of peace and justice studies; publications: *Critical Studies in Media Commercialism.*

OLIVER BOYD-BARRETT, director of school, professor in journalism and telecommunications, Bowling Green State University; Publications: *The International New Agencies: the Globalization of News, Media in Global Context.*

LIANE CLORFENE-CASTEN, cofounder and president of Chicago Media Watch; award-winning journalist with credits in national periodicals such as *E Magazine, The Nation, Mother Jones, Ms., Environmental Health Perspectives, In These Times,* and *Business Ethic;* author of *Breast Cancer: Poisons, Profits, and Prevention.*

GEOFF DIVIDIAN, Milwaukee investigative journalist; editor of the Putman Pit online newspaper.

LENORE FOERSTEL, Women for Mutual Security; facilitator of the Progressive International Media Exchange (PRIME).

ROBERT HACKETT, professor, School of Communication, Simon Fraser University; codirector of News Watch Canada since 1993; recent publications include *Democratizing Global Media: One World, Many Struggles* (coedited with Yuezhi Zhao, 2005), and *Remaking Media: The Struggle To Democratize Public Communication* (with William K. Carroll, 2006).

CARL JENSEN, professor emeritus, communication studies, Sonoma State University; founder and former director of Project Censored; author of *Censored: The News That Didn't Make the News and Why* (1990–1996) and *20 Years of Censored News* (1997).

SUT JHALLY, professor of communications and executive director of the Media Education Foundation, University of Massachusetts; publications: *The Spectacle of Accumulation: Essays in Media, Culture & Politics.*

NICHOLAS JOHNSON,* professor, College of Law, University of Iowa; former FCC Commissioner (1966–1973); author of *How to Talk Back to Your Television Set.*

RHODA H. KARPATKIN, president emeritus of Consumers Union, non-profit publisher of *Consumer Reports*.

CHARLES L. KLOTZER, editor and publisher emeritus, *St. Louis Journalism Review*.

NANCY KRANICH, past president of the American Library Association (ALA); senior research fellow, Free Expression Policy Project.

DEEPA KUMAR, assistant professor, Department of Journalism and Media Studies, Rutgers, State University of New Jersey; author of *Outside the Box: Corporate Media, Globalization and the UPS Strike*.

MARTIN LEE, investigative journalist, media critic and author; an original founder of Fairness and Accuracy in Reporting in New York and former editor of *Extra Magazine*; author of *Acid Dreams: The Complete Social History of LSD—The CIA, the Sixties and Beyond*.

DENNIS LOO, associate professor of sociology at California State University Polytechnic university, Pomona; coeditor of *Impeach the President: The Case Against Bush and Cheney* (2006).

WILLIAM LUTZ, professor of English, Rutgers University; former editor of *The Quarterly Review of Doublespeak;* author of *The New Doublespeak: Why No One Knows What Anyone's Saying Anymore* (1966).

MARK CRISPIN MILLER, professor of media ecology, New York University; director of the Project on Media Ownership.

BRIAN MURPHY, associate professor Communications Studies Niagara University specializing in Media Programming and Management, Investigation and Reporting, Media History and Theory and International Communication.

JACK L. NELSON,* professor emeritus, Graduate School of Education, Rutgers University; author of sixteen books, including *Critical Issues in Education* (1996), and more than 150 articles.

NANCY SNOW, professor of public diplomacy and communications at Syracuse University and Senior Fellow at the USC Center on Public Diplomacy; publications include *Persuader-in-Chief, Propaganda, Inc., Information War, War, Media and Propaganda* (with Yahya Kamalipour) and the *Routledge Handbook of Public Diplomacy* (with Philip M. Taylor).

SHEILA RABB WEIDENFELD,* president of D.C. Productions, Ltd.; former press secretary to Betty Ford.

ROB WILLIAMS: Action Coalition for Media Education (ACME) Board copresident, Champlain College.

*Indicates having been a Project Censored judge since our founding in 1976

PROJECT CENSORED 2008 AND 2009 FACULTY, STAFF, AND COMMUNITY EVALUATORS AT SONOMA STATE UNIVERSITY AND REGIONAL AREA

Bob Alpern, Community Expert on Peace and Social Justice
Jeff Baldwin, PhD Geography
Philip Beard, PhD Modern Languages
Jim Berkland, PhD Geology
Stephen Bittner, PhD History
Barbara Bloom, PhD Criminal Justice Admin.
Cynthia Boaz, PhD Political Science
Andrew Botterell, PhD Philosophy
Maureen Buckley, PhD Counseling
Kelly Bucy, PhD Political Science
Elizabeth Burch, PhD Communications
Noel Byrne, PhD Sociology
James R. Carr, PhD Geology
Liz Close, PhD Nursing (Chair)
G. Dennis Cooke, PhD Zoology
Bill Crowley, PhD Geography
Victor Daniels, PhD Psychology
Laurie Dawson, PhD Labor Education
James Dean, PhD Sociology
Randall Dodgen, PhD History
Stephanie Dyer, PhD Cultural History
Carolyn Epple, PhD Anthropology
Gary Evans, MD
Michael Ezra, PhD Chemistry
Tamara Falicov, MA Communication Studies
Fred Fletcher, community expert, labor
Dorothy (Dolly) Friedel, PhD Geography

Ben Frymer, PhD Sociology/Liberal Studies
Ajay Gehlawat, PhD Liberal Studies
Nick Geist, PhD Biology
Patricia Leigh Gibbs, PhD Sociology
Robert Girling, PhD Business Economics
Mary Gomes, PhD Psychology
Myrna Goodman, PhD Sociology
Keith Gouveia, JD Political Science
Karen Grady, PhD Education
Diana Grant, PhD Criminal Justice Admin.
Debora Hammons, PhD Liberal Studies
Janet Hess, PhD Liberal Studies
Laurel Holmstrom, Academic Programs; MA (English)
Jeffrey Holtzman, PhD Environmental Sciences
Mickey Huff, MA History
Pat Jackson, PhD Criminal Justice Admin.
Tom Jacobson JD, Environmental Studies & Planning
Sherril Jaffe, PhD English
Paul Jess, Community Expert Environmental Law
Susan Kashack, SSU Vice President Communications and Marketing
Cheri Ketchum, PhD Communications
Amy Kittelstrom, PhD History
Patricia Kim-Rajal, PhD American Culture
Mary King MD Health
Paul Kingsley, MD
Jeanette Koshar, Nursing
John Kramer, PhD Political Science
Heidi LaMoreaux, PhD Geography—Liberal Studies
Wingham Liddell, PhD Business Administration
Jennifer Lillig Whiles, PhD Chemistry
Ron Lopez, PhD Latino Studies
Rick Luttmann, PhD Math (Peace Studies)
Robert Manning, Peace Issues
Ken Marcus, PhD Criminal Justice Admin.
Perry Marker, PhD Education
Elizabeth Martinez, PhD Modern Languages
Chip McAuley, PhD Communication Studies
David McCuan, PhD Political Science
Eric McGuckin, PhD Anthropology—Liberal Studies

Robert McNamara, PhD Political Science
Andy Merrifield, PhD Political Science
Mutombo M'Panya, PhD International Studies
Catherine Nelson, PhD Political Science
Leilani Nishime, PhD Ethnic Studies Department
Linda Nowak, PhD Business
Tim Ogburn, International Business (State of California)
Tom Ormond, PhD Kinesiology
Wendy Ostroff, PhD Psychology, Liberal Studies
Ervand M. Peterson, PhD Environmental Sciences
Jorge E. Porras, PhD Modern Languages
Robert Proctor, PhD Political Science
Jeffrey T. Reeder, PhD Modern Languages
Rick Robison, PhD Library
R. Thomas Rosin, PhD Anthropology
Andrew Roth, PhD Sociology
Richard Senghas, PhD Anthropology, Linguistics
Rashmi Singh, PhD American Multicultural Studies
Cindy Stearns, PhD Sociology
Greg Storino, American Airlines Pilot
Meri Storino, PhD Counseling
Elaine Sundberg, MA Academic Programs
Jessica Taft, PhD Sociology
Laxmi G. Tewari, PhD Music
Karen Thompson, PhD Business
Suzanne Toczyski, PhD Modern Languages
Carol Tremmel, MA Extended Education
Charlene Tung, PhD Women's Gender Studies
David Van Nuys, PhD Psychology
Francisco H. Vazquez, PhD Liberal Studies
Greta Vollmer, PhD English
Alexandra (Sascha) Von Meier, PhD Environmental Sciences
Albert Wahrhaftig, PhD Anthropology
Mary Ann Walker, Adult Education
Tim Wandling, PhD English
Tony White, PhD History
Elaine Wellin, PhD Sociology
John Wingard, PhD Anthropology

PROJECT CENSORED NATIONAL AND INTERNATIONAL AFFILIATE COLLEGE AND UNIVERSITY FACULTY

Mickey Huff, Diablo Valley College, CA
Rob Williams, Champlain College
Natalie P. Byfield, St. John's University, Jamaica, NY
Carl Bybee, University of Oregon
Ken Burrows, San Francisco State University
Bill Griggs, Eastern Oregon University
Brian Murphy, Niagara University
Kevin Howley, DePauw University
Jeanette Pope, DePauw University
Tom Huckin, University of Utah
Bryan Sacks, Immaculata University
Michelle Ronda, Marymount Manhattan College, NY
Stephanie A. Flores-Koulish, Loyola College in Maryland
Julie Andrzejewski, St. Cloud State University
Patricia Gibbs Stayte, Foothill College, CA
Christina Knopf, SUNY Potsdam
Kathleen de Azevedo Feinblum, Skyline College, CA
Victoria Johnson, University of Missouri-Columbia
William Dinan, University of Strathclyde, Glasgow
James F. Tracy, Florida Atlantic University
William Du Bois, Southwest Minnesota State University
Sangeeta Sinha, Southwest Minnesota State University
B.C Franson, Southwest Minnesota State University
Douglas Anderson, Southwest Minnesota State University
Duane Macha, Siena College
Elliot Cohen, Indian River State College
Samual Mikhail, Indian River State College
Jaime Becker, University of San Francisco
Peggy Lopipero-Langmo, City College of San Francisco
Linda Bowen, California State University Northridge
Carl Grossman, SUNY, Long Island
Marla Donata, Columbia College, Chicago

SONOMA STATE UNIVERSITY SUPPORTING STAFF AND OFFICES

Ruben Arminaña, president, Sonoma State University and staff
Eduardo Ochoa: chief academic officer and staff
Melinda Bernard: vice provost, Academic Affairs
Elaine Leeder: dean of School of Sciences and staff
Erica Wilcher: administrative manager
Katie McCormick: operations analyst
Holly Sautner: dean's assistant
William Babula: dean of School of Arts and Humanities
Barbara Butler and the SSU Library Staff
Paula Hammett: Social Sciences Library Resources
Elisabeth Burch, and Faculty in Communications Studies
Susan Kashack, Jean Wasp and staff in SSU Public Relations Office
Eric McGuckin and the Faculty in Hutchins School of Liberal Studies
Associated Students Productions, Bruce Berkowitz
Media Services, Bruce Carpe, Bill Bayley

Acknowledgments for coeditor Mickey Huff

I would like to acknowledge the following people for their support and participation: Teaching and Research Assistants Frances A. Capell, Elliot van Patten, and Rebecca Barrett, with special thanks to Frances for her additional work as a Project Censored intern and public speaker.

Thank you to the students from History 122: Critical Reasoning in History courses at Diablo Valley College; also, from DVC, Dr. Bob Abele, Dr. Lyn Krause, Matthew Powell, Greg Tilles, Dr. Manual Gonzales, Katie Graham, Adam Bessie, and students from the SDS DVC chapter whom I had the pleasure of advising.

Thank you also to Berkeley City College, Dr. Charles Wollenberg, and Joan Berezin; and from St. Mary's College, Dr. John Ely and Dr. Paul Rea and Dr. Marc Sapir, formerly of Retropoll.

A special thanks to Dr. Peter Phillips for his belief in me and inclusion with such a great project, one that I've followed since 1993. It's been a dream come true for me to be involved as much as I have the past few years. I thank family and friends for their patience and kindness, especially my late father, without whom I would not be where I am today;

and finally, most significantly, my wife and best friend, Meg, who helps me in everything I do, and daughter Molly Luna, whose presence in my life is a constant reminder of why I do what I do and what makes life worth living. Thanks again to everyone.

About the Editors

PETER PHILLIPS is a professor of sociology at Sonoma State University and director of Project Censored. He teaches classes in Media Censorship, Investigative Sociology, Sociology of Power, Political Sociology, and Sociology of Media. He has published thirteen editions of *Censored: Media Democracy in Action* with Seven Stories Press. Also from Seven Stories Press is *Impeach the President: The Case Against Bush and Cheney* (2006) and *Project Censored Guide to Independent Media and Activism* (2003).

In 2009, Phillips received the Dallas Smythe Award from the Union for Democratic Communications. Dallas Smythe is a national award given to researchers and activists who, through their research and/or production work, have made significant contributions to the study and practice of democratic communication.

Phillips writes op-ed pieces for independent media nationwide and has been published in dozens of publications, newspapers and websites, including Common Dreams, BuzzFlash, Dissident Voice, Global Research, and Minute Man Media. He frequently speaks on media censorship and various sociopolitical issues on radio and TV talk shows including *Talk of the Nation*, Air America, Talk America, World Radio Network, and *Flashpoints*.

Phillips has completed several investigative research studies that are available at Projectcensored.org, including "The Global Dominance Group: 9/11 Pre-Warnings & Election Irregularities in Context," "A Study of Bias in the Associated Press," "Practices in Health Care and Disability Insurance: Deny Delay Diminish and Blame," "US Electromagnetic Weapons and Human Rights," "Building a Public Ivy: Diversity at Three California State Universities," and "The Left Progressive Media Inside the Propaganda Model."

Phillips earned a bachelor's degree in social science in 1970 from Santa Clara University, and an master's degree in social science from California State University at Sacramento in 1974. He earned a second MA in sociology in 1991 and a PhD in sociology in 1994. His doctoral dissertation was entitled "A Relative Advantage: Sociology of the San Francisco Bohemian Club" (http://libweb.sonoma.edu/regional/faculty/Phillips/bohemianindex.htm).

Phillips is a fifth-generation Californian who grew up on a family-owned farm west of the Central Valley town of Lodi. Phillips lives today in rural Sonoma County with his wife, Mary Lia.

MICKEY HUFF is associate professor of history at Diablo Valley College and associate director of the Media Freedom Foundation and Project Censored, which was the recipient of the 2008 PEN Oakland National Literary Censorship Award. He is the Media Freedom International's College and University Affiliates Coordinator, working in conjunction with Project Censored (http://mediafreedominternational.org). He is also a former adjunct lecturer in sociology at Sonoma State University, and the previous codirector of the alternative public opinion research agency Retropoll, in Berkeley, CA (http://retropollorg).

Mickey has been interviewed for several documentaries and news programs around the country, including NPR, Air America, Pacifica, Republic Broadcasting, the *Santa Rosa Press Democrat*, New Standard News, and others, and has been published on numerous media and news websites, including Global Research, *CounterPunch*, *Z Magazine*, BuzzFlash, and even a few corporate media outlets (which he routinely critiques). He teaches courses in US Media History, Sociology of Media and Censorship, Propaganda and Media Studies, 9/11 and American Empire, and Popular Culture. Mickey codesigned and taught classes on the History of US Media at Berkeley City College, including Critical Reasoning in History; America, 9/11, and the War on Terror: Media Myth Making and the Propaganda of Historical Construction; and American Popular Culture and Mass Media in Historical Perspectives.

Mickey has co-organized and presented at numerous national academic conferences on media and recent historical events, including in Berkeley, Santa Cruz, Minneapolis, and Sonoma County on Truth Emergency and Media Reform (see http://truthemergency.us). He has given public addresses at colleges, community halls, and bookstores across the US on media censorship and American history, and was the host of the Modern Media Censorship Lecture Series at Sonoma State University in the fall of 2008. In spring 2009, Mickey was the Visiting Scholar for the Academic Library at the University of Nebraska, Lincoln, discussing media censorship, historiography, and democracy.

Mickey has been published most recently in *Censored 2009* from Seven Stories Press, coauthoring the chapters "Media Reform Meets Truth Emergency" and "Deconstructing Deceit: 9/11, the Media, and

Myth Information." He is currently working on several articles on the truth emergency, post-9/11 propaganda studies, and collective memory. Mickey will be continuing to work with Dr. Peter Phillips on Validated Independent News and the Project Censored College and University Affiliates Program at Media Freedom International. When he has time, he blogs at http://mythinfo.blogspot.com and http://dailycensored.com.

Mickey is also a musician and composer of over twenty years and lives with his wife, Meg, their daughter Molly Luna, and their cat Abigail, near Berkeley, CA.

How To Support Project Censored

NOMINATE A STORY

To nominate a *Censored* story, send us a copy of the article and include the name of the source publication, the date that the article appeared, and page number. For Internet news stories of which we should be aware, please forward the URL to Censored@sonoma.edu. The final deadline period for nominating a Most Censored Story of the year is March of each year.

CRITERIA FOR PROJECT CENSORED NEWS STORIES NOMINATIONS

1. A censored news story is one which contains information that the general United States population has a right and need to know, but to which it has had limited access.

2. The news story is timely, ongoing, and has implications for a significant number of residents in the United States.

3. The story has clearly defined concepts and is backed up with solid, verifiable documentation.

4. The news story has been publicly published, either electronically or in print, in a circulated newspaper, journal, magazine, newsletter, or similar publication from either a foreign or domestic source.

5. The news story has direct connections to and implications for people in the United States, which can include activities that US citizens are engaged in abroad.

SUPPORT PROJECT CENSORED BY MAKING A FINANCIAL GIFT

Project Censored is supported by Media Freedom Foundation 501-C-3 non-profit organization. We depend on tax-deductible donations and foundation grants to continue our work. To support our efforts for freedom of information send checks to the address below or call 707-664-2500. Visa and Mastercard accepted. Donations can be made through our website at: www.projectcensored.org.

Media Freedom Foundation
P.O. Box 571
Cotati, CA 94931
e-mail: censored@sonoma.edu

MEDIA FREEDOM FOUNDATION AND PROJECT CENSORED WEBSITES

www.projectcensored.org

http://mediafreedom.pnn.com/5174-independent-news-sources

www.Mediafreedominternational.org

http://dailycensored.com/

Index

al-Bashir, Omar, 78, 80
Bastidas, Carlos, 212
Bastidas, Edmundo, 212
Batista, Fulgencia, 212
Bauer, Mary, 127
Beck, Glenn, 252–53, 258
Belarus, 243–44
Bergsten, C. Fred, 287
Berman, Howard, 65
Berman, Rick, 86
Bernays, Edward, 218n14
Between Two Ages: America's Role in the Technetronic Era (Brzezinski), 97
Bevelacqua, Robert, 228
Biden, Joe, 14, 165
Biggers, Jeff, 143
Bin Laden, Osama, 255
bin Mahfouz, Khalid, 250
Bishop Don Magic Juan, 346–47
Black Agenda Report (Ford/Dixon), 82
Black Box Voting, 57–58
Black Noise (Rose), 345
Black Star News, 82
Blackwater: The Rise of the World's Most Powerful Mercenary Army (Scahill), 137
Blackwater Inc., 137–38, 277–78
Blackwell, Kenneth, 57
Blair, Dennis, 35, 94
Blank, Rebecca, 93
Blay, Gina, 246
Blumenthal, Michael, 287
Bolivia, 48, 107
Bolozier, Roger, 308
Bolton, John, 254
Bonds, Barry, 157–59
Bonifaz, John, 299
Boone, Pat, 256
Boston Globe, 140, 208
bottled water, 184–85
Bourgeois, Roy, 116–17
Bradley, David, 97
Bradshaw, Adam P., 235
brain function, 181
Brazil
    economic exploitation of, 107–9
    food-as-a-right policy in, 178–79
    sex industry in, 349–50
Bright, David, 298
Brinded, Malcolm, 145
Broken Hearts Club, 375–76
Brown, Chris, 163–64
Brown, Harold, 287

Brown, Mano (MC), 349
Brown v. Board of Education, 17, 169, 318
Bryson, John, 203
Brzezinski, Zbigniew, 37, 94, 97, 287
Bush, George H. W., 33, 226, 277
    military spending under, 201
Bush, George W., 36, 60, 82, 119, 128–29, 265–67, 270–72, 275–78, 280–86
    military spending under, 201–2, 268–69

cable companies, Internet neutrality and, 138–39
Caldeira, Teresa, 348–49
campaign donors strike, 177
campaign finance reform, 87, 177
Campbell, Kurt, 94
Canada, 178, 244
carbon credits, 68
carbon tax, 71
Carbon Trade Watch, 70–71
carbon trading, 67–71
Cardenal, Jaime Chamorro, 248
Cardoso, Fernando Henrique, 113, 195
The Caribbean, 40. *See also* Cuba; Haiti
Carlson, Tucker, 168
Carrero, Carmen, 210
Carter, Jimmy, 89, 97, 286–87
Carter, John, 64
Casey, George W., 225
Casey, William, 33
Castro, Fidel, 212
Cavanaugh, Warren, 26
CBS Evening News, 237
CCR. *See* Center for Constitutional Rights
CDM. *See* Clean Development Mechanism
Celluloid Closet, 369
censorship, of media, 206–7, 252–53
    Index on Censorship, 241–50
Central Appalachian Network, 185
Central Intelligence Agency (CIA)
    APA support of, 129–31
    Guantánamo prison and, torture in, 130
    politicization of, 33–34, 36–37
Center for Constitutional Rights (CCR), 113–14
Chad, 244
Chamber of Commerce, U.S., 30
Chapkis, Wendy, 352
Charleston Gazette, 236
Chávez, Hugo, 50, 211, 254
    as evil, 252–55

Kusherbayev, Almas, 247
Kyoto Protocol, 67–68

labor equity, 191
Lachey, Nick, 151
Lancaster, Brad, 365
Lancet, 122, 197–98
land trusts, as protection against
    foreclosures, 194
La'Onf ("No to Violence"), 176
Lasante, Zamni, 76
Lasseter, Tom, 160
Las Vegas Sun, 235
Latin America
    Amazon region in, economic
        exploitation of, 106–10
    CDM in, 68–69
    foreign debt in, 48
    ILEA in, 124–25
    PPPs in, 100
    U.S. drug war and, 113
    water rights in, 99
Latin American Commission on Drugs
    and Democracy, 195
Latino-Americans, segregation of, in U.S.
    schools, 17
Law & Order, 239
Lazare, Djekourninga Kaoutar, 244
League of Women Voters, 88–90
Leahy, Patrick, 216
Lebanon, demining in, 110–11
left progressive media, 209–10
Lekoto, Terror, 249
Leopold, Aldo, 360–61
Lerner, Stephen, 87
lesbians. media representations of. *See*
    homosexuality, in films
Letters to George Bush (Sheehan), 212
Levato, Roberto, 154
Levi, Primo, 344
Lewis, Alwyn, 203
Libby, Lewis "Scooter," 328
libel cases, international, 243–50
Libel Terrorism Protection Act (U.S.), 250
Lieberman, Joe, 65, 125
Life & Style, 234
Lim, Freddy, 249
Limbaugh, Rush, 234, 255–57
Liu Xinda, 244
Llamas, Gabriella, 167
Lloyd, Rachel, 344
lobbyists
    for automotive companies, 30–31

for CPD, 90
for defense contractors, 202
for electric utilities industry, 29
for finance industry, 3, 29
for insurance industry, 29
for Israel, 2, 29
for oil and gas industry, 29
for pharmaceutical/health industry, 29,
    325
TARP for, 32
U.S. Congress influenced by, 29–32
for U.S. Chamber of Commerce, 30
Lohan, Lindsay, 154
London Observer, 280
Long, Karen, 309
Los Angeles Times, 8, 75, 84
Lou Dobbs Tonight, 306
Louie, May, 194
Lugo, Fernando, 50
Luke, Keith, 258
Lynch, Marc, 230
Lynn, William, 34, 37–38, 202

Mabrouk, Mohammed, 244–45
Madinov, Romin, 247
Mair, Rafe, 244
Manufacturing Consent, 209
Marchant, Kenny Ewell, 64
Marcus, Bernie, 86–87
Margil, Mari, 83, 85, 196
Markey, Ed, 139
Marti, Jose, 212
Martin, Kevin, 139
Marx, Karl, 257
al Massae, 248
Matheny, Virginia, 307
Matthews, Chris, 166, 168, 297
Maud'huy, Charles-Louis de, 360
Mayardit, Salva Kiir, 82
McBride, Kelly, 227
McCain, John, 60, 298
    campaign finance reform and, 87
    Wall Street donors to, 12
McCaskill, Claire, 166
McChesney, Robert, 288
McConiughey, Kolan, 167
McCorkindale, Douglas, 203
McGaffigan, Edward, 26
McIlmoil, Rory, 116
McKinney, Cynthia, 308
media
    advertiser influence on, 234–35
    aid to Haiti in, 75, 77

antidotes to propaganda in, 214–15
anti-war activism in, 207–9, 217n4
celebrities in, 147–61
censorship of, 206–7
corporate pressure on, 233–34
deregulation of, under Clinton, W. J.,
    282–83
FCC and, 283–84
global dominance groups and, 200–
    205
Gulf War coverage by, 205
hyperreality in, 251–59
Iraqi mortality coverage by, in Iraq War,
    121–22
junk food news in, 147–61
left progressive, 209–10
lesbian/gay films, 367–80
Media Freedom Foundation, 215–16
NAB and, 215
NCMR, 199–200
pay-to-play in, 235–36
Pentagon's influence over, 203–5, 221–
    32
privatization of, for radio frequencies,
    283–84
public relations and, 236–40
reform, 198–200
Somali piracy coverage by, 23
trustworthiness of, 4
Media Freedom Foundation, 215–16
meditation, neurology of, 181
Medved, Michael, 225
Mello, Felicia, 127
Melo, Mario, 85
Merz, Hans-Rudolf, 41
Mexican American War, 217n14
Meyer, Don, 222
Meyer, Todd, 227
Miami Herald, 77
Michel, Eddy, 73
Middle East. See Egypt; Gaza Strip, in
    Middle East; Israel; Lebanon,
    demining in; Palestine, occupation
    of; Turkey
Milazzo, Linda, 207
military, U.S. See also U.S. Air Force
    (USAF), coal energy use by
corporate media influenced by, 203–5
defense spending for, 37–38
Duncan, Arne, and, 111–12
Iraq War and, 1, 33, 36
U.S. dollar surplus effect on expansion
    of, 103–6

Military Commissions Act (U.S.), 206
military spending, 201–4. See also military,
    U.S.
    under Bush, G. W., 201–2, 268–69
    under Obama, B., 202
military weaponry
    in Africa, illegal shipments of, 82
    in Gaza, 42–46
Miller, Judith, 10
Miller, Mark Crispin, 58
Miller, Tracey, 160
Mills, C. Wright, 201, 327
MIneral Wells Index, 308
The Miner's Canary (Guinier/Torres), 319
mining, of uranium, 187
Mining Law (Ecuador), 84
MINUSTAH. See UN Mission to Stabilize
    Haiti
Mitchell, James Elmer, 129
Mohamad, Abdalmahmood Abdalhaleem,
    78
Mondale, Walter, 89, 287
Le Monde, 101, 268
Montag, Heidi, 156–57
Montague, Peter, 117
di Montezemolo, Luca, 97
Moore, Michael, 214, 252, 324
Mormon Church, election campaign
    infractions by, 157
Morocco, 248
Mortgage Bankers Association of America,
    30
MOSOP. See Movement of the Survival of
    the Ogoni Peoples
Mother Jones, 238
mountaintop removal (MTR), 142–43
Movement of the Survival of the Ogoni
    Peoples (MOSOP), 144
MSNBC, 148
MSNBC Live, 166
MTR. See mountaintop removal
Mumuni, Alhaji Mohammed, 246
Murtha, John, 66
Mustafa, Kemal, 247

NAB. See National Association of
    Broadcasters
NAFTA. See North American Free Trade
    Agreement
Naiman, Robert, 45
Nashua Telegraph, 302
NASRA. See North American Standards
    and Regulatory Area

Sanderson, Janet, 73
San Francisco Chronicle, 207
Sarki, Saidu Usman, 248
Saro-Wiwa, Ken, 144–45
Savage, Michael, 257
Save America's Forests, 107
Scahill, Jeremy, 137
Scales, Robert H., Jr., 228
Scarborough, Joe, 166
Schakowsky, Jan, 138
Schapiro, Mark, 27
Schlafley, Phyllis, 256
Schneider, Ann Kathrin, 355
schools. *See* segregation, in U.S. schools
Schwartz, Michael, 270
Scoop Weekly, 249
Scowcroft, Brent, 95
Seattle Post-Intelligencer, 8
Securities and Exchange Commission, 13–14
Security and Prosperity Partnership (SPP), 122–24
Seetaram, BV, 246
segregation, in U.S. schools, 16–19, 317–18
    income levels and, 18
    in rural areas, 18–19
    "separate but equal" and, 17–18
    in university system, 319–20
SEIU. *See* Service Employees International Union
Seldes, George, 214
Sensenbrenner, James, Jr., 63–64
"separate but equal," 17–18
Service Employees International Union (SEIU), 114–15
sex trafficking. *See* human trafficking, for sex
sexual exploitation, in worldwide slavery, 132
Sharpley-Whiting, Tracy, 349
Sharpton, Al, 168
Sheehan, Cindy, 212, 252
Shenkman, Rick, 217n4
Sherwood, Carlton, 228
Shih-Mingthe, 249
Shiva, Vandana, 358
Shuster, David, 351
Sicko, 214, 324
Siegelman, Don, 58
Silverstein, Michael, 351
Simpson, Jessica, 147, 151
Simpson, Kari, 244
SIPP. *See* Survey of Income and Program Participation
Sirota, David, 176

60 Minutes, 36–37
slavery, worldwide, 131–32
    for sexual exploitation, 132
Smart, Malcolm, 44
Smile . . . You're Under Arrest, 170
Smith, Anna Nicole, 148
Smith, Jack, 203
Smith-Mundt Act (U.S.), 221, 229–30. *See also* propaganda
Snoop Dogg, 346–47
Snyder, Mark, 150
Snyder, Matt, 236
social democracy, in Venezuela, 210–12, 253–54
solar energy, 189
Solomon, Norman, 204
Somalia, 21, 23
Somali pirates, 19–24
    IUU fleets, 19–20
    media coverage of, 23
    UNEP and, 20
    UN resolutions on, 22
Song Jude, 244
Soto, Hector, 211
South Africa, 249
Spanish American War, 217n14
Spears, Britney, 147, 159
Spears, Jamie-Lyn, 159
Spitzer, Eliot, 134–35
Spoonamore, Stephen, 57
SPP. *See* Security and Prosperity Partnership
St. Clair, Jeffrey, 26
Star (college newspaper), 320
Steele, Michael, 168, 256
Stein, Sam, 87
Steinberg, James, 94
Steiner, Achim, 189
Stern, Andy, 114
Stiglitz, Joseph, 50
stock fraud, 271–72
Stryker, Ted, 154
Sudan, 78–83
    civil war in, 80
    colonial history of, 79–80
    genocide in, 51–52, 79, 81–82
Suharto, Haji Muhammed, 35, 247
Suleman, Nadya, 162–63
Sunday Gazette-Mail, 307
Super Imperialism: The Economic Strategy of American Empire (Hudson), 106
Survey of Income and Program Participation (SIPP), 140
Switzerland, as tax haven, 40

UNRWA. *See* United Nations Relief and Works Agency
Upton, Fred, 64
uranium mining, 187
urban gardens, 182
U.S. Air Force (USAF), coal energy use by, 117–18
USAF. *See* U.S. Air Force (USAF), coal energy use by
US Agency for International Development (USAID), 72
USAID. *See* US Agency for International Development
US National Health Insurance Act, 181
Us Weekly, 156

Vance, Cyrus, 287
Van Gelder, Sarah, 196
Varma, Monika Kalra, 74
Velopoulos, Kyriako, 246
Venezuela, 48. *See also* Chavez, Hugo
  development of social democracy in, 210–12, 253–54
  Global Bonds payments by, 49
  media censorship in, 252–53
Verdier, Steve, 190
victimhood, human trafficking and, 339–44, 352
video news releases (VNRs), 224–25
vigilantism, after Hurricane Katrina, 61–62
Violent Radicalization and Homegrown Terrorism Prevention Act (U.S.), 125
Visa Reform Act (U.S.), 128
Viva Palestina, 55
VNRs. *See* video news releases
Volker, Paul, 94–95
von Brunn, James, 258
voter fraud, 56–60
voting reform, 176

Walker, William, 267–68
Wall Street, 12–16
  political party donations by, 12, 14–15
  TARP and, 13–15
Wall Street Journal, 8, 66
Wang Ting-yu, 249
war, as moral issue, 207–9
  media images and, 208
Warner, Douglas, III, 203
"War on Terror," 37, 136, 201. *See also* Iraq War
Washington Post, 66, 134–35, 207

water
  as commodity, 357–58, 366n5
  conservation measures for, 365
  control of, as source of power, 357–58, 366n6
  international issues, media sources for, 364
  as public trust, 357
Watermelon Woman, 375–77
water rights, 99–100, 102, 183–85
  acequias and, 184
  community, 183
  in Turkey, 361–62
Water War (Shiva), 358
Waxman-Markey bill. *See* American Clean Energy and Security Act
Webb, Jason, 194
Weinrich, Jens, 245
Weinstein, Adam, 238
welfare system, U.S., 91–93
Welsh, Robert, 93
Wentz, Ashlee-Simpson, 151
West Bank. *See* Gaza Strip, in Middle East
What's the Matter with Kansas (Frank), 217n4
Whistleblower Protection Enhancement Act (U.S.), 177
Whitman, Bryan, 228
wind energy, 188–89
  coal v., 116
Winehouse, Amy, 160–61
Winehouse, Mitch, 160
Winfrey, Oprah, 164, 291–92, 304
Wired, 309
Witt, Gallo Mora, 211
Wolfowitz, Paul, 328
Wood, Patrick, 98
wood and pulp industries, 68–69
Wooten, Jim, 168
World Bank, 48
  carbon trades and, 67–71
  CDM and, 69
  U.S. control of, 192
World Trade Organization (WTO), 105
World Water Council, 99–101, 355–56, 359–61
  corporate control of, 99–100, 359–60, 362–63
  PPPs under, 99
World Water Forum, 98–103, 355–65, 356
worldwide slavery. *See* slavery, worldwide
World Wildlife Fund, 68
Worster, Donald, 358

Wright, Ann, 54
WTO. *See* World Trade Organization
Wurzelbacher, Samuel "Joe," 164–66

Xie Jin, 244

Yes! Magazine, 196
Young, Andrew, 287

Zakaria, Fareed, 97, 135
Zedillo, Ernesto, 113, 195
Ziane, Mohammed, 248
Ziskin, Laura, 335
Zoelick, Robert, 95
Zoey 101, 159
Zogby, John, 297
Zorrilla, Carlos, 84–85
Zuckerman, Mortimer, 97
Zunes, Stephen, 45
Zwanziger, Theo, 245